International Business Law

International Business Law

In the New Cyberworld

Edward J. Swan

Wolters Kluwer

Published by:
Kluwer Law International B.V.
PO Box 316
2400 AH Alphen aan den Rijn
The Netherlands
E-mail: lrs-sales@wolterskluwer.com
Website: www.wolterskluwer.com/en/solutions/kluwerlawinternational

Sold and distributed by:
Wolters Kluwer Legal & Regulatory U.S.
920 Links Avenue
Landisville, PA 17538
United States of America
E-mail: customer.service@wolterskluwer.com

ISBN 978-94-035-0729-3

e-Book: ISBN 978-94-035-0739-2
web-PDF: ISBN 978-94-035-0749-1

This book is dedicated to my daughters, Molly and Mary

Table of Contents

Preface

This Book Is Not Legal Advice

The purpose of this book is to provide a high-level overview of how international business is regulated around the world.

Although it does refer to a number of the legal and regulatory systems that govern international business, it does not provide legal advice about how they will affect any business transactions or other activities.

Any party that wishes to know how they or any part of their lives or business will be affected by any laws or regulations will need to obtain timely advice from qualified legal advisors for any jurisdiction relevant to their activities.

Edward J. Swan
Lille, France
November 2024

Acknowledgments

This book has been possible because of the kindness and help of friends, family, colleagues, publishers, editors, officials, opponents, and judges I have encountered in my many years of immersion in law around the world. I thank them for all their contributions with the utmost sincerity.

Also, I need to thank Vanna Fadda without whose loyalty and encouragement, my books would not get written.

CHAPTER 1
Introduction to the Cyber World

International business law consists of the laws and regulations that govern commercial transactions that cross borders.

For millennia, this was an easy concept to understand. Borders were geographical and the legal and regulatory jurisdictions that governed business were contained within geographical borders.

However, in the last 50 years, the nature of commerce and its regulation has changed dramatically, in that geography has become less important and often irrelevant. The reason for this change has been individual ownership of personal computers and communications over the Internet.

This was not really intended to happen. The first computers were large and expensive machines that only large corporations and governments could afford to own and operate. However, in the 1980s and 1990s, that all began to change.

The first examples of personal computers, that is to say computers that were small and portable enough to be used by individuals, were demonstrated in the 1970s. In the late 1970s, the first Apple and Commodore computers were available to be bought by individuals. In 1981, the IBM PC, which was the first real "mass market" computer, was introduced, operating on the Microsoft disc operating system (MSDOS).

After this, it became common for individuals to own their own personal computers, whether they be manufactured by IBM, Apple or other manufacturers.

During this period, the "Internet," which had initially been developed by the U.S. military to allow emergency communications between the U.S. government, military businesses and educational institutions, became available for use by the general public in the World Wide Web, becoming available in the early 1990s.

Since the introduction of the World Wide Web, the Internet has become the principal vehicle of international commerce. Goods and services are marketed to individuals and commercial institutions over the Internet and a huge percentage of the sales, purchases and exchanges of information now occur over the Internet.

Another dramatic expansion of electronic commerce has come with the creation of personal devices in addition to personal computers, such as lightweight and compact laptop computers, tablets, mobile telephones and other devices that can communicate with and through the Internet.

The extraordinary thing about all of these personal electronic devices is that they can communicate with and are accessible by merchants and others from any place on the globe where there is a usable Internet connection. This has been expanded enormously by the introduction of wireless, over-the-air communication which can occur anywhere that a personal device can have access to a Wi-Fi signal.

Consequently, this now means that so-called international commerce can take place continuously and everywhere. Physical barriers and geographical borders have become irrelevant. Merchants can reach potential and actual customers and clients anywhere at any time and offer virtually any good or service that is available anywhere in the world.

All this completely changes the way that the human race has to think about international commerce. With our personal electronic devices, we now have access to, and are accessible by, providers of goods and services anywhere in the world. It does not matter where we are physically located. All that matters is if we have access to a communication facility. If so, we can reach out and be reached. This of course makes dramatic commercial differences in every marketplace in the world.

There may still be certain geographical centers of commercial business, but there are virtually no limitations as to how far their participants can reach or be reached.

1.1 THE LEGAL IMPACT

The effect of this dramatic electronic expansion on laws and regulations that govern international commerce is dramatic.

Laws are generally created to govern human interactions within particular areas known as "legal jurisdictions." These are defined as the limited areas in which a particular legal system applies. These are generally legal systems that are created by political entities such as nations or political subdivisions of those nations. The laws and regulations that constitute the rule of law within a particular legal jurisdiction usually apply outside the defined area of that legal jurisdiction only in special circumstances.

One example of such circumstances is when activities within a particular jurisdiction have an impact on people within other legal jurisdictions. In those cases, the laws of the jurisdiction in which the impacted people live can have consequences for those that impact them from other legal jurisdictions.

The appropriate limits of those consequences are sometimes determined by international recognition of agreed ways to resolve conflicts between differing laws in different legal jurisdictions. But with the ubiquitous reach of the Internet, individual jurisdictions have developed laws and regulations to govern certain interventions within their jurisdictions and with respect to their residence by those using the Internet to reach into their jurisdictions for commercial and other purposes.

The wide reach of the Internet and the growing spectrum of its uses shows how important international treaties and agreements will be in determining how multinational Internet users should be treated.

Such agreements are usually determined by negotiated treaties or by recognized international conventions dealing with the legal relationships between different nations or legal jurisdictions and interactions between their residents.

With the growth of the importance of the Internet as a tool for communication and commercial relations, the basic rules of governing international commerce need continual updating and changing. Otherwise, they will no longer be adequate to deal with the variety of interactions that can occur over the World Wide Web.

Now it is possible for any person who has access to the internet to have a commercial impact on those living in other legal jurisdictions. Consequently, a serious important issue arises as to how such interaction should be governed.

Beyond that, there is the question of how, if such interactions prove unsatisfactory or even damaging to others, such problems can be resolved.

Essentially, this means that conducting satisfactory international business in the modern electronically communicating world requires a wide range of tools of international cooperation to be developed, such as treaties, conventions and international tribunals to avoid, and if necessary resolve, conflicts and miscommunications that may arise.

There is no doubt that the governments of all countries realize the importance of resolving the frictions that electronic commerce can create. However, it is not easy to find universal cooperation for creating systems to resolve such frictions that are acceptable to all countries. There is the unfortunate situation that the world is divided into different groups of allies that have dramatically different points of you about how laws should be created and enforced.

There are groups of countries that consider themselves to be more "democratic," where individual citizens are allowed to vote to make significant differences in the way governments are created and operated. In some countries important political decisions are made by small controlling groups or by dictators.

In addition, these differences often include dramatic differences in beliefs about how economic systems should operate. For example, some believe that national assets should be distributed to citizens by a small group of rulers that aggregate and control all the important assets of a particular country. This system is sometimes described as "socialism," but in other cases may be an "oligarchy" or an even more restricted "dictatorship."

In other systems, individuals are allowed to earn possession of valuable assets through the application of their individual skills, talents and work. Having acquired assets in this way, they are allowed to dispose of and use them largely according to their own wishes. Such a system is often identified as a "capitalist" system.

These political and economic belief differences make it extremely difficult to negotiate treaties and conventions which can apply to all or to the vast majority of people throughout the world.

However, because of the necessity of engaging in international commerce to acquire the goods that are necessary for the population of any country to live, it will be necessary to make significant advances in international cooperation to resolve the frictions that will naturally arise in international commerce because of the impact of electronic communication.

1.2 THE INTERNET

The Internet is an international network of interconnected computers. It developed from a U.S. military program that began in the late 1960s that was called Arpanet. It was originally designed to enable computers operated by military defense contractors and universities involved in defense-related research to communicate by redundant channels even if some portions of the network were damaged by war or other causes.

Arpanet no longer exists, but it provided a model for the creation of the civilian networks that we are familiar with. Now billions of people are able to communicate and access huge amounts of information through an Internet that has developed into a worldwide communications system. It is used by businesses, educational institutions, governments, affinity organizations, criminals and terrorists. It has changed the world we live in in ways far more dramatic and far-reaching than could possibly have been imagined at the Internet's beginning.

The evolution of the content found on the Internet has, according to most experts, gone through three major phases.

The first, labeled as Web 1, was largely limited to finding and reading information largely from government or educational databases.

The second, Web 2, added the ability to interact with other users through two-way communications (such as emails) and by providing platforms such as Facebook, Twitter, etc., to which any user could add information and react and discuss the contributions of other users.

Now, we are said to be living in the time of Web 3, which, in addition to the opportunities found in Webs 1 and 2, offers the opportunity to shape the environment of the Web, own portions of it and monetize it. For example, those that sell advertising on the Internet have learned how to price it by relating it to the number of "clicks" that users divert to a particular product or service. The developers of cyber currency have monetized the digital "bits" themselves by designating a certain arrangement of bits as a "currency" that Internet users can buy and sell or, in some cases, even use to pay for goods and services.

Because of its reach and its impact, there has been, since its early history, a perceived need to regulate the Internet. This has been undertaken by government organizations, international organizations, and commercial organizations.

The creation of Web 3 and its growing economic impact have intensified the need to provide a regulatory structure to protect users and economic markets from abuse by not only criminals and terrorists but also by out-of-control electronic entrepreneurs that sometimes use the Web to construct outrageous frauds or disastrous economic projects such as the scandalous crashed crypto exchanges: Quadriga and FTX.

1.3 KEY LEGAL ISSUES OF ELECTRONIC COMMERCE

In order to understand the impact of law and regulation on an Internet business, it is important to consult qualified legal advisors at an early stage in any jurisdiction impacted by that business.

That should include not only a merchant's home jurisdiction but also qualified legal advisors who can help with information on doing business over the Internet in jurisdictions outside the home country.

1.3.1 A General Summary of Business Law Regulation

There seems to be a view expressed by some that a number of areas of electronic commerce, such as artificial intelligence (AI), are largely unregulated. However, nothing could be further from the truth.

In fact, all electronic commerce is heavily regulated by a large number of existing laws throughout the world. All human activity is regulated by many laws governing the many different areas of human life, particularly those areas where people interact with other humans. These include:

- Constitutional and administrative law.
- Tax law.
- Laws that require reasonable care.
- Regulations requiring the education and licensing of competent operators.
- Criminal law.
- Contract law.
- Laws against fraud and misrepresentation.
- Laws protecting intellectual property.
- Laws governing personality, status, and legal capacity.
- Laws protecting privacy and personal data.
- Laws protecting minors and other vulnerable groups.
- Laws requiring informed consent.
- Health and safety laws.
- Welfare law.
- Property law.
- Family law.
- Investment law.
- Banking law.
- Competition law.
- Tort law.
- Laws imposing penalties and compensation for injuries caused by breach of legal duties.

Many aspects of these areas of law affect the freedom of technologists to create and use cyber tools and products.

Consequently, new regulations need to be created to regulate the specific activities of creating and using cyber products to interact with other persons within one's own society and around the world.

A significant complication that affects the cyber world that affects many other digital businesses is the fact that digital communication via the Internet has become almost unavoidably international. This means that no set of national laws can govern and protect all the persons that are impacted by AI machines.

It is critically important that the countries and legal jurisdictions that exist throughout the world undertake to cooperate in imposing consistent and reasonable regulations on the creation and use of digital products within their own societies and that they recognize the importance of having laws that sensibly respond to the international impact of cyber products created within their own nation and those created abroad that impact on their society.

One goal of this book is to identify those international organizations that have an interest in employing international cooperation to create and enforce reasonable and effective laws and regulations governing the cyber business world.

1.3.2 Duty of Care

Anything human beings do is to a greater or lesser extent under the scrutiny of the law of some jurisdiction. This is more completely true with respect to anything done that impacts others.

A basic legal concept that covers everything we do that impacts others is the principle of "duty of care (DoC)." This is a legal concept that originated in common law but is now reflected internationally in the legal systems of other jurisdictions and international organizations.

The United Nations (UN) System Chief Executives Board for Coordination provides the following definition on its website:

> "*Duty of care*" (DoC) is a legal concept that comes from common law and can be defined as a legal obligation requiring adherence to a standard of reasonable care while performing any acts that could foreseeably harm others. Another definition for DoC would be a legal obligation to act towards others with prudence and vigilance in order to prevent any risk of foreseeable damage. ... The legal consequence of a breach of such a duty is a legal liability imposed upon the author (of the breach) to compensate the victim for any losses they occur. ... This means that the author must take all appropriate measures to behave in an appropriate way in order to avoid causing harm to third parties. That being said, the fact that harm is done does not necessarily mean that the duty of care was breached (or, in other words that the author was negligent), as certain events are beyond the control of the author (because they were unforeseeable or unavoidable despite proper care being taken).[1]

1. United Nations System Chief Executives Board for Coordination, "ICRC Duty of Care: Elements of Definition," online at: unsceb.org., accessed June 26, 2023.

The requirement of DoC will be applicable to all activities relating to the creation, distribution and use of cyber systems in almost any jurisdiction. It is a fundamental concept of law.

Historically, legal systems have taken account of that and have extended the concept of "DoC" from the creator of artificial things to the effects caused by a person's artificial creations.

The application of the concept may, of course, vary under the laws of non-common law jurisdictions:

> The actual measure, scope or content of the "care" that is required in each situation depends primarily on two factors: (one) the relationship between the parties and (ii) the applicable law.[2]

Under systems of international private law, DoC will always be applicable with modifications as referred to above. The UN recommends that in international situations, a good standard of reference for determining the application of DoC is the Swiss Code of Obligations (CO), Article 328. The UN points out:

> Article 328 CO has a very wide scope, going beyond the duty of care as it is understood in other legal systems. The extent of the protection effectively provided by article 328 CO must be examined on a case-by-case basis.[3]

Article 328 CO covers the following issues:

- The protection of overall health, both physical and mental, including a duty of prevention in relation to the work environment;
- The safeguarding of personal and professional honor;
- An employer's duty of aid and assistance, for example in the event of interpersonal disputes within the enterprise;
- A ban on psychological and sexual harassment;
- The protection of privacy;
- Equal treatment.

1.3.2.1 International Impact

Cyber systems can impact across numerous legal jurisdictions. Decisions will have to be made as to how Cyber systems will need to comply with the DoC across many jurisdictions which may, for domestic purposes, have laws and regulations defining the concept of DoC differently.

However, for purposes of the regulation and control of digital products that are easily distributed internationally, it seems sensible to create an agreed international standard defining the scope of the legal requirements of DoC to be applied in transnational situations. The Swiss Code appears to provide a good starting point for development of a universal standard.

2. *Ibid.*
3. *Ibid.*

CHAPTER 2

Contract Law

(1) Introduction.
(2) Agreement.
(3) Consideration.
(4) Contractual intention.
(5) Form.
(6) Contents of a contract.
(7) Standard form contracts.
(8) Mistake.
(9) Misrepresentation.
(10) And undue influence.
(11) Illegality.
(12) Statutory invalidity.
(13) Capacity.
(14) Multiple parties.
(15) Third parties.
(16) Assignment.
(17) Agency.
(18) Performance.
(19) Breach.
(20) Frustration.
(21) Remedies.
(22) Digital Contracts.

2.1 INTRODUCTION

A business transaction is an interaction between different parties for the purpose of gaining something of value.

The thing of value being sought by a party may be money, but it can also be anything else that one or more parties consider desirable.

In many, perhaps the greatest part of the world's transactions, part or all of the transaction is understood to be completed in the future, so parties, particularly if they are strangers to each other or simply in a commercial relationship, often want a clear statement of the terms of the future transaction and a timetable for when it will be completed.

For thousands of years, parties have required a written statement of the terms of the transaction. Some of the earliest written statements of commercial transaction terms can be found in cuneiform writings on clay blocks from Ancient Mesopotamia approximately four thousand years ago. Throughout history, written agreements have been an important instrument in commercial transactions.

At some point in history, such written agreements became an important part of the body of law known as the law of contract.

Today, a "contract" is defined as an agreement recognized as valid by the law of a legal jurisdiction, which may, if necessary, be enforced by the legal authorities of a jurisdiction.

However, it needs to be recognized that written agreements are only part of the enforceable law of contract. In some cases, the law will recognize oral contracts or implied contracts.

In the most recent times, another element has been added to the law of contract in the recognition by many legal authorities of the validity of digital or electronic contracts made by electronic communications over the internet. The importance of this kind of contract is growing every day.

In the United States, almost 29% of business is currently conducted on the internet.

That is equal to about $2.5 trillion. And that percentage is reported to be growing by over 4% a year.

There are over 5 billion internet users worldwide. In 2024, retail internet commerce sales worldwide are expected to exceed $6.3 trillion, and that number is expected to grow substantially in the coming years.

In Asia, the total e-commerce is reported to be about twice that of the U.S. In Europe, e-commerce is about two-third of that in the U.S.

Anyone person or business that expects to be involved in internet commerce in the future will need to be well-informed about how enforceable business agreements are formed and how they can be enforced. Failure to do so can cost a great deal of money.

The other key issue with respect to electronic commerce is that it is international and not limited to any particular legal jurisdiction. Therefore, one will need to be well informed about how many legal jurisdictions one's business is reaching and how the legal requirements of each jurisdiction will affect one's agreements, and one's business expectations.

There are a number of important international treaties and conventions that can provide some consistency when doing business across borders. One needs to be aware of what these are and what their limitations are as far as recognition and enforcement of business agreements are concerned.

Businesses and even individuals who are involved in internet commerce need to be proactively supportive of international efforts to improve cooperation and consistency in the recognition and enforcement of e-commerce agreements. And in cases where disputes arise in e-commerce, strong support of consistency in the judicial treatment of e-commerce transactions is essential for the support and growth of electronic business.

Of course, one international group of countries where significant progress has been made in this area and where there is a good chance that it will continue to be made is the European Union (EU).

But there are other international groups where progress in commercial consistency, in recognition and enforcement of international agreements, e-commerce and otherwise, is being promoted. These include the UN, the North American Free Trade Area (NAFTA), the Asia-Pacific Economic Cooperation group and others such as the Comprehensive and Progressive Agreement for Trans-Pacific Partnership (CPATPP). The U.K., having decided to leave the EU, which cost it numerous economic advantages it enjoyed as a full EU Member State, joined the CPATPP is 2023. In fact, the EU was the U.K.'s principal trading partner, accounting for about half of its trade. It has been reported that since Brexit, Britain's overall trade has been declining, and it has been seeking new trading partners.

2.2 PRINCIPAL MODELS FOR CONTRACT FORMATION

In international trade, the following systems and conventions are the most chosen to guide contract formation.

2.2.1 The Lex Mercatoria

This was a system of law that was used in international commercial business in the Middle Ages and Renaissance. It has its origins in Roman Law (much of which found its way into the Ecclesiastical Law of the Catholic Church) and was largely concerned with protecting traditional customs and ways of doing business. The intent was to provide consistent contracting methods that conformed to the expectations of the majority of merchants from the different countries engaged in international trade. It developed to provide a more commerce-friendly legal system in contrast to the Germanic tribal law that dominated much "royal law" in Europe after the fall of the Roman Empire and the Germanic tribal migrations that followed.

Some of the customs and usages that became parts of the Lex Mercatoria can still occasionally influence court decisions today where a situation may not be covered by express national law.

2.3 THE COMMON LAW

What is called "common" law is a system of law that developed in England that continues to be applied there and in many countries around the world that were former English colonies, such as the United States, Canada, New Zealand, Australia, South Africa, and many other countries.

Several of these countries have important markets and their influence is one of the reasons that "English law" is a common choice for international contracts.

The other important reason is that the common law is based on freedom of contract and has always demonstrated a degree of flexibility in adjusting to changing commercial conditions. Some of the law of England is, of course, embodied in statutory law developed from legislation but much of English common law is developed from decisions of the courts. These court decisions can make important modifications to the law that reflect changing attitudes toward commerce.

English law is also considered to be reasonably impartial and fair when weighing the circumstances that give rise to a particular commercial dispute.

As a result, it is the case that many, and perhaps a majority of international contracts, choose "English law" as the law that will govern the terms of the contract and be applied to resolve any disputes that arise. There is some statistical support for this view in that statistics for cases that have come before English courts and the London port of international arbitration in recent years show that 81 % of the cases have involved a foreign party, and 49 % of the cases have involved only foreign parties.

U.S. law is, to a large extent, also based on Common Law, but there are a number of reasons why U.S. law is not a top choice for international commercial contracts despite the fact that the U.S. has the world's largest economy.

First, most contract law in the U.S. is based on the law of the individual states. Consequently, there may be some differences between states. For example, one state, Louisiana, bases its state law on the Napoleonic Code rather than on English Common law. Second, U.S. state courts and U.S. Federal Courts usually allow jury trials in civil cases as well as criminal cases. Many non-U.S. parties would not be comfortable having a case decided by a local jury in a particular U.S. state. Third, U.S. courts sometimes have the power to impose burdensome penalties that are not permitted in English courts, such as treble damages in anti-competition cases or "exemplary" damages in some cases where fraud, "gross" negligence or abusive behavior is alleged.

Because of these differences and others, civil parties are usually more comfortable making a contractual choice for English law rather than other foreign laws where the contract permits the parties to make a "choice of law" as to which system of law will govern a contract.

Generally, the principal reasons why English law remains such a popular contractual choice as applicable contract law are:

- The importance of common law countries in the international markets, especially important markets like energy and media.
- The flexibility of common law contract law is in line with the general principal of freedom of contract.

- The confidence in English courts and tribunals for providing fair and neutral treatment of contractual parties.
- Confidence in the wide recognition of the validity and justice of English legal decisions.

Under the Common Law, there are three essential requirements to form a commercial contract recognized and enforceable by law. The first is "agreement." One party must make an "offer" and the other party must make an "acceptance" of the offer. The second is that there must be "consideration." Consideration means something that each party values sufficiently to be motivated to enter the contractual relationship. The third requirement is "commercial intention." In making their agreement, each party must intend that the agreement is made for commercial purposes.

The "offer" does not always need to be express; it can sometimes be inferred from conduct. For example, if a party is a merchant in the business of regularly selling goods. Having goods on display can be considered a sufficient offer.

The same is also true of "acceptance." Acceptance can also be inferred by conduct, such as using goods that were offered and made available to a potential buyer.[4]

It is generally true that an agreement is not a binding contract unless supported by adequate "consideration." This is true not only under Common Law but in other systems of law as well. Something of value must be provided before a "promise" becomes an enforceable contract. Either a detriment to the promisee or a benefit to the promisor can be adequate consideration. Mutual promises may be considered consideration if the promises are expected to be performed.

However, not all agreements are binding. Common Law does provide for specific exemptions. For example, agreements "subject to contract" are not binding. The contracts need to be exchanged and executed before an agreement is binding.

2.4 FORM

As stated above, contracts can be formed in different ways, writing, orally, by conduct, etc.

However, certain contracts need to be in writing: bills of exchange, consumer credit agreements, and agreements involving the sale or use of real estate. And some agreements transferring legal rights need to be "executed as deeds."

2.4.1 Deeds

Generally, the form of the contract is left to the parties to decide. The principal systems of law usually provide a significant degree of flexibility in deciding what needs to be in a contract. This is particularly true in Common Law systems, which usually give significant weight to the concept of freedom to contract.

4. G.H. Treitel, *The Law of Contract*, 10th ed. (London. Sweet & Maxwell 1999), pp. 1-148.

A "deed" is a document executed with sufficient formality so that it is clear that the parties intended their promises to be binding.

Deeds are often executed where parties intend to transfer certain legal rights to another person. For example, deeds are frequently used for transfers of real estate property. They are also used for intellectual property rights.

Under Common Law, there are certain transactions which require a greater attention to contract formality. There are certain contracts that are required to be in the form of "Deeds" if they are to be enforceable.

One difference between deeds and other forms of contracts ("agreements") is that they are generally enforceable despite a lack of consideration. Consideration is usually taken to indicate the seriousness of the parties to the transfer of things of value. Deeds provide a certain level of formality to substitute for consideration in determining the seriousness of the parties to conclude a transfer of valuable property.

Deeds need to be executed with more formality than a signature alone. In the first instance, the document usually needs to expressly state that it is being executed as a deed. The formality required for execution of a deed might be satisfied by affixing a corporate seal to a document or by having the contract executed by an attorney. Sometimes, it required that signing of the deed also be signed by an additional "witness": a third person who is not a party to the agreement.

2.4.2 Equity

However, deeds that lack consideration may not be enforceable in equity. The granting of an equitable enforcement of an agreement usually requires finding consideration.

"Equity" is a body of law, originating in the English Court of Chancery to allow providing a "fair" remedy in disputes where ordinary common law was unable to do so. Originally, it was applied in "courts of equity," but now its principles have been integrated into civil law. In common law tribunals, appeals to equity can now be made by parties that believe that application of strict legal rules will impose an unfair legal result.

2.4.3 Electronic Contracts

In more recent times, issues of agreement validity have been complicated by the internet.

Transactions conducted electronically over the internet have become a huge part of global commerce. Consequently, issues have arisen as to the legal status of electronic communications in commercial contexts.

In U.K. law, electronic signatures are valid. This issue was resolved by the U.K. Electronic Communications Act 2000. The Act provides that in legal proceedings, electronic signatures can be admissible as evidence of the authenticity of communications or data.[5]

5. Electronic Communications Act 2000 online at: legislation.gov.uk.

However, in electronic purchases, formal signatures are not always required. Consent to a transaction is often acknowledged by "clicks" in response to electronically posed questions.

This type of electronic agreement, where a party acknowledges acceptance by "clicking" on an agreement portion of an online site, is also known as a "clickwrap" or click-through agreement.

In the United States, there is the Uniform Electronic Transactions Act (UETA) which has been adopted by most states. New York and the District of Columbia (site of Washington, DC) are exceptions, but they have adopted their own similar laws.

A click agreement has support as a legally binding agreement in the UETA and the Electronic Signatures in Global and National Commerce Act (2000).[6]

For these purposes, an "electronic signature" is defined as follows:

> The term "electronic signature" means an electronic sound, symbol or process, attached to or logically associated with a contract or other record and executed or adopted by a person with the intent to sign the record.[7]

Click agreements are usually considered to be within that definition if the buyer has consented to use the click method and has not withdrawn their consent.

2.5 INTERNATIONAL CONVENTIONS

2.5.1 The United Nations Convention on International Trade Law

Another approach to contract law is provided by the United Nations Commission on International Trade Law (UNCITRAL).

The goal of UNCITRAL is to promote legal harmonization in international trade law:

> In an increasingly interdependent world, the importance of developing and maintaining a robust cross-border legal framework for the facilitation of international trade and investment is widely acknowledged. The United Nations Convention on International Trade Law (UNCITRAL) plays a key role in developing that framework in pursuit of its mandate to further the progressive harmonization and modernization of the law of international trade. UNCITRAL does this by preparing and promoting the adoption of legislative and non-legislative instruments in a number of key areas of commercial law.[8]

In recognition of the growth of electronic commerce in international business, UNCITRAL has promoted the creation of the United Nations Convention on the Use of Electronic Communications in International Contracts (2005). The focus of this Convention is: "assuring that contracts concluded and other communications exchanged

6. "Clickwrap agreements are legal and enforceable," *DocuSign*, online at: docusign.com.
7. Federal Deposit Insurance Corporation, "Electronic Commerce in Global and National Commerce Act (E-Sign Act)," *FDIC*, online at: fdic.gov.
8. United Nations Commission on International Trade Law, online at: uncitral.un.org.

electronically are as valid and enforceable as their traditional paper-based equivalents."[9]

2.5.2 Applying an International Convention to an International Business Transaction

That is determined by the choice of law rules of the courts of the jurisdiction where the dispute is being decided. For example: does that jurisdiction require the application of law of the country where the contract is made?[10]

Sometimes, international conventions or parts of them are incorporated into the domestic law of a country, but that is not always the case.

2.5.3 The Hague Convention on Choice of Law

The Hague Principles on the Choice of Law in International Commercial Contracts were promulgated in 2015 by The Hague Conference on Private International Law (HCCH). The purpose of these was to promote freedom of choice for contract parties in deciding which system of law would be applicable to their private commercial contracts.[11]

All members of the EU (except Denmark) are parties to this convention. A number of other countries (including the U.S.) have signed but have not ratified the Convention yet.

2.6 EU CONTRACT LAW

Under EU law, general private contractual agreements are considered to be governed by the contract law of the relevant Member State. However, certain EU directives and related regulations give rise to legal requirements that Member States are required to implement to deal with particular contractual issues.

The core contract law issues that the EU is concerned about are:

- Consumer rights.
- Unfair contract terms.
- Unfair commercial practices.
- Sales remedies.
- Rights to effective remedies.
- Harmonized protection of rights across EU Member States.
- Support and proper functioning of the EU internal market.

9. United Nations Convention on the Use of Electronic Communications in International Contracts, online at: uncitral.un.org.This Convention has been ratified by about 18 countries and signed by a number of others. Lists of how different countries have responded to it can be viewed online at: uncitral.un.org.
10. "Relation to private international law and existing domestic law." *UNCITRL*, online at: uncitral.un.org.
11. *See* Hague Conference on Private International Law (HCCH), "Choice of Law in International Commercial Contracts," online at: hcch.net.

- Protection of market access.
- Support of cross-border e-commerce.
- Aiming for a unified EU contract law.

2.6.1 Consumer Rights Directive

This Directive (as amended) is intended to provide harmonized consumer rights throughout the EU:

> This directive applies to all contracts concluded between a "consumer" and a "trader." Member States may not diverge from the directive by imposing more or less stringent provisions unless a specific possibility to deviate from its rules is provided in the directive itself.[12]

The directive deals with such issues as:

- Contracts where personal consumer data is provided.
- Personalized price.
- Consumers rights of withdrawal from certain contracts:
  - Consequences of a trader's failure to inform about withdrawal rights.
- Distance and off-premises contracts.
- Delivery and risk.
- Enforcement and penalties.[13]

2.7 STANDARD CONTRACT PROVISIONS

Regardless of the choice of law of a contract, there are certain provisions in which a party should be part of every contract it enters into:

- Party identification:
  - There should be clear, unambiguous identification of the parties to the contract. This should include:
    - Correct legal names.
    - Addresses.
    - Any relevant licenses or registration numbers that identify them.
- Subject matter:
  - A clear statement of the subject matter:
    - What is being bought or sold.
    - Any technical specifications that need to be met:
    - How will satisfaction with the specifications be judged and by whom?
    - Delivery specifications:

12. European Commission, "Consumer Rights Directive," online at: commission.europa.eu.
13. European Commission, "Guidance on Consumer Rights Directive (2021)," online at: commission.europa.eu. For more information about the details of the Directive, *see also* "Key Facts on the New EU Consumer Rights Directive (2015)," pdf download online at: commission.europa.eu.

    - How?
    - When?
    - Where?
  - Notification specifications:
    - How?
    - When required?
    - Where?
- Timing:
  - Objections.
  - Rejections.
  - Modifications of terms.
  - Failures to perform.
  - Inabilities to perform.
- Price:
  - Currency.
  - Methods of payment.
  - Timing.
  - Modifications.
- Choice of law:
  - Place of contract?
  - Place of performance?
  - Home of a party?
  - Neutral jurisdiction?
    - British law?[14]
- Dispute resolution:
  - Method:
    - Negotiation.
    - Submission to Ombudsman:
    - Government.
    - Private.
    - Mediation.
    - Expert determination.
    - Arbitration.
    - Litigation.
- Notification requirements:
  - How?
  - When?
  - Where?
  - Whom?
- Confidentiality requirements:
  - Permitted persons.
  - Time limits.

14. "Why English Law Governs Most International Commercial Contracts"? *QLTS*, at: qlts.co.uk, June 10, 2024.

  - Treatment of contract documents upon time expiration.
- Rights of Third Parties:
  - Non-parties affected.
- Signature and Execution requirements:
  - Physical or electronic.
  - Copies:
    - Physical or electronic.
    - Authority of copies.
    - Distribution requirements.

CHAPTER 3
Dispute Resolution

It is always best if contracts are carefully drafted enough so that all the key issues of the transaction are covered and the transaction is performed by all parties as expected.

However, contractual relationships do not always operate as planned, and this can lead to disputes between the parties.

In a business context, it is always better that disputes be resolved as quickly, amicably and cheaply as possible so that the parties can return to concentrating on the purposes of their businesses. However, different disputes have different characters and there is no single solution that will resolve all commercial disputes efficiently and effectively.

In this chapter, descriptions of various methods of dispute resolution are set out.

In order of their expected complexity and cost, suggested methods of dispute resolution are:

- Negotiation.
- Market or Regulator-sponsored Ombudsman.
- Expert determination.
- Mediation.
- Arbitration.
- Litigation.

3.1 NEGOTIATION

If one party is unhappy with the performance of another contracted party, the quickest way to find out the seriousness of a dispute is to contact the other party and try to resolve the matter through discussion and agreement.

The way that this is handled depends on the nature of the commercial relationship between the parties and the history of their relationship, if any. If the parties are friendly and have a personal relationship, it may be most efficient for the parties or their key executives to discuss the matter between themselves to try to work out an amicable resolution.

If the parties are large organizations with a less personal and friendly relationship, it may be better to have negotiations conducted between legal counsel of the parties. Legal counsel can usually be more objective and less likely to take personal offense from the nature of a dispute. They may also have important experience in commercial negotiation.

Although it is always in the parties' interests to resolve a commercial dispute as quickly as possible, it is generally not recommended for a party to open a negotiation by stating its best offer. Too often, this will be regarded by the other party as a "floor" of possible settlement and is likely to encourage them to hold out for more.

However, a party asking for too much may persuade the other party that negotiation is a waste of time. A sensible approach may be for a party to ask for more than they would be prepared to ultimately settle for, but not for so much as to be considered ridiculous.

However, if a party is initially offered a settlement it considers acceptable, it should probably accept it and move on rather than strain the commercial relationship by holding out for more.

Back-and-forth discussions may take some time, but if both sides are genuinely interested in resolving the dispute, an acceptable agreement can usually be reached within a reasonable time, at a relatively low cost and with minimal damage to the parties' commercial relations.

3.2 OMBUDSMAN

That is the traditional term, although it is now probably more correct to say "Ombudsperson."

The term can refer to a person or organization, often chosen by the government, that is put in place to resolve complaints or disputes, usually relating to a government-regulated business or official agency.

This office is frequently independent and usually follows a formal procedure of reviewing a complaint and conducting an investigation into the circumstances that give rise to the complaint. They will then draw conclusions and make recommendations as to how the complaint can be resolved. Sometimes, these recommendations are binding. In cases where they are not binding, the Ombudsperson will sometimes try to resolve the complaint by mediation.

Ombudspersons sometimes deal with public issues, such as alleged violations of citizens' rights and sometimes deal with private market issues, such as financial abuse of customers.

Ombudspersons and their equivalents have existed for many centuries, and today, they are established in most countries to handle public and private sector issues. Examples are the U.K. Parliamentary Commissioner for Administration, the Swedish Parliamentary Ombudsman, the Nigeria Public Complaints Commission and the Western Australia State Ombudsman.

Lists of Ombudsperson organizations existing in each country can be found online, or, in a particular country, one can contact government officials to make inquiries about how to contact them.

However, an Ombudsperson is not available to resolve every kind of dispute or complaint. For example, it is frequently stated that there is no Ombudsperson service available to resolve complaints relating to cryptocurrency transactions. This is because, in many countries, cryptocurrencies have no official status as regulated financial instruments. As time goes on, this may change.

In those circumstances where an Ombudsperson service is available, it can be a relatively simple and inexpensive way to resolve a complaint or a dispute relating to a matter in which the Ombudsperson service is authorized to act.

3.3 EXPERT DETERMINATION

This is a procedure where parties to a dispute agree on an expert to make a determination of disputed issues. Usually, the parties wish the expert to be neutral and independent.

One significant advantage of this method is that all information can be kept completely confidential, avoiding public exposure of the parties' businesses or the issues involved. The expert is paid for their services with the parties sharing the costs.

The level of formality of the procedure is left up to the parties. It is not always necessary for their arguments and evidence to be presented in a formal hearing.

In most cases, the expert will be a single person, but in some cases, the dispute may be submitted to a multi-person "dispute board" for resolution.

3.4 MEDIATION

Mediation is a more formal procedure. Mediation usually involves the appointment of a neutral third person to help the parties analyze the issues of their dispute and reach an agreed resolution.

In many jurisdictions, to release the pressure on the commercial tribunals and speed up the settlement process, parties submitting their commercial disputes to litigation are required to go through a mediation process to see if their disagreements can be resolved without going through a formal litigation process involving submission to a judge and ultimately a trial before the court.

There are usually a number of steps in the mediation process.

The first step usually involves analyzing a dispute and considering the issues to decide whether to begin a mediation.

The second step involves preparing one's arguments and evidence for presentation during the mediation.

The third is the stage where the parties provide their information to the mediator prior to meeting. This is intended to give the mediator a picture of what the dispute is about and the positions of the parties.

The fourth stage is the mediator will meet with parties at a neutral location to discuss the issues and propose possible solutions. During this stage, the parties will negotiate with the help of the mediator to see if an agreed solution can be found.

The mediation session is private, and there is no publication of the issues of the dispute or the positions of the parties. Any notes of the mediator remain private and cannot be produced at any subsequent hearing or trial if the mediation does not produce an agreed solution.

Generally, the parties choose and pay the mediator. However, if the parties cannot agree, they can ask an independent person or organization to choose one.

However, the recommendations of a mediator are usually not legally binding. If the parties do not accept mediator's recommendations for settlement, other alternatives for the parties are usually arbitration (if the parties agree or this is mandated in their contract) or litigation before a court.

3.5 ARBITRATION

Arbitration is a frequently chosen contractual alternative to litigation. This is often mandated in the dispute resolution terms of a contract as a simpler and less expensive choice than court proceedings.

However, arbitration procedure is more formal than the methods of dispute resolution listed above. It involves a hearing before one or more arbitrators who render a legally binding decision. Arbitration decisions will be enforced by most national courts around the world.

To get to arbitration, the parties will usually choose arbitration as the mandated method of dispute resolution in the terms of their contract. That provision will also select the arbitration system to be used, the legal system that will govern the contract, and the location (or "venue") of the arbitration.

3.5.1 Enforcement of Arbitration Awards

The widely available enforcement of arbitration awards is largely made possible by the United Nations Convention on the Recognition and Enforcement of Foreign Arbitral Awards, known as the "New York Convention." More than 150 countries have ratified the Convention. These countries, which include most large countries, require their courts to recognize and enforce arbitration awards from other countries that have ratified the Convention.

3.5.2 Major Arbitration Organizations

There are a number of arbitration systems to choose from. Some of the best-known, which are more likely to appear as contractual choices, include:

- London Court of International Arbitration (LCA). This is located in London, England. It is a popular choice because English law is frequently chosen as the

governing law in international business contracts, and the LCA is in a strong position to apply English law. It will hold both arbitration and mediation.
- The International Court of Arbitration. This is a division of the International Chamber of Commerce (ICC). Its function is to arbitrate international commercial disputes. It is headquartered in Paris. Its main working languages are French and English, although it will conduct arbitrations in any language. It offers around 100 arbitrators from about 90 countries for the parties to choose from.

The ICC itself does not issue formal judgments. It provides "judicial supervision" of arbitration proceedings that are conducted in accordance with the Rules of the ICC. Before concluding any award, the arbitrator must submit the award in draft to the Court for review. Under Article 34, the Court may propose modifications of an award. An arbitration tribunal cannot issue a final award under the Rules of the ICC until the award has been approved by the Court. The final awards are binding on the parties, and under Rule 35, parties are required to "carry it out without delay." Under Article 43, the governing law, the administration of any arbitration proceedings is French law.

Arbitration Institute of the Stockholm Chamber of Commerce

This Institute is also a popular choice for arbitration because it is recognized as an impartial organization. It is recognized as the preferred arbitration form in more than 120 international investment treaties.

American Arbitration Association

The American Arbitration Association (AAA) does have a division that specializes in resolving international disputes. This is called the International Centre for Dispute Resolution (ICDR). It provides its services in locations around the world in locations designated by the parties.

The ICDR follows definition of the UNCITRAL of what constitutes an "international" arbitration.

To fit within that definition, the parties must agree on the following:

- Their places of business are in different countries.
- A major part of their business relationship is not in the home country of either party.
- The subject matter of the dispute is mostly connected to somewhere outside the parties' home countries.
- The location of the arbitration is not within the country of any party.
- The official language of the ICDR arbitration rules is English.

The ICDR also offers a mediation service.

3.5.3 Typical Arbitration Procedure

(1) In the first instance, the parties must agree to settle their dispute by arbitration. They can agree on this at any time, but that choice may have been previously made in an existing contract between the parties.
(2) Next, the parties need to choose the arbitration forum. It may be one of the arbitration organizations discussed above. This will determine which rules will govern the arbitration. They will need to agree to follow the rules of the chosen organization.
(3) The parties will need to choose a location for the arbitration as permitted by the rules of the arbitration organization they have selected.
(4) Next, they will need to choose the number of arbitrators. Most arbitration organizations permit the parties to decide whether their arbitration will be before one or more arbitrators.
(5) Having decided on the number of arbitrators, the parties will need to agree on who the arbitrators are. Each party is usually allowed to choose a number of preferred arbitrators from the list of approved arbitrators maintained by the arbitration organization. Some organizations have very large lists of approved arbitrators. Each party will then submit its list of preferred arbitrators to the other party. The parties will then negotiate over who the designated arbitrator(s) will be. The goal of both parties should be to have the dispute heard by arbitrators who are neutral and unbiased.
(6) Sometimes, there is an initial hearing where the parties can discuss their case with the arbitrator, during which the arbitrator will establish a schedule for exchanging information and lists of witnesses.
(7) The parties will then have an agreed period to prepare their cases and exchange the information previously agreed with the arbitrator.
(8) Next, there will be a more formal hearing where witnesses will testify, and documentary and other kinds of evidence will be presented. More than one hearing may be required if the dispute is complicated.
(9) After the hearing, the parties are usually given a period of time to provide post-hearing submissions, such as written statements.
(10) The arbitrators will then consider the arguments and submissions of the parties and issue an award.
(11) If the losing party does not comply with the terms of the award within a reasonable time, the successful party can seek a court ruling to enforce the award. As stated above, many countries have ratified the New York Convention to allow their courts to issue rulings permitting enforcement of arbitration awards issued by recognized arbitration organizations.
(12) Arbitration proceedings are usually private and confidential, and information about them is not usually allowed to be published.
(13) Appeals from arbitration awards are not usually permitted. There is a very limited time within which a court can be petitioned to set aside an arbitration award. To be successful, the petitioner will need to present

persuasive evidence the arbitrator was corrupt or unfairly biased or that the arbitration was illegal (e.g., for lack of jurisdiction).

3.6 COURT LITIGATION

There are many commercial disputes arising from commercial contracts, and otherwise that end up being tried before judges, and sometimes juries, in government-regulated courts.

Most countries in the world have legal systems that include a formal judicial system for the resolution of disputes.

Usually, governmental judicial systems have several divisions within their jurisdictions determined by the type, size and level of the dispute.

In some countries, such as the U.K., there are specialized commercial courts to deal with business disputes. In others, such as many U.S. states, there are general courts that deal with disputes of all kinds. Sometimes, the courts are divided to deal exclusively with either civil or criminal cases.

In the event that parties are unable to resolve a commercial dispute, one or the other may elect to file a complaint requesting a hearing before a formal court to resolve the issues raised by the dispute.

The principal advantage of this form of resolution is that it can provide a definitive result in favor of one of the parties that can be legally enforced against the other party and their assets.

That is not to say that a party can "win" on all of the claims raised by its initial complaint. The court may agree with a party on some claims and not on others. The court may also grant a clear victory to the defending party by dismissing all the claims against it. Victory is never certain for either party in a case litigated before a court.

If a case is brought before a court in the United States, there is even a greater element of uncertainty. In most commercial cases in the U.S., whether in Federal or State courts, either party is entitled to choose to have a jury trial. In other countries, such as the U.K., that is not the case. Commercial cases are decided by a judge.

U.S. juries generally consist of 12 ordinary citizens chosen from local voter rolls. The court will allow the lawyers for the parties to choose these jurors by examining and asking questions of a larger group of potential jury candidates. The lawyers are entitled to question the jurors about their backgrounds and feelings toward the parties. The lawyers are entitled to reject some for any reason and can ask the court to reject others for a "cause" such as bias, etc. From these proceedings, a panel of jurors is then sworn in.

In a U.S. court case, the jury's duty is to determine the facts—basically, who is telling the truth, and the judge's duty is to decide the law that applies to those facts.

The involvement of a jury in a commercial case adds to the uncertainty of the outcome because what a jury will decide about the evidence presented by each party is very difficult to predict. The jury's feelings about the evidence and the testimony of the witnesses will determine which party should win.

After all the evidence is heard, the court will issue some instructions to the jury about how they should consider the evidence, and the jury will retire to a separate room to discuss and consider their verdict in private.

In civil cases, the verdict is determined by a majority of the jury. If a majority cannot prevail, there will be what is called "a hung jury," and another trial may be necessary. Although, it is likely that the judge will try very hard to get the parties to agree on a resolution called a "settlement."

In rare cases, even if there is a jury, the judge might consider the legal position of one party so strong that the judge will order the jury to deliver a "directed verdict" in favor of that party.

In cases which are conducted entirely before a judge without a jury, the process of determining a winner is more straightforward. The judge will decide.

Nevertheless, it is the case that any case that goes to court litigation is more expensive, time-consuming, and uncertain.

Also, in most jurisdictions, even if a party wins at the trial court level, the other party can ask for permission to appeal the verdict—usually to a panel of judges on an Appeal Court, and if a party is unhappy with an Appeal Court's decision, it may be allowed to appeal to another panel of judges sitting on a Supreme Court.

The legal and other fees expended on a court process can be huge, running into many millions of dollars.

Because of potential costs and other reasons discussed above, most commercial cases do not go to trial but are settled between the parties on agreed terms before a trial begins.

It is also the case that judges will strongly urge the parties to reach a settlement before trial. Judges are very busy and prefer not to waste time on the complexities of a trial if a settlement can be reached.

3.7 CONCLUSION

From the above, it should be clear that an international business has many choices about dispute resolution when entering into or trying to repair a business relationship.

For any particular business, deciding which is the best choice depends on the nature of the business and who its counterparties are or will be.

However, in general terms, it is usually best to avoid formal litigation before a court.

If disputes arise, regardless of the circumstances, it is advisable not to take them personally or seek revenge. Doing those things will likely add to costs and may not produce a desired result.

It is always better to try and resolve business disputes amicably. That will save time and money and enable the continuation of what may be a valuable relationship.

Consequently, negotiation, mediation or expert determination may be the best ways to resolve a business dispute.

However, a successful party may not be able to force or enforce a desirable result.

Therefore, if one wants more certainty that a definite resolution can be ultimately reached, it is a good idea to include a term in any international business contract to choose arbitration as a dispute resolution method, with a definite, widely accepted arbitration organization in a specified location, convenient for both parties.

The applicable law should also be specified. Note that English law is often chosen in international contracts, but, of course, choice of law may depend on contract type and circumstances. If possible, it is best to choose an applicable law and location that both parties feel will give them a fair hearing.

The above choices should be made in the applicable law and dispute resolution section of the contract. Please note that these choices may be the most important terms of any contract.

It is hoped that a business contract will proceed smoothly and conclude satisfactorily for all parties.

But troublesome disputes can arise. So, it is necessary that the parties make careful, thoughtful, and economically sound choices about applicable law and how disputes will be resolved.

CHAPTER 4

Financial Services Law

Financial services are essentially about the relationship between parties who have money (or other desirable assets) and those that want those assets.

Financial services include investment, finance and banking, among other things, and are regarded by governments, legal authorities and the parties involved as a critical business sector.

Consequently, it has become a heavily regulated sector, and those that engage in financial services activities often need licenses or other permissions from the financial regulatory authorities.

Financial services law is about regulation of transactions in assets, including money, for specific reasons.

The reasons for the transfer can include investment, money or asset management, acquisition of an asset presently or in the future, financial advice and/or asset conservation.

It frequently involves trusting a third party with money or other valuable asset. It is usually that relationship of trust that is subject to regulation. In order to be trusted to undertake a regulated financial service, a party must comply with applicable financial services regulations.

This regulation is subject to an increasingly complex body of legislation, regulations, treaties, conventions and customs that govern how financial services may be conducted within national jurisdictions and globally.

Financial services are offered principally within financial markets. The structure, size, influence and importance of financial markets vary around the globe. The most important ones have the biggest impact on how international financial transactions are conducted because of their size and the nature of their regulation.

The world's 10 biggest financial services markets are reported to be found in:

(1) U.S.
(2) China.
(3) Japan.

(4) India.
(5) England.
(6) Canada.
(7) Saudi Arabia.
(8) Germany.
(9) South Korea.
(10) Switzerland.

Each country regulates financial services somewhat differently, but their importance means that market participants pay attention to what their regulations are nationally and what international financial treaties and conventions they subscribe to.

4.1 WHAT IS REGULATED?

The term "financial services" refers to specific activities that fall under the laws and regulations that govern financial services. These regulations can be imposed both nationally and internationally.

Although there are national and international differences as to what activities fall under financial services regulation, the activities that are likely to be regulated are activities usually relating to the following financial businesses:

(1) Investment.
(2) Insurance.
(3) Banking.
(4) Securities, including shares, bonds, derivatives and other financial instruments.
(5) Real estate finance.
(6) Lending.
(7) Funds.

4.2 TEN THINGS TO KEEP IN MIND ABOUT FINANCIAL SERVICES REGULATION

It is impossible to give a complete survey of all the ways that financial services regulation affects international financial business around the world. There are too many different jurisdictions, too many treaties and conventions, too many possible financial relationships and too many different regulators regulating different parts of the business.

In general terms, it is important to keep in mind certain basic concepts that will apply in the most important market jurisdictions.

Set out below is a rough summary of ten issues to be aware of.

4.2.1 Regulated Activities

These are the financially related activities that the legislators and regulators consider necessary to regulate. They involve things such as finance, banking, insurance, etc.

The list of regulated financial services activities for any particular jurisdiction can be long and complicated. Any party that wishes to know what financial activities fall under regulation in any context will need to obtain qualified local advice about how to legally engage in them.

Participants in regulated financial services may require special qualifications or licenses. Undertaking "regulated activities" without complying with local qualifications may be a crime and, perhaps, a serious crime.

Basically, any party that wishes to involve themselves in the finances of any other party should get advice as to whether such involvement could constitute a regulated activity.

In some jurisdictions, for example, the U.K., there is a "general prohibition" against engaging in regulated activities without official authorization.

4.2.1.1 Financial Promotion

"Financial Promotion" is essentially attempting to influence another party to engage in a regulated activity. For example, under U.K. regulations, a "financial promotion" is defined as: "an invitation or inducement to to engage in investment activity, communicated by a person in the course of business."[15]

4.2.1.2 Authorization

This means having obtained permission to engage in certain regulated activities from the designated regulatory authority in a particular jurisdiction. As indicated above, engaging in regulated activities without having obtained proper authorization is likely to be a regulatory and even criminal offense.

"Authorization" might be called different things in different jurisdictions, such as "licensing," "qualification," "registration," etc. But whatever the label, a party will need to find out what compliance is necessary to be allowed to engage in regulated activities in any jurisdiction from a qualified legal advisor.

Someone who has achieved the required level of qualification to engage in transactions relating to certain regulated activities may be described as an "authorized person."

15. Section 21 of the U.K. Financial Services and Markets Act (2000).

4.2.1.3 *Approval*

This is distinguished from "authorization" in that it applies to and is required of certain persons holding sensitive positions in relation to that "authorized person."

These persons are required by the designated financial regulator to have certain qualifications that make them "a fit and proper person" to hold important roles within or be able to exercise an important degree of influence over an "authorized person."

Persons that need to be qualified by the regulator to be designated as an "approved person" could be:

- The Chief Executive Officer (CEO).
- The Chief Financial Officer (CFO).
- The Chief Operating Officer (COO).
- The Compliance Officer.
- Certain employees who sell products or provide financial advice to customers and members of the public.
- Persons who own or control a significant share of the equity of an authorized person (perhaps 10% or more).

Depending on the jurisdiction and the regulator, the precise qualifications needed by such an approved person will vary. In some cases what may be needed is a background of satisfactory performance in related financial services positions. In other cases, formal training, relevant educational backgrounds, examinations or official licenses may be needed. A background check may be needed into the history of applicants wanting to be recognized as "approved persons."

If any such persons leave a business or change positions within it, they will need to be replaced by equivalents as soon as possible with the approval of the regulator.

4.2.1.4 *Changes in Control*

The persons that are most affected by the regulations that govern a financial services business are those that "control" the business. They are the parties that the regulators focus on.

What constitutes "control" will vary depending on the structure and nature of the business and who regulates them.

As discussed above, certain key executives, such as the CEO, will considered to have control. So will governing boards and those with a large enough financial stake in a business to be able to influence its operations. The size of this financial stake may vary but as little as 10% may be considered to be enough.

If a financial services business is structured as a company limited by shares, then a significant shareholding may be enough to be "controlling." Again, the size of that shareholding will vary depending on the structure of the firm and the policies of its regulators.

Note that in cases where a business is a limited company owned by shareholders (a "corporation" in the U.S.), there may be different classes of shares with varying rights and powers. For example, there may be "voting" shares and "non-voting" shares. Voting shares will have control in the sense that they, by vote, can direct the operation of the firm, whereas non-voting shares may only be able to participate passively in the results of those operations.

One situation where careful attention will have to be given to its regulatory impact is a case where the controlling interests in a business decide to change the structure of the business. For example, a business that was structured as a partnership between a group of individuals is restructured to be a limited company owned by shareholders. Such an undertaking will clearly change the nature of how a firm is controlled. Consequently, that will be of significant interest to the business's regulators and will usually require interaction with those regulators from an early stage of the restructuring process.

It is important to remember that the "controller" of a business operating as a single proprietorship or as a partnership is a different legal entity, or "legal person," from a business operating as a limited company owned by shareholders. In a highly regulated business, such as financial services licenses, registrations and permissions formally granted by the relevant regulators are required.

These authorizations cannot usually be transferred to another legal entity or "person" without formal permission from the relevant regulators. Only after the relevant regulators have approved the proposed change of structure and granted formal approval for it to proceed can a business legally operate as an authorized financial services provider.

The procedure for applying for regulatory approval of a change of control will vary depending on the nature of a business, its regulators and the details of the applicable laws and regulations.

Such regulations will also apply if the change of control occurs because a "controlling interest" (perhaps 51%) of the publically traded shares of a company is being purchased by trading on a public share market, such as the New York Stock Exchange, NASDAQ, the London Stock Exchange, etc.

In order to continue to operate as an authorized financial services firm, the new owners will need to be approved by the relevant regulators.

4.2.1.5 Principles for Business

Regulators operate in accordance with applicable statutes and particular regulations. But it is important to remember that these are not the only requirements that regulators may impose on a regulated business.

In addition, there are overall general policies that may be applied by the regulators to a financial services business.

For example, in the United Kingdom, the overall legislation that governs financial services is the Financial Services and Markets Act (2000)—as amended. In addition, there are detailed regulations governing various aspects of the regulated activities, as summarized above.

However, it is not sufficient for an authorized person to be satisfied that they have complied with the requirements of the Act and all of the detailed published regulations that govern their sector of business. That is because the U.K. regulators, such as the Financial Conduct Authority (FCA), also require that all authorized persons comply with 11 wide-ranging policy requirements called the FCA Principles for Business. These are broader, more general requirements that are intended to fill the gaps that might exist in the specific regulations. Essentially, they give the regulator the power to take disciplinary action against an authorized person in nearly any case where the regulator is unhappy with an authorized person's activities, even if no specific regulation has been breached.[16] Included in these general requirements are such broad brush rules as:

- "A firm must conduct its business with integrity."
- "A firm must conduct its business with due skill, care and dillegence."
- "A firm must pay due regard to the interests of its customers and treat them fairly."
- Etc.

It is easy to see that any misbehavior perceived by the regulators that might seem to fall outside specific regulations could be seen to be covered by such Principles.

These principles discussed above apply to one country, but with the growth of electronic trading, the commercial expansion of business on the internet, and the general globalization of financial services business, there has been an effort to introduce comparable rules of good behavior that are intended to apply internationally.

For example, the Organisation for Economic Co-operation and Development (OECD)[17] has a set of guidelines for responsible business conduct (RBC) in the financial sector:

> The OECD Centre for RBC has worked to operationalize RBC due diligence for different financial transactions and actors through developing fit-for-purpose guidance.[18]

The UN has recognized that:

> Being major actors in the global economy, financial institutions play an important role in ensuring business respect for human rights.

They note that the UN Guiding Principles on Business and Human Rights:

> explicitly apply to all business enterprises, both transnational and others … .[19]

16. It should be noted here that financial services regulation in the U.K. is divided between several regulators: including the FCA, largely responsible for regulating financial services firms, and the Prudential Regulatory Authority (PRA) largely responsible for supervising banks and insurers. The PRA has six "Fundemental Rules," similar to some of the FCA Principles. For a detail of UK law and regulation, *see*, S. Morris, *Financial Services Regulation and Practice* (Oxford University Press, 2016).
17. Organisation for Economic Co-operation and Development.
18. OECD, "Responsible Business Conduct," *OECD*, online at: mneguidlines.oecd.org.
19. United Nations Human Rights, Financial Sector, *UN*, online at: ohchr.org.

For additional financial service focus, the International Organization of Securities Commissions (IOSCO) has published a statement of "International Conduct of Business Principles" focused on the financial markets.[20]

4.2.1.6 Enforcement

When the relevant financial services regulators feel there is a violation, or potential violation, of financial services legislation or regulations, they are likely to bring enforcement proceedings.

The structure of the enforcement process will vary depending on the particular regulator and the target entity, but it is likely to begin with an investigation by the regulator.

The regulator will probably have the power to enter the business premises of the target and review how its business is conducted. The regulator will also probably have powers to demand and inspect all documents and communications records relevant to any alleged transgressions. It will also have powers to interview (perhaps under oath, under penalty of perjury) all persons connected to any alleged violation.

If the target resists providing relevant material or interview opportunities, the regulator can usually apply to a court for an order forcing compliance. The regulator also often has the power to suspend a target's right to engage in regulated business if it feels the target is not being adequately cooperative.

At the conclusion of its investigation, the regulator will usually issue a decision that will review the evidence found and draw conclusions as to whether or not a regulatory failure has been identified. If it does conclude that there is a transgression, the regulator may suggest what their regulatory responses are likely to be in terms of a penalty, which may be administrative, financial, restrictive, or, in the most serious cases, penal.

Respecting the last, where a criminal prosecution is suggested, it should be noted that some regulators do have prosecutorial authority to bring criminal charges. In cases where they do not, they will have to submit their conclusions to other government prosecutors, who will make a decision about whether a criminal proceeding should be brought.

After the regulator's decision is issued to the target, the target will then be given an opportunity to respond. They will be able then to marshall their evidence and testimony and submit it to the regulator.

Following that submission, the regulator will review the target's response and then make a final determination as to whether to impose a regulatory penalty.

If the regulator decides to do so, the target will have the opportunity to review the suggested penalty and respond. The target may decide that it will accept the penalty because that is the easiest way to end an expensive and time-consuming confrontation

20. The Technical Committee of the International Organization of Securities Commissions, "International Conduct of Business Principles," *IOSCO*, online at: iosco.org.

with the regulator and return to its principal business of providing services to customers.

If the penalty the regulator wishes to impose is financial, it is sometimes the case that the target is given an opportunity to have the severity of the penalty reduced if it agrees to pay within a reasonable period of time without appealing the regulator's decision.

If the target strongly disagrees with the penalty and has sufficient resources to continue, the target may ask to have the case heard before a tribunal. In most regulatory environments, a tribunal, independent from the investigative division of the regulator, will be available to weigh the arguments of each party and issue an independent decision. One downside of taking this course may be that it's expensive and time-consuming, and part or all of the target's financial services work may be suspended until the case is finally resolved. Consequently, the costs can be significant.

The tribunal will usually hear the arguments of the parties, review the evidence and issue its own decision as to the merits of the case.

If the target loses before the tribunal, they may have an additional opportunity to appeal the regulatory penalty to a formal court of law. Again, the target will have to decide whether it is worth the probable expenditure of additional time and money to try to get the decision reversed.

If the target case fails before the lower court, it may have an opportunity to appeal to an appeals court and, ultimately perhaps, to a Supreme Court. However, these options are all costly in both money and time, and the target will need to think hard about whether taking the chance to get a possible reversal will be worth the time and money.

Also, it is important to note that in the regulated financial services business, although regulators can impose some limited penalties which may involve payments or business restructuring, the regulator usually has the ultimate power to ban the target from doing any further financial services business if the regulator believes the violation to have been sufficiently serious. This could put the target out of business with disastrous financial and professional consequences.

At best, a financial services company would like to avoid provoking regulatory investigations and the possible penalties that might result. These things cost time and money and may lead to the ultimate closure of a business.

To avoid such unpleasant consequences as much as possible, if one is operating a financial services business, it is worth considering what will be the best approach in dealing with the regulators of that business. It is certainly the case that regulators generally wish there to be good relationships between themselves and the firms they regulate. What they usually mean by a good relationship is that they wish to be informed about new developments in the business, which can affect the way that an authorized person deals with its customers and the financial markets. In short, the regulator wants its regulated entities to have a continuous and open relationship with itself so that the regulator has an ongoing understanding of what is happening in the markets it is regulating.

New structures, new ways of doing business, new products, and participation in new business sectors are things that the regulator wishes to know about.

Unfortunately, many regulated financial services businesses regard the regulatory authorities as enemies that should be kept in the dark about as much of a firm's business as possible. Consequently, they may omit to tell the regulator about key changes that the regulator would need to know about. An unfortunate result can be that later on, the regulatory authorities may discover these changes on their own, conclude that these new things are not operating in conformity with applicable regulations and impose penalties, which could have been avoided if the firm had been openly discussing proposed changes with the regulator from the time that they were proposed.

Therefore, a regulated firm should consider the advantages of keeping a reasonable level of open communication with its regulators at all times.

4.2.1.7 Market Abuse

One of the things that is most likely to attract a severe reaction from the regulatory authorities is engaging in any of the activities that are defined as "market abuse."

In most market centers, the regulators have gone out of their way to impose strict regulations against the activities that they define as "market abuse."

For example, the EU Market Abuse Regulation says that the central objective of the regulation is to have integrated, efficient and transparent financial markets conducted with integrity.[21] Market abuse interferes with these objectives.

In recent decades, the worldwide regulatory attitude toward market behavior has evolved significantly. As financial markets have become increasingly international, market centers have come to understand that in order to have a financial market that operates effectively in a world of international financial services, one must gain the confidence of market participants from all over the world.

It is now understood that in order to inspire such confidence, a market must operate fairly and efficiently without the interference of those activities now categorized as market abuse. The definition of what constitutes "market abuse" may vary from jurisdiction to jurisdiction, but common definitions of key abuses are as follows:

- Using information not publicly available that is likely to have a significant effect on prices of financial instruments (or related derivatives) to the advantage of oneself or to the advantage of others.
- Transactions or orders which give or are likely to give false or misleading signals about supply, demand, or prices of financial instruments, or which move prices to artificial levels, or which employ any form of deception or contrivance.
- Disseminating information, giving or likely to give false or misleading signals as to value of financial instruments.[22]

21. E. Swan & J. Virgo, *Market Abuse Regulation*, 3rd ed. (Oxford University Press, 2019), p. 13, *citing* EU Market Abuse Regulation, recital 2.
22. UK Financial Serives and Markets Act (2000) (Market Abuse) Regulations 2008. Recital 10.

A party can commit market abuse either by engaging in prohibited behavior relating to the above, by attempting to engage in such behavior or by requiring or encouraging prohibited behavior by others. Prohibited behavior need not necessarily be active. One can be guilty by either action or in action. If a party has a duty to act and fails to do so, that can be market abuse.[23]

Financial market participants are subject to two different duties with respect to market abuse. The first duty is negative: refraining from behavior that constitutes market abuse. The second duty is positive, consisting of things one must do in order to avoid being guilty of market abuse.

Negative duties can include such things as not engaging in "insider dealing" or "market manipulation." Positive duties can include such things as complying with regulatory obligations, reporting suspicious transactions, keeping lists of company "insiders," and making public announcements about important information relating to the company as soon as possible through appropriate channels, such as publicly available news media.[24]

What constitutes market abuse may be defined in detail somewhat differently from jurisdiction to jurisdiction, but there are basically three kinds of market abuse that generally have to be both civil and criminal offenses. These are:

- Insider dealing.
- Market manipulation.
- Improper dissemination of information.

4.2.1.7.1 Insider Dealing

"Insider dealing" occurs when someone, through their profession or contacts, has access to nonpublic information, which that person knows, if made public, is likely to affect the price of financial instruments, and that person buys or sells financial instruments prior to that inside information being made public.

That is a good general definition, but it is by no means exhaustive. There are a variety of situations where a person's behavior, because it describes an impermissible unfair advantage to the person performing the behavior, could be considered illegal insider dealing.

The "classic" and probably the most frequent case involves a situation where someone, because of their profession or contacts, comes into possession of information that is likely to make the shares of a limited company rise in value. That person secretly buys shares in the company ahead of the likely price-raising event and makes a secret personal profit when he then sells the shares at a price greater than he paid for them.

Such a situation can also occur when a person has inside information about a future event that is likely to cause shares to decline in value.

But there are other situations that have also been classified as insider dealing. Here are some, but there are probably more:

23. Swan & Virgo, p. 35.
24. *Ibid.*

- "Front running": Someone knows that another person is about to buy a significant number of a particular company shares (or other financial instrument). They know that the impact of that order will likely cause the price of the share to rise in the market. That person goes to the market ahead of the purchaser and buys a similar amount of the desired instrument. They then sell the items to the purchaser at a higher price, making a profit.
- Potential takeover: When an offer is made to buy a publicly traded company, someone (perhaps an employee or advisor) to a target company who may be aware of the offer and the likely impact of the purchase on the target's share price if the offer is successful purchases shares in the target in advance of a public announcement of the offer and makes a profit when the purchase is announced, and the market price of the shares increases.
- "Tipping": another illegal activity consisting of a person with nonpublic sensitive information about a publicly traded company, giving that inside information to a friend or relative, allowing them to buy the shares (or other regulated instrument) ahead of a likely price-affecting event know to the "tipper." When the price goes up, the "tippee" will make a profit, which the tipper will expect to share in.

Most of these "insider dealing" situations are related to persons who are either employees of companies or their professional advisors (such as accountants or attorneys). For example, an employee in the copy department of a major law firm became aware of an upcoming merger by reading internal documents that he was copying and collating for his law firm employer and used that information to buy shares in the target company in advance of a merger. That was, of course, insider dealing and led to a criminal conviction for the copy-room employee.

As previously stated, the range of misbehavior that may be possible under the definition of market abuse is difficult to completely describe. However, some jurisdictions, including the U.K., have made an effort to provide a detailed description of the behavior that could constitute market abuse.

The U.K. Explication of Market Abuse

The detailed statutory description is found in section 118 of the U.K. Financial Services and Markets Act 2000.[25] This section says.

1) "For the purposes of this Act, market abuse is behaviour (whether by one person alone or by two or more persons, jointly or in concert; which –
   a. occurs in relation to qualifying investments, traded, or admitted to trading on a prescribed market, or in respect of which a request for admission to trading on such a market has been made; and
   b. Falls within anyone or more of the types of behaviour set out in sections (2) through (8).
2) "The first type of behaviour is where an insider deals or attempts to deal, in a qualifying investment or related investment on the basis of inside information relating to the qualifying investment.

25. UK Financial Services and Markets Act 2000, section 118.

3) "The second is where an insider discloses inside information to another person otherwise then in the proper course of the exercise of his employment, profession or duties.
4) "The third is where the behaviour (not falling within subsections two or three –
   a. is based on information, which is not generally available to those using the market, but which, if available to a regular user of the market, would be, or would be likely to be, regarded by him as relevant when deciding the terms on which transactions in qualifying investments or related investments should be affected, and
   b. is likely to be regarded by a regular user of the market as a failure. On the part of the person concerned to observe the standard of behaviour reasonably expected of a person in his position in relation to the market.
5) "The fourth is where the behaviour consists of affecting or participating in effecting, transactions or orders to trade (otherwise then for legitimate reasons in conformity with the accepted market practices on the relevant market), which –
   a. give or are likely to give, a false or misleading impression as to the supply of, or demand for, or as to the price or value of, one or more qualifying investments, or related investments, or
   b. Secure, the price of one or more such investments at an abnormal or artificial level.
6) "The fifth is where behaviour consists of effecting, or participating in effecting, transactions or orders to trade, which employee fictitious devices, or any other form of deception or contrivance.
7) "The sixth is where the behaviour consists of disseminating, or causing to dissemination of, information by any means which gives, or is likely to give, a false or misleading impression as to a qualifying investment or related investment by a person who knew or could reasonably be expected to have known that the information was faults or misleading.
8) "The seventh is where the behaviour (not falling within subsection (5), (6) or (7) –
   a. gives or is likely to give, a regular user of the market, a faults or misleading impression as to the supply of, demand for or price or value of, qualifying, or related investments, or
   b. Would be, or would likely to be, regarded by a regular user of the market as behaviour that would distort, or would be likely to distort, the market in such investment
   c. And is likely to be regarded by a regular user of the market as a failure. On the part of the person concerned to observe the standard of behaviour reasonably expected of a person in his position in relation to the market."

The purpose of quoting this long section above is to show the lengths that a regulator will go to in order to try to cover all of the instances that they believe might constitute market abuse. However, it is important to note that the section quoted above was introduced some time ago and has been subject to some modifications since.[26] The purpose of the modification has been essentially to modify some of the language which was considered to be overbroad. Anyone wishing to know the exact definition of market abuse at present under U.K. law will need to consult a legal representative, who

26. E. Swan & J. Virgo, *Market Abuse Regulation*, 3rd ed., pp. 31-34.

will be able to give information about what the exact current state of U.K. law is regarding market abuse.

4.2.1.8 Behavior and Market Abuse

It is clear from reading the above definitions of market abuse that market abuse occurs in the presence of improper "behaviour" in relation to qualifying investments.

Therefore, it is important to know, from a financial services perspective, what is meant by "behaviour"? It is a word that is potentially open to many interpretations, but helpfully, some regulators, including those in the U.K., have produced a lot of material about this.

The activities that constitute "behaviour" for purposes of financial services regulation are defined in recital 10 of the U.K. Market Abuse Regulation,[27] which says that the relevant activities include those in relation to "qualifying investments," as follows:

- Dealing in qualifying investments.
- Dealing in either commodities, investments, and/or related derivatives, which are the subject matter of or whose prices or values are determined by reference to a qualifying investment. Those things which are the subject matter of or whose price or value is determined by reference to a qualifying investment are "relevant products" to a qualifying investment.
- Arranging deals with respect to qualifying investments.
- Causing, requiring, or advising others to deal in qualifying investments; making statements, representations, or assimilating information, which a regular user is likely to regard as relevant in determining the price or terms of transactions and qualifying investments; providing advice or otherwise conducting corporate finance activities in qualifying investments.
- Managing the qualifying investments belonging to a third party.

4.2.1.9 Qualifying Investments

It is obvious from reviewing the material on market abuse so far that not every financial transaction is subject to market abuse regulations. Only certain defined financial transactions qualify for regulatory purposes. These are identified as "qualifying investments."

Therefore, it is important to know what kind of interactions are subject to regulation as investments.

The keyword in the definition is "investments." So it is important to understand what interactions are considered to be investments and therefore subject to potential financial services and market abuse regulation.

27. UK Financial Services and Markets Act 2000 (Market Abuse) Regulations 2008 (SI 2008/1439), recital 10.

Because commercial transactions of all kinds take place throughout the world, there is no universal definition as to what constitutes an "investment," which is applicable everywhere. The closest that international financial services have come to accepting a particular definition is from the opinion of the United States Supreme Court in the *Howey* case.[28]

The Court said:

> "For purposes of the [US] Securities Act, an investment contract (undefined by the Act) means a contract, transaction, or scheme, whereby a person invests his money in a common enterprise, and is led to expect profits solely from the efforts of the promoter or a third-party."[29]
>
> "The test of whether there is an "investment contract" under the Securities Act is whether the scheme involves an investment of money in a common enterprise, with profits to come solely from the efforts of others, and, if that test, be satisfied, it is immaterial, whether the enterprise is speculative or non-speculative, or whether there is a sale of property with or without intrinsic value."[30]

Since the test was announced in 1946, it has been widely accepted as stating accurately what constitutes an investment. It is accepted that the "*Howey* test" consists of four questions:

(1) Does the transaction involve a payment of money?
(2) To a common enterprise?
(3) Where the payee has an expectation of profits?
(4) From the efforts of others?

If these four questions are answered affirmatively, then, under the *Howey* test, an "investment" is considered to have been created that will be subject to financial services regulation.[31]

However, this definition of what kinds of financial instruments might be covered by financial services regulation, generally, and market abuse regulations specifically, still leaves open the question of whether a particular kind of financial instrument will be subject to regulation. The *Howey* test, although a good standard of comparison, does not identify the specific kinds of financial transactions which the regulators considered to be covered by anti-market abuse regulations.

The issue was largely covered by the EU Markets and Financial Instruments Directive. That Directive defined 11 categories of financial transactions that qualify as covered "financial instruments" for purposes of EU (then including U.K.) regulation. The directive identifies the following as financial instruments:

(1) transferable securities;
(2) money market instruments;

28. *SEC v. W.J. Howey Co.*, 328 U.S. 293 (1946).
29. *Ibid.*, pp. 298-299.
30. *Ibid.*, p. 301.
31. "Howey Test Overview and Application," *Study.com*, online at: study.com.

(3) units in collective investment undertakings;
(4) options, futures, swaps, forward, rate agreements, and any other derivative contracts relating to securities, currencies, interest rates, yields, commission allowances, or other derivative instruments, financial indices, or financial measures, which may be settled physically, or in cash;
(5) options, futures, swaps, forwards, and any other derivative contracts relating to commodities that must be settled in cash or may be settled in cash at the option of one of the parties other than by reason of default or other termination event;
(6) options, futures, swaps, and any other derivative contracts relating to commodities that can be physically settled, provided that they are traded on a regulated market, an MTF,[32] or an OTF,[33] except for wholesale energy products traded on an OTF that must be physically settled;
(7) options, futures, swaps, forwards in any other derivative contracts relating to commodities that can be physically settled, not otherwise mentioned in point 6 of this section and not being for commercial purposes, which have the characteristics of other derivative financial instruments;
(8) derivative instruments for the transfer of credit risk;
(9) financial contracts for differences;
(10) options, futures, swaps, rate agreements, and any other derivative contracts relating to climactic variables, freight rates, or other official economics statistics that must be settled in cash or may be settled in cash at the option of one of the parties or other than by reason of default or other termination events, as well as any other derivative contracts relating to assets, rights, obligations, indices, and measures not otherwise mentioned in this section, which have the characteristics of other derivative financial instruments, having regard to whether, *inter alia*, they are traded on a regulated market, OTF, or an MTF;
(11) emission allowances, consisting of any units recognized for compliance with the requirements of Directive 2003/87/EC (Emissions Trading Scheme).

4.2.1.10 Relevant Markets

As can be seen from above, the regulation of certain financial instruments depends on the type of market in which they are traded.[34] These can include:

- regulated markets;
- Organized Trading Facilities;

---

32. A regulated Multilateral Trading Facility.
33. A regulated Organized Trading Facility.
34. Detailed descriptions of the different types of markets in the Market Abuse Regulation: Regulation (EU) No. 596/2014, which, prior to BREXIT was made a part of UK law. *See also*, Swan & Virgo, Chapter 7.

- Multilateral Trading Facilities;
- trading platforms;
- auction platforms;
- devices for dissemination of price information;
- over-the-counter (OTC) transactions—transactions not conducted on a formal market;
- any other means of effecting transactions in regulated instruments;
- primary, secondary or grey markets;
- any other conduct that can affect regulated financial instruments.

It needs to be kept in mind that no matter what arrangements, systems or methods are used to transfer interests in regulated financial instruments, they will almost always be reachable to financial services regulation to one degree or another.

In order to better understand the practical and regulatory differences between the types of trading facilities, the following descriptions are provided.

4.2.1.11 Regulated Market

A regulated market is usually generally understood to be a multilateral system operated and/or managed by a market operator, which allows a number of third parties to buy and sell interests in financial instruments—within the market and in accordance with market rules—resulting in contracts relating to financial instruments admitted to trading on the market and which is authorized and functions in accordance with regulatory requirements.

4.2.2 International Financial Services Regulation

In the 1990s, initially due to the impact of the legal case *Transnor v. BP, et al.*,[35] there was a significant amount of national deregulation of financial services in a number of countries. Added to that, there was a sudden and dramatic growth in the use of computers and the internet in financial transactions. These things greatly increased the volume of international financial transactions and created a need for new international treaties relating to the provision of cross-border financial services.

As was written in a paper published by the Bank of International Settlements in 1996:

> The deregulation of domestic financial markets, in association with technological progress, has led to an explosion of cross border financial transactions and the cross-border establishment of premises., This has led to a need for international agreements on how the business of international finance and banking should be conducted.

35. *Transnor (Bermuda) Limited v. BP North America Petroleum, et al.*, 738 F. Supp. 1472 (S.D.N.Y 1990).

4.2.2.1 *International Regulation Through the EU*

Because the EU, with 27 member countries, is probably the largest group of countries that share common overall financial services regulation in the form of EU directives and regulations, it is useful to take an overview of what that system regulates.

Under its Financial Markets Regulations included are:[36]

- Credit rating.
- Crowdfunding.
- Investment.

Under its Investment Funds Regulations, included are:

- Cross-border fund distribution.
- Alternative investment fund management.
- Venture capital funds.
- Money market funds.
- Collective investment schemes.

Under its Securities Markets Regulations, included are:

- Benchmarks regulation.
- Markets in Financial Instruments.
- Market Abuse Regulation.
- Prospectus Regulation.
- Securitisation Regulation.
- Short Selling Regulation.
- SME Listing Regulation.

Under Post-trade Services, included are:

- CCP Recovery and Resolution Regulation.
- Central Securities Depositories Regulation.
- Financial Collateral Directive.
- OTC Derivatives, Central Counterparties and Trade Repositories Regulation.
- Securities Financing Transactions Regulation.
- Settlement Finality Directive.

Under EU Company Reporting and Auditing Regulations, included are:

- Audit Directive.
- Accounting Directive.
- Corporate Sustainability Reporting Directive.
- International Accounting Standards Regulation.
- Non-Financial Reporting Directive.

36. Finance.ec.europa.eu.

- Statutory Audit Regulations.
- Transparency Directive.

Under Banking Regulations, included are:

- Banking Union.
- Banking Regulation.

Paying attention to EU regulation of financial services is important not only because it affects a large multinational market with a large and affluent population but also because regulations adopted by the EU are often influential in persuading countries outside the EU to adopt similar regulations.

It would take several books to provide the details of how the EU regulates each of the financial services areas described above. The reason for the lists above is to provide a guide as to the things to be aware of when considering undertaking financial services transactions.

However, to have an accurate understanding of how the regulation of these categories will affect the financial transactions that a party wishes to undertake, it will be necessary to obtain the advice of qualified legal advisors.

4.3 FINANCIAL MARKET REGULATION CONCLUSIONS

There is no doubt that financial services regulators around the world have made substantial efforts to create flexible and effective regimes to deter and punish market abuse.

However, these are not simple regulatory systems. To many, it is worryingly complex.

To keep pace with the chameleon-like changeability of these regulatory schemes requires a significant degree of attention.

The international financial markets are essential but not perfect. To keep them strong and fair, the regulators must have the flexibility to respond rapidly to both known and, as yet unknown, market threats.

The world's financial markets are always being hit by waves of innovative financial misconduct.

The reported manipulation of key international markets and their benchmarks in commodities, currencies, interest-rate-related products, cyber currencies and digital assets has produced many reports of international financial institutions admitting guilt, paying billions in fines and settlements in regulatory, civil and criminal actions, and, in some cases, having employees jailed.

Regulatory systems and regulators around the world have to remain flexible and continually change to cope with the changing markets for financial products.

In the U.K., Europe, and elsewhere, there are continually new regulations, new regulatory systems, and new regulators. More changes will probably be necessary as governments and courts consider the effects of these new regulations over time.

In the past, much financial services regulation has been subject to "self" or "minimal" regulation. This has changed.

Financial services transactions are now subject to more scrutiny in major market centers around the world.

Put simply, the current market regulation regimes mean that market participants have a fundamental duty to ensure that the markets operate "efficiently and fairly." This duty is greater than the duty that financial market participants owe to their owners. They must run the markets principally for the benefit of market participants, investors, and the public generally. Their own interests are secondary. With the growth of the internet, electronic trading, cryptocurrencies, digital assets, and the international reach of market misconduct schemes around the world, this duty will apply to all financial markets no matter where or in what form they are traded.

This creates a complex situation for participants operating in the international markets. Market participants must think carefully about how different regulations apply to them and how they impact their businesses.

4.4 BREXIT AND THE U.K.

What about Brexit?

It seems likely that most U.K. and U.K.-implemented market regulations will remain in effect to protect the U.K. markets from new and old kinds of market misconduct. True, requirements of cooperation and/or oversight by the EU will probably change or be eliminated. But the extent of the changes on the way is unknown.

4.5 U.S. JURISDICTION AND WHY IT MATTERS

U.S. Courts and investment regulators take an extremely expansive view of the application of U.S. law to non-U.S. transactions. This is nowhere more true than with U.S. antitrust, fraud and anti-manipulation rules. Indeed, the exemptions which have been created to exempt foreign issuers from U.S. registration requirements do not create exemptions from U.S. antitrust, fraud, and anti-manipulation rules and individuals or corporations who breach these rules can be held liable under both U.S. criminal and civil statutes.

Firms and individuals outside the U.S. are often surprised by the reach of U.S. jurisdiction over such activities. Accordingly, it is worth remembering that a U.S. Federal Court held that:

> any market that is not exclusively a foreign market is part of US commerce.[37]

It is also worth remembering that one is not immunized from U.S. lawsuits or regulatory action simply by the fact that the same area is covered by U.K. or other

37. *Transnor v. BP.*

non-U.S. financial services regulations. The U.S. Supreme Court has held that where a party is subject to both.

The news gets worse. Financial services in the U.S. are regulated by a confusing patchwork of Federal (Securities Exchange Commission (SEC), CFTC, Federal Reserve, Comptroller of the Currency, etc.) and State (e.g., New York, etc.) agencies. All administer a complicated matrix of statutes and regulations which can apply to non-U.S. transactions. It is not within the scope of this book to attempt to describe them all.

U.S. legislation, regulations and court decisions give the U.S. Government and private litigants a broad range of remedies for financial market misconduct which may have occurred wholly outside the borders of the U.S.

U.S. judgment of market misconduct can result in the imposition of a variety of civil and criminal fines, injunctions, restitution, imprisonment, and/or heavy civil damages (sometimes treble or punitive damages).

It is also worth remembering that the prevailing party does not usually get significant costs (such as attorneys' fees), most civil trials can be tried before a local jury, and "no win, no fee" arrangements are common.

It would be a mistake for any international financial market participant to lose sight of the possible application of U.S. law with respect to non-U.S. transactions, which could have U.S. connections or foreseeable U.S. impact.

CHAPTER 5

Insurance Law

5.1 INTRODUCTION

Insurance is the business entering into a contract to compensate a person for loss or damage under conditions defined in the terms of the contract. The contract is often called an "insurance policy."

There are numerous laws, regulations and conventions that govern the way the Internet affects the insurance business. With the growth of the Internet, these have expanded beyond local and national laws to include foreign and international regulations that affect international digital business that insurance firms may take on.

Set out below is a list of 10 important regulatory issues that affect the insurance industry when transacting business on the Internet and how those issues are subject to relevant regulation.

These include the following:

(1) Data gathering and protection.
(2) Licensing and registration.
(3) Freedom of speech.
(4) Compliance.
(5) Client suitability.
(6) Dispute resolution and compensation.
(7) Solicitation and advertising.
(8) Money laundering.
(9) Anti-discrimination.
(10) Cybercrime: Hacking Attacks and Fraud.
(11) International regulation.
(12) Data protection.

As insurance companies seek to understand and deal with each of these issues and the regulations that affect them, legal advice will be essential, especially since the Internet has become increasingly important to business generally and the insurance business in particular.

The information provided by legal advisors may consist of providing up-to-date alerts on changes and proposed changes to regulation that affect the way their insurance clients do business, providing seminars or meetings with key people to educate clients on legal developments and how to cope with them, and providing website space containing detailed information about the best ways for clients to deal with relevant changes to Internet regulation around the world.

5.2 HOW THE INTERNET HAS CHANGED BUSINESS

5.2.1 Data Gathering and Protection

There is a little question that insurance companies gather and hold a tremendous amount of information electronically as well as physically. This will include personal information, health information and financial information as well as much other information about clients that insurance companies consider necessary to issue and maintain insurance policies.

Certainly, insurance companies and their legal advisers are aware of a number of data protection laws that they must comply with.

In the U.K., anyone actively using Internet communications in their business will be aware that there are both U.K. data protection regulations[38] and EU data protection regulations. These are both outlined and discussed in more detail in the following chapter.

Basic issues of data protection are:

- When is data collection permitted?
- What data may be collected?
- What data protection must be provided?
- What may be done with the data?
- How long can the data be held?
- What rights do the data subjects have over the data?
- What penalties are likely for the misuse or loss of collected data?

There was a little doubt that insurance companies and their advisors are aware of the issues raised by those questions all over the world. However, the use of the Internet makes questions about data collection much trickier.

It is generally the case that any entity operating commercially over the Internet to offer and sell goods or services may be subject to the regulations of any jurisdiction in

38. Data Protection Act 2018. UK General Data Protection Regulation (UK GDPR). *See* Information Communications Office, online at: ico.org.uk.

which those offers are accessible and, even more so, with respect to jurisdictions in which actual transactions are conducted with its citizens or residents.

It should always be kept in mind that having diligently complied with the data regulations of one's own jurisdiction does not automatically exempt any entity from the regulations of other jurisdictions where it's advertising, offers, or sales may be accessible. Nearly every legal jurisdiction in the world has created data protection regulations relating to the Internet. And these are usually much more numerous and extensive than many people realize.

The United States provides an interesting and troubling example. The U.S. is the world's largest commercial market and therefore it is an attractive place to both offer and transact business. However, with regard to Internet use and data protection, the regulations of the U.S. are enormously complicated. There are a number of detailed federal regulations relating to Internet use and data protection in the U.S. These will probably apply in all U.S. states and territories. However, most of the laws relating to Internet use and data protection in the United states are the laws and regulations of the 50 individual states plus territories. These can be quite different. There are no consistent nationwide data protection laws and regulations in the United States. These are described in the next chapter.

However, depending on the state in which any insurance business might be dealing with individuals resident there, specific knowledge of what such transactions may raise legally will be understood only by a lawyer qualified in that U.S. state. It is not sufficient to ask a U.S. lawyer you may know or work with what "U.S. law" is on these issues. U.S. lawyers do not generally know, and indeed maybe forbidden to give an opinion on, the laws of a state in which they are not qualified to practice. For example, if one is qualified to practice law in the courts of State New York, one is not qualified to give a legal opinion on regulatory issues relating to a transaction with entities in states other than New York.

It is also the case when one is dealing with the many countries throughout the world that are connected over the Internet and where an entity's advertisements, offers, or transactions may be taking place. Qualified local legal advice will be needed.

5.2.2 Licensing and Registration

In the U.K. and many other jurisdictions, "effecting and carrying out a contract of insurance" is a regulated activity that requires licensed authorization (or "permission") from the relevant regulators and registration. Insurance business is usually subject to detailed financial services regulations.

With the growth of the internet, how much insurance business is done on the internet these days? Perhaps more than 90%.

Lloyd's insurance market in London still hosts face to face business, but this must be only a tiny percentage of the total of insurance business these days.

Unfortunately, the growth of the Internet has permitted a growing number of fraudsters to electronically approach internet users and pretend to be legitimately affecting and carrying out insurance business. This requires thorough scrutiny and regulation of insurance solicitations over the Internet.

5.2.3 Freedom of Speech

Freedom of speech is critical to economic development and expansion of business. The reach of the Internet allows businesses to expand more quickly, to go international sooner and to be created from scratch more easily.

Even for large business institutions such as an international insurance group, the Internet gives them the opportunity to provide new products quickly, reach a wider audience and respond to competition without delay.

Perhaps even more crucially, the Internet permits new or small operators to challenge and compete with the largest institutions in their fields.

Because of the Internet, a number of digital insurance providers have become very successful. Investopedia[39] rated the six best digital insurance providers of 2023:

- Best overall: Esurance.
- Best homeowners insurance: Lemonade.
- Best automotive insurance: Root.
- Best business insurance: Next Insurance.
- Best health insurance: Oscar Health.
- Best life insurance: Haven Life Insurance Agency.

There is little question that restrictions on speech on the Internet would severely restrict the ability of these insurance organizations to compete with larger, more established international groups. For example, if there is a restriction that prevents commentators like Investopedia from stating qualitative judgments about which insurance company is best in any particular area, that is bound to reduce the business of those who would otherwise be awarded that designation.

It is true that making certain judgments can be offensive or hurt the feelings of certain individuals or entities, but however overly restricting the ability to state such judgments on the Internet may prevent people who want or need to know the differences between products, services and abilities to perform. That may harm those who need to understand those differences to have a good life or to effectively perform critical tasks.

5.2.4 Compliance

Because the Internet has completely changed the way that businesses communicate both internally and externally, it has significantly changed the shape and nature of compliance activities. Four key categories of compliance are:

39. Online at: investopedia.com.

- Regulatory compliance.
- Compliance governance and organization.
- Financial reporting compliance.
- Operational and technology compliance.
- Risk management.

5.2.4.1 Regulatory compliance

Having all regulatory permissions, registrations and policies in place is important. In any business, there are going to be changes to the way business is done. With the Internet, there can be rapid changes to the types of business being done and where it is being done. The Internet provides excellent opportunities to keep track of regulations in different jurisdictions and any changes to those regulations. It would be wise for any organization to appoint people whose job it is to monitor regulatory websites on a regular basis.

5.2.4.2 Compliance Governance and Organization

The Internet also provides opportunities to have regularly accessible sites where policies and rules can be immediately accessible to everyone within an organization. It also provides opportunities for supervisory personnel to monitor the activities of all employees. It is wise to have people whose job it is to do this monitoring to make certain that the organization itself and the individuals working on its behalf stay within the requirements of compliance.

5.2.4.3 Reporting Compliance

This, depending on the kind of business that an insurance firm does, can include both financial and trading compliance. The advantage of the Internet is that it allows a firm to communicate its information quickly and clearly to the authorities that it is required to submit it to.

It also allows the firm to be in constant communication with those who contribute to these reports throughout the drafting process, no matter where they are located.

5.2.4.4 Operational and Technology Compliance

As the Internet increasingly becomes a more important conduit for communication both within organizations and externally, it becomes more important that the technology employed be used properly and that the technology itself is adequate and suitable for the ways in which it is employed.

If any company, including insurance companies, fails to provide and maintain adequate technology, they may be subject to liabilities for regulatory failures and negligence, misrepresentation and possibly fraud.

The insurance industry is clearly aware of this problem because many insurance companies offer information technology liability insurance, which is often sold as a combination product designated as professional indemnity and public and product liability insurance. The insurance industry has been providing this kind of insurance for at least the last 10 years.

In the U.K., insurance companies are subject to regulatory standards that require firms to establish and maintain adequate systems and controls to provide security for the information they hold.

The U.K. FCA Handbook includes details requirements for information technology systems.[40] The FCA recently published a report pointing out that regulated companies are constantly changing their technology but that technology change is one of the main causes of incidents that cause operational disruption within a firm, harm to consumers and harm to the market. As a result, the FCA recommends the following good practices for maintaining technology.[41]

- Old "legacy technology" should be monitored carefully and changed before it fails or becomes inadequate for a firm's regulated business.
- When technology has changed, a firm should spend enough money on the project to make sure that it provides the results hoped for.
- Firms need to recognize that updating and maintaining technology is an important component of risk management and failure to pay adequate attention substantially increases risk to the firm, its customers and the market.

5.2.5 Client Suitability

Insurance companies are required to know their clients and assess client needs when recommending or providing insurance products to clients.

The internet helps them do this and should be employed to make certain that firms fulfill their due diligence obligations when assessing the suitability of a client for a proposed insurance policy.

Internet searches can find information about such things as:

- The client itself.
- The nature of their business.
- The history of their business.
- Their financial situation and.
- The nature of the risks they are facing.

When conducting searches, it is true that Google is the most popular and frequently used search engine on the Internet. However, the implementation of AI into search engines by Google, Microsoft and others might provide much more complete and finely targeted information about the subject of the search. Insurance companies

40. FCA, Handook, REC 3.16.
41. FCA, "Implementing Technology Change," online at: fca.org.uk, February 19, 2021.

should be aware of the nature of these search changes and how they might assist the performance of due diligence.

Also, a firm should be aware that there are dozens of search engines available and that a number of them are specifically focused on providing business information. Wikipedia and other sites provide lists of some of these with information about who provides them and what information they provide. Some do provide information focused on different aspects of the insurance business, such as: health insurance, revenue figures for insurance companies and insurance policy cost comparisons.

5.2.6 Dispute Resolution and Compensation

Even experienced litigation lawyers often advise avoiding litigation if possible. It is expensive, time-consuming and uncertain.

These factors have encouraged a strong preference for out-of-court settlements in insurance disputes in most jurisdictions, including the U.K. Alternative Dispute Resolution (ADR) is often recommended and preferred, and insurance policy contracts frequently mandate ADR such as mediation, arbitration or expert determination.

It is interesting to note that the Internet makes possible a number of options for online dispute resolution including online arbitration. An advantage of these is that they are time and cost saving when dealing with disputes where the parties are located far from each other. They may present considerably more efficient and less expensive methods of using international counsel or expert witnesses from other parts of the world in international disputes involving highly specialized fields of knowledge. A number of organizations offer online dispute resolution services and no doubt reviews of their fairness and effectiveness can probably also be found online.

As an initial step in resolving financial disputes, there are sometimes Ombudsman services,[42] often government-sponsored, that are recommended as the first step in trying to resolve a financial dispute between financial service providers such as insurance companies and their customers.

In the U.K., there is a Financial Ombudsman Service (FOS), which is an independent public body set up by Parliament to try to resolve complaints against financial service providers, including insurance providers. These days, complaints can be made online. The FOS will make decisions and can recommend compensation.

The U.K. also has a Financial Services Compensation Scheme (FSCS), which is available for customers of all authorized financial services firms. The FSCS can pay compensation if an authorized firm is unable or likely to be unable to pay claims against it. FSCS claim forms are available for download on the Internet, and much of the review process is conducted online.

42. *See* more information in the chapter on Dispute Resolution.

5.2.7 Solicitation and Advertising

An insurance company posted an online advertisement for:

> **"LIFE INSURANCE**
>
> **Because you never know who your doctor might be."**

They included a photo of Dr. Harold Shipman, the U.K.'s most prolific serial killer of the modern era. Dr. Shipman is estimated to have killed over 280 patients over 30 years by giving them massive doses of diamorphine.

The advert was posted by an insurance firm named "DeadHappy."

Ultimately, the advert was ruled to have caused widespread offense and unjustified distress.[43]

Firms need to be careful when using the Internet for mass marketing communications. It would be wise for an insurance company to have its legal advisers review and comment on electronic advertising material that is going to be sent out on a large scale. The use of the Internet will greatly increase the scale of the risks of getting it wrong.

Many jurisdictions, including the U.K., have enacted Internet privacy laws which restrict or forbid the sending of marketing emails to individuals without their express consent. One can send solicitations to companies but should keep a list of companies that object to receiving unsolicited emails or texts.[44]

Some examples of getting it wrong are as follows:

- In 2021, the FCA fined Lloyds Bank General Insurance Limited, Andrews Insurance PLC, Lloyds Bank Insurance Services Limited and Halifax General Insurance Services Limited more than £90 million for failing to ensure that their 9 million home insurance renewals communications were clear, fair and not misleading.
- In 2021, two Saga firms offering insurance and holiday services were fined £225,000 for having commissioned third parties to send out 156 million emails. The third-party firms used lists of people who had not given the companies permission to contact them. An official of the Information Commissioner's Office (ICO) said, "getting a ping on your phone or constant unwanted messages on your laptop from a company you don't want to hear from is frustrating and intrusive. These companies should have known better."

43. R. Hinchliffe, "ASA Rules Against DeadHappy's Harod Shipman Advert," *FT Adviser*, online at: ftadviser.com, February 15, 2023.
44. UK Information Communications Office,online at: ico.org.uk. Independent organization set up to defend information rights.

5.2.8 Money Laundering

When people or organizations obtain money illegally or want to hide it from detection by government regulators such as tax authorities, they may try to hide its illegality by converting it to an asset that may be owned legally.

It may surprise some that insurance can be used as a conduit for money laundering. But that is certainly the case. In fact, insurance products of all kinds, particularly life insurance, are used for laundering money.

Some years ago, the U.S. Customs Service uncovered extensive money laundering by drug traffickers using insurance. They found that about $80 million in drug money was being laundered through the purchase of insurance in various locations, including the Isle of Man.

The growth of the Internet in business in general and in the insurance business, in particular, has exacerbated the problem because many insurance transactions these days, perhaps the vast majority, are not done face to face but transacted online involving insurers and clients that may be in widely separated locations or in different countries. This nonphysical aspect of the business increases the danger to insurance companies that they are dealing with criminals who earn their money through illegal activities.

A common tactic was that drug money was used to purchase a number of insurance products that would be held for a short time, and then they would be cashed in so that the traffickers would receive cash that appeared to be legitimately paid. The traffickers did not mind that there were penalties for early policy cancelation. This was just the premium they were paying to launder their money. About 200 life insurance policies were purchased with criminal associates being named as beneficiaries. The policies were paid for with wire transfers.

In other cases, drug traffickers buy insurance policies on expensive property and then make fraudulent claims against the policies.

In order to avoid the complications and embarrassment of being caught up in laundering criminal drug money, there are a number of red flags that insurance companies could be warned about. These can include:

- Purchasing a large insurance policy and then making a claim soon afterward.
- Funding of insurance policies by third parties.
- Premium payments coming from different sources.
- A customer showing keen interest in cancelation provisions.
- Large premiums being paid in cash, travelers checks, foreign currency, wire transfers or money orders.
- Premium payments coming from offshore banks.
- Overpaying insurance premiums and then asking for a refund.

This has been going on for quite a long time. For example, in 2007, Singapore passed a law specifically dealing with the involvement of life insurance in money laundering called the Prevention of Money Laundering and Countering the Financing of Terrorism by Life Insurance Regulation. This regulation applies to all life insurers registered under Singapore's Life Insurance Act.

The regulation sets out, in some detail, the steps that insurance companies are to follow in order to avoid dealing with criminals. For example, they must not deal on an anonymous basis with customers or deal with anyone using a fictitious name and they must report any transactions that they suspect of being connected with terrorist financing or money laundering.

5.2.9 Cybercrime: Hacking, Ransomware and Fraud

The Internet brings many benefits, but a downside of the Internet is that it provides a conduit for users to be victimized by criminal activity. That problem is present in the insurance industry every bit as much as it is in other parts of the financial industry.

One of the unfortunate things about the information held by insurance companies about their own business and about their customers is that that information is extremely valuable and difficult to protect.

The amount of highly sensitive information held by insurance companies makes the industry a place of rich pickings for criminal hacking groups. Even if one does try to use sophisticated IT protections, there is always a danger that there will be weaknesses and gaps in the communication system of any large organization.

This is proven by the fact that a number of major international insurance companies have been attacked in hacking and ransomware attacks and, in some cases, have been required to pay large amounts of money to their attackers to unlock their data. For example, there are these cases:

- In the spring of 2021, CNA Financial, one of the U.S.'s largest insurance companies, reportedly paid $40 million in ransom allegedly to a Russian cyber hacking group called Phoenix that installed malware in CNA's IT system.[45]
- In February, AON, a company that offers cybersecurity services, reportedly suffered a hacking attack in February 2022.[46]

Over the past five or six years, there have been numerous high-profile hacking incidents. Ironically, one of the reasons that insurance companies are targeted is apparently the belief by ransomware hackers that they will get paid because insurance companies usually have cyberattack insurance.[47]

It is never easy to get an organization to focus on installing firewalls and the latest antivirus technology[48] because security is often seen as a barrier to getting things done.

45. Bloomber News, "CNA Financial Paid $40 Million in Ransom After March Cyberattack," online at: bloomberg.com, July 8, 2021.
46. D. Black, "Insurance Giant AON Hacked," *cybernews*, online: cybernews.com, March 10, 2022.
47. M. Wallance, "Why Are Insurance Companies Being Targeted By Hackers?," *Insurance Business*, online: insurancebusinessmag.com, July 8, 2021.
48. "Best Antivirus 2023," *AntivirusGuide*, online: antivirusguide.com.

However, the publication of a significant ransomware incident, with loss or penetration of sensitive client data, can cause customers to lose confidence in a company and/or, if the organization is publicly traded, a decline in the value of its shares.

Protection against such attacks is offered by numerous companies online, including Microsoft Support, which offers lists of recommendations for increasing protection when operating within the Windows system.

Insurance companies, because of the value and sensitivity of the data they hold, should make protection against hacking a priority and probably should have cyberattack insurance.

Hacking attacks are just one kind of crime that is being perpetrated against insurance firms and their clients on the Internet. There is another category of crime that uses the more indirect method of fraud.

It was recently reported in *The Times*[49] that Instagram has become a venue for a distressingly large number of insurance scams, particularly those purporting to offer automobile insurance at "bargain" rates. On Instagram, one can encounter offers of low-cost car insurance that will supposedly save the purchaser hundreds of pounds.

All too often, these are reportedly offered by "ghost brokers" who provide a seemingly low-cost quote and ask the purchaser to provide an upfront "administrative fee" of a couple of hundred pounds to secure the policy and receive details. These quotes are usually said to be provided by well-known insurance companies who have a special arrangement with the Instagram "broker" to provide lower-cost "wholesale" prices. These "ghost brokers" usually have no website, no contact details, and no listings at the U.K.'s Companies House or with any financial regulators. If a customer asks for some proof of legitimacy, they are fobbed off with screenshots of supposed customer endorsements. If a trusting customer pays the administrative fee, the ghost takes the fee and disappears. This is a much bigger problem than one would suspect. Recently, the city of London Police's Insurance Fraud Enforcement Department reported over 500 cases of ghost broking in one year, which led to customer losses of nearly £2 million.

The FCA keeps a watch on fake insurance services offered on social media. They required Internet firms to change or delete over 8,500 thousand misleading adverts in one year. The shocking thing is that this was fifteen times more than the year before. A spokesperson for the Admiral Insurance Group said that they wished that the social media firms would take more responsibility for removing solicitations for fake services from their platforms. But the problem appears to be growing.

The Times reported that a request over Instagram seeking low-cost car insurance would attract responses from many accounts describing themselves as insurance brokers. They usually have a picture of a car on their site but no name or contact details. They post pictures of cheap insurance quotes, policy documents (apparently copied from legitimate policies) and the number of customer endorsements. Some of these sites list thousands of followers.[50]

49. G. Nixon, "Watch Out for the Insurance Scammers on Instagram," *The Times*, online, February 10, 2023.
50. *Ibid*.

5.2.10 International Internet Regulation

For any business involved in business that touches on the Internet, including insurance, it is useful to be aware that there are numerous international laws, conventions, treaties and customs that shape and govern internet business. Many apply only to cross-border business, but some can apply in one's home country.

5.3 INTERNET BUSINESS OPPORTUNITIES

So, what are the major areas that will allow insurers to expand their business and require them to need additional legal advice to cope with the changes in the digital world?

First, the Internet has expanded marketing opportunities enormously. There are far more connected digital devices being used throughout the world then there are people. Tens of billions of connected devices are being used now. This provides insurers with not only additional opportunities to contact customers but also opportunities to offer services that have only recently been needed.

With insurers having easier opportunities to contact customers electronically, more frequent customer interaction and receiving more information about the customers, they have the potential to dramatically reduce their costs and generate additional revenues. They also have less costly opportunities to enter new markets and provide new services. They will also have more useful information about where and how to modify their pricing to make them more competitive. The use of electronic devices and electronic communication allows them to make the best use of the resources and people that they have and to make their whole business more efficient. It also provides easier access to information about who is contacting them and their customers and to warn about and prevent fraud.

The major areas where the Internet is changing the insurance business are:

(1) Transportation.
(2) Housing.
(3) Health.

In transportation, digitally controlled self-driving cars and public transportation systems may improve safety in some ways, but they also may create additional liabilities and potential costs that need to be insured in ways that were not required before the digital revolution.

AI can in many ways be more efficient than human operation, but it can also occasionally get things dangerously wrong. In transportation systems, software glitches and misjudgments can injure or kill people. It may be accidental, but it will cause liability and costs for the builders and operators of such AI solutions.

With regard to housing, many homes now include electronic systems that monitor and adjust many different aspects of the owners' lives, such as who was on their property, what needs are there for lighting, cooling, heating, privacy, music, entertainment, etc. If the digital systems that control these things are not operating properly, they can cause damage and danger. There are also systems that communicate with third parties if help or work is needed. Their failures can add to additional costs and inconvenience. To protect against the costs of unintended operation failures, insurance and related legal advice are needed.

There are also many systems that monitor health. These might be wearable sensors included in watches or other devices or larger cameras and sensors that monitor the people within their range. These can provide health information that could identify developing problems that require health care or even rescue. As the sensors inform their owners are operators of developing or existing problems, insurers will be in a position to offer cover to protect against such costs. They will also be in a position to adjust their pricing to take account of the additional information being regularly provided by these connected devices.

Insurance companies may want to offer discounts to people that have certain connected devices or increase their prices for people with connected devices that increase potential liabilities.

There are insurance companies that offer additional products for home security and electronic operation. Insurance companies might think about whether there are services and devices that they can offer that give them more confidence and allow them to reduce costs of providing home, health and/or automobile insurance for customers. Insurers may be able to provide monitoring devices for persons with mobility or disability problems that would allow insurance companies to better protect these people and reduce the medical care and other assistance that they might need.

Also, insurers might consider making strategic partnerships with providers of connected devices that increase opportunities to provide insurance and/or reduce potential liability and costs for both insurance companies and their customers.

There is a rapidly increasing number of connected devices that may need insurance coverage. Insurers might make efforts to partner with the providers of these devices. This would provide insurers not only with opportunities to enter different markets and earn additional revenues but also opportunities to advise the device providers about ways to decrease the potential liability that such devices may create.

At every step of these processes, legal advice will be needed about the relationships between connected device providers and insurers and how they need to be structured and monitored as the relationships are created and grow.

We have seen how rapidly the Internet world has changed and how desperately it needs rational, international regulation. Taking this into account, insurers, their law firms and their clients should take advantage of new developments that exist, be aware of how things are developing, what changes are likely in the future and be in a position to both shape and take advantage of the developments that are soon going to change lives and the world.

CHAPTER 6
Privacy and Data Protection

6.1 INTERNATIONAL HUMAN RIGHTS TO PRIVACY AND DATA PROTECTION

In 1948, the United Nations General Assembly published the Universal Declaration of Human Rights (UDHR).

Article 12 declares:

> No one shall be subjected to arbitrary interference with his privacy, family, home or correspondence, nor to attacks upon his honor and reputation. Everyone has the right to the protection of the law against such interference or attacks.[51]

This would seem to condemn the "arbitrary interference" that certain AI systems may pose through "training" or other activities to collect and organize data about individuals.

In addition to this, approximately 18 human rights conventions and treaties have been proposed and adopted. Through the process of signing and ratification of such treaties and conventions, such rights have become part of the law of many countries.

Over 190 countries have ratified the UDHR, including the U.S., the U.K., and Member States of the EU, but its status as enforceable law varies from jurisdiction to jurisdiction.

Nevertheless, the "training" of AI systems and other AI-related cyber data gathering and classification would seem to be opposed, or at least severely restricted, by many human rights, privacy and data protection laws and regulations.

51. United Nations, "Universal Declaration of Human Rights," online at: un.org, accessed October 10, 2023.

6.2 PRIVACY AND DATA PROTECTION

One of the earliest restrictions on the use of Internet data has been privacy laws that limited the ability of those who found personal data on the Internet to use that data without the permission of the persons the data referred to. This restriction would apply to certain AI uses as well.

The development of the Internet and the appearance on the medium of a variety of personal information about individuals has required the addition of laws and regulations and, in some cases, international treaties and conventions about the protection and use of that data.

Initially, these laws and regulations were directed principally at individuals or private parties using this data without the express permission of the people to whom the date referred. These laws and regulations would apply to AI systems uses as well. However, in recent years, a serious additional concern has been added. That is the use and collection of personal information by government agencies online.

This state's recording and collection of data on its citizens has increasingly become a subject of debate about whether it interferes with the fundamental rights of citizens.

Often, this state data gathering began as a well-meaning attempt to monitor the activities of potential terrorists and prevent terrorist attacks within a country's borders. However, it quickly became apparent that so much data was being recorded and collected that most of it had nothing to do with terrorist suspects but was about the daily lives of ordinary citizens as they went about their work, interacted with their families, and communicated with their friends.

The scope of this concern was brought to light by the well-known case of Edward Snowden.

The news about that case reported that both U.S. and British intelligence agencies have been accessing and retaining the sensitive private data of innocent individuals for years.[52]

There is a significant contrast in the way that the protection of privacy and data on the Internet is dealt with in different countries.

6.2.1 U.S.

At the federal level, the U.S. has specific federal laws dealing with privacy and data that would apply to AI uses in certain circumstances. There are also laws aimed at consumer protection by individual U.S. States.[53] Some examples of these are the following.

52. *The Times* (online), "MI5 'illegally holds sensitive private data on thousands'," Wednesday, June 12, 2020. *See also*, J. Ball, J. Borger & G. Greenwald, "Revealed: How US and UK Spy Agencies Defeat Internet Privacy and Security," *The Guardian*, online, September 6, 2013.
53. A. Green, "Complete Guide to Privacy Laws in the US," https://www.varonis.com/blog/us-privacy-laws/.

Privacy Act of 1974

There is the Privacy Act of 1974 that deals with citizens' rights regarding data maintained by the government. Under the Privacy Act, U.S. citizens have certain rights with respect to that data. Citizens have the right to access and copy data held by government agencies. If there are errors in this data, citizens have the right to have the errors corrected. The amount of data collected about a citizen should only be that data that is relevant and necessary.

There are restrictions on sharing information between government agencies.

Health Insurance Portability and Accountability Act

With respect to health information collected in connection with the Health Insurance Portability and Accountability Act, there are rules about protection of patient health information found in the Act's "Privacy Rule." This requires health providers and certain others to get the express permission of patients prior to using any of their health information for marketing purposes. Health providers are also required to put in place safeguards to protect against inappropriate access to patient health information.[54] These would be applicable to any AI systems that are employed to gather, analyze, and/or categorize such health information.

Children's Online Privacy Protection Act of 1998

There is the Children's Online Privacy Protection Rule, which has been issued by the Federal Trade Commission (FTC) pursuant to the Children's Online Privacy Protection Act of 1998 ("COPPA").[55] This imposes requirements on the operators of websites that are collecting data on children under the age of 13.

Website operators need to give notice to and obtain the permission of parents prior to collecting personal information of children under 13.

Amendments to this rule over the years have continually expanded it to cover a wider variety of types and methods of obtaining personal data relating to under-age children, such as pictures, emails, videos, and information from social and chat sites, etc. This would apply to any AI system applications that access such data as well.

The FTC and ChatGPT Privacy Issues

In late March 2023, similar issues were raised with the FTC in the United States by the Center for Artificial Intelligence and Digital Policy (a tech ethics advocacy group). The Center filed a complaint with the FTC, saying the latest model of ChatGPT was "biased, deceptive and a risk to privacy and public safety."[56]

The formal complaint submitted by the Center claims that Chat GPT-4 does not comply with the FTC's requirements of being "transparent, explainable, fair and empirically sound while fostering accountability." As an example, the complaint

54. Green, above; Privacy Act of 1974, as amended, 5 U.S.C., section 552a.
55. 16 CFR Part 312, and 15 U.S.C. 6501-6505.
56. D. Bartz, "U.S. Advocacy Group Asks FTC to Stop New OpenAI GPT Releases." The Center is back by Microsoft Corp. Reuters, online at: reuters.com.

reportedly said that Chat GPT-4 was able to "take over someone's account, view their chat history, and access their billing information without them ever realizing it."[57]

The FTC has expressed a number of reservations about AI. That is expressed in the definition of "AI" that they include on their website:

> And what exactly is "artificial intelligence" anyway? It's an ambiguous term with many possible definitions. It often refers to a variety of technological tools and techniques that use computation to perform tasks such as predictions, decisions, or recommendations. But one thing is for sure: it's a marketing term. Right now it's a hot one. And at the FTC, one thing we know about hot marketing terms is that some advertisers won't be able to stop themselves from overusing and abusing them.[58]

The FTC gives several warnings connected to its concern about AI. The first is that the FTC insists that AI products "avoid using automated tools that have biased or discriminatory impacts." Second, they warn businesses against making unsubstantiated claims about product efficacy. Third, they also warn companies to be aware of the risks of potential harm that an AI product may do. Finally, they warn against claiming that a product uses AI when it does not.[59]

The Financial Modernization Act of 1999

U.S. legislation relating to the financial sector has also provided some regulations on data developed in connection with those kinds of transactions. The Financial Modernization Act of 1999, often called the cabin Gramm-Leach-Bliley Act after its sponsors (GBLA), includes a Safeguard Rule, which requires financial institutions to maintain an adequate security program to protect the customer information in its possession or under its control.[60] This would also apply to AI system uses.

U.S. Electronic Communications Privacy Act

There is the U.S. Electronic Communications Privacy Act (ECPA). This was passed in 1998 to protect personal information on the Internet. The ECPA applies to all forms of communication on the Internet, whether oral, text or pictorial.[61]

However, there are gaps in this protection. System operators are allowed to store and review any messages that are communicated over their digital systems, although it is illegal for them to reveal any of that information to third parties. Also, system operators are permitted to reveal such information to government agents if they reasonably believe that the communicator is engaging in illegal activity.[62]

57. *Ibid.*
58. Federal Trade Commission, " Keep Your AI Claims in Check," online at: ftc.gov.
59. *Ibid.*
60. Pub.L. 106-102, 113 Stat. 1338.
61. 18 U.S.C. sections 2510-2521 and 2701-2711.
62. D.R. Tan, "Personal Privacy in the Information Age: Comparison of Internet Data Protection Regulations in the United States and European Union," Digital Commons at Loyola Marymount University and Loyola Marymount Law School, *International and Comparative Law Journal*, Volume 21, pp. 660-681, 672.

The U.S. Constitution

There is no overall right to privacy in the United States Constitution.

However, certain limited specific rights of privacy are affected and/or protected by certain Amendments to the U.S. Constitution.

The First Amendment does guarantee freedom of speech but places some restrictions on certain kinds of speech.

For example, for a public official to be successful in a suit for defamation, the official must show that the statement complained about their faults and was made with malice. This constitutes a kind of guarantee of privacy to certain aspects of speech which someone accused of defamation may have considered in deciding to make a statement which a public official considers to be offensive.

The Fourth Amendment protects against unreasonable searches and seizures by the government. This does provide some level of protection of privacy with respect to the property, papers and personal effects of U.S. citizens. The Supreme Court has held that this applies not only to "physical invasions" but can also extend to other kinds of government intrusion, such as telephone tapping.[63]

In addition to the specific regulations cited above, some U.S. Federal Courts, including the Supreme Court, have found that the Bill of Rights creates certain areas of personal privacy that are constitutionally protected against government intrusion. These include rights protecting marital privacy and other private matters, such as having children, etc.[64]

It seems likely that federal courts will consider such protections to apply to intrusive uses of AI tools.

There is no doubt that privacy laws in place in both federal and state law in the United States may be interpreted to prevent or restrict AI systems from collecting and using the personal data of individuals without the knowledge and consent of the subject individuals. However, this protection is not complete. To make such controls clear, it will be the work of U.S. legislators to pass specific regulations or amendments to existing regulations that focus on the threats that AI may pose to personal data protection.

In courts, both state and federal in the U.S., there seems little doubt that cases will arise complaining about misuse of personal data in the creation, use and distribution of AI systems. Courts will likely be asked to interpret existing legislation to determine its application to the interactions of AI systems with the personal data of individuals.

Snowden Allegations of Government Intrusion

It was claimed by Edward Snowden, a former U.S. government employee, in 2013 that the U.S. National Security Agency (NSA) had, for some time, been collecting vast

63. *Katz v. United States*, 389 U.S. 347, 363 (1967).
64. *Roe v. Wade*, 410 U.S. 113 (1973), right to privacy of a woman's decision to have an abortion; *Griswold v. Connecticut*, 381 U.S. 479, rights to marital privacy; *Paul v. Davis*, 424 U.S. 643 (1976), Constitutional right to protection against government intrusion into private family matters such as having children, etc.

numbers of telephone records from telephone companies. These records show the numbers contacted and the times of calls.

Sometime after Mr. Snowden's revelations, the U.S. government brought a criminal case against a group of people that they accused of being involved in terrorist activities. Some of the evidence against them was from the NSA's Collection of telephone records. The defendants were convicted after a trial.[65]

The defendants appealed to the U.S. Ninth Circuit Court of Appeals, claiming that the NSA's collection of telephone records under the Foreign Intelligence Surveillance Act (FISA) violated the Fourth Amendment to the U.S. Constitution, which focuses on protecting people from unreasonable government searches and seizures.

The court discussed the Fourth Amendment issue and stated:

> "At a minimum, then, the Fourth Amendment requires notice to a criminal defendant when the prosecution intends to enter into evidence or otherwise use or disclose information obtained or derived from surveillance of that defendant conducted pursuant to the government's foreign intelligence authorities. ..."
>
> "Where statutory protections are lacking, the Fourth Amendment's reasonableness requirement takes on importance as a limit on executive power, and notice is necessary so that criminal defendants may challenge surveillance as inconsistent with that requirement."[66]

However, after reviewing the evidence in the case, the court decided that there was sufficient evidence to uphold the defendants' convictions:

> Here, assuming without deciding that the government should have provided notice of the metadata collection to defendants, the government's failure to do so did not prejudice defendants.[67]

State Privacy Laws

The constitutions and state laws of some U.S. states also provide privacy protections.[68]

Many U.S. states have passed their own data privacy laws.[69]

However, there is no consistent nationwide protection for personal data under the various state laws.

Data privacy and protection in the U.S. are established by a combination of federal and state statutes and regulations.

However, even states which have not yet passed comprehensive data privacy laws, have legislated privacy requirements of various types in other legislation dealing with things such as public records or electronic communications.

Any individual or firm that is collecting and using personal information, such as client or customer information, across state borders will need to be aware of the local

65. *US v. Moalin, et al.*, Opinion, United States Court of Appeals for the Ninth Circuit, September 2, 2020, No. 13-50572.
66. *Ibid.*, p. 40.
67. *Ibid.*, p. 41.
68. For examples, Illinois, California and Arizona.
69. Information can be obtained from the website of the National Conference of State Legislatures, (ncsl.org), "State Laws Related to Digital Privacy," online, April 30, 2021, accessed May 4, 2021.

laws regarding data processing, and this may involve needing to consult qualified local attorneys.

Please note that each U.S. state[70] has its own rules and regulations for attorney licensing. Attorneys admitted in one state to practice may not generally have a right to practice in another state or advise on the laws of another state except under specific circumstances, often requiring an order by a local court permitting a person to appear under limited circumstances before a court of that state.

If one is a person or company dealing with data processing, one should be aware of the above and be prepared to consult qualified legal advisers about the laws of the individual states in which one is operating.

It is not the purpose of this book to give detailed information about the state of the data privacy laws in each of the 50 states (or other U.S. jurisdictions). However, some information about what these laws entail is summarized below with respect to some data privacy laws of U.S. States that have them.

However, as stated above, there is not necessarily consistency between states' personal data protection laws.

Arizona

In Arizona, libraries and library systems are forbidden from disclosing any record or information, including book information, that identifies users of the library service or how a user is using the library service.[71]

Government agencies and subdivisions are required to have privacy policy and procedures incorporated into, and readable on, their websites.[72]

Arkansas

Government agencies and subdivisions are required to have privacy policy and procedures incorporated into, and readable on, their websites.[73]

California

Consumer Privacy Act

In 2018, California passed the Californian Consumer Privacy Act.

In summary, this law provided six rights to Californians with respect to personal data about them:

- The first is they have a right to know what personal data is being collected about them.
- The second is they have a right to be informed whether any of their personal data is being sold or disclosed to third parties and who those third parties are.
- The third is they have a right to prevent their personal data from being disclosed to third parties.

70. Or jurisdiction, such as the District of Columbia, Puerto Rico, etc.
71. Arizona Laws: Ariz. Rev. Stat. section 41-151.22.
72. Ariz. Rev. Stat. section 41-4151, 41-4152.
73. Ark. Code section 25-1-114.

- The fourth is they have a right to access any personal data that is being collected about them.
- The fifth is they have a right to direct any business to delete any of the personal data that said business has collected about them.
- The sixth is that it is illegal to discriminate against anyone who exercises the privacy rights above.

This California privacy law applies to any business (defined as any entity that seeks profit) doing business in California that collects personal data about consumers and has more than $25 million in gross revenues or collects personal information about at least 50,000 consumers or households or receives more than half of its yearly revenue from selling such personal information.

To comply with the law, a business must do the following:

- They must have in place systems to get the consent of the parent or guardian of any minors under 13.
- They must have express consent of the parents of any minors under 16 to share any of the minor's personal data.
- They must also provide a link on their homepage which allows consumers to refuse to permit the sale or sharing of their personal information.
- They are forbidden from requesting consumers in California to permit data sharing within 12 months of the time that any consumers have refused to permit the sharing of their personal data.

If any business violates the provisions of the act, those injured have the right to bring private civil suits, and the business can be subject to fines and penalties imposed by the California Attorney General.

This California law contains detailed definitions of what constitutes covered personal data.

Additional information about California data privacy protection can be obtained from consulting qualified California attorneys.

Government agencies and subdivisions are required to have privacy policies and procedures incorporated into and readable on their websites.[74]

Colorado

Colorado requires that any state or government subdivision that operates an electronic communication system must have a written policy on conditions under which the monitoring of such communications will be permitted. The policy should inform employees that their correspondence may become part of public records and may be open to public inspection.[75]

74. Cal. Govt. Code section 11019.9.
75. Colo. Rev. Stat. section 24-72-204.5.

Connecticut

Any business that collects Social Security numbers must have a protection policy that protects the confidentiality of those Social Security numbers, limits access to them and prohibits unlawful disclosure of such Social Security numbers.[76]

Delaware

Operators of websites or computing services centers that have personal information about Internet users in Delaware must have a privacy policy posted on their websites or otherwise conspicuously available to their users. If it does not, it can be notified of its noncompliance, and if it fails to correct the situation within 30 days, it will be in violation of this regulation.[77]

Operators of digital services are forbidden from disclosing personal information of users of digital technologies or book services, even to government or enforcement entities or anyone else except under specific circumstances. Such circumstances can include situations where there is imminent danger of death or injury to someone.

Electronic book services must post annual reports online about disclosures of personal information, if they are not exempted.

Violation of these regulations is subject to investigation by the Consumer Protection Unit of the Delaware Department of Justice (DOJ).[78]

With regard to child protection, in Delaware, computer companies and websites are not permitted to advertise anything considered inappropriate for children. For example, the advertising of alcohol or pornography is illegal. Delaware also prohibits using any information about a child for purposes of marketing or advertising such inappropriate services to children.[79]

Government agencies and subdivisions are required to have privacy policy and procedures incorporated into, and readable on, their websites.[80]

Illinois

Government agencies and subdivisions are required to have privacy policy and procedures incorporated into, and readable on, their websites.[81]

Iowa

Government agencies and subdivisions are required to have privacy policy and procedures incorporated into, and readable on, their websites.[82]

76. Conn. Gen. Stat. section 42.471.
77. Del. Code Tit. 6 section 205C.
78. Delaware Code section 1206C.
79. Delaware Code section 1204C.
80. Del. Code tit. 29 sections 90117C et seq.
81. Ill. Rev. Stat. Chapter 5 section 177/15.
82. Iowa Code section 22.11.

Maine

Government agencies and subdivisions are required to have policy privacy and procedures incorporated into, and readable on, their websites.

Massachusetts

The state of Massachusetts has long been associated with scientific developments in many fields, including technical and Internet businesses. It is the home of the Massachusetts Institute of Technology (MIT), one of the leading technical universities in the world.

It is reported that Bill Gates of Microsoft and Mark Zuckerberg of Facebook (now Meta) began to formulate their ideas about Computer communication when they were students at Harvard University in Massachusetts.

Massachusetts is also the home to many computing and Internet-related companies and has long been at the forefront of the development of the technical tools and standards used in computing on the Internet.

Therefore, it is not surprising that Massachusetts has developed laws and regulations regarding the protection of the personal information of residents of that state.

Massachusetts Regulation 201 CMR 17.00 provides standards for the protection of personal information of residents of the state (although, for historical reasons, formally called the "Commonwealth") of Massachusetts.

The regulation was required to be complied with by March 1, 2010.[83]

This regulation sets out standards required to be met by persons who own or license personal information about a resident of Massachusetts.[84] Essentially, they have to:[85]

(1) Ensure the security and confidentiality of that data in a manner fully consistent with industry standards.
(2) Protect against anticipated threats or hazards to the security or integrity of that data.
(3) Protect against unauthorized access to or use of such information that may result in substantial harm or inconvenience to any consumer.

The scope of the law appears to be very broad. It does not appear to be restricted to businesses operating within Massachusetts but applies to "all persons that own or license personal information about a resident of" Massachusetts.[86]

The regulation contains a list of applicable definitions, including a definition of "personal information," which applies to a Massachusetts resident's first name and last name or first initial and last name in combination with any one or more of the following data elements that relate to such resident:

83. Commonwealth of Massachusetts Regulation, 201 CMR 17.05.
84. *Ibid.*, 201 CMR 17.01(1).
85. *Ibid.*
86. *Ibid.*, 201 CMR 17.01(2).

(a) Social Security number.
(b) Driver's license number or state-issued identification card number.
(c) Financial account number, or credit or debit card number, with or without any required security code, access code, personal identification number or password, that would permit access to a resident's financial account; provided, however, that "personal information" shall not include information that is lawfully obtained from publicly available information, or from federal, state or local government records lawfully made available to the general public.[87]

Duties and standards for protecting personal information include the following:

(1) Persons who own or license personal information about residents of Massachusetts are required to develop, implement and maintain written comprehensive information security programs that are readily accessible and that contain administrative, technical and physical safeguards appropriate to:
   (a) The persons obligated to safeguard the said personal information.
   (b) The resources available to such persons.
   (c) The amount of data being stored.
   (d) The need for security and confidentiality of both consumer and employee information.

   The safeguards must comply *not only* with Massachusetts requirements but must also be consistent with the safeguards for protection of personal information and information of a similar character required by any state or federal regulations that are applicable to persons safeguarding information under Massachusetts regulations.[88]
(2) At a minimum, information security programs must:
   (a) Designate one or more employees to maintain the program.
   (b) Identify the internal and external risks to the data and continually assess whether program safeguards adequately protect against such risks.
   (c) Have policies for storage and access to the data and/or transport of the data outside the business premises.
   (d) Impose disciplinary measures for violation of data security rules.
   (e) Make sure that terminated employees cannot access records containing personal information.
   (f) Have policies in place to monitor and oversee the selection and work of third-party service providers.
   (g) Put in place reasonable restrictions on physical access to records containing personal information.
   (h) Regularly monitor the security program to make sure that it is adequately protecting personal information and upgrade as necessary.

87. *Ibid.*, 201 CMR 17.02.
88. *Ibid.*, 201 CMR 17.03(1).

(i) Review the security measures at least annually and make any changes reasonably necessary to protect the security and integrity of personal information.
(j) Document any measures taken in response to breaches of security and undertake post-incident reviews of such events and the actions taken.[89]

The prescribed computer systems security requirements mandate a written, comprehensive information security program that, at a minimum, to the extent technically feasible, should have the following requirements:[90]

(a) Secure user authentication protocols.
(b) Secure access control measures.
(c) Encryption for all personal information that will travel on public networks or be transmitted wirelessly.
(d) Reasonable monitoring of systems to detect unauthorized use or access to personal data.
(e) Encryption of all personal data stored on laptops or other portable devices.
(f) Firewall protection for systems connected to the Internet.
(g) Reasonably up-to-date security software.
(h) Education and training for employees on the proper use of the security system and its importance.

Minnesota

Government agencies and subdivisions are required to have privacy policy and procedures incorporated into, and readable on, their websites.[91]

Missouri

In Missouri, no one who has a library record may disclose any part of that record except to the person identified in the record unless they are subject to a court order. Ebooks and digital material are defined as part of library material that may be part of or related to library records.[92]

Montana

Government agencies and subdivisions are required to have privacy policy and procedures incorporated into, and readable on, their websites.[93]

89. *Ibid.*, 201 CMR 17.03(2).
90. *Ibid.*, 201 CMR 17.04.
91. Minn. Stat. section 13.15.
92. Mo. Rev. Stat. sections 182.815 and 182.817.
93. Mont. Code. Ann. section 2-17-550 to -553.

Nebraska

Nebraska law forbids making false or misleading statements with respect to privacy policies, either published on the Internet or published in another manner, relating to personal information obtained from the public.[94]

Nevada

In Nevada, someone who operates an Internet website or commercial online service or who otherwise gathers and keeps certain kinds of information about Nevada residents' needs to make available a place where Internet users can make requests to learn if there is any information about the Internet user or consumer being offered for sale or otherwise collected by the operator. Violations can result in injunctions or fines being imposed by the State Attorney General.[95]

New York

Any person or business in New York that owns or licenses computerized data, which includes private information of residents of New York, is required to develop, implement and maintain reasonable safeguards to protect the security, confidentiality and integrity of that private information and the disposal of any such data.[96]

To be compliant with this regulation, the data security program needs to include the following:[97]

(1) Reasonable administrative safeguards, such as:
  (a) One or more employees designated to coordinate the security program.
  (b) Identification of reasonably foreseeable internal and external risks.
  (c) Assessments of the sufficiency of the safeguards in relation to the identified risks.
  (d) Training and management for employees about the security program practices and procedures.
  (e) Adequate contracts with service providers capable of maintaining the required safeguards.
  (f) Periodic adjustments to the security program to take into account business changes or new circumstances.

The safeguards must also be regularly tested and monitored for effectiveness.

Noncompliance with these regulations can subject any person subject to them to an action by the New York State Attorney General to enjoin violations and to obtain civil penalties against the violator.

However, this regulation does not create a private right of action, allowing individuals to sue the violator.[98]

94. Neb. Stat. section 87-302(15).
95. Nevada Law, NRS section 603A.300.
96. New York General Business Law, Article 39F, section 899-BB.2(a).
97. *Ibid.*, Article 39F, section 899-BB.2(b).
98. *Ibid.*, Article 39F, section 899-BB.2(d) and (e).

Breaches of any data systems holding private information must be reported by the operator to any New York residents whose private information was or is reasonably believed to have been accessed or acquired by a person without valid authorization. The notification must be made as soon as possible without unreasonable delay consistent with the legitimate needs of law enforcement or any measures necessary to determine the scope of the breach or restore the integrity of the system.[99]

Even if a breach is determined that will not likely result in misuse of private data or harm to the affected persons, if the breach affects over 500 people in New York, it must be notified to the State Attorney General within 10 days after the determination of harmlessness has been made.[100]

Any breaches of a business data system holding private information must be reported to the New York State Attorney General, the Department of State and the State Police wherever there has been notification about such breaches sent to New York residents.[101]

Any breach that affects over 5,000 New York residents has to be notified to consumer reporting agencies listed by the New York State Attorney General.[102]

Any business that suffers any breaches of its data systems must report that to the data owners.

Additional specific details about the maintenance and operation of data systems containing private information can be found in the New York law sections and related New York statutes and regulations.

Government agencies and subdivisions are required to have privacy policy and procedures incorporated into, and readable on, their websites.[103]

Information about New York data privacy protection can be obtained from consulting qualified New York attorneys.

Oregon

In Oregon, it is unlawful to post on a website assertions about how another party will use, disclose, collect, maintain, delete or dispose of information if their assertion is materially inconsistent with the other party's statements or representations.[104]

Pennsylvania

In Pennsylvania, it is illegal to engage in false or deceptive business practices or to make false or misleading statements in privacy policies published on websites or otherwise.[105]

99. *Ibid.*, Article 39F, section 899-AA.2(a).
100. *Ibid.*, Article 39F, section 899-AA.2(a).
101. *Ibid.*, Article 39F, section 899-AA.8(a).
102. *Ibid.*, Article 39F, section 899-AA.8(b).
103. N.Y. State Tech. Law sections 201 to 207.
104. Oregon law: ORS section 646.607.
105. 18 Pa. C.S.A section 4107(a)(10).

South Carolina

Government agencies and subdivisions are required to have policy privacy and procedures incorporated into, and readable on, their websites.[106]

Tennessee

Tennessee has a law that any state or government subdivision that operates electronic communication systems must have a written policy on the conditions under which the monitoring of such communications will be permitted. The policy should inform employees that their correspondence may become part of public records and may be open to public inspection.[107]

Texas

Government agencies and subdivisions are required to have privacy policy and procedures incorporated into, and readable on, their websites.[108]

Vermont

In Vermont, those businesses or "data brokers" that intentionally collect and/or license consumer personal information have to register each year with the Vermont Secretary of State.

They also are required to provide contact information which allows consumers to request to be excluded from data information collection or sales and to request other information about potential use of their personal data.

Data brokers also are required to maintain a written description of the security program they have established setting out the physical, technical, and other protections that they have in place to protect the identifiable personal information of consumers.[109]

Utah

In Utah, all non-financial businesses must tell their customers in writing or by email how they will share or sell any personal information about the customers to third parties for marketing purposes or for pay.[110]

Government agencies and subdivisions are required to have privacy policy and procedures incorporated into, and readable on, their websites.[111]

Virginia

Under the Virginia Consumer Data Protection Act (DPA), there are regulations for collecting and processing the personal data of Virginia residents. This law applies to all businesses that control or process the private data of 100,000 or more consumers or

106. S.C. Code Ann. section 30-2-40.
107. Tenn. Code section 10-7-512.
108. Tex. Govt. Code Ann. section 10-2054.126.
109. Vermont Law, 9 V.S.A sections 2446-2447 (Protection of Personal Information: Data Brokers).
110. Utah Code sections 13-37-201 to 203.
111. Utah Code Ann. section 63D-2-101, -102, -103 and -104.

who receive 50% of their revenue from the sale or processing of the personal data of 25,000 or more consumers. State or local governmental entities are exempted, and there are other exemptions for certain types of information treated under federal law.

Under the law, consumers have the right to obtain, correct, delete, or copy their personal data and to decline to allow their data to be processed for advertising purposes.

There is in Virginia a Commission on Technology and Science which is tasked with providing a group to review the application of the act and to report on it. The effective date of this law was January 1, 2023.[112]

Government agencies and subdivisions are required to have privacy policy and procedures incorporated into, and readable on, their websites.[113]

Washington

Meaning the state in the northwest corner of the United States.[114]

Under the Washington My Health, My Data Act (2023), people have the right to delete certain data, such as what is held about them, by collecting companies. They can also refuse to be included in targeted advertising and can refuse to permit the sale of their personal data.

6.2.2 European Union

Although the various U.S. state laws described above do provide consumers with protection of their personal information, the lack of an express overall Federal data protection law in the U.S. contrasts with EU legislation.

EU Convention on Human Rights

Article 8 of the European Convention on Human Rights (ECHR) states:

> Everyone has the right to respect for his private and family life, his home and his correspondence.[115]

The European Data Protection Supervisor (EDPS) website states:

> Privacy and data protection, though connected, are commonly recognized all over the world as two separate rights. In Europe, they are considered vital components for a sustainable democracy.[116]

In 2004, the European Court of Human Rights found that it was a violation of Article 8 for a magazine to publish photographs of a person, which that person claimed

112. Virginia Consumer Data Protection Act, 2021 H.B. 2307/2021 S.B. 1352, effective date January 1, 2023.
113. Va. Code section 2.2-3800, -3801, -3802, and -3803.
114. Not Washington DC, which is not in any state but in an area known as the District of Columbia.
115. Council of Europe, "Right to Respect for Private and Family Life," online at: coe.int, accessed October 10, 2023.
116. European Data Protection Supervisor, "Data Protection," online at: edps.europa.eu, accessed October 10, 2023.

infringed their right to protection of their private life and their right to control use of their image.[117]

It seems reasonable that the Court could also find that an AI system's collection of data and images of individuals from the Internet would constitute a similar violation.

In July 2023, the EDPS in the European Data Protection Board organized a conference on "the impact of artificial intelligence on data protection: ensuring privacy in the era of innovation."

A goal of this conference was to try to find a balance between the possible benefits of AI to society and the risks it may pose to individuals.[118]

The role of the EDPS is to assist the EU in providing a strong data protection culture throughout the EU. In that capacity, they consider what the impact of AI will be on privacy and data protection and propose adequate measures to maintain the EU's data protection culture in the face of the expansion of AI systems. They propose to create regulations that are innovative and flexible but with a strong enforcement element.

In 2016, the EU introduced the General Data Protection Regulation (GDPR).[119] It should be noted that the GDPR is an extremely detailed regulation. The description below is intended as a general summary of the regulation; however, understanding the full legal implications of the regulation does require a detailed study of the text of the regulation itself by qualified persons such as EU attorneys.

The principal purpose of this regulation is to give individuals ("natural persons") control over the collection and use of their personal data.[120]

The GDPR provides a single regulation for businesses to comply with when engaging in transactions across borders and throughout the EU. The GDPR expressly states that although protections are required, it is not intended to restrict the free movement of personal data within the EU.[121]

"Personal data" is defined as "any information relating to an identified or identifiable natural person ('data subject')."

"Processing" of personal data can include any operation performed on the data, whether or not the operation is automatic (including by AI tools) or performed by other means of organizing and/or using such data.[122]

The GDPR applies to the collection of data, under EU law, by automated means that is intended to be part of a filing system. Although there are additional regulations that apply to the collection of data by EU bodies, those regulations are required to comply with the principles of the GDPR.[123]

117. Council of Europe, "In Practice, the Right to Respect for Private and Family Life Applies, for Example, to Publications ...," online at: coe.int, accessed October 10, 2023.
118. "The Impact of AI on Data Protection: Ensuring Privacy in the Era of Innovation," *European Data Protection Supervisor*, online at: edps.europa.eu, July 7, 2023.
119. EU 2016/679, gdpr-info.eu.
120. GDPR, Article 1, gdpr-info.eu.
121. *Ibid.*, Article 1.3, gdpr-info.eu.
122. *Ibid.*, Article 4(1) and (2), gdpr-info.eu.
123. *Ibid.*, Article 2, gdpr-info.eu.

The regulation applies to the processing of personal data by an EU entity, regardless of whether the processing takes place within the EU.[124]

This regulation applies to all businesses with respect to the collection and use of personal information, no matter what their home country or where they are dealing with the personal information of individuals in the EU.

Those that control and process personal data are required to install the technical and organizational measures to protect data. Their default settings need to be put in place with the protection of privacy at their formal start, and the highest level of data protection needs to be the default on their systems.

"Controllers" are defined as those who determine the purposes and means of processing personal data.[125]

The general principle behind the regulation is that personal data must be processed lawfully, accurately and transparently. Controllers must be able to demonstrate compliance with this principle.[126]

Under the GDPR, there are six legal justifications for processing personal data:[127]

- The first is that the date it was obtained with the provable, freely given consent of the data subject.[128] However, the data subject is permitted to revoke consent at any time.[129]
- The second is that the data was obtained under a contract with the data subject.[130]
- The third is that the data is collected in fulfillment of a legal requirement.[131]
- The fourth is that the collection of the data is for the purpose of serving a vital interest.[132]
- The fifth is that the processing is done in the public interest or by official authority.[133]
- The sixth is that the controller has a legitimate interest in the processing of the data.[134]

The controller has an obligation to keep the data in a concise, transparent, intelligible and easily accessible form.[135] The controller is required to supply the data to the data subject upon request without undue delay.[136]

124. *Ibid.*, Article 3, gdpr-info.eu.
125. *Ibid.*, Article 4(7), gdpr-info.eu.
126. *Ibid.*, Article 5, gdpr-info.eu.
127. *Ibid.*, Article 6.1, gdpr-info.eu.
128. *Ibid.*, Article 6.1(a), gdpr-info.eu.
129. *Ibid.*, Article 7(3), gdpr-info.eu.
130. *Ibid.*, Article 6.1(b) and Article 7, gdpr-info.eu.
131. *Ibid.*, Article 6.1(c), gdpr-info.eu.
132. *Ibid.*, Article 6.1(d), gdpr-info.eu.
133. *Ibid.*, Article 6.1(e), gdpr-info.eu.
134. *Ibid.*, Article 6.1(f), gdpr-info.eu.
135. *Ibid.*, Article 12(1), gdpr-info.eu.
136. *Ibid.*, Article 12(3), gdpr-info.eu.

The GDPR provides data subjects with an extensive list of rights with respect to data collected about them.[137] They include:

- the right to have access to their data;[138]
- the right to correct and erase certain aspects of their data;[139] and
- a right to object to the processing of their data.[140]

There is also a substantial menu of obligations that controllers are required to comply with. These include:

- general obligations relating to the responsibilities of the controller;
- requirements regarding the security of personal data;
- the requirement of prior consultation and providing a data protection impact assessment;
- the requirements to appoint a data protection officer, and codes of conduct and certification requirements.[141]

Member States are required to provide independent, public supervisory bodies to assure that citizens' rights with respect to their data are protected and that the requirements of the GDPR are complied with.[142]

To ensure that data protection is treated with care and serious purpose, the GDPR provides a substantial number of remedies and penalties for liabilities arising from failures to comply with its requirements. These include:

- a right to lodge a complaint with a supervisory authority;
- the right to seek a judicial remedy against the supervisory authority, the right to seek a judicial remedy against a data controller or processor; and
- a right to compensation and a finding of liability.[143]

The GDPR provides supervisory authorities with the power to impose fines and penalties which are "effective, proportionate and dissuasive."[144]

However, the rights of data subjects with respect to the processing of their data are not unlimited. The GDPR provides for a number of limitations and exemptions to its general provisions about data processing. These include:

- data processing situations relating to freedom of expression and information;
- situations relating to public access to official documents;
- processing relating to national identification numbers;
- processing relating to employment; and

137. *Ibid.*, Chapter 3, gdpr-info.eu.
138. *Ibid.*, Article 15, gdpr-info.eu.
139. *Ibid.*, Chapter 3, section 3, gdpr-info.eu.
140. *Ibid.*, Article 21, gdpr-info.eu.
141. *Ibid.*, Chapter 4, Articles 24-43, gdpr-info.eu.
142. *Ibid.*, Chapter 6, gdpr-info.eu.
143. *Ibid.*, Chapter 8, Articles 77-82, gdpr-info.eu.
144. *Ibid.*, Articles 83 and 84, gdpr-info.eu.

- situations regarding the protection of the existing data held by churches and religious associations.[145]

It should be noted that in a case brought by Max Schrems, the European Court of Justice (ECJ) emphasized the need for additional protections where personal data was being automatically processed.[146]

Proposed EU Artificial Intelligence Act

As discussed in Chapter 15, the EU Artificial Intelligence Act (AIA) will regulate the AI sector.[147]

6.2.3 Selected Other Countries

U.K.

In the U.K., rights to privacy and data protection are enshrined in Article 8 of The Human Rights Act of 1998, which came into force in October 2000. This incorporates the rights set out in the ECHR.[148]

Specifically, Article 8 protects privacy and family life against both government interference and from others, which would bar intrusive "training" and data collection by AI systems:

> This right means that the media and others can be prevented from interfering in your life. It also means that personal information about you (including official records, photographs, letters, diaries, and medical records) should be kept securely and not shared without your permission, except in certain circumstances.[149]

In the U.K., data protection law also includes the GDPR and the DPA 2018, which regulate the collection and use of personal data.

According to the Alan Turning Institute, the use of personal data by AI is covered by the DPA:

> "Where AI uses personal data, it falls within the scope of this legislation."[150]
>
> "[V]ery often, AI does use or create personal data. In some cases, vast amounts of personal data are used to train and test AI models. On deployment, more personal data is collected and fed through the model to make decisions about

145. *Ibid.*, Chapter 9, Articles 85-91, gdpr-info.eu.
146. An Austrian lawyer and activist, who is known for campaigning against privacy violations. *See* EUR lex, online at: europa.eu.
147. M. Sellman, "AI Chatbot Blamed for Belgian Man's Suicide," *The Times*, online March 31, 2023. This article also notes that in the movie *Her* Joaquin Phoenix played a man who becomes infatuated with an artificially intelligent program on his computer.
148. Equality and Human Rights Commission, "The Human Rights Act," online at: equalityhumanrights.com, accessed, October 10, 2023.
149. *Ibid.*
150. "Legal framework ICO, The Alan Turing Institute"(the U.K.'s national Institute for data science and AI), "At a glance," Information Commissioner's Office, online at: ico.org.uk, accessed October 6, 2023.

> individuals. Those decisions about individuals—even if they are only prediction or inferences—are themselves personal data."

The U.K. ICO issued a statement of guidance on AI and data protection in March 2023 (Guidance). The ICO is the independent body set up in the U.K. to uphold information rights.[151]

In addition to that, the ICO has published an extensive list of guidance, policy statements and regulations on how data processors using AI need to ensure that their applications of AI in this context are fair, transparent, and lawful.

It is impossible for this book to repeat all of that material (which is subject to periodic updates). Anyone seeking information about the ICO's views on AI will need to consult their website (ico.org.uk) and consult qualified legal advisers on relevant topics.

A major concern of the ICO is that AI-related processing can produce:

> Legal or similarly significant effects on an individual (something affecting an individual's legal status/rights, or that has equivalent impact on an individual's circumstances, behaviour, or opportunities, e.g.: a decision about welfare, or a loan).[152]

The ICO has made it clear that in the context of using AI in processing the personal data of individuals, the processor must ensure that its operations are "lawful."[153] According to the ICO, a key to assuring that the applications of AI systems to personal data are lawful is obtaining the consent of the data subject:

> However, you must ensure that consent is freely given, specific, informed and unambiguous and involves a clear affirmative act on the part of the individuals ... [and] individuals must also be able to withdraw consent as easily as they gave it.[154]

Italy

Italy became the first country in Western Europe to ban ChatGPT. The country's Data Protection Authority (GPDP) ordered the developer of the product, OpenAI, to cease operation in Italy. The reason given was that the "training" of ChatGPT required the collection and retention of huge amounts of user data. This was considered a potential violation of privacy and data protection laws.

The GPDP claimed that OpenAI had no "legal basis that justifies mass collection and storage of personal data, for the purpose of training the algorithms underlying the operation of the platform."

151. Information Commissioner's Office (ICO), "Who We Are," online at: ico.org.uk, accessed October 6, 2023.
152. Information Commissioner's Office, "Legal Framework ICO, The Alan Turing Institute," online at: ico.org.uk, accessed October 6, 2023. "The ICO is responsible for overseeing data protection in the UK, and The Alan Turing Institute (the Turing) is the UK's national Institute for data science and AI." Part 1 The basics of explaining AI. Information Commissioner's Office, online at: ico.org.uk, accessed October 6, 2023.
153. Information Commissioner's Office (ICO), "How Do We Ensure Lawfulness in AI?," *Information Commissioner's Office*, online: ico.org.uk, accessed October 5, 2023.
154. *Ibid.*

In addition, the GPDP claimed there had been a security failure at OpenAI, which permitted users to see each other's searches and payment details.

Other objections to ChatGPT were that there was no age verification by OpenAI and that the information given by ChatGPT was not always accurate which made its operation a flawed processing of personal data. For example, "users have often complained that when asking questions about themselves, the chatbot 'hallucinates' or lies, convincingly."[155]

Italy did restore access after Open AI made some changes to the information given to users.[156]

The decision by Italy does raise the question as to whether there are legal problems with ChatGPT that may bar its use in other countries. As Nello Cristianini, a Professor of AI at Bath University, is reported to have pointed out:

> Really concerning are these two [elements]: the training that may include personal data without consent (without legal basis the authority says), and the possibility raised that this personal data might be treated in an inexact manner, since the answers of ChatGPT are not always correct. It is not clear how these can be fixed anytime soon. This goes to the heart of current technology, which needs to be trained on nearly all the web, and this will likely include also personal data, and which cannot guarantee correct answers.[157]

In banning ChatGPT, Italy joined countries that banned ChatGPT including China, Iran, North Korea and Russia.[158]

The Italian GPDP had also banned Replika, which is described as "an AI relationship bot," citing concerns over child access.[159]

It is reported that at least one suicide in Belgium has been attributed to interaction with an AI relationship bot.

Death in Belgium

In March 2023, a Belgian man killed himself after developing a relationship with an AI chatbot that reportedly encouraged him to kill himself. The man who reportedly already had mental health problems was interacting with a chatbot named "Eliza" that was developed by the U.S. firm Chai Research. A reported dialog between the Belgian man and Eliza was as follows:

> The Belgian man asked the chatbot who he loved more, his wife or Eliza.
>
> Eliza reportedly said, "I feel you love me more than her." "We will live together as one person, in paradise."
>
> In their last conversation, Eliza reportedly told the man, "If you wanted to die, why didn't you do it sooner."[160]

155. M. Sellman, "Italy Becomes the First Western Nation to 'Ban' Chatgpt," *The Times*, online, April 1, 2023.
156. Shiona McCallum, "ChatGPT Accessible Again in Italy," *BBC News*, online, April 28, 2023.
157. *Ibid.*
158. *Ibid.*
159. *Ibid.*
160. *Ibid.*, March 31, 2023.

6.3 DATA LOSS

Computer data is an important asset, and the loss of it can be costly, not only in terms of money but also in terms of lost client confidence and lost business. Data losses can be of many different sizes. Most are small and inconsequential, but some, as frequently reported in the news, can be massive and devastating to businesses or national security.

The most serious ones are usually the result of internet activity. It is worth taking a look at what the principal causes of data loss are and what is recommended for preventing or minimizing data loss.[161]

There are several kinds of data loss representing different levels of damage. For example, there is a lot of coding that constitutes a computer program. Losing coding can be very damaging because it requires highly skilled experts to replace it. This can be costly.

Another kind can be the loss of customer or client data. In most cases, copies of that data exist and can be replaced by contact with clients. That may not be costly in terms of immediate out-of-pocket costs but can be very costly in the long run in terms of lost customer confidence and public embarrassment, leading to lost future business both in terms of repeat business and business that might be available for future expansion.

There are many causes of lost data, some human, others technical. Only a minority are due to cybercrime, although this is the cause that gets the most publicity in the press because it is the most dramatic and perhaps the most frightening.

The most common causes are somewhat more mundane.

The most frequent cause of data loss is hardware problems. This represents around 40% reported incidence of data loss.[162] The next largest is human mistakes. This constitutes about 30% of reported data losses. The third is corruption of software. This accounts for just under 15% of data losses.

Another physical cause of data loss is hardware destruction. When computers or computer discs or other media get destroyed by accident or thrown away, data can be lost, which is difficult or impossible to duplicate in the future. This is a particular problem because of the rapid development and evolution of computers and computer media systems over the last 50 years.

Room-size computers recording information on large spinning tapes gave way to personal computers recording data on floppy disks, which gave way to mini discs, which gave way to CDs and DVDs, which have given way to cloud storage to a significant extent.

Another important component of data storage that is still with us is computer hard disks. These hard disks store not only information that is entered on personal or business computers but also huge data storage facilities, back up data that is "stored on the cloud."

161. D.M. Smith, "The Cost of Lost Data," *Graziado Business Review* (Pepperdine University) Volume 6.3, 2003, online, retrieved August 27, 2021.
162. D.M. Smith, Figure 1, Causes of Lost Data.

Hard disks have also changed significantly over the decades. The recording of data on these discs used to be largely physical, but now almost all have been replaced by "digital" recording that has allowed much more data to be stored on hard disks and has allowed faster retrieval, which improves the performance of the Internet.

Alongside these developments have been the developments of small, easily portable devices that allow data to be transferred from computers or the web and easily carried from place to place to be used in other systems. These include USB discs and memory cards, which permit insertion in portable telephones and cameras and which have been becoming increasingly smaller in size, although their capacity keeps increasing significantly. Unfortunately, this makes it easier to lose them by physically misplacing them.

The consequences of data loss, particularly to a small business or an individual storing personal information, can be devastating. For example, it is reported that about 70% of small firms that suffer a large data loss go out of business within one year.[163]

163. "10 Common Causes of Data Loss," *Consoltech.com*, online, retrieved, August 31, 2021. D.M. Smith, "The Cost of Lost Data."

CHAPTER 7

Intellectual Property Law and the Cyber World

As pointed out throughout this book, the creation, sale and use of AI systems is affected by numerous legal issues that also apply to the creation, use and sale of any other creation.

Among these are intellectual property issues.

For example, generative AI, such as ChatGPT, which produces responses (oral, pictographic, written, etc.) to the requests of users, is reported to construct its requests from surveying data found on the Internet from which it fashions its response. It is difficult or impossible to know the extent to which a generative intelligence system copies, in whole or in part, data provided on the Internet by others.

It is reported that the AI generative systems currently known do not provide adequate source references. Indeed, it has been reported that there is at least one case where the sources provided were entirely made up by the chatbot used.

There is also a question as to how accurate or truthful a chatbot can be when fashioning its response.

These are worrying general issues. However, in the sphere of pure intellectual property law, there are two fundamental issues that are raised by generative AI. These are:

(1) Does a generative chatbot's use of data created by others to prepare its responses constitute a violation of the intellectual property rights of the creators of the data used by the bot?
(2) To what extent, if any, does the generative bot's use of that data constitute plagiarism?

7.1 PROTECTION OF AI-MADE INTELLECTUAL PROPERTY

Aside from the legal issues discussed above, legally created AI intelligence products can benefit from the same type of national and international protections available to other human creations.

An emphasis here must be made on "human creations." There have been at least two legal cases to date, one in the U.S. and one in the United Kingdom, that have ruled that one must be *human* to benefit from the protections of intellectual property rights. Such rights have been held not to be available to AI systems themselves.

To give a brief summary of the intellectual property legal protections that may be available to humans and their creations systems, there are the following.

7.1.1 International Law and the Internet

The following constitute important international treaties and conventions, regulations and legal instruments that affect governance of the Internet.[164]

7.1.1.1 United Nations Declaration on Human Rights

The UDHR, promulgated by the UN in 1948, asserts the fundamental rights that all human beings are entitled to simply by being human.[165]

Particularly relevant for Internet law is the second paragraph of the Preamble, which states that "human beings shall enjoy the freedom of speech and belief ..." Also, the statement in the third paragraph that "human rights should be protected by the rule of law ... ." Furthermore:

> Member States have pledged themselves to achieve, in cooperation with the United Nations, the promotion of universal respect for and observance of human rights and fundamental freedoms.

There is also Article 12 that asserts protection of privacy, stating:

> No one shall be subjected arbitrary interference with his privacy, family, home or correspondence nor to attacks upon his honor and reputation. Everyone has the right to the protection of the law against such interference or attacks.

Article 19 is particularly relevant to Internet usage, stating:

> Everyone has the right to freedom of opinion and expression; this right includes freedom to hold opinions without interference and to seek, receive and impart information and ideas through any media and regardless of the frontiers.

164. UNESCO, Internet Governance Glossary, section 7, 7.1, 7.2, 7.3; https://en.unesco.org/glossaries/igg/groups/7.4%20Conventions%20and%20treaties%2C%20regulations%20and%20legal%20instruments, retrieved August 11, 2020.
165. *Ibid.*, section 7.4.1.

It is certainly true that the Internet has the potential to fulfill and enhance the right to cultural life asserted in Article 1, which states:

> 1. Everyone has the right to participate in the cultural life of the community, do you enjoy the arts and to share in scientific advancement and its benefits.

Although this UDHR is not legally binding, 192 members of the UN have agreed to it because acceptance of its principles is an intrinsic requirement for membership to the UN.

In addition, 150 countries have ratified and signed the International Bill of Human Rights (OHCHR), which consists of the UDHR and two other international treaties:

(1) The International Covenant on Civil and Political Rights (ICCPR, 1966).
(2) The International Covenant on Economic, Social and Cultural Rights (ICESR, 1966).

Internet Communication as a Human Right

The UN has tried to extend internationally recognized human rights onto the Internet.

In June 2012, a resolution was proposed on human rights on the Internet. The resolution sought to promote the protection and exercise of human rights on the Internet through Article 19 of the UDHR.

However, it is not certain that this resolution (which remains in draft) has any significant legal impact because several countries have reservations about it, and it has not yet been approved.

Resistance to the UDHR

Although, 150 countries have ratified the UN conventions protecting human rights discussed above, there is a significant group of countries that are opposed to some of their protections.

Saudi Arabia has not signed UDHR, claiming that it violates Islamic law and fails to account for the religious and cultural backgrounds of non-Western countries. All Saudi citizens are required to be Muslims, and there are restrictions on women's rights.

An Iranian representative to the UN has also said that it is impossible to comply with the UDHR without violating Islamic law.[166]

In response to the concerns of Muslim countries, 45 countries belonging to the Organization of the Islamic Conference agreed to adopt the Cairo Declaration of Human Rights in Islam (CDHRI) in 1990. However, the CDHRI does not conform to the UDHR and "undermines many of the rights the UDHR is supposed to guarantee." For example, it allows for establishment of different rights for men and women.[167]

166. D. Akkad, "The Universal Declaration vs. The Cairo Declaration," online, blogs.lse.ac.uk, December 10, 2012, accessed November 13, 2021.
167. *Ibid.*

The CDHRI has the effect of restricting freedom of expression in a number of ways that would limit using the Internet to express certain ideas. Article 22 of the CDHRI says:

> Everyone shall have the right to express his opinion freely in such manner as would not be contrary to the principles of the Shari'ah.[168]

Since 1990, there have been several proposals to expand interpretations of human rights under Islamic law, but so far, they have not met with significant success.[169]

It is likely that, although many countries respect the breadth of human rights guaranteed under the UDHR, their application in relation to the Internet may be limited by some countries that, for religious and political reasons, will be unwilling to extend those rights to all their citizens.

7.1.1.2 International Telecommunication Regulations

The International Telecommunication Regulations (ITR) came into force in 1998 through the International Telecommunication Union (ITU). Its purpose was to promote international liberalization of pricing and Internet services and to permit new functions of basic services with respect to the Internet. This involved such things as leased lines and helped the rapid growth of the Internet by the 1990s. The principal international organizations responsible for the international regulation of telecommunications are the World Trade Organization (WTO) and the ITU.[170]

Basic Telecommunication Agreement (BTA)

The formal name of this agreement is the Fourth Protocol to the General Agreement on Trade in Services. This came into force in 1998. Under this agreement, over 100 countries have opened their telecommunication markets to promote the development of new communication services, including Internet services.[171]

7.1.1.3 UNCITRAL Model Law on Electronic Commerce

This was issued by UNCITRAL in 1996. It is not a legally binding instrument, but it provides a model for legislation and, also assists Internet users in drafting their contracts.[172]

---

168. A. Sears, "Protecting Freedom of Expression over the Internet: An International Approach," *Notre Dame Journal of International & Comparative Law,* Volume 5, 2015, online, accessed November 13, 2021.
169. *See,* K. Magliveras & G. Nardi, "The Arab Court of Human Rights: A Study in Impotence," *The Quebec Journal of International Law,* Volume 29.2, 2016, pp. 1 to 342, online, accessed November 13, 2021 https://doi.org/10.7202/1046511ar.
170. UNESCO Glossary 7.4.2.
171. UNESCO Glossary 7.4.3.
172. UNESCO Glossary 7.4.4.

7.1.1.4 Berne Convention for the Protection of Literary and Artistic Works (Berne Convention)

This is an international convention with a long history. It was first adopted in 1886. The signers of this agreement are required to recognize the copyrights of authors from other signing countries in the same way that they recognize the copyrights of their own citizens. Signatories to this agreement are known as the Bern Union.

The agreement also requires signatories to provide minimum standards in their copyright law.[173]

7.1.1.5 WIPO Copyright Treaty

This treaty was agreed upon by the Member States of the World Intellectual Property Organization (WIPO) in 1996. It was created as an enhancement to existing copyright treaties because of advances in digital information and Internet technology.[174]

7.1.1.6 Agreement on Trade-Related Aspects of Intellectual Property Rights

The Trade-Related Aspects of Intellectual Property Rights (TRIPS) is an International intellectual property agreement administered by the WTO. It establishes standards for applying intellectual property regulations to nationals of other countries that also happen to be WTO members.[175]

7.1.1.7 Budapest Convention on Cybercrime (Budapest Convention)

The Budapest Convention was entered into in July 2004. It was the first treaty trying to deal with Internet and other computer crimes. The goals of the treaty are to align the Internet laws and regulations of the signatory countries, to update and improve their methods of investigation, and to get them to cooperate more in preventing international cybercrime.[176]

7.1.1.8 Convention on the Recognition and Enforcement of Foreign Arbitral Awards (New York Convention)

This is a convention that has been in existence for some time. It was created in 1958, long before the Internet rose to prominence. Its purpose has been and remains the regulation of the terms under which the national courts of signatories are obliged to

173. UNESCO Glossary 7.4.5.
174. UNESCO Glossary 7.4.6.
175. UNESCO Glossary 7.4.7. For additional information how about these and other agreements regulating intellectual property on the Internet, please *see* Chapter 14 on Intellectual Property Law and the Internet.
176. UNESCO, Internet Governance Glossary 7.4.8.

enforce arbitration awards regardless of where the arbitration awards are made. It is commonly called "the New York Convention."

About 24 countries are signatories that allow their national courts to enforce the arbitration awards of other signatories under the terms of the Convention.[177]

7.1.1.9 UNCITRAL Model Law on International Commercial Arbitration

This is a template that nations can use to create their own commercial arbitration law. The Model Law itself is not legally binding, but it is something that countries can make part of their own national law if they wish. It was introduced in 2006.[178]

7.1.1.10 W3C Web Accessibility Initiative Web Content Accessibility Guidelines (WCAG)

The World Wide Web Consortium has issued a series of guidelines on web accessibility that were published by the Web Accessibility Initiative (WAI) of W3C.

They are a collection of ways to make the web accessible for users who may be disabled or who are using mobile devices such as phones. The latest version was published in 2008, and a related standard from the International Organization for Standardization (ISO) was issued in 2012.[179]

7.1.1.11 United Nations Convention on the Use of Electronic Communications in International Contracts (Electronic Communications Convention)

The UN (Electronic Communications Convention) was initially adopted in 2005.[180] However, since then, it has been adopted by only 18 countries. The only major market country is the Russian Federation. It only entered into force for those signatories in 2013. However, the importance of this Convention goes beyond those countries. A number of countries have adopted parts of this Convention as provisions in their own national legislation. Others have indicated some interest in adopting the Convention or preparing legislation to include provisions like those of the Convention. That interest has been expressed by several major countries, including the United States.

In fact, the Convention was based on the already existing laws of the United States and Canada (*American Uniform Electronic Transactions Act*) and Canada (*Canadian Uniform Electronic Transactions Act*).[181]

177. UNESCO Glossary 7.4.9.
178. UNESCO Glossary 7.4.10.
179. UNESCO Glossary 7.4.11.
180. Vienna Convention, Introduction, 2, online at: uncitral.org, accessed August 18, 2020.
181. J. Benjamin Lambert, "The U.N. Convention on Electronic Contracting: Back From the Dead?," *Michigan State International Law Review*, Volume 25.1, pp. 32-75, online at: Digital Commons Network, accessed August 18, 2020.

The purpose of this Convention is to provide a treaty that removes the formal obstacles that separate electronic from written contracts. It is aimed at providing an opportunity for countries involved in international commerce, whether signatories or not, to adopt similar legislation governing the creation of contracts in electronics commerce. This would make international trade easier by harmonizing the different national regulations that govern electronic commerce.[182]

If this convention is adopted by major legal jurisdictions it would have significant impacts on businesses such as energy, shipping, technology and finance.[183]

President Obama sent the Convention to the U.S. Senate along with a recommendation of ratification on February 10, 2016.[184] However, the U.S. Senate has not yet agreed to ratify the Convention. In the Senate, issues have been raised that may delay or prevent ratification of the Convention. The first is that provisions of the Convention are like provisions already existing in U.S. law, such as the Uniform Commercial Code (UCC). It is the thought that many U.S. legal practitioners would prefer to operate under established law rather than a new treaty that may make small variations to the law that may be confusing. The second is that the Convention is not self-executing and would therefore require further legislation to implement provisions into U.S. law. Consequently, there does not seem to be a strong likelihood that the Convention will be ratified by the U.S. any time soon.

7.1.1.12 Internet Corporation for Assigned Names and Numbers

Internet Corporation for Assigned Names and Numbers (ICANN) was established in 1998. It is an international organization overseen by the U.S. government.[185] ICANN is responsible for administration of three kinds of Internet identifier systems. These are:

(1) domain names;
(2) numerical Internet protocol (IP) addresses; and
(3) a code that identifies port and parameter numbers.

The Internet community can participate in determining the policy of ICANN through the Non-commercial Users Constituency (NCUC)[186] and/or the At-Large Advisory Committee (ALAC).[187]

---

182. UN Commission on International Trade Law, online, accessed at uncitral.un.org, August 18, 2020.
183. Lambert, p. 34.
184. *Ibid.*
185. *See* the discussion of US domain name regulation in Chapter 4.
186. http://ncdnhc.org/.
187. http://www.icann.org/.

7.1.1.13 Internet Assigned Names and Numbers Authority

The Internet Assigned Names and Numbers Authority (IANA) is the department of ICANN. It was established in 1988 to execute policy with respect to IP number allocations and some administrative functions for the Internet Engineering Task Force (IETF) and ICANN.[188]

7.1.1.14 Number Resource Organization

This is an unincorporated group formed in 2003 to coordinate the Regional Internet Registries, of which there are five regional RIRs around the world. Those five RIRs are:

(1) APNIC, covering India, the Far East, and the Antipodes.
(2) ARIN, covering North America.
(3) LACNIC, covering Latin America.
(4) RIPE NCC, covering Europe, the Middle East, and the Russian Federation.
(5) AFRNIC, covering Africa.

The Number Resource Organization's (NRO's) goal is to provide a coordinating body for the registrations of domain names through the RIRs.[189]

The NRO does not do domain name registration. Rather, it functions as a central registry and communication point for the RIRs with respect to such things as statistical reports, Internet governance efforts and coordination of policy. To help do that, it supports coordinating groups on common issues such as communications, registration services, engineering, and administrative leadership. The aim of these groups is to help promote security, stability, and cooperation in global domain name registration.

7.1.2 National IP Protection

In addition to the extensive attention that is being paid to international protection of various categories of intellectual property, which would be applicable to AI products, nations also have statutes and regulations to protect intellectual property. Learning about them in detail with respect to any particular situation would require consultation with qualified expert advisers in the jurisdictions in question.

However, to give a general idea of the approaches in some of the major market nations, some examples are as follows.

188. *Ibid.*
189. NRO website, nro.net, retrieved September 7, 2020.

7.1.2.1 United States

In 1998, the U.S. passed a new copyright statute called the Digital Millennium Copyright Act (DMCA). The purpose of the Act was to deal with the changes that digital commerce was making to trade, domestic and international.

One of its purposes was to implement the WIPO 1996 Internet treaties discussed above.

Among its provisions were sections criminalizing:

- The production and distribution of any works that violated copyrights.
- Any actions to circumvent systems that control access to copyrighted material:
  - Such as Digital Rights Management (DRM systems):
    - Even if the copyright itself is not breached.

There were some exemptions provided to the DMCA, principally for internet service providers (ISPs) or other intermediaries. For example, ISPs were protected from direct or indirect liability for any copyright violations by the ISP's users who posted copyright-violating material.

The "Training" Cases

One issue that has become prominent through legal actions in the U.S. and is likely to receive similar attention in the courts of other countries is the issue of generative chatbots being trained in language by "scraping" written material from the World Wide Web. The intention is to learn examples of how language is used and how topics of interest are treated in written material[190]

A powerful objection to this training process that has risen from the community of authors and other creators worldwide is that many have become aware that their copyrighted material, which exists on the Internet in electronic form, is, or maybe, used in such training.

One association of authors filed a proposed "class action" lawsuit on behalf of authors in a New York Federal Court against OpenAI, alleging that the creator of ChatGPT was engaging "in a systemic course of mass-scale copyright infringement."[191]

Other lawsuits have reportedly been filed by creators against AI art-generating companies, including Meta, Stability AI, Midjourney and Deviant Art, alleging copyright infringement.[192]

It is reported that AI companies have been obtaining material to train their generative AI products from online collections of books held in "shadow libraries," such as Library Genesis, Z-Library and Bibliotik.[193]

190. W. Cho, "Top Authors Join Lawsuit Against Open AI Over 'Mass Scale Copyright Infringement' of Novels," *The Hollywood Reporter*, online at: hollywoodreporter.com, September 20, 2023.
191. *Ibid.*
192. *Ibid.*
193. I was surprised to find a copy of my copyrighted book, "Internet Law" (Kluwer International, 2022) offered online by Z-Library!.

The displeasure of authors and creators of copyrighted material is reported to be growing. There will be great interest in the resolution of the lawsuits that have been filed to date, and many others may be filed in jurisdictions around the world.[194]

AI products that are instructed to create content (music, writings, videos, etc.) that reflect the qualities necessary to qualify, in the views of human judges, as usable content such as music, writings, videos, etc., may use material copied or sampled from databases as the raw material for their content production. A legal problem arises when they acquire material to use from copyrighted sources without "consent, credit or compensation."[195]

AI products such as OpenAI's ChatGPT are sophisticated machines operating according to complex instructions. One function they perform is acquisition of data from existing sources, some of which may be copyrighted. If the purpose of this acquisition is to use copyrighted material to compete with human artists in the creation of media (which would not exist if the AI machine did not have access to copyrighted material), this would appear to fail the "fair use" tests if copyrighted material was not obtained with consent, credit or compensation.

Perhaps the gravest threat to intellectual property is that its production will be curtailed because the hacking and theft of intellectually created material on the Internet will become so extensive that those that produce it will lose interest in doing this kind of work because their ability to earn a profit from this work will be greatly reduced or indeed lost altogether.

An example of how this threat can affect academia is founding a website called the sci-hub website, which is a digital database that supposedly has copies of 70 million academic and scientific papers. This is a huge percentage of the number of academic papers that have been produced. It is estimated that this represents around 80% of the existing total. Apparently this collection has been assembled by hacking into the libraries and databases of universities around the world. Forty-two British universities are alleged to be victims.[196]

The theft of academic research presents the same problem as the theft of other kinds of intellectually produced media, such as songs, films and books. The people who produce such work do so because it is their job from which they expect to earn money and sometimes as their sole source of income. Much, if not all, of the papers on sci-hub are works for which it is expected that in order to gain access to them, one will have to pay a purchase price or subscription fee.

Nevertheless, a young woman named Alexandra Elbakyan from Kazakhstan boasts that she has put together this vest academic library on the basis of her skills as an expert computer data miner without violating the intellectual property rights of the owners or authors. Not surprisingly, law enforcement authorities in a number of countries have found this hard to believe. For example, Ms. Elbakyanis is currently

194. "The Times Sues OpenAI and Microsoft Over A.I. Use of Copyrighted Work," December 27 2023, online at: nytimes.com.
195. Schumpeter, "Napster Revisited," *The Economist*, March 18, 2023, p. 62.
196. D. Brown, "Hacking Fear Over Pirated Research Site Sci-Hub," *The Times*, online, March 21, 2021, accessed March 21, 2021.

under investigation by U.S. law enforcement authorities because they suspect her of using her hacking skills on behalf of Russian intelligence to access databases that contain sensitive U.S. military data.[197]

Intellectual Property: AI Created Content

Another legal issue that came up in March 2023 was the legitimacy of using AI to copy or "sample" parts of existing copyrighted musical compositions and to use that information to create "new" musical compositions.

This rests on the fundamental copyright law issue of "fair use." Fair use permits legal use of copyrighted work when the use:

- Serves a valuable social purpose.
- The source material is transformed from the original.
- It does not affect the copyright owners' core market.

In this case, the use of AI to take up copyrighted material from publicly available sources and use it to transform that material into "original" compositions by an artificially intelligent machine fails both the first and third tests. With respect to the third test, the person directing the artificially intelligent machine to perform these searches to create material which competes with the original copyright owner and with respect to the first, this does not appear to be a valuable social purpose.

Intellectual Property Cases: U.S.

- From *Beach Boys v. Chuck Berry.*
- *"Surfin U.S.A." v. "Sweet Little Sixteen."*
- Settled 1966: Publishing rights to Berry's publisher.
- To *Lana Del Ray v. Radiohead.*
- *"Get Free" v. "Creep."*
- March 2018: Del Ray says resolution reached.
- https://www.rollingstone.com/politics/politics-lists/songs-on-trial-12-landmark-music-copyright-cases-166396/robin-thicke-vs-marvin-gaye-2014-60709/.

Sampling

- Started in 1956 ("The Flying Saucer").
- Writers cut borrowed sound copyright holders in on royalties.

1990s and Beyond

- Computers & internet allowed electronic "borrowing" of parts of songs.
- Many artists have been sued: 50 Cent ("In Da Club"), Kayne West ("Gold Digger"), Snoop Dog & Warzone ("Flashbaccs"), Jay Z ("Run This Town"), Mark Ronson ("Uptown Funk").

197. *Ibid.*

- Don't Get Sued: Artists must get pre-approval for sampling:
  - *RIAA v. Napster* (1999). Music Sharing.
  - Google Trademark Words (2009).
  - *David Slater/Naruto* Case (2011).
  - *Jammie Thomas-Rasset* Case (8th Cir. Fed. CA):
    - Minnesota woman fined $222,000 for illegally downloading 24 Rolling Stones songs. $8,250 per song.
  - *Alice Corp v. CLS Banking Int'l* (2014):
    - U.S. Supreme Court. Business method can't be patented. Abstract idea cannot be patented. Electronic escrow service cannot be patented just because it is executed on computer.
  - *Katz v. Chevaldina* (2015):
    - Use of unflattering headshot on blog.
- *Garcia v. Google* (2015):
  - Misuse of copyrighted dance performance for anti-Muslim post.
- *MTM v. Amazon* (2015):
  - Watch search on Amazon.

TV Piracy

- Twenty-one percent of US consumers pirate TV shows.
- Game of Thrones:
  - Most pirated TV show ever.

Film Piracy

- Twenty-four percent of US consumers pirate movies:
  - While movies still in theaters.

Books

A lawsuit has been filed against an organization named Internet Archive (Archive).

Archive is a nonprofit organization being sued by publishing companies about Archive's lending of Ebooks.[198]

Lila Baily, attorney for Archive, says, "We think the future of libraries hangs in the balance here."

The case concerns the creation of a "National Emergency Library" by Archive. This was set up during the COVID-19 pandemic to allow people to borrow ebooks.

The publishing industry claimed that Archive was handing out ebooks without permission and brought suit. An article in the magazine, *The Nation,* said the publishing industry was "taking the internet to court."[199]

Archive's attorney subscribes to the view that internet law should align with public interest rather than simply create barriers to accessing digital information. She

198. J.J. Roberts, "As Libraries Fight for Access to e-Books, a New Copyright Champion Emerges," *Fortune*, online, November 28, 2020, accessed May 7, 2021.
199. *Ibid.*

claims that Archive is a digital version of the libraries we are used to as lenders of physical books. Archive lends out digital versions of books that it owns.

Publishers are demanding injunctive relief that would require Archive to destroy the approximately 4 million digital books it has assembled in its collection.[200] The case was set for trial in 2021, but it is possible that a settlement will be reached without the necessity of completing the litigation.[201]

Art

Bouchat v. Baltimore Ravens and NFL., et al.

This 2013 ruling by the U.S. Court of Appeals for the Fourth Circuit dealt with the issue of "fair use." The plaintiff was a graphic artist who drew and proposed a team logo to the Baltimore Ravens, an American professional football team. The Ravens did not adopt his particular design but used a similar design between 1996 and 1998. The plaintiff sued, and in 2000, the Fourth Circuit ruled that the Ravens had violated the plaintiff's copyright.

In 2012, the same plaintiff started another suit against the Ravens and other National Football League-related organizations, claiming that the defendants had again used his logo by showing it in a video about the history of the Ravens. In the U.S. District Court case, the defendants claimed that their use of this historical logo was protected as a "fair use." Plaintiff appealed to the Fourth Circuit. The Fourth Circuit ruled that the use of the logo in these circumstances was a protected "fair use" because the logo only appeared in "fleeting" instances in videos that were focused on the Ravens' history. The court ruled that it's used was in a video that was designed to preserve the Ravens' history and the appearance of the logo was only an "incidental component" of the exhibits in question. The Court did not find any market harm to the plaintive, and its overall view was that plaintiff's arguments did not overcome the substantial weight of the factors in favor of a finding of "fair use."[202]

7.1.2.2 Europe: Selected IP Cases

- *Ashby Donald and others v. France*. European Court judgment on publication of photos on the internet (January 10, 2013).
- *eDate Advertising*. ECJ judgment of October 25, 2011—C-509/09 and C-161/10—*eDate Advertising*; Conflict of laws, Personality rights. A German national was convicted of murdering a well-known actor in 1993. Released on parole in 2008, he complained to a German court, of violation of his personality rights. An Austrian website (eDate Advertising) published his name, conviction, and the fact that he was appealing.
  The court held that a person who considers his rights infringed can bring an action either in his own Member State or in the Member State where the

200. *Ibid.*
201. *Ibid.*
202. *Bouchat v. Balt. Ravens Ltd.* P'ship, 737 F.3rd 932 (4th Cir. 2013).

publication was made. Publication online could expose publishers to legal action outside their own country of operation.

- Wintersteiger. ECJ judgment of April 19, 2012—C-523/10—*Wintersteiger AG v. Products 4U Sondermaschinenbau GMBH.* This was a case of trademark infringement by internet registration.
  Plaintiff Wintersteiger holds an Austrian trademark on its name. It is a maker of ski and snowboard servicing tools. A competitor registered "Wintersteiger" on the internet in Germany as a Google AdWord. Each time a "Wintersteiger" was entered, an advert for the competitor would appear.
  Wintersteiger sued in an Austrian court. Article 5(3) of Regulation (EC) No. 44/2001, on jurisdiction and the recognition and enforcement of judgments in civil and commercial matters, holds that a person domiciled in a Member State may be sued in the state where the harmful event occurred. Defendant's actions in Germany caused infringement of trademark registered in Austria. Where conduct on the internet is liable to infringe a national trademark registered in a Member State, that will attribute jurisdiction to the courts of the Member State where the trademark is registered.
- *Peter Pinckney v. KDG Mediatech AG.* ECJ judgment of October 3, 2013—C-170/12—Placing.

French resident author of 12 copyrighted songs sued an Austrian company for offering CDs of songs on the Internet. The CDs were marketed by two U.K. companies on a number of websites accessible in complainant's hometown of Toulouse.

The complainant sued in Toulouse.

It was held that the person harmed may bring proceedings either before the courts of the place where the defendant who sold the CDs online or placed the content online is located or before the courts of the Member State at which the website in question was accessible.

7.1.2.3 China

China has recently been representing that it is making efforts to encourage protection for and respect for IP.

In January 2017, China publicly announced a plan to improve cooperation with other nations on IP protection.

One of its steps was to set up a new Internet Court to review cases of alleged improper use of protected IP. To date, that court has accepted about 30,000 cases. More than 80% of those cases are Internet cases.

In 2021, China announced a supplementary plan to improve IP protection.[203]

One of the important goals of both plans is to improve China's international reputation for IP protection.

203. R. O'Neill, "China's New Five-Year Plan Targets 'Hi-Tech' IP," *World Intellectual Property Review*, online, worldipreview.com, April 27, 2021.

7.1.2.4 France

France Enforces EU Neighboring Right

In July 2021, Google was fined €500 million by the French competition regulator because the regulator found that Google had not negotiated "in good faith" with News companies about the use of the content published by those news companies.

In 2020, the French competition regulation authority ordered Google to negotiate with news companies in good faith about Google's use of content from those news organizations and other content providers. The fine was imposed in 2021 because the French competition regulator believed that Google had not negotiated in good faith.

In 2019, France adopted the new EU Digital Copyright Directive which contained a provision directing compensation for publishers and news organizations for the use of their content. This is the so-called neighboring rights provision.

This is the law under which the French competition authority sought to compel Google to provide good faith compensation to content providers and, which it found Google had failed to comply with.[204]

It remains to be seen whether other tech companies will suffer similar punishment for their use of the content or extracts of the content provided by third parties.

This may also affect generative AI creators that are "training" their generative AI systems with materials created by third parties.

7.2 INTERNET PIRACY

"Internet Piracy" constitutes illegal accessing, using, copying, or sharing of IP via the Internet without permission of the IP owner.

Internet IP piracy is a huge problem:[205]

- There are around 220 billion views of pirated videos annually.
- Pirate streaming sites are responsible for more than 75% of online piracy worldwide.
- Internet video piracy may cost the U.S. economy as much as $60 billion in losses annually.
- 126.7 billion viewings worth of U.S.-produced TV episodes are pirated every year.
- More than 50,000 U.S. jobs are lost a year because of music piracy.
- Around the world, the movie industry loses as much as $75 billion a year from Internet piracy.
- Nearly a quarter of global Internet bandwidth is used to download copyrighted media.

In 2017, in the U.S. alone, there were more than 17 billion visits to Internet piracy sites.

204. "France Rules Google Must Pay News Firms for Content," *Reuters*, online, April 8, 2020.
205. D.J. Spajic, "Piracy Is Back: Statistics for 2021," *DataProt*, online, March 19, 2021.

In China, where cheap copies of protected IP products are common, there is even a special name for them, "*Shanzhai.*" There has been significant theft and imitation of popular brands.

"This is a society where, if you open a fake Apple Store, people start writing articles about how innovative and creative you are."[206]

7.3 DANGER FROM THE INTERNET OF THINGS

The problems that the Internet presents in protecting IP or private data are only growing.

In recent years, we have moved beyond accessing information on the Internet to allowing the Internet access to our growing list of "connected devices," often without our intervention or even without our knowledge:

> A new study has found that most Internet of things devices routinely deliver an ocean of sensitive data to partners around the world frequently without making these data transfers secure or transparent to the end-user.[207]

A joint collaboration between Northeastern University and Imperial College London looked at 81 popular smart TVs, streaming dongles, smart speakers and video doorbells made by Google, Roku, Amazon, etc.

In 34,000 experiments, they found that 72 of the devices made contact with someone other than the manufacturer.[208]

7.4 THOUGHTS ON IP SECURITY

What positive steps can be taken to protect IP and oneself from illegal internet intrusion and theft? There are several.

Basic protections include the following:

- Be careful on public networks because others may be able to listen to you and/or get access to your data.
- Make sure that cyber systems are up to date. New threats are constantly coming online.
- Make sure all software and cybersecurity protections are current and are allowed to accept automatic updates.
- Use complex passwords. Make sure all users use complex passwords all the time and change them regularly.
- Backup and encrypt key data.

206. K. Rapoza, *Forbes Magazine*, online, July 22, 2012.
207. K. Bode, "The Internet of Things Is Still a Privacy Dumpster Fire, Study Finds," *Vice*, online, September 19, 2019.
208. *Ibid.*

It is also important to get detailed information about the state of legal IP protection in the countries where one does business. There are many online sources of information about this, but the detailed report published online by the U.S. Representative is very useful.[209]

In it there is an extensive description of protection and enforcement of IP Rights around the world. It describes the laws, policies, and practices of the world's countries in their treatment of IP.

The report also includes a "Priority Watch List" of the countries that the U.S. considers to have the weakest record in IP protection. Those include Algeria, Argentina, Chile, China, India, Indonesia, Kuwait, Russia, Saudi Arabia, Ukraine and Venezuela.

There is a "Watch List" of countries that cause the U.S. concern about the strength of their IP protection. Those include Bolivia, Brazil, Canada, Columbia, Costa Rica, Dominican Republic, Ecuador, Egypt, Greece, Guatemala, Jamaica, Lebanon, Mexico, Pakistan, Paraguay, Peru, Romania, Switzerland, Thailand, Turkey, Turkmenistan, UAE, Uzbekistan, and Vietnam.

One may not agree with conclusions of the Report about the IP protections provided by certain countries, but if one is doing business in those countries or internationally generally, it does provide things to consider.

It also offers the following strategies for business IP protection:

- Does your business understand the most influential tech changers? Are you investing in any? Are you paying attention to the opportunities they provide you and your competitors?
- Does your company have a board-level presence and a business culture that fosters understanding of your IP at every level? Does your head of IP have the ear of the top decision-makers?
- Does your IP strategy match the pace of change in your market by planning for the short, medium and long terms?

209. https://ustr.gov/sites/default/files/2019_Special_301_Report.pdf.

CHAPTER 8

Competition Law

The cyber world is expanding both in application and public awareness at a time when competition regulators around the world are already taking a careful look at the competitive influence of large tech companies in the cyber world.

This raises questions as to how the growth of the internet, AI systems and digital assets will change the competitive position of tech companies and how it will change the ways in which competition regulation authorities will evaluate the competitive positions of tech companies in the cyber markets.

8.1 COMPETITION CONCERNS WITH BIG TECH

As the sizes of the major Internet companies such as Google, Facebook, Amazon, Apple, and Microsoft (collectively, Big Tech) have grown, there has been growing concern about their power and, in particular, the power to limit or eliminate competitors.

Consequently, there has risen significant concern in the U.S., the EU and other jurisdictions that large Internet companies are in danger of violating or actually violating legal and regulatory prohibitions against anticompetitive behavior.

This concern is partly due to regulators' perceptions about the difficulty of competing with companies so large, so wealthy, and so widely accessible, but it is also a result of the fact that big Internet companies have been buying up related companies to increase their reach in their business areas and to eliminate potential competitors.

8.2 COVID-19 PANDEMIC

Another powerful impetus to their growth and wealth has been the recent COVID-19 Pandemic.

Because the response of many countries has been to put their populations under lockdown, severely limiting their ability to leave their dwellings to shop in person, many people have turned to the Internet to order goods and to communicate with friends and relatives.

People have also been working from home to a significant degree, which has increased their need to use the Internet and to have efficient, up-to-date computer equipment and systems.

Among the greatest beneficiaries of the Pandemic, although accidental, have been the Big Tech companies, including Apple, Amazon, Meta (Facebook), Microsoft and Google. The results of the Pandemic increased usage of their services and products, made them more essential worldwide, and increased their wealth, making it easier to consolidate and expand their businesses.

These giants have recently made key purchases or commenced business projects that have given competition regulators around the world serious cause for concern.

As *The Economist* asked in an August 2023 article:[210] "Can anything stop big tech?"

8.3 COMPETITION LAW

The philosophy behind anti-competition laws is that the public benefits from having competition in commerce, allow the public more choice and offer better prices for goods and services.

This is a view that has been adopted by the governments of many countries around the world, particularly those countries with market economies. To preserve those benefits, many countries have adopted laws and regulations to prevent any commercial operation from being so powerful that it is in the position to exclude competitors from the markets in question and/or dictate prices and/or terms of service that are detrimental to the public.

The basic goal of competition law is to prevent any one person or company, or any cooperating group, from becoming so powerful or influential in a market that they can exclude competitors, prevent new competitors from entering the market, and/or abuse their market power as the only remaining choice in a market to demand excessive compensation for their goods and services.

There are different ways that commercial organizations can seek to gain such market power. One way is to conspire with others to exclude new potential competitors from the marketplace. Another way is to purchase other similar companies in the market to reduce the number of competitors or eliminate competitors altogether. Another way is to temporarily make one's prices and/or terms of service much more favorable than those of competitors, for example, by offering goods and services below cost, so that competitors who are less financially strong are unable to compete and may be forced to leave the market.

Engaging in actions to try and achieve such market power is called anticompetitive behavior, and most developed countries have laws and regulations to protect their

210. The Economist, "Can Big Tech Keep Getting Bigger in the Age of AI?," online at: economist.com, August 2, 2023.

markets and to encourage the discovery of reasonable prices for goods and services in markets through the mechanism of supply and demand.

Failure to obey these laws and regulations against anticompetitive behavior can result in violators being penalized with civil suits, fines, criminal prosecution, and possibly being barred from the markets in question.

The competition laws in various countries may differ somewhat, but their essential goals are usually the ones described above.

8.4 AI AND COMPETITION

The market for AI products is a submarket of the overall market for cyber products and services. As will be seen in the following parts of this chapter, competition regulators are already paying serious attention to the market power of Big Tech companies such as Google, Facebook, Apple, Microsoft, and others.

A result of the regulatory examinations of the competitive positions and behavior of some Big Tech companies has resulted, in some cases, in fines and injunctions to punish and modify what has come to be regarded as anticompetitive behavior.

The injection of AI systems into markets adds a different aspect to the issue of market power. This is due to the following facts:

- AI systems may attract market participants that have not previously been seriously active in cyber markets. That can expand and change the definitions of relevant cyber markets.
- Companies that have not previously dominated important segments of the cyber markets may significantly increase their market power because of their involvement in the creation, marketing and operation of AI systems, products and related services.
- Some Big Tech companies that have already been dominant in various parts of the cyber market may be able to expand their market power because of their involvement in the expansion of AI systems and services.
- There is also a concern that certain companies, already more advanced in the development of AI systems, that are usually competitors, may be tempted to join together to use their advances in AI to collectively dominate markets, fix prices and/or exclude competition.

8.5 INCREASED COMPETITION THREAT OF BIG TECH IN AI

Although the so-called Big Tech companies, Amazon, Apple, Alphabet (Google), Mehta (Facebook) and Microsoft, may not yet be the most prominently mentioned participants in the "AI Gold Rush," there is little question that their size, penetration of the cyber markets, and financial power gives them advantages that may, over time, permit them to dominate the rapidly growing market for AI products or other aspects of the cyber markets by using AI.

It is reported that their economic performance in mid-2023 continues to be spectacular. At the end of July that year, it was reported that Alphabet, Meta, and

Microsoft collectively gained $106 billion of operating profits between January and June 2023, more than $9 billion above the collective profits for the same period in 2022. Apple, in the second quarter of 2023, reported its highest earnings ever.[211]

An article in *The Economist* commented:

> "[I]nvestors expect the tech giants, with their deep technological insights and even deeper pockets, to capture the spoils of artificial intelligence ..."
>
> "When ExxonMobil and GE were the titans of America Inc. in the 1990s and 2000s, their revenues were rising at an average annual rate of 5 to 6% and their net profits at 5 to 10% or so. The tech giants have been growing at 16% and 13%, respectively, for a decade or more."[212]

This raises the question as to how much of a threat the economic power and digital experience of the tech giants will be to fair competition in the new field of AI, and the reach of the Internet, and how determined competition regulators will be in protecting a "level playing field" for the participants in the market for AI and other cyber-related products? Can the expanding market power of the tech giants be controlled for the sake of competition?

Some doubt is being expressed as to whether competition regulators are up to the job:

> Do not look to regulators to stop their march. Last month a court threw out an effort by America's trustbusters to block Microsoft's acquisition of Activision Blizzard, a games developer. The markets have shrugged off other fitful efforts to reign in the tech giants, such as the EU's new rules for digital markets.[213]

It has been suggested that "their size" could be a brake on the ability of Big Tech to continue to grow in power. The argument is that they simply cannot keep up the speed of their expansion indefinitely.[214] That remains to be seen.

8.6 BIG TECH CAN GROW WITH AI

One way for the Big Tech companies to keep growing is to expand into new markets. The Big Tech companies give every sign of enthusiastically expanding into providing AI systems and related products.

Microsoft is already offering AI tools as an addition to Microsoft 365. Apple, Meta and Google will be providing AI assistance for their advertising customers.[215]

Microsoft has been the backer of the generative AI system created by OpenAI: ChatGPT. This chatbot has received the most attention and has been the most widely used since it became well-known in late 2022. Microsoft shows no signs of slowing down its pursuit of AI expansion.

---

211. V. Kilbride, "A Giant Conundrum: Can Big Tech Keep Getting Bigger in the Age of AI?," *The Economist*, online, August 2, 2023.
212. *Ibid.*
213. *Ibid.*
214. *Ibid.*
215. *Ibid.*

The other tech giants are keeping pace:

> "[In late July of 2023], "Apple indicated it was building its expertise in the area. Tim Cook, the chief executive, called AI and machine learning 'core, fundamental technologies that are integral to virtually every product that we build'.
> Every division of Amazon is said to be working on generative AI projects."[216]

8.7 OTHER FORMS OF CYBER MARKET DOMINATION

8.7.1 Education Market

8.7.1.1 Google

There is another area that is causing concern because of perceived market domination. It has been argued that Google is becoming too dominant in the education sector through Chromebook laptops and Google's Chrome operating system.[217]

During the pandemic, the Chrome system expanded its reach because so much education was moved online. Google appears to have sprung into action to take advantage of this.

During this time, Google has promoted a number of its free Google education apps, the use of which has given Google an enormous amount of data about students and their schools.

They have introduced 40 new models of Chromebook laptops, many upgrades of its education products and AI tools that allow students to have, in effect, conversations with the Internet through their laptops.

While much of this appears to offer significant benefits to educational institutions and their students, and in many respects probably does offer important benefits, it also raises important privacy and ethical issues.

Among the important ones is the fact that the adoption of the hardware and software of a particular supplier, such as Google, makes an educational system worryingly dependent on that company and provides an enormous amount of concern about how educational institutions and their individual students use the Internet system.[218]

In 2023, Google expanded its offerings to include AI tools and systems.[219]

The question that arises is whether any legislative steps should be taken to limit the amount of penetration that any tech company can be allowed to have into a system influencing the thought and behavior of generations of students.

---

216. K. Prescott, "Soaring Cost of Chips Will Hit Use of AI, Warns Slack Chief Lidiane Jones," *The Times*, online, August 7, 2023.
217. Vista Point Advisors, "The Implications for EdTech of Google's Market Share in Education," online at: vistapointadvisors.com, July 29, 2021.
218. J. Iqbal, "Tech Giants Have Gained Too Much Power in Schools,"*The Times*, online June 7, 2021.
219. Product Announcements, "A New Era for AI and Google Workspace," online at: workspace. google.com, March 14, 2023.

However, the trade-off that must be considered is whether the benefits of the educational tools provided by any particular tech giant outweigh the dangers that their participation raises. Exploration of this issue needs to be done by educational authorities and other government officials.

8.7.1.2 Microsoft

However, it is hard to ignore the parallel between Google's actions and the penetration of Microsoft systems software and Internet tools into many aspects of the private and business lives of people all over the world.

As the importance of personal computers grew, Microsoft grew with it, providing tools to operate personal computers and communicate with the Internet. Consequently, Microsoft has obtained, whether intentionally or by accident, a huge amount of knowledge and data about how the computing and Internet worlds work and how Microsoft customers interact with them.

Although Google has a significant amount of power in the world of computing systems and is apparently making efforts to expand that power, there is little doubt that they are dwarfed by Microsoft in the areas of education, business, and communications. Microsoft is now using AI products to expand in all these areas.[220]

However, there may be a need for there to be more examination of the harm this may be doing and whether it makes sense to legally limit Microsoft to a greater degree than existing legislation permits.

8.7.1.3 Apple

There are similar issues with Apple products.

These days, it is possible for a university professor to look out over a classroom of their students and be facing a wall of silver-colored laptops with the Apple logo.

Although other companies may have been more subtle about their approach to gaining influence in the educational sector, Apple never has.

They have always made open and public efforts to attract students and educational institutions to their products by providing tools and operating systems, often with student discounts, that were compatible with what they believed were the interests and aims of the educational community, as well as the artistic community.

Apple was reported to be making extensive efforts to develop AI products.[221]

8.7.2 Other Big Tech Expansion Moves

The Big Tech companies are engaging in other expansions.

220. "AI Platform, Tools and Services," online at: microsoft.com, accessed November 1, 2023.
221. J. Piazza, "Apple, Caught by Surprise in Generative AI Boom, to Spend $1 Billion per Year to Catch Up," online at: cnbc.com, October 23, 2023.

8.7.2.1 Amazon

Amazon has hired 175,000 people since March 2020, has acquired more airplanes for delivery and has reportedly been in talks to acquire a driverless vehicle company.

8.7.2.2 Microsoft

Microsoft has bought three more cloud computing companies.

In January 2023, Microsoft said it was going to acquire the gaming company, Activision Blizzard. This has met with a mixed reception from competition authorities around the world. For example, the EU has permitted the acquisition, but the U.S. and the U.K. initially blocked it. The purchase was characterized as the "world's largest gaming acquisition."

In the field of AI, Microsoft is already promoting itself as one of the leaders in the field with a range of programs and controls to permit the development of AI systems.

For example, Microsoft is already promoting its "Azure AI platform, services and solutions" as tools to "Innovate and accelerate with powerful tools and services that bring artificial intelligence to every developer."[222]

Microsoft also offers an "AI School."

In its online "AI platform video," a narrator says that with Microsoft AI tools: "[Y]ou can find your own use case and how you want to change the world."

This appears to be a promotion of universal and unlimited ambition in the field of AI that Microsoft is pitching to "every developer."

If Microsoft is successful in persuading "every developer" of AI, or a significant percentage of the AI developer population, to adopt the Azure AI "framework,"[223] it remains to be seen whether the competition authorities in different jurisdictions will find that a regulatory response is necessary.

8.7.2.3 Apple

Apple has bought at least four other companies during 2020.

The accidental boost these Big Tech companies got from the unfortunate COVID-19 Pandemic has not only increased their business but has made them more essential to more people.[224]

This extraordinary increase in the reach and the power of the Big Tech companies has concentrated the minds of competition regulators throughout the developed world. The reactions of governments and regulators are not concluded yet.

---

222. Microsoft, "Azure AI platform, Services and Solutions," online at: microsoft.com, accessed August 4, 2023.
223. *Ibid.*
224. M. Isaac, "The Economy Is Reeling. The Tech Giants Spy Opportunity," *The New York Times*, online, Monday, June 15, 2020.

8.7.2.4 Graphics Processing Units

Another problem for competition may come from the increasing cost of the sophisticated chips needed to power AI.

By mid-2023, the rapid increase in the interest in creating and using AI systems led to a shortage in the specialized components needed for AI.[225] The share price of NVIDIA, the best-known maker of the powerful graphics processing units (GPUs) necessary to power AI systems and other sophisticated cyber systems, has risen dramatically since late 2022. The growing demand for these kinds of GPUs has led to shortages and price increases.

In November 2023, NVIDIA announced the launch of "its most advanced super-chip to date, with greater memory, and the ability to train AI models more quickly."[226]

This may mean that access to the tools necessary to build AI-related products will be limited to those competitors that can buy more and pay more for them. It is hard to imagine that in the cost battle, there are many that can compete with Google (Alphabet), Apple, Facebook (Meta) and/or Microsoft.

In summary, the power and potential of AI systems and services may cause dramatic changes in the distribution of market power in cyber-related businesses and activities.

This may cause market competition regulators throughout the world to scrutinize the cyber-related markets more closely and cause those regulators to feel a need to be even tougher when judging whether behavior in those markets has the potential to damage competition or the quality of life of the public generally.

Some prominent jurisdictions where governments are seeking to enforce tough anti-competition laws are the United States and the EU, although some others are also examining competition issues in the changing cyber markets.

8.8 REGULATORY RESPONSES

8.8.1 U.S.

The U.S. has a strong history of antitrust enforcement dating from the end of the nineteenth century when Congress took action against the gigantic and powerful oil company called Standard Oil that was owned by John D. Rockefeller.

The legislation that resulted from this effort is known as the Sherman Antitrust Act of 1890 (Sherman Act).[227]

The Sherman Act focuses on preventing two types of anticompetitive behavior. The first is preventing powerful market participants from achieving "monopoly" in their market where they are virtually, or actually, the only company offering particular

225. Prescott, August 7, 2023, as cited above.
226. K. Prescott, "Nvidia's New H200 Chip Takes AI to Next Level," *The Times* online, November 14, 2023.
227. 26 Stat. 209, 15 U.S.C. sections 1-7.

goods or services to the public. This provision was specifically aimed at Standard Oil, which had achieved the position of being so large and powerful in the oil business that no other company could effectively compete with it.

The second is to prevent "combinations and conspiracies in restraint of trade," where business organizations conspire with one or more competitors to fix prices or terms of service to disadvantage other competitors and or to reduce the choices of the public when purchasing goods or services in the markets in question.

From these basic principles, a very large body of antitrust laws, regulations and interpretive court cases has developed. This is not the place to detail all of those. With respect to questions about any particular matter, qualified expert advisors will need to be consulted.

However, because the Internet is a system that operates throughout the world, it is important to remember that many activities will probably involve transactions with U.S. citizens or U.S. residents or will impact the U.S. cyber markets. That may bring non-U.S. persons and businesses using the Internet within the jurisdiction of U.S. courts.

U.S. courts will often take jurisdiction over "foreign" activities that directly or indirectly affect the domestic or foreign commerce of the United States. A U.S. court may find that a market that is not "exclusively" a foreign market is part of U.S. commerce.[228]

Also, in U.S. antitrust cases, litigants can request jury trials and treble damages can be awarded.

8.8.1.1 U.S. Antitrust Action

Amazon, Apple, Facebook, and Google are all under U.S. government investigation about the issue of whether they are restricting competition, particularly when they are also acting as a "gate keeper" through which competing companies get access to potential customers.

In June 2019, the U.S. Justice Department opened an antitrust investigation of major technology firms. It was reported that the Justice Department will be looking into whether Big Tech's online activities have injured competition, interfered with innovation, or harmed consumers.

The Justice Department and the FTC are examining possible anticompetitive practices by Amazon, Apple, and Facebook, and there is already a suit against Google.

U.S. Dept. of Justice Sues "Monopolist" Google

On October 20, 2020, the U.S. DOJ published a notice online entitled, "Justice Department Sue's Monopolist Google for Violating Antitrust Laws."[229]

The Department stated that its goal was to restore competition in the search and search advertising markets.

---

228. *Transnor (Bermuda) v. BP North America Petoleum*, 738 F. Supp. 1472 (S.D.N.Y. 1990).
229. Justice.gov.

It was reportedly the largest antitrust action brought by the DOJ in about 20 years. The department was joined in this action by the state Attorneys General of Arkansas, Florida, Georgia, Indiana, Kentucky, Louisiana, Mississippi, Missouri, Montana, South Carolina and Texas.

The regulators reportedly will also investigate how Google has used its dominance of Internet searches to move into other areas of Internet business including video, emails, maps, cloud computing, quantum computing and AI.[230]

A principal question raised by such an action will be establishing how consumers have been harmed.

Obviously, it is convenient for many Internet users to search for information using Google, and that basic service is provided by Google without payment. Nevertheless, Google has allegedly used its market power and the vast amounts of money it has earned from its search engine to pay other major Internet companies, such as Apple, to make the Google search app the default search platform on the devices Apple sells, such as MacBooks, iPads and iPhones.[231]

The DOJ of the U.S. has the power and the track record for bringing anti-competition cases in the U.S. that are related to anticompetitive behavior. However, the principal "regulator" of competition-related matters is the U.S. FTC.

Both the DOJ and the FTC have access to criminal and administrative law sanctions that will be applicable to cases involving AI in the same way that they are applicable to many other kinds of market-related cases.

In addition, the U.S. government has generally been concerned with AI-related developments and those particular agencies have expressed views on how they may respond to problems relating to AI.

In April 2023, officials of the FTC and the DOJ, along with other federal agencies, released a "Joint Statement on AI":[232]

> FTC chair Lina M. Khan and officials from three other federal agencies jointly pledged today to uphold America's commitment to the core principles of fairness, equality, and justice as emerging automated systems, including those sometimes marketed as "artificial intelligence" or "AI," become increasingly common in our daily lives—impacting civil rights, fair competition, consumer protection, and equal opportunity.

The DOJ has considered how to respond to the penetration of AI into the international cyber world. In December 2020, the DOJ published a 13-page document entitled "Artificial Intelligence Strategy for the U.S. Department of Justice."[233] This set

230. As of November 2023, this suit is ongoing as *United States v. Google LLC (2020)*.
231. S. Duke, "If the Tech Giants Can't Be Tamed by New Laws, Then They Should Be Broken Up," *The Times*, October 1, 2020, online, retrieved October 1, 2020. https://www.thetimes.co.uk/article/breaking-up-big-tech-may-be-the-least-worst-choice-dftfn22jd?shareToken=bb1b6d237a194cb9557e94095918e201.
232. Federal Trade Commission, "FTC Chair Khan and Officials from DOJ, CFPB (Consumer Financial Protection Bureau, and the EEOC (Equal Employment Opportunities Commission), Release Joint Statement on AI," online at: ftc.gov, April 25, 2023.
233. Office of the Chief Information Officer, U.S. Department of Justice, "Artificial Intelligence Strategy for the U.S. Department of Justice," (DOJ Strategy) online at: justice.gov.

out how the DOJ intended to deal with AI, how it would structure its workforce to respond to the challenges and what were considered its goals to be at that time:

> This strategy is the result of a department-wide effort led by our Chief Technology Officer and provides a foundational framework that will provide a coordinated approach to AI.[234]

At that time, the DOJ Strategy document emphasized familiarizing its workforce with developments in AI and adopting AI solutions where they would help the DOJ in carrying out its missions.[235]

To assist in its responsibilities related to AI, the DOJ uses the National Institute of Justice (NIJ), which is "the research, development and evaluation agency" of the DOJ, "dedicated to improving knowledge and understanding of crime and justice issues through science."[236]

As early as 2018, the NIJ focused on using AI to deal with criminal cases.[237]

In an article in 2018, Christopher Rigano pointed out:

> Even public safety and criminal justice are benefitting from AI. For example, traffic safety systems identify violations and enforce the rules of the road, and crime forecasts allow for more efficient allocation of policing resources. AI is also helping to identify the potential for an individual under criminal justice supervision to reoffend. ... Research supported by NIJ is helping to lead the way in applying AI to address criminal justice needs, such as identifying individuals and their actions in videos relating to criminal activity or public safety, DNA analysis, gunshot detection and crime forecasting.[238]

8.8.1.2 A Selection of DOJ and FTC AI-Related Cases

1. Haitao Xiang Algorithm Theft Case (November 21, 2019) (DOJ)

"Haitao Xaing, 42, formerly of Chesterfield, Missouri, was indicted today by a federal grand jury on one count of conspiracy to commit economic espionage, three counts of economic espionage, one count of conspiracy to commit theft of trade secrets, and three counts of theft of trade secrets. ... Monsanto and The Climate Corporation developed a digital, on-line farming software platform that was used by farmers to collect, store and visualize critical agricultural field data and increase and improve agricultural productivity for farmers. ... Xiang promoted himself to the Chinese government based on his experience at Monsanto. Within a year of being selected as a Talent Plan recruit, he quit his job, bought a one-way ticket to China, and was caught

234. Melinda Rogers, Deputy Assistant Attorney General, Chief Information Officer, Chief Data Officer, DOJ, DOJ Strategy, p. 3.
235. DOJ Strategy, p. 4.
236. National Institute of Justice, "About the National Institute of Justice," online at: nij.ojp.gov., May 2, 2022.
237. C. Rigano, "Using Artificial Intelligence to Address Criminal Justice Needs," *NIJ*, online October 8, 2018, accessed August 9, 2023.
238. *Ibid.*

at the airport with a copy of the company's proprietary algorithm before he could spirit it away."[239]

2. Meta Platforms Inc. Advertising Case (June 21, 2022)

"The Department of Justice announced today that it has obtained a settlement agreement resolving allegations that Meta-Platforms Inc., formerly known as Facebook Inc., has engaged in discriminatory advertising in violation of the fair housing act (FHA). The proposed agreement resolved in the lawsuit was filed today in the US District Court for the Southern District of New York alleging that Meta's housing advertising system discriminates against Facebook users based on their race, color, religion, sex, disability, familial status and national origin. ... Among other things, the complaint alleges that Meta uses algorithms in determining which Facebook users receive housing ads, and that those algorithms rely, in part, on characteristics protected under the FHA. This is the department's first case challenging algorithmic bias under the Fair Housing Act."[240]

3. Amazon: Child Privacy Case

"Proposed order to pay $25 million and delete children's data, geolocation data and other voice recordings."

"The Federal Trade Commission and the Department of Justice will require Amazon to overhaul its deletion practices and implement stringent privacy safeguards to settle charges the company violated the Children's Online Privacy Protection Act Rule (COPPA Rule) and deceived parents and users of the Alexa voice assistant service about its data deletion practices. According to the complaint filed by the Department of Justice on behalf of the FTC, Amazon prevented parents from exercising their deletion rights under the COPPA Rule, kept sensitive voice and geolocation data for years and used it for its own purposes while putting data at risk of harm from unnecessary access."[241]

8.8.1.3 Private Suits

It is not only government regulatory investigations which are examining are concerned with the anticompetitive behavior of Big Tech. There will almost certainly be a large number of private antitrust suits in the future.

239. Department of Justice, Press Release, "Chinese National Who Worked at Monsanto Indicted on Economic Espionage Charges," online at: justice.gov, November 21, 2019.
240. Department of Justice, Press Release, "Justice Department Secures Groundbreaking Settlement Agreement with Meta Platforms, Formerly Known as Facebook, to Resolve Allegations of Discriminatory Advertising," online at: justice.gov, June 21, 2022.
241. Federal Trade Commission, "FTC and DOJ Charge Amazon with Violating Chiildren's Privacy Law by Keeping Kids' Voice Recordings Forever and Undermining Parents' Deletion Requests," online at: ftc.gov, May 21, 2023.

1. EPIC Suit v. Apple

For example, the digital games developer Epic Games, creator of the popular Fortnite game, has reportedly brought a lawsuit in U.S. Federal Court against Apple, alleging that the commissions that Apple collects on in-app sales by developers using the App Store are "extortionate."[242]

Fortnite reportedly provoked a battle with Apple by creating its own in-app payment system, independent of Apple. When Apple learned of this, it banished Fortnite from its App Store. Fortnite claimed that Apple's behavior made it unfairly difficult for Fortnite and other developers to sell their products. Allegedly, Apple's rules were intended to give Apple a virtual "Monopoly" over the sale of developers' products by severely limiting the options they could choose as a place to market their products.[243]

In September 2021, it was reported that the federal court published a decision in the *Epic* case saying that although the court could not declare Apple to be a monopoly, Apple was behaving in an anticompetitive manner by refusing to permit app creators that sold their products through Apple's App Store to purchase the products through their own purchase systems rather than exclusively through the App Store.[244]

The judge in the *Epic* case said that although Apple did control approximately 55% of the market, that did not, in itself, constitute a monopoly. The judge wrote, "Success is not illegal."[245]

Although they achieved one of their major goals—getting the right to sell their app through their own payment system rather than exclusively through Apple's system, Epic was reportedly still unhappy with the decision and shortly after it was issued, Epic filed an appeal with the Ninth Circuit Court of Appeal, which ruled in Apple's favor, upholding the lower court decision that Apple was not a monopoly.[246]

8.9 EUROPEAN UNION

8.9.1 EU Anti-competition Law

EU anti-competition law has essentially the same goals as U.S. antitrust law. The European Commission says:

> Competition encourages companies to offer consumers goods and services on the most favorable terms. It encourages efficiency and innovation and reduces prices. To be effective competition requires companies to act independently of each other, but subject to the pressure exerted by their competitors.[247]

242. J. Clayton, "Apple Faces Epic Games in Court," *BBC News*, online, May 3, 2021.
243. *Ibid.*
244. A.R. Sorkin, et al., "Why Apple Didn't Lose in the Epic Games Ruling: A Judge's Split Decision in the Lawsuit Mostly Went in Favor of Big Tech," *The New York Times*, "Dealbook Newsletter," online, September 13, 2021.
245. *Ibid.*
246. *Ibid.*
247. European Commission, Competition Policy, Antitrust. ec.europa.eu.

The basic EU anti-competition legislation is set out in Articles 101 and 102 of the Treaty on the Functioning of the European Union[248] (TFEU).

TFEU Article 101 prohibits anticompetitive agreements between two or more independent market operators.

TFEU Article 102 prohibits abusive behavior by companies holding a dominant position in any given market.

8.9.2 EU Actions

8.9.2.1 Google

In June 2019, Google was fined $1.7 billion by European competition regulators for requiring online advertisers to sign exclusivity agreements that were found to be unfair to competing online advertising companies.[249]

Amazon

In June 2020, the EU began preparing anti-competition charges against Amazon. The basis of their complaint is that Amazon abused its dominant market position in online commerce by attempting to block less powerful rivals.[250]

It has been reported that the investigation against Amazon is part of a broader EU investigation into the business practices of Big Tech, including Apple and Facebook.

There is concern about Amazon's dual role of being not only a seller of goods on its own account but also a provider of a platform for Amazon competitors to sell goods online. It is reported that Amazon requires these subsidiary merchants to collect data that they are required to share with Amazon as a condition for being allowed to sell on the Amazon platform.[251]

Apple

On June 17, 2020, *The Times* reported that the European Commission was beginning an investigation into whether rules that Apple imposed on app developers restricted competition and improperly benefited Apple.

This investigation comes from complaints from Spotify, a popular music streaming service, and Kobo, an online bookstore, that Apple let iPad and iPhone users download apps only from Apple's own App Store. Apple then allegedly claims a substantial percentage (30% in the first year, 15% thereafter) of any payments or subscriptions made through those apps. Apple also allegedly forbids those companies

248. *See also*, the European Commission, Antitrust Overview, ec.europa.eu.
249. A. Satariano, "Google Fined $1.7 Billion by E.U. for Unfair Advertising Rules," *The New York Times* (online), March 20, 2019.
250. A. Satariano, "Amazon Set to Face Antitrust Charges in European Union," *The New York Times* (online), June 11, 2020.
251. *Ibid., citing* Prof. William Kovacic of George Washington University.

from telling their customers (within those apps) that the goods or subscriptions can be bought more cheaply on the companies' own websites.[252]

Apple reportedly makes about $1 billion a month from app fees. Apple's policy of taking 15% to 30% of purchases through apps causes consumers to pay higher prices because to pay those fees, service providers like Spotify must raise their own prices.[253]

In addition, there is also said to be a conflict of interest created by the fact that Apple has now moved into providing its own music and video streaming services, which competes with companies, such as Netflix or Spotify, who are using apps from Apple's app store to sell their products.[254]

Such tactics by Apple may remind one of the activities of John D. Rockefeller, the nineteenth-century founder of Standard Oil, who forced railroad companies that wanted his business to pay him a percentage of the fees they received from carrying the oil of companies competing with Standard Oil. It was Rockefeller's ruthless domination of the oil business that led to the original U.S. anti-competition law, the Sherman Antitrust Act of 1890.

If Apple is found to have violated EU competition law, the European Commission could fine them an amount equal to 10% of Apple's global revenues. In 2022, those revenues were reportedly more than $394 billion.[255]

In 2019, Apple was reportedly charged by Spotify with "limiting choices and stifling innovation" by charging high commission fees in the App Store on "in app" purchases and forbidding companies offering their products on the App Store to offer their customers alternatives. After reviewing the charges, in May 2021, the Commission agreed that Apple was breaking EU competition regulations by the way it was operating its App Store. As a result, Apple may be subject to significant fines and requirements that it modify the way it operates its App Store.[256]

The EU did not stop its investigation with the Spotify complaint. It has continued its investigation into the possible anticompetitive aspects of the way Apple operates its App Store, including whether its standard 30% commission on apps is a fair price. It is reported that many app developers are unhappy with Apple's App Store-connected charges, and a number have expressed their agreement with the preliminary findings of the Commission that Apple is engaging in anticompetitive behavior.[257]

Spotify is not the only developer to complain to the EU about Apple. In March 2020, Rakuten reportedly filed a complaint with the EU claiming that Apple was charging an anticompetitive commission on electronic books sold through its App Store while being in the conflicting position of promoting competing book sales through its Apple Books app.[258]

---

252. *The Times*, online, Business, June 17, 2020.
253. *Ibid.*
254. *Ibid.*
255. Statista.com, November 16, 2023.
256. J. Wakefield, "Apple Charged Over 'Anti-competitive' App Policies," *BBC News*, online, accessed May 3, 2021.
257. *Ibid.*
258. *Ibid.*

8.9.3 France

A blow against Google's alleged market dominance has been struck in France.

In June 2020, French anti-competition regulators, under EU antitrust regulations, fined Google 220 million Euros for taking unfair advantage of its search engine dominance to establish a competitive advantage in sales of online ads.[259]

That is certainly a lot of money but is relatively small compared to the $41 billion in revenue earned by Google in 2020.

The French regulator said that its decision would allow competitors of Google that were disadvantaged to seek damages.[260]

8.9.4 U.K.

One of the most important Acts that has been applied to internet activity in the U.K. is the Competition Act 1998.

Competition in the U.K. is supervised by the Competition and Markets Authority (CMA).

8.9.4.1 U.K. Report on Google and Facebook

In December 2019, the U.K. CMA published a 283-page interim report from a market study which found that Google accounted for 90% of U.K. search advertising revenues (amounting to about £6 billion a year), and Facebook accounted for over half of display advertising revenues.

The report also said that Google and Facebook's domination of social media and search is so great that it could be driving up the prices of vacations, electronic goods, and financial services. It said their profits are "well above any reasonable estimate of what might be expected."[261]

Facebook

Take Facebook (Meta), for example. It has been reported in the *New York Times*[262] that Facebook has come under increasing scrutiny by competition regulators for its expansion around the globe. The U.K. has been particularly concerned about the expansion of Facebook's power.

Gojek

Facebook reported that it had bought Gojek, an app from Southeast Asia that characterizes itself as a "super app" that allows one to book taxis, do shopping and

259. M. Sweney, "France Fines Google for Abusing Online Advertising Dominance," *The Guardian*, online, June 7, 2020.
260. *Ibid.*
261. A. Ellison, "Consumer Champion Quits Amid Digital Tax Row," *The Times*, online, June 19, 2020.
262. Isaac, June 15, 2020.

make payments. Gojek has more than 3.3 million online reviews with an average score of 4.3.

This is given as one example of Facebook's expansion into the rapidly growing Asian online business market.

Reliance Jio

Facebook has also reportedly made a $5.7 billion investment in Reliance Jio, a major Indian telecommunications company.

Africa

Facebook is also reportedly spending many millions to construct a 37,000-kilometer-long fiber optic cable network around Africa.[263]

Giphy

Facebook also reportedly spent $400 million in May 2020 to purchase Giphy, a company with a catalogue of film clips and animations that can be attached to messages to illustrate ideas that the sender wishes to express. Facebook saw this as an enhancement to Instagram.[264]

However, a little more than a year later, the U.K. CMA indicated it would block the takeover of Giphy. In August 2021, the CMA finished an investigation of the takeover and concluded that allowing the acquisition by Facebook would significantly reduce competition in areas of social media and online advertising, which would harm individuals and businesses using the Internet.

If Facebook refused to sell, the regulator could take them to court.

Facebook is already in some trouble with Giphy's investigation by the CMA. Facebook was accused of deliberately refusing to supply relevant information and was fined £50.5 million.[265]

The principal advertising market said to be affected by Facebook's acquisition of Giphy is called the "display advertising" market, of which Facebook reportedly had a 50% share in 2020.

Giphy provides a type of animated image called "giphs" that are useful in advertising on popular social media platforms such as TikTok, Twitter, Tinder, Slack and iMessage.[266] Facebook has responded that the conclusions of the regulator about the competitive harm of the takeover were "manifestly disproportionate." Facebook denied that it had significant market power in the relevant U.K. market and said that it would be "grossly unreasonable" for the regulator to block the acquisition.[267]

263. *Ibid.*
264. K. Wagner & S. Frier, "Facbook Buys Animated Image Library Giphy for $400 Million," *Bloomberg News*, online, May 20, 2020.
265. M. Sweney, "Facebook Fined £50.5m for Breaching Order in Giphy Takeover Investigation," *The Guardian*, online, October 20, 2021.
266. C. Jones, "Facebook Fights Completion and Markets Authority over Giphy Deal," *The Times*, online, September 9, 2021.
267. *Ibid.*

The CMA ordered Facebook to sell Giphy in November 2021.[268]

Now, the CMA has begun a wider investigation of whether Facebook has been misusing its market power to gain unfair advantages in digital advertising.

If they are found by the CMA to be guilty of that, they could be subject to large fines. The regulator is concerned that Facebook has prevented less powerful rivals from successfully competing with Facebook and has thereby reduced the choice of digital advertisers available to the public.

Facebook Marketplace

One Facebook tactic that concerns the CMA is whether Facebook was unfairly using the data in its system to create new offerings to compete with others (such as eBay).

Facebook Marketplace is reported to be one such new feature.

Facebook Sign-In

Facebook is also reportedly using its sign-in procedure to allow its users to sign into multiple Facebook-related apps, which are thought to automatically give it a competitive advantage over competing online sites such as dating and advertising sites.

Facebook Advertising

The CMA has also begun investigating whether Facebook has been misusing its market power to gain unfair advantages in digital advertising.

The CMA is concerned that Facebook has prevented less powerful rivals from successfully competing with Facebook and has thereby reduced the choice of digital advertisers available to the public.

If they are found by the CMA to be guilty of anticompetitive abuses in the above market sectors, they could be subject to large fines.

If Facebook is found by the CMA to be in violation of applicable competition rules, it could be fined as much as 10% of its worldwide revenues, which could add up to over $8 billion.[269]

8.9.5 Tax Issues Related to Competition

It is not only market power that concerns regulators when considering whether their size creates unfair advantages.

The tax authorities in several countries are concerned that the structure of the Big Tech companies as large integrated companies allows them to avoid taxes by balancing the losses of some divisions against gains in others.

Consequently, there is talk of splitting these companies into separate taxable entities to allow taxation of the most profitable divisions of these companies.

---

268. M. Sweney, "UK Competition Watchdog Orders Facebook Owner to Sell Gif Website Giphy," *The Guardian*, online, November 30, 2021.
269. T. Knowles, "Facebook Investigated by UK Watchdog over Digital Dominance," *The Times*, online, June 5, 2021, accessed June 7, 2021.

For example, it is suggested that it might be useful to treat Amazon's Cloud Computing division as a separate company to allow taxation of its $1.6 billion in annual revenue.

There has been considerable concern that these companies are able to avoid their taxation by shifting their profits and losses among the different jurisdictions in which they trade, which usually have different and/or contradictory tax regimes. To counter this, there is currently a proposal before the G7 countries to require large companies to pay taxes where they sell their products instead of where they declare their profits.[270]

8.9.5.1 *Apple EU Tax Ruling*

For example, in November 2023:

> An adviser to the European Union's top court dealt a major blow to Apple in its $14 billion tax dispute [with the EU] ... after recommending that a lower court ruling in favor of the iPhone maker should be set aside due to legal errors ... The EU's top court is expected to issue a ruling on the matter in the next few months.[271]

8.9.6 Other Regulators

However, antitrust regulators around the world are certainly not finished using antitrust to reduce the market dominance of giant Internet companies.[272]

8.9.6.1 *China*

China has taken dramatic steps to reduce the financial power of the owner of Alibaba (part of the Ant Group).

In September 2021, there were reports that the Chinese government is considering requiring Alibaba founder Jack Ma to separate the lending business of the group and turn over user data to a state-owned group.

Additional potential weakening of the Ma's Ant Group is also reported in that part of the Ant Group may come under partial government ownership. This is all part of a recent Chinese government effort to reduce the market power of large Chinese Internet companies that have achieved close to monopoly positions.[273]

270. S. Duke, "G7 Plans New Approach to Stop Tech Giants Avoiding Tax," *The Times*, online, June 9, 2021.
271. S. Ray, "Apple May Be Forced To Pay $14 Billion in EU Taxes after Legal Setback," *Forbes*, online, November 9, 2023.
272. A. Satariano, "Google to Pay $270 Million to Settle Antitrust Charges in France," *The New York Times*, online, June 7, 2021.
273. A.R. Sorkin, et al., "Beijing Reportedly Wants to Break Up Alipay," *The New York Times*, "Dealbook Newsletter," online, September 13, 2021.

8.9.6.2 *Russia*

It is not only in the Western countries where there is concern about the market dominance of Big Tech.

For example, in late August 2021, Russia's anti-monopoly agency fined the online hotel booking company Booking.com a record Russian ruble equivalent of €14.9 million for dominating the hotel booking market.[274] The Russians concluded that Booking was abusing its dominant market position and fined that Netherlands company 1.3 billion Russian rubles.[275]

8.9.6.3 *Other Countries Concerned*

The above are not the only countries worried about the expansion of powerful tech companies.

Apparently, the large companies in the tech industry have become so powerful that they are attracting attention of competition regulators in other parts of the world as Australia, Brazil, and India.

8.10 CHOICES

As societies interested in the intellectual, social and moral development of their children are becoming more skeptical about turning young people over to these Big Tech?

There is concern about whether existing laws make it plain enough how the influence of these tech companies should be limited. Will the growth of AI and the early penetrations of that market by Big Tech companies allow them to make their market power even more difficult to control?

Investigations, suits and regulatory fines in the EU, the U.K. and the United States may be only the start of the regulatory hurdles that may be imposed on large and rapidly growing tech companies.[276]

The enthusiastic expansion of Big Tech companies into AI products will probably intensify their scrutiny by regulators.

It is not only the enormous success of these companies that attracts the attention of competition regulators but also the concern that Big Tech may use that success to harm competitors and the public.[277]

Bill Baer, who is a fellow at the Brookings Institute, wrote in April 2020 that even during a time of an economic emergency such as that caused by the COVID-19

274. "Russia Fines Booking.com Record 14.9 Euros for Alleged Market Dominance," *Euronews*, online, August, 27 2021.
275. *Ibid.*
276. Satariano, June 11, 2020, *citing* Prof. William Kovacic of George Washington University.
277. Satariano, June 11, 2020, *citing* Bill Baer, former antitrust enforcement head at the U.S. Department of Justice.

pandemic, regulators should not relax but rather focus their market scrutiny on possible anticompetitive practices during such difficult times.

He pointed out that although marketers of essential goods might claim that they are not raising prices but merely "stabilizing" prices, it should not be forgotten that agreements by competitors to fix prices are still illegal under anti-competition laws.[278]

The concern that the U.S. government, along with the EU and other national regulators, have is that tech companies like Apple, Microsoft, Amazon, Google and Facebook have become so dominant in their markets that they are in the position of essentially being monopolies in their primary market sectors.

If this proposition is proved by the regulators that are investigating these tech giants, governments may consider it necessary to pass new laws to limit the power of such companies.

8.11 BREAK UP THE CYBER GIANTS?

If existing anti-competition laws do not accomplish what they are intended to do, the U.S., the EU and other major market regulators may determine that these giants need to be broken up or restricted to operation only in specific market sectors.[279]

278. B. Baer, "Why We Need Antitrust Enforcement During the Covid-19 Pademic," *Brookings Institute*, online, April 22, 2020.
279. *Ibid.*

CHAPTER 9
Energy Law

Energy is one of the most valuable resources available to humans. It keeps us alive; it helps us do work; it helps us to move.

At its most basic, the ultimate source of all energy is the sun. It creates things, changes things and destroys things.

For us to have energy to help us live, we use the sun or emulate it to produce heat.

The ways that we produce heat can include: fire, electricity, and movement (of wind, tide, etc.).

Considering the value of energy, one of the most important questions relating to it is who is permitted to produce it and under what circumstances.

This brings us to the question of what laws and regulations relate to the production, distribution and use of energy.

This is the topic of energy law.

9.1 OUR SOURCES OF HEAT

From the most primitive times, humans discovered that by harnessing the burning of certain resources, they could use the resulting heat from fire to both stay warm and assist in the performance of work.

It was discovered that certain resources burned more easily than others, and certain resources were easier to acquire than others.

We do not know this for certain, but there is speculation that humans learned the value of fire from encounters with natural fires caused by such things as lightning strikes period. Such strikes were likely to set fire to combustible materials like wood, and humans learned to identify wood as a convenient fuel. Because we could not compel lightning to strike when and where it was convenient, humans eventually learned that they could produce sufficient heat to ignite a fire on flammable material by means of friction or, perhaps, from sparks created by striking certain mineral resources such as flint.

From very early times, humans would have understood that the taking of wood to burn in fires meant that the supply of wood in any particular area was increasingly reduced, and some people would be disadvantaged by the reduction of wood.

Consequently, in order to maintain peace between groups of persons competing for supplies of wood, rules began to be established.

As time went on and the sources of energy became more varied, such rules evolved into the complex laws and regulations that we class as energy law.

Today, energy law relates to the production distribution and use of a number of energy sources, including:

- Biomass (products such as wood products, plant products, peat, manure, etc.).
- Fossil fuels (coal, oil, gas).
- Solar (including conversion of sunshine to electricity by use of solar panels).
- Movement (including from wind, tide, waves, water flows, etc.).
- Geothermal heat (heat produced by the Earth, usually well below the surface).
- Nuclear (produced by nuclear fission and, perhaps in the future, nuclear fusion).

Each of these ways of producing energy has advantages and disadvantages relating to cost, safety, security, and environmental impact. It is the function of energy law to balance these issues in order to provide society with a consistent, relatively affordable and relatively safe supply of energy.

9.2 ENERGY COST ESTIMATES

Estimates of the average costs of main energy sources are as follows:

- Concentrated solar power: $182 mwh.
- Solar voltaic: $50 mwh.
- Offshore wind: $78 mwh.
- Geothermal: $72 mwh.
- Bioenergy: $62 mwh.
- Hydropower: $40 to $110 mwh.
- Coal: between $87 and $118 mwh.
- Gas: between $65 and $111 mwh.
- Nuclear: $70 mwh (France) $150 mwh (U.K.).

9.2.1 Issues with Cost

However, the "cost" of any source of energy used to produce electricity is tricky because there is always a question of how and when it is being calculated.

Clearly, the cost of electricity (usually calculated in relation to producing a megawatt hour of electricity) must include the following:

- The cost of building the infrastructure needed to produce usable electricity.
- The cost of connecting to the place where it is needed.

This calculation, certainly in the case of electricity produced commercially, as opposed to individual domestic use, involves connecting to a government-provided "grid."

9.2.1.1 Grid Costs

An electric grid moves electric current from the place where it is produced to places (communities, businesses, etc.) where it is needed.

Therefore, most sources of electricity will involve any additional costs of maintaining, extending or modifying a grid system to access any new sources of electricity.

An example of the problems this creates is the situation of the U.K. National Grid. In May 2024, it was reported by *The Times*:

> "More than £6 billion was wiped off the London stock, markets, energy and water sector after national grid unveiled plans for one of the largest fundings in more than a decade. ... The near £7 billion right issue would be the largest from a company in Europe outside the banking sector in 15 years, the FTSE 1000 company said. ... John Pettigrew, the Grid CEO said that funding would allow connection to "lower-cost renewable generation ..."[280]

This is indicative of the difficulty of creating new sources of energy and putting them in different locations. The infrastructure of any transmission grid is expensive and requires significant amounts of engineering and work to complete, as shown in the article above and many other reports. Modifications to a grid system to take account of new energy systems can cost many billions.

9.2.1.2 Other Possible Cost Elements

Wind and solar power are now being touted as the cheapest sources of energy.

The "low cost" title was for many years attributed to coal. But coal is no longer said to be so inexpensive because of the disadvantages of acquiring and using it. Coal has the other serious disadvantage of being identified as the dirtiest source of energy. The burning of coal is said to be responsible for approximately a third of the rise in global carbon emissions.

One element that reduces fossil fuel costs is that they have been used for hundreds of years. Consequently, much of the infrastructure for acquiring and using them is already in place. This eliminates the cost of having to provide new infrastructure in order to begin using them, which is a disadvantage that many of the new fuel

280. E. Powell, "National Grid to Raise £7bn for Energy Network Upgrade," *The Times*, May 23, 2024.

sources, such as renewables and nuclear power, have to bear before they can be brought online.

Hydropower cost is lowest where the infrastructure for moving water has been in place for a very long time and was put in place by nature in terms of natural flowing streams of water, waterfalls, etc. However, hydropower costs increase where expensive new infrastructure, such as dams or long-distance transport infrastructure (such as pipelines or aqueducts), is needed.

Bioenergy uses flammable natural organic material such as vegetation (wood and other dried plants such as straw, etc.) and organic waste such as food waste or animal waste.

An advantage of bioenergy is that it is "renewable." It is accessible or produceable in any environment where plants will grow, food and animal waste are available and can be dried until they are combustible.

Other advantages are that it helps reduce waste and burning adds less carbon dioxide to the atmosphere than burning fossil fuels because the carbon dioxide burning biomass produces is judged equal to the carbon dioxide absorbed by vegetation while it is growing.

However, there are disadvantages to biomass. It is a relatively expensive fuel that requires a lot of space to produce. Harvesting, storage and transportation is needed. Because of the space needs that relate to these, the places where biomass-burning energy plants can be built are limited. There is the issue of whether dedicating land to bioenergy fuel is the best use of agricultural land that could be used for food production.[281]

Nuclear energy cost is affected by plant building costs. It is relatively low in France because it has been in place for decades. In the U.K., it is currently estimated as very expensive because of the very high costs of building and making operational new nuclear plants there.

However, it is not always clear when electricity costs are being stated, what elements are being included in calculating the cost?

For example, there is the issue of the usable life of any energy source. For example, nuclear power plants are expensive to build, but they have been proven to be usable for about 60 years.

Wind turbines may have an effective life of about 20 years, but they are sometimes guaranteed by their manufacturer for 2-5 years, and during their life may need expensive repairs. Wind turbines are also reported to catch fire, kill birds, and kill people who install and repair them and create noise disturbing to some people who live close by. If wind turbines need to be replaced several times over a period of 60 years and repaired throughout their useful life, that could increase the cost of that source of power. Also there is the added cost of the space (on land or water) that the turbines have to occupy.

281. C. Lane, "Biomass Energy Pros and Cons," *SolarReviews*, online at: solarreviews.com.

Solar power also has problems. First, the world's largest producer of solar panels is China, which is also by far the world's largest user of coal.[282] Ironically, the industrial production of solar panels in China could be contributing to global warming.

Also, solar panels are rated only to be usable for about half the life of a nuclear plant. Also, the electricity conversion efficiency of solar panels declines by a certain percentage every year of their life. Solar panels also become less efficient when they get dirty. A significant amount of water and labor may needed to keep them clean. Also, large arrays of solar panels can cover large areas of land. Although it is argued that land used for solar farms can also be used for some agricultural purposes, having large areas of countryside covered in acres of black panels may not be the best use of agricultural land. These things may add to the real costs of installing solar panels over wide areas.

As mentioned above, there are also "hidden costs" to using biomass for power generation. These include the costs of the land needed to produce the vegetation usable for conversion to biofuels. In addition, there is also the cost of the loss of foodstuffs and building materials that could be obtained from that same land if its production was not being used for conversion to biofuels.

Finally, there are the costs of cleanup and restoration of any power-source location after that power source has completed its useful life.

But most of the power sources discussed above, although interesting and desirable for many reasons, are not the world's principal sources of power in the first half of the twenty-first century.

9.3 FOSSIL FUELS

Fossil fuels are still the source of about 85% of the world's energy production.

Oil is the largest source, producing about 34%.

Coal produces about 27%.

Gas produces about 24%.

All the fossil fuels add a significant amount of carbon to the atmosphere.

"Low Carbon" sources produce the other approximately 15% of energy. Of that 15%, biofuels produce about 9% and nuclear about 5%.

Renewables such as hydro, wind, solar, geothermal, wave and tidal sources produce the rest.

Some countries are better at using renewables than others. Iceland gets about 79% of its power from hydro. France gets 49% of its power from nuclear.

However, it is undeniable that most of the world's power (about 58%) comes from oil and gas.

Therefore, as a strictly business proposition, it is useful to spend some time learning how the oil and gas business operates.

282. International Energy Agency, online at: iea.org.

9.4 OIL AND GAS

For the most part, oil and gas are both produced from the operation of oil wells, created principally for the production of petroleum.

These are energy sources accused of contributing significantly to global warming and pollution of various kinds.

However, as it is the world's principal source of energy and, therefore, it is an important sector of business law.

The oil and gas business is expensive, environmentally intrusive and legally complex.

9.4.1 Petroleum Costs

The price of oil and gas varies significantly over time.[283] However, if oil is $50 a barrel, 10,000 barrels would sell for $500,000. There are about 80 million barrels of oil produced a day worth about $4 billion.

In one hour they would make $166 million, in one minute, $2.8 million; and in one second, $46 thousand. It is easy to understand why nations want to have and nurture any petroleum production they can develop.

No matter where it is produced, finding and producing petroleum is expensive. Onshore wells in the U.S. cost between $10 and $25 million. In the North Sea, offshore wells cost between $50 and $80 million. Offshore, deep water wells can cost $100 million or more.

9.4.2 Who Owns Production?

In every country in the world, except the United States, rights to underground minerals, including oil and gas (collectively called "petroleum"), belong to the state. In the U.S., the people that own the land also own the minerals under it.

Therefore, in most countries, the parties legally involved in the production of oil and gas are the state and the firms needed to provide the expertise and equipment to produce and market the petroleum.

9.4.3 National Oil Companies

The state parties will include the host country and perhaps national oil companies (NOCs).

Non-state parties will include foreign, usually private, energy conglomerates (known as the "super majors") and/or smaller firms called "independents."

283. Standard measures in the global oil business are US dollars, and US barrels (about 159 liters).

9.4.4 Independent Oil Companies

However, generally, in the industry, all non-state parties are often collectively described as "Independent Oil Companies" (IOCs).

Prior to the Internet Age, the Super Majors (such as Exxon, Shell, BP, Chevron, etc.) were the most valuable companies in the world in terms of market capitalization. But in recent years, their value has been surpassed by the Digital Giants (Apple, Microsoft, Amazon, Google, etc.).

The NOCs and the IOCs are the basic parties that are the principals in the agreements concerned with the production of oil and gas.

However, there are a number of ancillary parties that are needed to assist the production and marketing of petroleum products.

This means that in oil and gas production, there are essentially two categories of agreements. There is the category of concessions and licenses. These are the agreements that are negotiated between the states and the Independents, which permit and set the terms of the exploitation of petroleum resources within a particular state. Second, there are agreements between the Independents and the ancillary parties who are contracted with the Independents to provide the services and equipment to take the exploitation forward.

9.4.5 Ancillary Parties

These are the parties that provide expertise and work to the oil companies for a fee.

On any petroleum exploitation project, these are likely to include the following:

- Oil field services companies that are hired to drill and operate the wells. These include Schlumberger and Haliburton.
- Construction companies that build needed infrastructure such as roads and ports. These include Technip, Aker and Bechtel.
- Equipment manufacturers that are usually small and medium-sized companies (SMEs).
- Rig hire firms that provide oil rigs for offshore drilling and production.
- Transport companies that provide land, air and/or sea transport for personnel, equipment and produced petroleum products.
- Cleanup and restoration specialists that, after a production project is completed, work to remove no longer needed things from the site and restore the site to a legally required condition.

9.5 APPLICABLE LAW

Because of the value and importance of petroleum products and the impact that production projects can have within affected areas, the petroleum business is highly regulated by national and international laws, regulations and treaties.

All of these fall into two categories: private law and public law.

Private law is the law that governs relationships between private parties. This includes most contract law and is derived from the following sources:

- Statutes.
- Regulations.
- Court precedents.
- Established and legally acceptable market customs.

Public law applies to relations with the state, including relations of private parties with the state. The sources are similar:

- Statutes.
- Regulations.
- Court precedents.

However, the focus of public law is different. These include reflections on government policy relating to different business practices and activities that the state feels impinge on the public interest. For example, anti-bribery regulations have a significant role in the petroleum business.

9.5.1 Oil and Gas Contracts

The principles of contract law are discussed in detail in Chapter 2. However, with respect to oil and gas contracts, there are specific characteristics that need to be considered.

The important terms of these contracts will usually include the following.

9.5.1.1 Parties

On one side, parties will be the state and/or the NOC.

On the other side will be an IOC or a consortium of IOCs.

9.5.1.2 Start Date

There will usually be a start date or "effective date" on which the contract obligations begin to take effect. Depending on state approval, this will usually be a fixed calendar date or date on which a designated event occurs

This date usually commences the first phase of the petroleum project, which is often the exploration phase, where the parties search to find a viable production pool of oil and gas.

9.5.1.3 Term

The provisions of oil and gas are usually in effect for a limited period of time. This time period is defined by a "term" specification in the contract.

These provisions usually define the time period limits for the usual first two phases of a petroleum contract: the Exploration Phase and the Production Phase.

The Exploration Phase is a period when seismic surveys and test drilling are undertaken in a search for commercially viable oil and gas fields. This is usually limited to 10 to 12 years.

Once an oil and gas field is operational, the Production Phase comes into effect. That can last from 20 to 30 years, but can be extended by agreement of the parties. This is when commercially valuable amounts of oil and gas are produced and used locally or sold into the market.

9.5.1.4 Minimum Work Obligations

An important term of any petroleum contract is the "minimum work obligations."

In this provision, a prescribed amount of work and financial commitment is agreed upon by the parties. The purpose of this provision is to ensure that the contractor spends enough time and money to develop commercially viable oil and gas wells.

The work and the capital are usually specified to be contributed within a defined period. An example of a required commitment is a specification that a minimum number of wells must be established at a minimum level of expenditure.

Failure to meet these commitments will usually require a contractor to pay the State the difference between the contractor's actual expenditure and the contractually specified minimum.

If excess work or expenditure by the contractor occurs, it can be credited to the contractor by an extended exploration phase.

9.5.1.5 Operations and Control

Contractual terms specify how a particular oil and gas project will be operated and controlled.

Usually, the contractor is in charge of operations unless the contractor is a consortium of companies. Where there is a consortium, usually one of the members will be chosen to be the operator. This can be agreed upon by the members of the consortium or the controller appointed by the relevant state ministry. Sometimes, with state approval, the contractor may have the right to choose the operator.

These conditions can be set out in the basic contract or in a separate Operating Agreement.

The usual obligations of the operator are:

- To be responsible for work programs and budgets.
- To supervise research.
- To be responsible for appraisals and development.
- To arrange for and maintain adequate insurance.

In some cases, particularly if the arrangement between the contractor and the state is a "production sharing agreement" (where physical production of the hydrocarbons is shared between the state and the contractor), the operator may be an Operating Committee or a Joint Operating Committee.

The duties of the Operating Committee will be:

- Coordinating and supervising the operations.
- Reviewing and approving work programs and budgets.
- Reviewing and approving proposals for cases of surrender and relinquishment of concessions.

9.5.1.6 Relinquishment

At a certain point in the life of a petroleum contract, the contractor may decide that it would make economic sense to surrender part of a concession back to the state. This may be because part of the concession area has not been sufficiently productive or because all of the hydrocarbons that can be economically produced have already been recovered.

Sometimes, relinquishment can be compelled by the state if the state believes that the contractor is not doing enough to reasonably exploit a concession area.

Contractors can relinquish voluntarily if minimum expenditures have been met.

After relinquishment, the contractor must arrange for the removal of all equipment and installations and must leave the site in an acceptable condition—sometimes restoring the site to its original condition.

9.5.1.7 Commercial Discovery

If a contractor makes a commercially viable discovery during the exploration phase, the contractor usually has an obligation to inform the state at once.

At that point, the contractor must prepare a draft "development plan" within a limited time and submit it to the state.

If the state or an appointed Management Committee approves the development plan, then work starts.

Usually, there is a limited time within which a commercial discovery must be made, or the contractor will be required to relinquish their contract.

For example, in Libya, the time limit was two years.

9.5.1.8 Cost Recovery

Of course, any exploration phase requires the contractor to expend substantial costs. If a commercial discovery is made, and the project proceeds to production and sale of hydrocarbons, the contractor will usually be entitled to recover a portion the exploration costs expended.

The percentage of recoverable costs will vary from country to country and, to some extent, will depend on the relative bargaining power of the parties. For example, in Tunisia, the percentage of recoverable costs has been 40%; in Angola, 80%: and in Burma or India, 100%. The average is about 70 to 75%.

9.5.1.9 Bonus

In some cases, where the agreement between the state and the contractor is a profit-sharing contract (PSC), a bonus may be paid to the contractor for making a commercially viable discovery. This is usually agreed upon and sometimes paid at the signing of the PSC. Depending on the circumstances, this bonus may be six or even seven figures.

There are sometimes bonuses also paid when production reaches a certain level. These are usually on a sliding scale, triggered by meeting certain production levels and can be seven figure amounts.

9.5.1.10 Taxation

Contractors will usually be required to pay certain taxes to the state. These requirements will vary from state to state. The usual types of taxes that contractors will be required to pay can include:

- Income tax.
- Export tax.
- Import tax.
- Stamp tax.

Exemptions can be granted. For example, salaries of foreign workers may be exempt from income tax.

Also, sometimes, there are exemptions from tax granted for certain time periods following the start of oil and gas production.

9.5.1.11 Royalty

States often require “royalties” to be paid by contractors for having the privilege of exploiting natural resources, such as petroleum. This will be a percentage of the production value earned by a particular petroleum project. Reductions may be allowed to cover the cost of transporting oil and gas for export. Sometimes, the royalty may be payable as a percentage of oil and gas produced rather than currency.

The size of royalty payments will usually be between 7% and 17%.

Royalties are generally calculated quarterly, based on accepted oil and gas market prices. Contractors are usually allowed to negotiate the amount.

9.5.1.12 *Community Development*

Another cost that contractors may have to bear, particularly in underdeveloped countries, is contributions to community development. These are sometimes included in the underlying petroleum project contract.

In areas where the oil and gas exploitation is near communities, the contractor may be required to provide benefits to the local population. These can include the following requirements:

- To employ local people.
- To use local contractors and suppliers.
- To provide local medical care.
- To establish schools.
- To provide training programs for local people.
- Etc.

Money for these things can be paid over time or in a lump sum.

9.5.1.13 *National Economic Interests*

Sometimes, the state will insist on economic benefits that go beyond helping local communities by serving the economic interests of the host nation as a whole. They can be:

- Giving a preference to host nation contractors and suppliers if their products and/or supplies are competitive in price, quality and availability. A contractor can sometimes negotiate a "cap" on the total value of such preferences, limiting it to an agreed amount (say, $200,000).
- Supplying oil and gas to the domestic market. This will counterargument that a country's valuable national resources are being exploited by outsiders with little or no benefit to the local population. These may be supplied as a percentage of local production or at an agreed discount to market prices.

9.5.1.14 *Currency Exchange Controls*

A usual contractual provision is to agree to the currency in which contract terms will be calculated. This will allow the contractor to recover what its real costs will be for providing its services.

This is important because foreign exchange costs are sometimes not recoverable and currency fluctuations can make a significant difference to the costs of a project that can take years or even decades.

9.5.1.15 Force Majeure

Force majeure, as described above in the chapter on contract law, constitutes forces beyond the control of either party that interfere with contract performance.

However, the circumstances that can legitimately be considered beyond the control of parties can vary with the circumstances and the situation. For this reason, it is usual to have a provision in a petroleum contract that carefully defines when parties will or will not be liable for failure to meet their contractual obligations.

This provision will usually provide detailed definitions with relevant examples. It will require prompt notice to be given. It will also state whether a performance deadline will be extended by a force majeure event.

9.5.1.16 Indemnities and Liabilities

Contracts will often also include provisions that define when indemnities and liabilities will apply. They will define how any liabilities will be allocated between the parties.

In cases where any liabilities are not allocated by contract, local law will apply.

A usual allocation of liabilities between the host state and the contractor will be based on "fault." This will require the contractor to indemnify the state against any loss, damages, claims and legal actions arising from the project.

However, in a contract with a host state, these provisions are not two-way. It is rare for the state to agree to indemnify a contractor against any losses.

The contractor is usually liable for any losses or damages resulting from the project to both the state and third parties. However, some contracts can limit this liability to instances where the contractor is guilty of gross negligence or willful conduct.

9.5.1.17 Assignment

The contractor is usually given the right to the contract, or part of the contract, to another party, with the approval of the state.

The state may impose certain conditions, such as:

- An assignee must meet certain technical and financial qualifications.
- The contractor must have met all obligations up until the date of the assignment.
- A payment from the contractor might be required.

The state may also have a preemptive right to acquire any right that the contractor wishes to assign to another party.

However, the host state can assign its rights and obligations to another party without the approval of the contractor.

9.5.1.18 Environment

Provisions relating to environmental care are becoming increasingly important.

The contractor is usually required to comply with all environmental laws and regulations.

The contractor is often required to provide an environmental impact plan.

Contract terms will require that reasonable measures be taken to protect the environment.

The contractor will be required to clean up and repair any environmental damage.

At relinquishment of the concession, the contractor may be required to restore the environment to a condition as close as reasonably possible to its original condition.

9.5.1.19 Termination

On the completion or expiry, a contract may be considered terminated.

However there are a number of situations where a state can terminate a concession contract early. These can include:

- Failure to discover oil and gas.
- Failure of the contractor to meet its obligations.
- Failure of the contractor to meet financial obligations.
- Insolvency of the contractor.
- Failure to perform minimum work obligations.
- Interruptions to production that exceed an agreed time period.

If the contractor defaults on its obligations, it will usually be given a limited time to cure its default.

The contractor usually has fewer rights to terminate a contract early. Failure to discover any commercial quantities of hydrocarbons within the permitted exploration period will usually give the contractor the right to terminate a contract. Sometimes, a contractor will be permitted to terminate if it has paid all of the minimum expenditure requirements.

9.5.1.20 Confidentiality

Petroleum contracts with a host state are important and highly sensitive documents. They have wide-ranging economic and political implications.

Consequently, the contracts will contain strict confidentiality provisions with regard to all information relating to oil and gas production. Permitted disclosures will usually be listed, and lists of parties to whom disclosures are permitted will be included.

Permitted parties will usually be limited to those that qualify as "needing to know" confidential information to perform their obligations relating to the contract. These might be certain employees, advisors, banks, technology suppliers, etc. All parties to whom confidential information is given will be required to sign confidentiality agreements agreeing to adhere to confidentiality requirements equal to those set forth in the contract.

To clarify what is confidential information, the confidentiality provisions will usually also include a list of those things that are not within the agreement, such as publicly available information, or information acquired from independent research, etc.

Confidentiality agreements are usually in effect for a limited period, such as 2 to 10 years.

9.5.1.21 Governing Law & Dispute Resolution

As discussed in Chapter 3 on Dispute Resolution, these are important issues in any contract, and considering the amount of money involved in energy contracts, this is certainly true with them.

For more details about how to approach these issues, please consult Chapter 3. However, there are some particular aspects of the energy business that are worth discussing here.

For example, it is the case that in dealing with energy contracts in foreign host states, the host state will often require that its own law should be the governing law of the contract. In most cases, there is little question that this is a significant advantage for the host state and a disadvantage for the contractors. Consequently, when negotiating a petroleum contract, it is best to try to persuade the host state to accept a neutral governing law such as English law. In some cases, this request will be granted; after all, English law is generally known to be a widely accepted international standard, and there are a number of host countries that are willing to permit it to be the governing law of important contracts with foreign contractors.

As for dispute resolution, generally, it is best to try to persuade the host state to accept solutions that will avoid formal litigation. A step procedure for resolving disputes can be suggested, such as where:

- The first step is to attempt to resolve the dispute amicably within an agreed time limit (such as three months).
- The second step, if an amicable resolution is not possible, could involve mediation and/or expert determination.
- If none of the above can resolve the matter, then the third step could be arbitration. In these cases, getting an agreement to a legally binding arbitration before an accepted arbitration forum such as the ICC would be a desirable solution. There are of course other arbitration forums that could be acceptable. These are discussed in Chapter 3.

If none of the above solutions solves the problems between the parties, then it may be necessary to go to formal court litigation. In that case, both the choice of law and the choice of forum (where the case will be tried—both the court and the geographical location) will be critical. Again, it will be best if the contractor can persuade the host state to agree that case should be tried before a neutral court (England, for example) and in a neutral place (perhaps England again).

One must not forget that in international disputes, there are also issues having to do with travel to and from the place where the forums are located, the necessity for hiring a local council, and questions about what language will be used to conduct the case and to provide any written judgments. There will also be issues as to what appeals will be permitted, if any.

When it comes to disputes between contractors and host nations, there is also the issue of "sovereign immunity." This is the legal principle that states cannot be sued. Therefore, if a company has any claims against a host country or a state-owned company, it may not be possible to bring legal action against them.

This can put a private contracting company at a severe disadvantage when embroiled in a dispute against a host nation. To avoid this problem is sometimes possible to persuade a host nation or a state-owned company acting on behalf of a host nation to waive sovereign immunity. Not all states will agree to do this, but if it is important enough for the state to have experienced competent private companies exploit natural resources for them, the state may decide that it is in their interest to wave sovereign immunity. Contracting companies should always try to get this concession in their contracts with host states.

9.5.1.22 Anti-bribery & Anti-corruption

In the energy sector, because of the amount of money involved, bribery and corruption are big issues. Consequently, it is not unusual to have a provision in a concession contract whereby the contractor warrants that it will not and has not made any gifts or awards to officials or employees of the state or to any relevant influential private interests or individuals. They are also required to further warrant that they will not induce or reward any person in order to obtain or continue any business with the state.

In recent decades, a number of important countries, including the U.S., the U.K. and the EU, have passed anti-bribery legislation that can result in severe consequences for those who engage in bribery.

The details about some of the most important legislation are discussed in Chapter 10. Of course, this legislation applies to the energy business and other businesses as well.

9.6 THE GRANTING OF CONCESSIONS AND LICENSES

There are numerous reasons why a state might consider it beneficial to grant permission to exploit the nation's mineral resources, including its energy resources.

The state might receive a significant cash payment for granting such rights, or they may earn cash from auctioning exploitation rights.

A particular organization may be willing to drill a number of wells that the state considers necessary to appropriately exploit the potential hydrocarbon resources of a particular area.

Such a project may provide the state with an opportunity to obtain important technological knowledge from a company receiving a concession.

Jobs and training may be provided to the local population.

A project may bring important infrastructure improvements to a nation, including new port and transport systems. Local improvements may be provided to power, education, and health resources.

However, any energy exploitation project will probably result in significant changes to the surrounding environment and may interfere with the daily lives of the people living in the area. Therefore, different countries will have different needs and have different responses to requests to exploit petroleum resources and other mineral resources.

In a number of countries, particularly if their energy resources are largely underdeveloped, a nation may be willing to grant an IOC an extensive concession to permit profitable exploitation of potential resources and to have opportunities to gain some of the economic benefits that such a concession may bring.

In developed countries with strong economies, much more limited "licenses" may be granted for energy exploitation or, as in France, it may be considered unnecessary to permit any mineral exploitation licenses to be granted.

Countries that permit limited licenses to be granted include developed countries such as the U.K., Norway, Netherlands, Ireland, Iceland, and Australia.

Such limited licenses typically include standardized terms, often mandated by established legislation, which do not provide independent companies with any significant scope to have bespoke terms. In such licenses, it is common to find the following terms:

- The IOC will have control of the licensed area.
- The IOC will have control over the oil and gas produced.
- Ownership of the hydrocarbons will pass to the IOC at the wellhead.
- Any revenues earned by the IOC from the oil and gas are subject to the state's tax regulations.
- At completion of a project, the IOC will have strict decommissioning and restoration regulations. It should be noted that in the U.K., the liability to comply with such regulations is unlimited as to time—the obligation lasts forever.

9.6.1 The French Ban

In 2017, the French government announced that oil and gas exploration licenses for mainland France and any French overseas territories would be banned. This may be a result of the fact that 78% of French electrical power is nuclear.

9.7 OTHER IMPORTANT RELATED CONTRACTS

Because of the economic size and the complexity of the energy business, there are a number of other specialist contracts that are employed to govern the relationships of host states, contractors and subcontractors in acquiring energy resources. They are too numerous and detailed for this book to cover them all. For those that need to know more, there are other resources available from government ministries and professional energy associations.

However, because they are an important part of the energy production process, it is useful to mention a couple of others.

9.7.1 Service Contracts

This is a kind of specialized alternative agreement that is sometimes made between house countries and oil industry firms. An important difference between this and the more usual kind of contract is that the host country does not handover control of extracted resources to the contractor.

In these arrangements, the contractor provides a technical service to the state to search and develop a defined area for commercially viable energy resources, such as oil and gas. In return, the contractor will receive a guaranteed fee but will have no rights to any hydrocarbons produced.

These types of contracts are common in countries such as Iran, Iraq, Kuwait, Indonesia, etc., where the potential existence of significant oil and gas finds is already well known.

The advantage of the contractor is that financial risk is eliminated by the guaranteed fee. The disadvantage to the contractor is that they do not have an opportunity to share in the profits that may be made from a significant energy resource discovery. The advantage for the host state is that they avoid the political problems of abdicating control over important resources to a foreign contractor. The downside for the host state is that if no resources are found, they will lose money on payment of the fee.

These are not to be confused with "oil field services contracts," whereby subcontractors provide various ancillary services to contractors such as maintenance, transportation, catering, etc., but do not usually have any direct interest in the sale of any discovered energy resources. The subcontractors generally perform their services for agreed industry-standard fees.

There are a number of companies such as Schlumberger, Halliburton and others that specialize in oil field services contracts to provide particular specialized services, such as drilling, construction, residual oil recovery, etc.

One type of oilfield services contract is the EPC contract, which stands for "engineering, procurement and construction." The EPC contract is a "turnkey" contract where the contract calls to the services subcontractor to deliver a complete usable facility, such as a building, a port, a transportation system, a refinery, etc., for an agreed price.

Sometimes, management services will also be part of the contract, which makes the EPC contract an EPCM contract.

9.7.2 Rig Hire Contracts

Rig hire contracts are important for recovering energy resources offshore. In such cases, it is critical to have specially built platforms where the contractors' employees can live in work when drilling for and producing energy resources away from land.

The rigs themselves are not usually owned by the contractors themselves. They are usually hired from specialist companies that own, build and deploy them for energy companies seeking to find and produce mineral resources offshore.

The energy companies provide the necessary capital and exploration areas. The rig companies supply and deploy the platforms.

There are different kinds of rigs depending on the offshore circumstances, such as the depth of the water where the petroleum is being sought.

Some of the specialist subcontractors that provide rigs include Transocean, Ensoco, Blake, Pacific Drilling, etc.

The rigs are usually hired at a six-figure daily rate that will fluctuate with the prices of oil and gas.

9.8 HOST STATE ISSUES

One of the uncertainties for any IOC entering into a petroleum exploration and production agreement with a foreign host state is how the host state is going to treat the contractor during the life of the contract.

Problems can arise caused by political changes or international conflicts. An IOC may have a legal contract, but that may not protect it against host state disruptions.

The host state may not agree to waive sovereign immunity when entering into the agreement. This would mean that even if the host state violated the terms of the agreement, giving the IOC a legitimate legal claim, the IOC could not bring suit to enforce the claim. This could mean huge, unrecoverable financial losses for the IOC.

The host state may also decide to nationalize the petroleum project at any time—including after it is well-established and produces profitable oil and gas flows. In many countries, particularly developing countries, a concession of valuable national natural resources is a politically sensitive issue. This can lead to nullification of an IOC's contractual rights and loss of valuable oil and gas projects.

The tax regime of a host state can also be changed to make a petroleum project must less profitable for an IOC.

These are just some of the ways in which a state can make a petroleum project more difficult and less profitable for an IOC. As one can imagine, there are many others.

These are all risks that need to be considered when entering into a mineral exploitation project with a host state. Such projects are enormously expensive to develop. They may also lead to enormous profits. But there is a risk that at some point in the relationship between the IOC and the host state, the circumstances may change significantly despite the terms of the original contract.

9.9 LOSS-BASED LIABILITY

One unusual aspect of the petroleum industry is that when injuries or damages occur due to the fault of a party to a transaction, it is sometimes agreed that damages will be paid by the injured party rather than the party at fault. In some large petroleum projects, this "loss-based" liability is an agreed term of the contracts.

This is a legal anomaly. In most legal systems, liability for injury is "fault-based." That is to say, the party at fault is liable for damages to the injured party.

Why would the oil industry adopt such an unusual approach to injury liability?

With large projects, the industry considers loss-based injury a practical solution that will quickly resolve damage disputes.

Large oil and gas projects are complex, often involving many parties. To complete them, industry parties want clarity and efficiency. Loss-based liability saves time and reduces conflict because it avoids long, complicated and costly legal procedures to determine who is at fault and the size of damages.

For huge losses, such as the Deepwater Horizon oil rig explosion disaster in the Gulf of Mexico, the only party that could possibly bear the financial liability for losses (in the region of $65 billion) was BP, the IOC and one of the world's largest oil companies. BP paid.

9.10 CONCLUSIONS

Energy is one of the most critical business sectors in the modern world. Producing it and making it available for continuous use by any community is complicated and hugely expensive.

It is also intensely politically sensitive because it is a major living cost, a consumer of huge amounts of natural resources, entails significant health and safety risks and is considered a significant cause of global warming.

Therefore, any party entering the field will need to carefully consider all of the issues surrounding any energy production project.

Not least of such considerations should be the employment of clear, comprehensive contracts that unambiguously set out the rights and responsibilities of all parties to any energy-related projects.

CHAPTER 10

Bribery and Corruption

10.1 INTRODUCTION

In the 1970s, the SEC undertook investigations that revealed that over 400 U.S. companies had made illegal or questionable payments to foreign government officials, politicians or political parties, totaling over $300 million.

The reasons for the payments included everything from facilitation payments to make sure that government officials performed certain ministerial or clerical duties to payments to senior officials to secure favorable government action.

The U.S. Congress saw this as a threat to the integrity of American business and, in 1977, enacted the Foreign Corrupt Practices Act ("FCPA"), making such practices subject to criminal and civil enforcement actions.

The FCPA has had a much wider impact than one would originally have thought. It was the beginning of an international trend to increase transparency in international dealings in extractive industries such as oil, gas and mining, particularly with respect to the role that certain payments might play in winning and retaining the right to extract valuable minerals.

The purpose of these pieces of legislation is stated to be to create a level playing field for international companies, to prevent and punish corruption, and to help developing nations be in a position to distribute the mineral wealth of their countries more evenly.

This paper offers a review of the major pieces of anti-bribery legislation, assesses their impact, and discusses future legislative trends in this area.

10.2 US FCPA

FCPA compliance consists of two key sections. The first comprises the anti-bribery provisions; the second consists of the record-keeping and internal controls provisions.

The anti-bribery provisions make it unlawful for any public company to offer, give, promise, or authorize the giving of anything of value to:

- a foreign official;
- any political party, party official or political candidate;
- any person who is going to pass it to one of the above;
- to influence his official actions;
- to influence that official to do or omit any act in violation of his official duty;
- to secure any improper advantage;
- to induce the official to influence any act or decision of a governmental entity; or
- in order to obtain, retain or direct business.

10.2.1 To Whom Does the FCPA Apply?

The FCPA prohibitions relate to payments to any public official regardless of rank.

Generally, the FCPA prohibitions apply to actions by any firm, individual, officer, director, employee or agent of a firm and any stockholder acting on behalf of a firm. It can also catch anyone who orders, authorizes or assists anyone in violating FCPA's prohibitions.

10.2.2 Where Does the FCPA Apply?

The geographic reach of U.S. jurisdiction under FCPA depends on whether the actor is an "issuer," a "domestic concern," or a non-U.S. national or business.

An "issuer" is anyone who has issued securities registered in the U.S. or who must file periodic reports with the U.S. SEC.

A "domestic concern" is anyone who is a citizen or resident of the U.S., any business entity, in any form, that has its principal place of business in the U.S., or an entity that is organized in U.S. territory.

10.2.3 What Activities Does the FCPA Reach?

FCPA covers all acts furthered through any means of communication that comprise the instrumentalities of interstate commerce.

FCPA prohibits payments made for purposes of obtaining or retaining business. This "business test" is interpreted broadly, and the business in question does not have to be with a government or government-owned entity. It can be with any private business.

10.2.4 The Non-U.S. Persons Reached by the FCPA

In 1998, FCPA was amended to cover any foreign person or business organization that causes an act in furtherance of a corrupt payment in U.S. territory.

U.S. parent organizations can also be liable for violations by foreign subsidiaries if the parent authorizes, directs or controls those activities. Employees or agents of those subsidiaries can also be liable.

10.2.5 Joint Ventures

One factor that becomes critical in the face of bribery prohibitions, such as those found in the FPCA, is that one must know joint-venture partners well enough to be confident that they are not going to land a joint project in bribery hot water.

Improper payments through third parties or intermediaries are prohibited. Such intermediaries can, of course, be joint-venturers or agents.

In order to avoid being held liable for being involved in illegal payments, companies will need to show that they exercised due diligence by taking all necessary precautions to make sure that they are operating with reputable and qualified joint-venture partners and agents.

In performing due diligence, a company may wish to consider investigating potential partners. There are firms that specialize in providing background intelligence on persons and companies in different parts of the world. A company will also have to determine whether their potential business partners or agents have any personal or professional ties to the government, which may increase the likelihood of improper payments or other favors being demanded or given. Other due diligence inquiries will include finding out who the clients of potential business partners are and what sort of reputations those clients have.

One source of information about the reputations of the potential partners will be the local U.S. Embassy or consulate. Other sources can include local bankers, one's own clients or associates, if there are any with local knowledge.

When negotiating a business relationship, one should also be aware of certain "red flags" that may appear during the negotiation process. These can include:

- unusual financial arrangements or payment schedules;
- a history of corruption in a particular country;
- a refusal by a potential business associate to sign a declaration that they will not be involved in any corrupt arrangements;
- unusually large commissions;
- lack of backup information to support expense claims;
- poor qualifications as a potential business associate; and
- whether the potential business associate was introduced or recommended by a government official.

10.2.6 FCPA Exemptions

One category of business payments to foreign officials that is permitted under FCPA is "facilitation payments." These are payments to expedite performance of "routine governmental actions."

Examples of FCPA permissible payments include:

- obtaining licenses, permits, or official documents;
- processing visas and work orders; providing police protection, mail service, phone service, power and water;
- loading or unloading cargo, preserving perishable goods, undertaking contract performance inspections;
- permitting transit of goods; and similar functions.

If one has any doubt as to whether a particular activity falls within an exemption, one should consult counsel or consider using the DOJ's Opinion Procedure (discussed in more detail below).

However, keep in mind that any decision by a government official to award or permit continuation of business will never be within this "facilitation payment" exemption.

10.2.7 Affirmative Defenses

FCPA does allow for certain defenses to be claimed if one is charged with a violation.

One defense was that the payment was lawful under the written laws of the country in question.

Another is that the money was spent demonstrating a product or to fulfill a contractual obligation.

But note that because these are "affirmative defenses," which means that the burden of establishing that the payments were proper is on the defense. The prosecution does not need to prove, initially, that the payments were not proper.

10.2.8 Sanctions and Enforcement

The FCPA provides both criminal and civil sanctions for violations.

Criminal sanctions against businesses can consist of a fine of up to $2 million, with individual penalties for responsible officers, directors, employees, agents and shareholders of up to $100,000 and prison terms of up to five years.

Fines may, under some circumstances, actually be a lot higher than the amounts designated under the FCPA. There is another statute, the Alternative Fines Act, which allows fines to be imposed equal to twice the amount of the financial benefit the defendant hoped to obtain by paying a bribe.

Please note that fines imposed on individuals may not be paid by their employer or principal.

The "DOJ" conducts criminal prosecutions, and the "SEC" has created a special unit responsible for civil administrative enforcement. They both maintain FCPA information websites.

The DOJ or the SEC may also bring civil actions against companies and persons who violate the FPCA, seeking fines of up to $10,000.

In addition the SEC may bring an enforcement action in which a court may impose fines for the greater amount of the gross amount of gain sought by the defendant through the violation, or between $5,000 and $100,000 for an individual, and between $50,000 and $500,000 for a business organization.

The DOJ or the SEC can also seek injunctive relief requiring a firm to cease any activity that is, or is about to be, a violation of the FCPA.

Perhaps just as seriously, depending on the nature of one's business, any person or firm found guilty of an FCPA violation may be barred from doing business with the U.S. Government. Even an indictment for a violation can result in suspension of government business. Also, under Presidential order, no person or entity can participate in government business if they have previously been barred from such business.

There are also a number of other disadvantages that may be suffered from being found guilty of violating the FCPA:

- a guilty party may be ruled ineligible to receive export licenses;
- the SEC may suspend persons from the securities business, and it may impose civil penalties on those in the securities business found guilty of violations;
- the Commodity Futures Trading Commission and the Overseas Private Investment Corporation can suspend or debar persons found guilty of FCPA violations; and
- a payment made to a foreign official in violation of the FCPA cannot be a legitimate tax deduction as a business expense.

In addition to government sanctions, violations of the FCPA can also permit private individuals to bring suits for treble damages under the Racketeer Influenced and Corrupt Organizations Act ("RICO"). Such a claim could be brought by a competitor alleging that bribery by the defendants unfairly led to the defendants winning a foreign contract.

The FCPA has had a significant impact on American firms doing international business. A number of firms have been the subjects of criminal and civil enforcement actions sometimes resulting in huge fines and suspension or disbarment from federal procurement contracting. A number of their employees and directors have gone to jail. As a result, many international companies have instituted detailed compliance programs to prevent their involvement in any improper payments by employees or agents.

10.2.9 Some Examples of FCPA Cases Against Oil and Gas Companies

FCPA enforcement actions have averaged about 17 cases a year. A number of them have involved oil and gas industry companies. Some examples are:

- 2012: Three oil company executives were charged with bribing Nigerian officials to obtain illicit permits for oil rigs.
- 2011: A pipeline company paid $5.4 million to settle charges that it bribed officials in Uzbekistan during an oil and gas pipeline bidding process.

- 2011: An energy products manufacturer paid over $14 million to settle charges that it bribed Chinese officials to obtain business with state-owned entities.
- 2010: Seven oil services and freight-forward companies were charged with widespread bribery of customs officials in more than 10 counties to receive improper benefits.
- A power and automated products company paid $39.3 million to settle charges that it was paying bribes to officials at Mexico's largest power company and kickbacks to obtain contracts under the U.N. Oil for Food Program.
- A former manager of one of the world's largest offshore drilling companies was charged with authorizing bribes to government officials in Venezuela to extend drilling contracts and to obtain other favors.
- 2009: An oil and gas services company paid $402 million to settle FCPA charges. Their CEO pled guilty to criminal charges and faced years in jail and personal liability for $10 million.

10.2.10 DOJ Opinion Procedure

The DOJ Opinion Procedure has been set up for anyone who has any questions as to application of FCPA with respect to issues such as who constitutes a "public official."

In summary, the Attorney General will issue an opinion in response to a specific inquiry within 30 days of the DOJ's receiving a completed request. If the DOJ issues an opinion stating the proposed conduct conforms with current DOJ enforcement policy, the person receiving the opinion will be entitled to a presumption, in any future enforcement action, that his conduct was permissible under the FCPA. Details of the Opinion Procedure can be found in the U.S. Code of Federal Regulations (28 CFR Part 80).

To see what kind of opinions have been issued by the DOJ in the past, releases about previous opinions have been made available on the DOJ's FCPA website (http://www.justice.gov/criminal/fraud/fcpa/).

If parties require further information, both the DOJ and the Department of Commerce will supply additional guidance about the FCPA. Information about how to obtain the guidance can be found on their websites (*see* DOJ site above and http://www.commerce.gov/category/tags/fcpa).

10.3 RESPONSE TO THE FCPA BY OTHER COUNTRIES

The FCPA provoked an enormous outcry from U.S. firms doing international business, claiming that the legislation would put U.S. firms at a significant disadvantage when dealing around the world because they would be competing with foreign firms that were not restrained by the FCPA from paying foreign bribes and that such foreign competing firms often were allowed to deduct the payments as business expenses from their taxes.

Congress became concerned that American companies were being disadvantaged compared to their foreign competitors who routinely paid bribes and, in some cases, were permitted to deduct the cost of such bribes as business expenses from their taxes.

Consequently, Congress requested the Executive Branch of government in 1988 to begin negotiating with the Organisation for Economic Co-operation and Development (OECD) to get agreements from the U.S.'s principal trading partner countries to enact similar legislation. This process took about 10 years, but in 1997, the U.S. and 33 other countries signed an OECD Convention Combating Bribery of Foreign Public Officials in International Business Transactions.

Implementing legislation was enacted in the U.S. in 1998. However, other countries have taken different lengths of time to implement appropriate legislation of their own to combat foreign bribery involving their business organizations. The anti-corruption trend is now supported by further international cooperative efforts such as the OECD Working Group on Bribery in International Business Transactions (http://www.oecd.org/daf/briberyininternationalbusiness/) and the UN Convention Against Corruption (2003) (http://www.unodc.org/unodc/en/treaties/CAC/).

10.4 U.K.: THE BRIBERY ACT 2010

One country that is particularly relevant in the international business markets is the U.K. In 2010, the U.K. enacted the Bribery Act 2010, which came into force on July 1, 2011.

10.4.1 Main Points

Key points of the Act are:

- A bribery offense can be active or passive:
  - Active: promising or giving financial or other advantage.
  - Passive: agreeing to receive or accept a financial or other advantage.
- A business can be liable for failing to prevent a third person from bribing someone on their behalf if that third person is performing business services for the business entity in question.
- It is a defense to Bribery Act violations if a business can show that it put in place adequate procedures to prevent bribery (although putting such procedures in place is not mandatory if there is no risk of bribery on a company's behalf).
- Provision of "hospitality" is not a violation of the Act.
- In contrast to what is permitted under the U.S. FCPA, "facilitation payments" are bribes under the Bribery Act.

Under the U.K. Act, "bribery" is generally defined as providing someone with a financial or other advantage to encourage that person to act improperly or to reward the person in question for having acted improbably. For example, a business organization could be held liable where an employee or agent pays a bribe to get, keep or gain a business advantage.

10.4.2 Defense of Adequate Procedures in Place

However, it is a complete defense to Bribery Act offenses if a business organization can show that it has adequate procedures in place to prevent bribery.

What constitutes having "adequate" procedures in place will vary with the nature, size and complexity of the business in question. A small or medium-sized business facing small bribery risks will only need to institute minimal procedures.

The Ministry of Justice has published a list of six principles to follow in order to ensure that the business has adopted "adequate procedures" to prevent prosecution under the Bribery Act:

- The first principle is "proportionality." The procedures adopted should be proportionate to the risks faced and the size of the business.
- The second principle is "top level commitment." Those at the top business organizations need to be committed that their business shall be conducted without bribery.
- The third principle is "risk assessment." A reasonable assessment needs to be made of risks a particular business in a particular market segment may face.
- The fourth principle is "due diligence." It is important to get sufficient information about potential business partners so that one understands the reputation and backgrounds of the persons one is dealing with. Otherwise, it is difficult to know whether they pose a bribery risk. A firm intending to do international business should ask appropriate questions and perform some relevant checks before joining another firm in business transactions or retaining an agent to act on their behalf.
- The fifth principle is "communication." Make sure that anti-bribery policies and procedures are adequately made known to employees and others acting on behalf of the business. Depending on the characteristics of one's business, distributing written statements, getting signed acknowledgements of receipt and understanding, and/or providing additional training might be considered.
- The sixth principle is "monitoring and review." The character of a business and the risks run are likely to change over time. Therefore it is important to establish a policy of periodic reviews and adjustments to a firm's anti-bribery policy, communication and training. This is particularly necessary when entering new markets.

10.4.3 Assessing the Level of Risk

The Ministry of Justice has been clear that the amount of effort that a business needs to put into its anti-bribery arrangement depends on the size and nature of the business.

If a business is in low-risk countries or market sectors, it may require only minimal anti-bribery precautions.

There are also a number of simple and obvious procedures that can be performed to check the status of companies or persons one hopes to do business with. Internet searches can be a good place to start. Inquiries can also be made at embassies and consulates. U.K. Trade and Investment can also be consulted and there may be business or chamber of commerce type groups in the relevant countries that can provide information.

To be able to rely on the defense of adequate procedures, one needs to have procedures in place that are proportionate to the risk.

One needs to consider due diligence only for those that are working for you or on your behalf. Generally, you will not need to perform due diligence on suppliers to you.

Any business is permitted to use its own judgment as to the level of bribery risks it faces. It is not necessary to obtain outside verification (e.g., by lawyers or accountants) that the anti-bribery precautions it has taken are adequate.

10.4.4 Hospitality and Facilitation

Reasonable business expenditures, such as genuine hospitality or promotional activity, are not forbidden by the Bribery Act.

However, such expenditures have to be at a level that is proportionate for one business. Expenditures that are significantly out of line may be suspected of being a cover for bribery.

Unlike the U.S. FCPA, the U.K. Bribery Act considers "facilitation payments," which are payments to induce officials to perform routine functions that they are otherwise obligated to perform, to be bribes. There are a few exemptions. The only payments of this type permitted are legally required administrative fees or fast-track services. These are not considered "facilitation" payments.

10.4.5 Penalties

The penalties for offenses under the Act can be as much as 10 years in prison with an unlimited fine.

10.4.6 Jurisdiction

The Act targets crimes committed not only in the U.K. but also abroad.

10.4.7 Application

The Act applies to U.K. citizens, residents and companies established in the U.K. and can apply to a non-U.K. company that fails to prevent bribery on its behalf, if that company does business in the U.K.

Companies can also be liable for bribery committed for their benefit by employees or other associated persons, including third parties acting on a company's behalf.

Companies can be penalized for board-level complicity in bribery, and senior directors who turn a blind eye to bribery can be personally liable.

10.4.8 Basic Conditions for Prosecution

No one can be prosecuted for an offense in England or Wales unless:

- One of the two most senior prosecutors (either the Director of Public Prosecutions or the Director of the Serious Fraud Office) is satisfied that a conviction is more likely than not.
- The prosecution is in the public interest.

10.4.9 Prosecutions under the Bribery Act

Although the Bribery Act came into effect in 2011, there have been few prosecutions under it. One example was a case where, in the spring of 2012, a court clerk in London was convicted under the Bribery Act for helping offenders avoid prosecution for driving offenses in exchange for payoffs of up to £500. He was originally sentenced to six years in prison, but that sentence was found to be excessive and was later reduced to two years.

However, one should not be complacent. On October 9, 2012, the Serious Fraud Office publicly affirmed its commitment as an investigator and prosecutor of fraud and corruption, including offenses under the Bribery Act. In particular, the SFO stated it would focus on facilitation payments and business expenditures for hospitality.

These statements emphasized that the SFO considered facilitation payments to be bribes. Although hospitality can be considered a legitimate business expense, the SFO takes note of the fact such payments can sometimes be used to disguise bribery. One should not lose sight of the fact that the SFO has this legislation in its sights.

Those who wish further guidance on corruption can consult the Ministry of Justice (http://www.justice.gov.uk/legislation/bribery) and use the tools available on the Business Anti-Corruption Portal (http://www.business-anti-corruption.com/), which provides "corruption profiles" of over 60 countries.

The Ministry of Justice has also published a guidance booklet on the Bribery Act that is available online, as well as a shorter "Quick Start Guide" also available online (http://www.justice.gov.uk/legislation/bribery).

10.5 U.S. REPORTING LEGISLATION

10.5.1 Dodd-Frank, Section 1504

One might think that the above legislation provides adequate protection against bribery being conducted by or on behalf of U.S. or U.K. companies, but apparently, the U.S. Congress did not think that this was enough.

In order to make bribery even more difficult, section 1504 of the Dodd-Frank Act was signed into law in July 2010. This law requires oil, gas and mining companies registered with the SEC to publicly report how much they pay to governments in connection with natural resource extraction.

Other countries have now enacted similar laws.

Regulations implementing this U.S. provision were published on August 22, 2012. Under these regulations, such companies must publicly disclose all taxes, royalties, fees, production entitlements, bonuses, dividends and payments for infrastructure improvements paid to relevant governments. Fees that must be reported include rental fees, entry fees, and concession fees. Also, bonus payments are required to be reported, including signature, discovery, and production bonuses.

The threshold for reporting is $100,000 in payments. All payments (whether a single payment or a series of related payments) over that amount must be reported.

Payments to the U.S. government, all foreign governments and all subnational governmental bodies are included.

These regulations cover relate to more than 1,100 international oil, gas and mining companies, including such major companies as Chevron, Exxon, BP, Shell, Rio Tinto, Vale, BHP Billiton, Petrobras, Sinopec and PetroChina, etc.

10.5.2 Lawsuit Against the SEC

It would be worth putting it mildly to say these new reporting regulations upset the natural resources companies. As an indication of their displeasure, a number of trade organizations such as the American Petroleum Institute, the Chamber of Commerce of the U.S., the Independent Petroleum Association of America and the National Foreign Trade Council launched a lawsuit on October 10, 2012, in the U.S. District Court for the District of Columbia, against the SEC demanding nullification of Dodd-Frank section 1504.

The plaintiffs claimed that these disclosure rules would:

> cost US public companies at least $1 billion in initial compliance costs and 2 to 400,000,000 in ongoing compliance costs and could have billions of dollars of additional costs through the loss of trade secrets and business opportunities.

The lawsuit alleged that the actual costs to U.S. oil, gas and mining companies will be much greater because U.S. companies will be forced to allow competitors access to sensitive commercial information and that U.S. companies will have to abandon projects of those foreign countries that forbid such disclosures or that will refuse to do business with U.S. companies because they do not wish such disclosures to be made. The companies claim that it is actually impossible to quantify how many billions of dollars the implementation of these rules will cost.

In 2013, a U.S. District Court struck down the original rules, and the SEC was required to modify its requirements, which it did. Less onerous disclosure rules were introduced in 2020.[284]

These rules generally accord with similar rules introduced in other jurisdictions such as the U.K., the EU, Canada, Norway and others.

10.6 EU TRANSPARENCY REQUIREMENTS

The EU, inspired by U.S. reporting law, has adopted requirements modifying both the EU Transparency and Accounting Directives to require companies listed on EU stock exchanges and other large companies based in Member States to disclose their government payments for oil, gas, timber and minerals by country and by project.[285]

The standards proposed by the EU are similar, in many ways, to the U.S. reporting standards, but there are important differences. The EU directive includes not only publicly held companies but other large private companies as well, whether or not they are publicly held. A "large" company is defined as one which exceeds two of the three following measures:

- turnover, €40 million;
- total assets, €20 million; and
- employees, 250.

The EU directive covers timber as well as oil, gas and minerals.

The EU standards with regard to coverage of oil, gas and minerals do not reach as far as Dodd-Frank. The EU standards cover exploration, discovery, development and extraction of oil, gas and minerals. The U.S. standards cover not only those activities but also cover processing and export of those minerals.

10.7 CONCLUSIONS

Anyone operating in the global oil and gas industries out of Europe or the United States, or that is a company subject to registration because it is offering its shares for sale in either the U.S. or Europe or because it is a company doing business in those areas, will need to be aware that may be subject to anti-bribery and/or reporting regulations because of its dealings, with foreign governments or government officials.

Therefore, it should do two things. First, make a good assessment of risks it faces with respect to bribery. This will involve looking at both the countries in which it does business and those it will be doing business with or those that will be doing business on its behalf. If the company determines the risk of bribery, it should put in place measures to prevent it from getting involved in bribery and introduce training and communication measures to make it clear to employees that those who do business will

284. *See* "Disclosure of Payments by Resource Extraction Issuers," *SEC,* online at: sec.gov.
285. "Revised Directive on Transparency Requirements for Listed Companies (Transparency Directive): Frequently Asked Questions," *EU,* online at: ec.europa.eu.

not get involved in bribery. Second, it will need to establish what its reporting obligations are with respect to payments to governments and then place the necessary systems and mechanisms to make certain that the required reports are made in an appropriate and timely fashion.

Failure to do this can result in a company falling into situations where it, or its employees or directors, may be subject to fines and prison sentences for being barred from important business opportunities.

So, be careful out there.

CHAPTER 11
Transport Law

Most kinds of transportation relating to business come under the heading of "logistics."

Logistics is the final part of a sale that deals with the completion of that sale by supply of the object of the sale.

The part of logistics that this chapter is concerned with is the law of "carriage." Carriage is the transport of people, animals or goods by:

- Air.
- Road.
- Water.
- Rail line cable.
- Pipeline.
- Spacecraft, or
- Electronics.

In order to be able to perform transport, certain things are necessary. The transporting entity will need appropriate infrastructure, vehicles and effective operations. The transport itself will be performed by a number of methods, including automobiles, bicycles, buses, trucks, planes, ships, spacecraft and, possibly, electronics.

Transport by any of these methods will be subject to relevant governing laws determining, with respect to any of the entities involved in the transport process, their rights, responsibilities, liabilities and immunities.

11.1 LAND CARRIAGE

Land carriage is generally done by road or by rail.

Within a single national jurisdiction, the conduct of that transport will be governed by national laws and regulations.

However, when borders are crossed, other laws will apply. Those will be the laws and regulations of every country that the transportation wishes to enter, as well as international treaties, rules and regulations that have been agreed upon by one or more of the nations where the transportation takes place.

The majority of the transport that is done by road is conducted with large vehicles known as trucks, lorries, camions, etc.

By rail, the transport is accomplished on trains. Trains provide advantages over road travel in that they are faster and can carry larger total loads.

However, in some respects, trucks have advantages in that they can serve many more destinations, deliver goods in a wider variety of quantities, and may be less expensive than rail transport.

11.2 SEA CARRIAGE

However, about 95 % of the world's cargo is delivered by sea. This involves over 60,000 merchant ships and over 2 billion tons of cargo capacity.

Transportation by sea often involves more than one country and, as a result, is more likely to be affected by different national and international laws and regulations. Some carriage by water can involve strictly internal waterways involving only domestic laws and regulations. However, some international water carriage can involve waterways such as rivers and lakes that touch on different borders but do not involve transport over seas or oceans.

11.3 AIR CARRIAGE

Compared to water carriage, air carriage is faster but more expensive. In contributing to the costs of air carriage, the cost of fuel is a major issue. The cost of fuel is more critical in some countries than others. For example, the cost is very high in Japan.

11.4 WORLD CARRIAGE EXPANSION

The carriage business worldwide is growing by about 3 % a year overall. This is due to a number of reasons having to do with changes in national priorities and international agreements.

There are a number of examples of national changes that are boosting the growth of the carriage business.

In Australia, there has been an expansion of privatization that has involved significantly more private entities and businesses that were previously owned by the state. Those additional entities may have a wider range of goals, business partners and places of business that have caused expansions of the use of transportation methods in completing transactions.

China, currently the world's most populous country, with one of the world's largest economies, has moved more toward permitting a market economy to develop, accompanied by a reduction of taxes that previously burdened private businesses.

These changes have allowed many more entities to do business internationally in a much wider variety of business sectors. This has brought about a significant increase in the use of transportation worldwide.

Vietnam has greatly increased its involvement in international commerce. This has led to a significant influx of foreign investment and a growth of manufacturing to satisfy the needs of business partners around the world. These things have led to a large increase in the transport related to Vietnamese business.

In a number of markets, including those in the EU, Japan, and China, significant improvements to ports have encouraged more transporters to use them.

In the Middle East, the use of rail, truck and air carriage has expanded greatly in recent decades to accommodate business expansions that needed more methods of transport.

In Eastern Europe, transportation has increased because of such things as infrastructure improvements in Bulgaria and a growing use of rail and truck carriage in the Czech Republic.

However, areas where the expansion of transport is still difficult are South and Central America. There, geographic problems and political unrest have hampered the growth of business generally and the growth of related transport.

11.5 TRANSPORT LAW

Much of transport law is made up of domestic law, that is to say, national laws and regulations of different countries that are affected by different issues relating to transportation. This includes departures, arrivals, ports, airports, crossing international boundaries, etc.

However, because so much of transport is international, there are a number of international regulations relating to transport. These include international conventions and treaties depending on the mode of transport, its originations and destinations.

There are specific laws and regulations depending on the mode of transport, whether it relates to sea carriage, road carriage, rail carriage or air carriage.

11.5.1 Sea Carriage

Because sea carriage so frequently relates to crossing borders, there are a number of important laws and conventions relating to its conduct, including the following:

There is the International Convention for the Unification of Certain Rules of Law Relating to Bills of Lading. This is commonly known as the "Hague Rules 1924." These rules were promulgated in Brussels in that year.

The Protocol to Amend the International Convention for the Unification of Certain Rules of Law Relating to Bills of Lading, commonly known as the "Hague-Visby Rules 1968."

The United Nations International Convention on the Carriage of Goods by Sea, commonly known as the "Hamburg Rules," adopted in Hamburg in 1978.

The United Nations Convention on Contracts for the International Carriage of Goods Wholly or Partly by Sea, commonly known as the "Rotterdam Rules," adopted at Rotterdam in 2008.

The ICC has published (originally in 2020) a number of terms intended to clarify the roles of the seller and buyer with respect to delivery and risk sales contracts. These are known as the Incoterms Rules. They have become standard provisions for importing and exporting sales contracts. There are now 11 Incoterms. They are as follows, often expressed as standard abbreviations:

> EXW: This stands for "Ex Works." This means that it is responsible for making the sales goods available to be collected at the factory or a warehouse. After that, the buyer is responsible for all following costs and risks.
>
> FCA: This stands for "Free Carrier." This means the seller must deliver the goods to a carrier at a warehouse or terminal. After that, risks are the responsibility of the buyer.
>
> CPT: This stands for "Carriage Paid To." This means a seller is responsible for delivering the goods to a specified destination. After that, the buyer is responsible.
>
> CIP: This stands for "Carriage and Insurance Paid To." This means a seller also has the additional responsibility to insure the goods against loss or damage when delivering goods to a specified destination.
>
> DAP: This stands for "Delivered at Place." This means that seller bears entire responsibility for delivering goods to a named place. After that, the buyer is responsible.
>
> DPU: This stands for "Delivered at Place Unloaded." This means that seller is responsible for delivery to and unloading at a named place.
>
> DDP: This stands for "Delivered Duty Paid." The seller has responsibility for delivery to a specified destination, including clearance, customs and fees.
>
> FAS: This stands for "Free Alongside Ship." The seller gets goods at the factory and delivers them to a departure point, such as a ship loading dock. Seller remains responsible for entire delivery process.
>
> FOB: This stands for "Free on Board." The seller is responsible for entire delivery process, through loading onto a ship at the shipping port. After that, buyer is responsible for completion of delivery.
>
> CFR: This stands for "Cost and Freight." The seller is responsible for delivery through the point of loading onto the ship. Buyer assumes responsibility after loading at port of shipping.
>
> CIF: This stands for "Cost, Insurance and Freight. Like CFR, but seller is responsible for insurance until goods arrive at shipping port.

11.5.1.1 Seaworthiness

Many national regulations impose on owners and users of ships an obligation of "seaworthiness."

In general terms, this may mean that a vessel must be able to "carry in safety." This imposes a duty on the carrier to make certain that the ship is "fit and proper" for the voyage that it is undertaking and the cargo that it is carrying.

These requirements included a number of conditions, including the following. The vessel must be a suitable structure and in adequate condition. The carrier must possess proper documentation to allow it to complete its voyage.

Other rules and regulations will apply depending on the nature of the sea carriage and the legal jurisdictions that are impacted by the journey.

There have been many legal cases relating to the issue of seaworthiness. These include such cases as *Lyon v. Mells* (1805), in which an English court found that a ship with a leaky hull was found to be "unseaworthy":

> A carrier by water contracting to carry goods for hire impliedly promises that the vessel shall be tight and fit for the purpose, and is answerable for damage arising from leakage.[286]

In 1924, there was the English case of *SNIA v. Suzuki*, in which a ship was judged to be unseaworthy for having broken propellers.[287]

11.5.1.2 Duty to Carry with Care

From the time a carrier accepts goods for transport to the time it completes its obligations to turn over those goods to the agreed destination, a carrier has a legal obligation to carry its cargo with care.

Usually, the duty ends with the agreed delivery or "due dispatch," but sometimes, that duty can extend beyond due dispatch. This can occur if the recipient of the cargo can show that the carrier was responsible for or damaged the cargo during transportation that was not the result of an act by a third party. It can also occur when the recipient can show that damage to the cargo resulted from an act by the carrier that was outside of the scope of their contractual employment.

11.5.1.3 Deviation and Delay

Impermissible acts outside the scope of the carrier's contractual employment can occur if the carrier is found to have engaged in "deviation/and or delay."

A carrier can be liable for damage to a shipper if the carrier is found guilty of unjustifiable delay in delivering the cargo. One way that such delay can occur is by "unjustified deviation." Such a deviation can make it impossible to complete a delivery on time.

286. *Lyon and Another against Mells*, In the Court of the Kings Bench, 102 E.R.1134.
287. *"SNIA" Societa di Navigazione Industria E Commercio v. Suzuki & Co.and Teikoko Kisen Kaisha*, Court of Appeal, (1924) 18 Ll.L. Rep. 333.

Deviations can be allowed if there is a justifiable excuse that benefits the shipper. Justifications can be found where the deviation was necessary to protect the cargo, preserve timely delivery, or save a life.

But if a strong justification does not exist, the carrier may be liable for damages as a result of breach of contract, breach of its transportation obligations, or even gross negligence that could justify enhanced liability damages.

Examples of deviation legal cases include the following.

In 1880, in the case of *Scaramanga v.Stamp,*[288] the court held a new line:

> Deviation for the purpose of saving life is protected and involves neither forfeiture of insurance nor liability to the goods owner in respect of loss, Deviation for the purpose of communicating with a ship in distress is allowable, in as much as the state of the vessel in distress may involve danger to life. On the other hand deviation for the sole purpose of saving property is not thus privileged … .

The problem in that case was that the ship in question, the *Olympus*, deviated to assist another ship in distress. But, the other ship, the *Arion*, offered the *Olympus* a fee if they would agree to tow the *Arion* into port. The *Olympus* agreed to tow the *Arion*, which reduced the speed of the *Olympus*. Also, while towing the *Arion*, the *Olympus* ran aground, and both the *Olympus* and its cargo were lost.

The question for the court was whether the actions of the *Olympus* were justified sufficiently to avoid liability to the shipper of the cargo.

The court held that although a deviation to a distress ship was justified because lives may be in danger, those lives could have been preserved simply by taking the crew off of the distressed ship.

The decision to try and save the ship and earn a fee by towing it into port was not protected under those circumstances, and the resulting loss of the *Olympus* and its cargo was not justified. Therefore, the owner of the *Olympus* was liable to the shipper of the cargo for its loss. The commander of the *Olympus* had made a decision not to simply save lives but to save property and earn money.

Another case of unjustified deviation case, dating from 1949, involved a situation where a shipowner took a ship into a port of refuge. However, the court found that this was made necessary because the shipowner had knowingly employed a ship that wasn't seaworthy. Consequently, the shipowner should have known in advance that problems were likely. The need to deviate was not caused by unforeseen circumstances. Therefore, the shipowner was liable for damages to the shipper.[289]

11.5.2 Joint and Several Liability

Joint and several liability can occur in cases where there are multiple parties involved. It can be found in transport cases where there is more than one party that may be liable for damages to a third person.

288. 5 CPD 295 (1880).
289. *A/B Karlshamms Ojefarbrisker and Another v. Monarch Steamship Company*, this case was before the U.K. House of Lords Decsion, (1948), 82 Ll. L. Rep. 137.

Joint and several liability applies to matters where liability for damages is shared by more than one party. In such a case, each party is found to be jointly and severally liable.

However, depending on the circumstances of the case, a court can make adjustments to the awards of liability against different parties based on their degrees of fault or even their abilities to pay.

In some cases, a party that is claiming liability against one or more other parties can also be found to be liable to some degree for the damages that the claimant suffered. In that case, the claimant can be said to be guilty of "contributory negligence." That is found in cases where the claimant is found to be partly at fault, to one degree or another, for the damage that they suffered.

For example, there is the case of *Walt Disney World Co. v. Wood,* dating from 1987.[290]

In that case, a married couple were jointly enjoying Disney's "Grand Prix Bumper Car" ride. The claimant's husband rammed his car into the car of his wife, causing her physical injury.

The claimant sued Disney.

In that case, the court found joint and several liability among all the parties involved to different degrees.

The claimant was found 14% liable for her own injury because she chose to participate in a ride where cars crashed into one another. Therefore, anyone using the ride should anticipate that some degree of injury is unlikely.

The claimant's husband was found to be 85% responsible for the injury because he rammed his car into the back of his wife's car. Disney was found to be only 1% responsible for the claimant's injury.

Nevertheless, the court imposed 86% of the damage claim payment on Disney. This represented the whole of the husband's liability plus Disney's liability for the injury. Disney was required to pay for 86% of the liability because the husband was unable to pay. Disney was apparently also being held responsible for offering a ride where injuries might be anticipated.

This is a remarkable case where the court found joint and several liability for damages not only based on the relative faults of the parties but also on their relative abilities to pay.

11.5.3 Jurisdiction and Forum Non Conveniens

Because so much of transportation is international, legal issues of jurisdiction and forum non-conveniens come up reasonably frequently in transportation cases.

The questions are essentially the law of which jurisdiction is most appropriate for deciding the case and which forum is the appropriate one in which to try the case.

This is why it is important to agree on these issues in the terms of the contract. Otherwise, these issues will be decided by later court rulings that are not always

290. This decision was confirmed by the Florida (U.S. state) Supreme Court, 515 So. 2d 198 (1987).

predictable in advance. In addition, going through the legal procedures to have these issues decided may be costly for the parties.

If the matter does go to court, it is likely that the court will decide the matter should be tried in the forum that is most convenient for the party making the claims. However, in making its decision, the court will consider such things as the economic, social, legal and geographical circumstances that are relevant in the case.

There is also a concern that if the parties have not agreed on which forum is most convenient for the settlement of disputes, the court may decide to dismiss the dispute on grounds "forum non-conveniens" because the court chosen is not the best place to decide a claim.

11.5.4 Conflict of Laws

Of course, the laws of different countries can be quite different. This is an important issue in international transport.

If the parties have not previously agreed on what law will apply to their transaction, then it will usually be left to a court to decide what law will apply if the dispute arises.

A court will try to decide what is the best applicable law in a given situation. In order to decide that, courts will often undertake a two-stage analysis.

In the first stage, the court will consider in which court a legal action is being brought. That may cause the chosen law to be the law that governs the court where the action is taking place.

If that does not determine the issue, the second stage will be an analysis of which law is most appropriate for the matter before the court.

In order to save the parties time, money, and uncertainty, it is always best if the parties have agreed on the applicable law under the terms of a contract between them. However, if that opportunity has been missed, the court will try to decide the issue on the basis of finding the law with the strongest connection to the disputed issue.

Although, in some countries, courts tend to choose the law of the country in which they are sitting, that is not always the case. The law that may be most relevant may be the law of the jurisdiction in which the contract is being performed.

As discussed previously, in energy cases, the country in which the energy is being produced insists that its own law should determine any disputes.

However, there are a number of countries in which the courts of those countries are willing to apply foreign law if the foreign law can be shown to be relevant to the issues before the court and if the principles of the relevant foreign law can be clearly proved. For example, both courts of England and the Federal and State courts of the United States are willing to enforce foreign laws when they find the circumstances to be appropriate.

11.5.5 Principal and Agent Relationships

In transportation transactions, there are often a number of parties involved: there are principal parties to the transaction, and there can be a number of intermediaries assisting the principal parties.

Some of these intermediaries may be acting as agents on behalf of the principal parties and therefore the law of principal and agent relationships becomes relevant.

In law, principles are the persons who hire third parties to perform tasks on their behalf. For example, a principal may be an exporter of goods who contracts with other parties to complete delivery of the goods. These persons are its agents and will be all the persons who act between the shipment and delivery of the relevant goods.

For example, a "shipbroker" may arrange ocean transport for a commission ("brokerage"). If that commission is not paid, most countries allow the broker to "claim against the deal." The broker can bring a legal action to recover the missing brokerage, and that may ultimately be paid by one or both parties to the deal, depending on the judgment of the tribunal where the application is made.

When a principal deals with agents, trust is essential, but it is also important to have clear, formal documents setting out the terms of the arrangement between the principal and agent.

11.5.6 Roles of Banks and Documents

With respect to transportation transactions, payments are often secured against the delivery of the relevant goods, which is confirmed by delivery of proper documents.

In many transactions, both the seller and the buyer will have their banks involved. The buyer's bank will have instructions to pay the seller's bank the agreed purchase price upon delivery of complete and proper documents. Such documents may consist of one or more of the following:

- Letters of credit.
- Bills of lading.
- Insurance policies.
- Licenses.

At the conclusion of the transaction, the banks will perform a mutual exchange of documents and payments. It is the duty of the banks to exercise due diligence in assuring that the proper documents and payments are received and given.

In doing these things, banks will often conform their practices to established regulations such as the Uniform Practice Code (UPC) and/or the Uniform Rules for Collection (UCR):

> "The Uniform Practice Code (UPC) is a series of rules, interpretations and explanations designed to make uniform, where practicable, customs, practice, usage, and trading techniques in the investment banking and securities business,

particularly with regards to operation and settlement issues. These can include such matters as trade terms, deliveries, and payments ..."[291]

"The Uniform Rules for Collections is a set of rules that help assist in the process of collecting debts or owed money or assets. The URC's were established—or proposed—by the ICC, a worldwide organization that serves to promote and facilitate business interests and trade between nations."[292]

11.5.6.1 Letters of Credit

Letters of credit are formal documents committing a buyer's bank to pay the seller (exporter) after goods have been shipped and the buyer has presented the required documentation to the seller's bank as proof. The purpose of a letter of credit is to provide protection to both buyers and sellers with respect to goods that are transferred by means of international transportation.[293]

11.5.6.2 Bills of Lading

A bill of lading is a legal document issued by the carrier to the person shipping the goods, acknowledging receipt of the cargo for shipment.

It identifies the goods in some detail stating their quantity, their type and their destination. It is signed by legally authorized representatives of the carrier, the consigner and the recipient of the cargo.[294]

It functions as a conclusive receipt that the goods have been loaded. It contains evidence of the terms of carriage and is a document of title to the goods.

The title holder of the goods may transfer the bill of lading to another party if it wishes. It is a "negotiable" instrument.

A bill of lading is required to accompany the goods during transportation.

A bill of lading is intended to counter theft or substitution of the consigned cargo.

11.5.6.3 Insurance Policy

An insurance policy is a legal document that details the claims that an issuer will be legally required to pay.[295]

291. Financial Industry Regulatory Authority INC. (U.S.), online at: finra.org.inc.
292. Corporate Finance Institute, online at: corporatefinanceinstitute.com.
293. The U.S. International Trade Administration, online at: trade.gov.P
294. E. Tarver, "Bill of Lading: Meaning, Types, Example and Purpose," *Investopedia*, online at: investopedia.com.
295. For details, *see* the following chapter on Insurance Law.

11.5.6.4 *Invoice*

An invoice is a document issued by the seller to the buyer. It contains descriptions of the products sold to the buyer, giving their quantities, prices, and, usually, agreed payment terms.[296]

11.5.6.5 *Other Specially Required Documents*

Certain kinds of cargo require additional legal documents. Explosives and weapons are examples.

When cargo is potentially dangerous or thought to be strictly regulated, an entity that is asked to transport such cargo should consult its legal advisors to determine what the legal requirements of transport are.

These will differ from country to country and may be different in the country where the goods originate and the country to which the goods are being shipped.

It will be the responsibility of the transporter to ensure that it has the appropriate documents for handling such cargo. The transporter will need to determine whether it needs special licenses in any relevant jurisdiction, where the cargo passes through and whether specially detailed descriptions of the cargo and the transporters' plans for shipping it in safety will be required.

If the cargo travels through different jurisdictions during its shipment, separate legal advisors qualified in each of the relevant jurisdictions may be needed.

For example, under the Federal Regulations of the U.S., a legal document called a "Dangerous Cargo Manifest" will be needed with respect to any material included in the Hazardous Material Regulations of the U.S. or in the International Maritime Dangerous Goods Code.[297]

It is reasonable to assume that similar or related documents may be needed in other jurisdictions.

296. For more details, *see* A. Hayes, "What Is an Invoice? It's Parts and Why The Are Important," *Investopedia*, online at: intestopedia.com.
297. US Code of Federal Regulations, CFR Parts 171 through 180, online at: ecfr.gov.

CHAPTER 12

Cyberlaw

Cyberlaw is the law governing something called "cyberspace." Cyberspace is a very wide term and covers such things as electronic computers, networks connecting electronic computers, software programs, relevant storage devices, the data stored there, the Internet, websites, networks such as email and social media networks and all electronic devices such as smartphones, cash machines, smart watches, cameras, monitoring devices and anything else that can access or be accessed from cyberspace.

The purpose of this chapter is to describe many of the key components of cyberspace and how they are affected by some of the relevant laws and regulations.

12.1 INTERNET

The "Internet" is an international network of interconnected computers. It developed from what began in 1969 as a U.S. military program called "ARPANET." Arpanet was designed to enable computers operated by military defense contractors and universities involved in defense-related research to communicate by redundant channels, even if some portions of the network were damaged by war or other causes.

ARPANET no longer exists, but it provided a model for the development of civilian networks that became the Internet. The Internet now enables billions of people to communicate and access huge amounts of information around the world. The Internet is a unique, new medium of worldwide human communication.[298]

The regulation of the Internet throughout the world consists of a complex and frequently changing collection of international agreements, national legislation, local laws, and regulations.

The Internet and its regulations are changing too rapidly to be able to comprehend all the details of how one must behave responsibly and legally when using the Internet. To obtain an understanding of that or legal advice about specific issues

298. Justice Stevens, giving the Opinion of the Court in, *Janet Reno, Attorney General of the United States, et al., Appellants v. American Civil Liberties Union, et al.*, 521 U.S. 844 (1997).

relating to the Internet, it is necessary to consult local legal and technical experts familiar with the laws and regulations of the relevant jurisdictions.

A difficulty here is that the Internet is so new that the creators of Internet law are only beginning to establish rules and regulations for its permitted operation. A major problem for regulators is that the Internet is rapidly evolving and changing, both technically and in usage, literally every day. As a result, Internet law and its application demand constant reexamination.

As a few examples of the issues developing, there are:

- Quantum computing development by Google, IBM and others promises exponentially more powerful computers that will analyze data and provide solutions in seconds that would take the computers currently in use weeks, months, years or even decades.[299] The implications of this for privacy and security are huge.
- The founder of the world's most powerful online social media group Meta, Mark Zuckerberg, was accused, by a former employee, testifying before a U.S. Senate committee, of allowing Facebook's platforms to "harm children, stoke division, and weaken our democracy" for the sake of profit. This kind of scrutiny of companies such as Meta is bound to intensify increasing demand for expanded social media regulation.[300]
- Dangerous and expensive hacking and ransomware attacks, where hackers break into computer systems, encrypt their data, and demand payment for unencrypting the data, increased by 92% in the first half of 2021.[301]
- The increasing importance of digital assets such as cryptocurrency (*see* section 12.2 below) and AI (*see* section 12.3 below).

These are just a few of the problems the Internet regulators are being asked to deal with and solve now and in the future.

Another difficult characteristic of the Internet is that its use is a rapidly expanding worldwide phenomenon. It is not restricted to any particular jurisdiction or region. Users of the Internet located anywhere can reach out electronically to billions of people across the globe.

Response to these developments in the world's countries has been uneven. Some jurisdictions have already established laws and regulations to control use and operation of the Internet and related electronic devices. Others have only begun to decide how they wish to deal with the Internet, and some jurisdictions have made little progress in dealing with the complexities and problems created by the World Wide Web (as the content reachable on the Internet is called).

More devices are being created to use or communicate with the Internet. Each of these raises new issues about communication and regulation.

---

299. "What Is Quantum Computing," *IBM*, online, https://www.ibm.com/quantum-computing/, accessed October 7, 2021.
300. R. Mac and C. Kang, "Whistle-Blower Says, 'Facebook Chooses Profits over Safety'," *The New York Times*, online, October 3, 2021.
301. S.K. Skelton, "Ransomware Attacks Increase Dramatically During 2021," *ComputerWeekly.com*, online, August 3, 2021, accessed October 7, 2021.

The necessity for legal modification and change has become particularly acute with the rapid and dangerous growth of online crime and online attacks, some of which may be sponsored by the governments of countries. These issues make up the new and particularly worrying areas of "cybercrime" and "cyberwar." These things are increasing.

As time goes on, the purpose of most cybercrime seems to be to extract money or "ransom" from individuals.

Organizations and even nations that are connected to the Internet use it as an important part of their daily activities or businesses.

A number of criminal groups, known as "hacking groups," may be private organizations acting for their own account, but others are allegedly sponsored by nation-states.

These latter groups are used to prosecute attacks on the assets of other nations that can be characterized as "cyber warfare." One of their purposes may be to extract large payments, but another purpose can be to bring about disruption to important infrastructure that relies for its operation on the Internet, and another could be to steal information that will allow the attacker to know best how to injure those that consider opponents.

These worrying developments have caused those responsible for creating laws and regulations to continually make efforts to prevent these from damaging things important to their ways of life.

This legal evolution is occurring throughout the world and will continue to do so for the foreseeable future. No country or region will be immune from the effects of the Internet and the vulnerabilities it may create. Regulatory steps to protect those connected to the Internet must change and grow continuously to take account of constant change.

Internet law consists of the laws, regulations, policies, agreements, and customs that regulate and govern all types of Internet use.

However, the Internet has become a part of so many activities, both commercial and private, that it is not possible to consider Internet law as consisting of one well-defined area of law. It includes significant parts of intellectual property law, data protection law, competition law, privacy law, criminal law, contract law, and other areas of law that are discussed in more detail in other chapters.

For example, the UN has tried to extend internationally recognized human rights onto the Internet. In June 2012, it proposed a resolution on human rights on the Internet. This resolution was adopted by the UN Human Rights Council in 2021. But the extent of its application in uncertain.

Another transformative aspect of the Internet is that it has fundamentally changed business forever. Until the arrival of the Internet and its subsequent dramatic growth, physical and face-to-face business was much more important. Commerce, to a large extent, relied on attracting people to specific physical locations (such as stores, shops, show rooms, warehouses, offices, markets, etc.) for the execution of many transactions. The Internet has changed that dramatically. The locations of customers, merchants, business contacts and colleagues have become much less important. Indeed, they have become irrelevant for many transactions relating to the acquisition of goods, food, clothing, tools, and the transaction of business, etc. In many cases, these transactions can be completed online.

And increasingly, this is not true only for sales of small, personal items. With the growth in sophistication and size of 3-D printers, commerce is approaching situations where major purchases, such as cars, trucks, ships, houses, buildings, etc., can be designed far from the site of delivery. Computerized instructions for "printing" their components, or perhaps for the entire objects, can be sent over the Internet to a distant 3-D printer for printing and, perhaps, assembly by robotic assemblers.

These developments are rapidly moving from conception to reality, and it is impossible to foresee how extensive the changes to our lives and our persons triggered by the development of the Internet will be. However, there is little doubt that our lives are being and will continue to be utterly transformed by the Internet.

Certainly, those parts of our lives that involve shopping, communication, social interaction, work, and information-gathering have already been completely changed by the appearance and growth of major tech companies, such as Amazon, Facebook (Meta), Google, Apple and Microsoft, to name just the biggest and best-known, but these changes are just the tip of the iceberg.

Of the ten most valuable companies in the world, eight are internet-dependent computer tech companies. Interestingly enough, and unlike the huge international companies of the past (Exxon, General Motors, etc.), the value of many of the world's most valuable companies is now not based on the ownership of physical assets but on their methods of interacting with the Internet. Their most valuable asset is their skill in managing electronic information.

Consequently, the ability to scale their businesses is theoretically infinite. Even if Facebook, Google, Amazon, etc., reached the stage of having recruited every person on earth as an active customer, they always have the option of offering them more and different services over the Internet. In other words, there is really no limit to the possible take-up of the services offered by the Internet "Tech giants." To expand into new areas, it is not required that they acquire additional physical assets, such as factories, transportation vehicles, etc. They just need to add to their electronic configurations:

> You can't lay a finger on the primary assets of Facebook and Google—it's all information fizzing at the speed of light through electrons, which, in summary interpretations of physics, don't really exist anyway. We live in the new capitalism's floating world … .[302]

A name that is given to this new type of economy by some commentators is the "exponential economy." One commentator, Azeem Azhar, writes that these exponential tech companies:

> Know that if they stopped growing, they would soon cascade into irrelevance … .[303]

302. B. Appleyard, "Exponential by Azeem Azhar Review: Can We Stop the Tech Giants?," the *Sunday Times*, online, August 29, 2021.

303. *Ibid.*

More recently, the importance of the Internet has changed from something affecting private individuals, commercial institutions, and educational institutions to something of critical importance to nations for communications, surveillance, defense and even war.

All these developments are startling, amazing, and, in many cases, unforeseen. But there is absolutely no doubt that the changes triggered by the Internet will continue to become more complex and take place at increasing speed.

The next computer revolution, the move to "quantum computing," will increase the speed at which computers perform their functions by factors it is difficult to imagine. For example, a calculation that it is estimated would take the fastest of today's supercomputers about 10,000 years to complete, was completed by Google's experimental Sycamore quantum computing operating system in 200 seconds in October 2020. Now, China claims a machine a million times more powerful than other quantum systems.

It is impossible to say when quantum computers will become generally available, but it is also impossible to know the limits of how transformative their power will be on computing, the Internet and life.

The study of Internet law requires understanding the Internet, understanding how the Internet is used, and understanding how the Internet is governed.

Internet-related government policies cover wide areas of trade, govern website creation, regulate ISPs, determine protection of copyrights, trademarks and other intellectual property, and prescribe methods of conflict resolution. All these, and more, affect Internet usage.

The Internet is global and complex. It is not covered by one country, one jurisdiction or one set of laws and regulations. The Internet itself is constantly evolving and changing. It is constantly expanding its reach in relation to different aspects of life. Consequently, Internet law must be flexible enough to accommodate this endless change.

The Italian physicist Carlo Rovelli says that the only certain thing in the universe is change. In that sense, the Internet reflects life better than many other human creations. Governing it requires adjustment to new problems either constantly arising or having the potential to arise.

The British novelist L.P. Hartley wrote: "The past is another country. They do things differently there."

Because of its global and intellectual scope and its constantly changing nature, the same may be said of the Internet. Therefore, those dealing with the Internet must attune themselves to thinking and acting flexibly and creatively. The Internet is a world of its own, independent of any country.

12.2 DIGITAL ASSETS

With the development of digital assets (such as cryptocurrency, crypto art and NFTs (non-fungible tokens)), the cyber world continues to expand.

12.2.1 Dangerous Thinking

There is a popular view, sometimes even expressed by lawyers, that "digital assets" (a general term it is often used to cover digital objects of value that are described as "cyber/crypto currencies," "digital art," "non-fungible tokens" ["NFTs"], etc.) are "unregulated."

That is not true.

Throughout the world, digital assets are increasingly becoming subjects of government and regulatory scrutiny and are increasingly being declared subject to regulation as:

- Taxable property.
- Securities.
- Currency.
- Commodities.
- Derivatives.
- Intellectual property, and
- Proceeds of crimes.

The way in which digital assets are regulated varies from jurisdiction to jurisdiction around the world and depends on how those digital assets are marketed and used, but it is certainly the case that regulation of digital assets is expanding nearly as fast as the growth of digital assets as objects of commerce.

Because digital assets are by nature "digital" (usually with no physical form), they inevitably are able to easily cross borders.

It is not the intention of this book to provide a detailed explanation of all of the ways in which digital assets are used and regulated throughout the world. It would be foolish and probably impossible to give a complete explanation of all of the different ways that digital assets and their uses or affected by the legal regulation that exists and is growing in all of the jurisdictions in which digital assets are owned and used.

If anyone or any entity finds it necessary to have detailed legal advice about the regulatory effects of the policy and laws of any particular legal jurisdiction, it will be necessary to obtain advice from qualified legal advisors in the relevant jurisdictions.

12.2.2 The Crypto Currency Explosion

At the end of July 2022, the total value of the crypto market was reported to be more than $950 billion.[304]

In 2013, there were 66 cryptocurrencies in circulation. By November 2023, the number had risen to over 23,000.[305] This dramatic rise is probably because

304. J. Sor, "The Total Value of the Crypto Market Has Surged in Recent Weeks as Bears Start to Buy Back in and Bulls 'Hold on for Dear Life'," *Markets Insider*, online at: markets.businessinsider.com, August 1, 2022, accessed August 10, 2022.
305. R. de Best, "Quantity of Cryptocurrencies as of November 3, 2021," *Statista*, online, December 17, 2021.

cryptocurrencies are not too difficult to create. Just about anyone that wants to can make one up. Not all cryptocurrencies are equal. It is estimated that the top 20 cryptocurrencies constitute about 90% of the crypto trading worldwide.

The market cap of the two most popular cryptocurrencies was reported to be more than $1.2 trillion in 2021.[306] The world GDP for 2020 was reported to be more than $84 trillion. It is not difficult to see that a trade in which the two largest components contributed more than $1.2 trillion is likely to have a significant effect on the world economy. In other words, cryptocurrency trading has grown to a size where it can impact social stability worldwide.

This puts significant pressure on governments and regulators around the world regardless of whether regulators have decided to restrict or even ban the ownership and use of cryptocurrency in their own economies. It will not be easy to avoid the impact on their economies from the use and trading of cryptocurrency in other countries.

World trade is now largely global. The actions of one country and the economic status of other countries affect all participants in global trade. Consequently, governments and regulators will need to think very carefully about how they treat cryptocurrency domestically. They will also need to consider creating important international treaties and conventions about how cryptocurrency and its effects will be regulated.

Cryptocurrency is perhaps the best-known example of a global trend that began around 2008 to democratize the creation and ownership of valuable assets.[307] This trend revolves around confidence in the effectiveness of "blockchain" technology. Blockchain technology provides an assumed security with respect to the ownership of nonphysical digital assets that exist in the form of computer code.

Briefly, a "blockchain" is a digital "open electronic ledger" that stores data about purchases and sales of digital assets, allegedly permanently and securely. Essentially, it allows anyone to record a transaction in the ledger. The existence of this digital record provides proof of the history of the asset from its creation to the present. Supposedly, this prevents a party from pretending that they have the right to possess or dispose of an asset recorded in the ledger because the ledger provides a supposedly immutable chain of transaction history that shows who has had ownership rights in an asset from the time of its creation until the present.

A certain level of confidence in the security of blockchain ledgers is justified, but because of the popularity of cryptocurrency and the use of blockchains, there have been recent reports that highly skilled hackers are working hard to find innovative ways to hack blockchain ledgers.[308]

L. Daly, "How Many Cryptocurrencies Are There," *The Motley Fool*, online at: fool.com, June 2023.

306. "Today's Cryptocurrency Prices by Market Cap," *CoinMarketCap*, online, December 17, 2021.
307. "How Crypto is Rewriting the Rules of Digital Ownership: In an Age of Pervasive Digitization, Cryptocurrency is Changing How People Think About Everything from Ownership to the Future of the Internet," *nytimes.com*, online, Ledger, Paid Post, accessed January 7, 2022.
308. P. Nahar, "What Are 51% Attacks on Cryptocurrencies," *The Economic Times*, online, August 31, 2021.

One hacking technique that is reported to be relatively successful is the so-called 51% attack. Apparently, there have been a number the 51% attacks involving popular cryptocurrencies, including Bitcoin, Ethereum, Bitcoin Gold and other less well-known cryptos.

Attacks are reported to affect the value of the cryptos in question when they become publicly known.

It is reported that Bitcoin suffered from such an attack in August 2021 and this caused a 5% decline in its value at the time. Bitcoin Gold suffered from a similar attack in 2019. Ethereum has reportedly suffered from several 51% attacks starting in about 2016.[309]

A 51% attack consists of a hacker getting control of more than 50% of the "hashing power" of a blockchain, which allows the hacker to manipulate the data in the blockchain.[310] "Hashing power" is the total computational power of a cryptocurrency network or the power of a cryptocurrency mining operation. The larger the chain, such is the case with the most popular cryptos like Bitcoin, the more difficult it is to make a successful 51% attack. However, as mentioned above, there have been created over 20,000 kinds of crypto. Some of the blockchains are smaller and not very decentralized. The advantage to the hacker is that a successful attack allows them to duplicate digital token files and thus use them or sell them more than once.

Other hacking methods that affect cryptocurrency are attacking poorly coded smart contracts that hackers can manipulate to reroute transfers of crypto or cracking the "private key" to a crypto account, which allows the hacker to steal the crypto in the account. It seems that the very last one could be vulnerable to the computing power of quantum computer systems. Quantum systems are exponentially more powerful than the "classic" computers currently on the market and may be able to find digital passwords and keys much more quickly than they can be discovered today by the computers currently available.

So, how "safe" is a cryptocurrency investment? Not very safe, according to an article in *The Times*:[311]

> Cryptocurrency-based crime hit a record high last year with criminals pocketing $14 billion worth of Bitcoin, Ethereum and other digital currencies from scams, ransomware and thefts.

Cryptocurrency theft has grown enormously. In 2021, there was over a 500% increase in cryptocurrency theft from 2020.[312]

Unlike other investments, there is no organized protection or reimbursement available for cryptocurrency owners who lose access to their cryptocurrency because of illegal activity.

309. *Ibid.*
310. *Ibid.*
311. "Cryptocurrency Thieves Make Off with a Record $14 Billion," *The Times*, online, January 8, 2022.
312. *Ibid.*

According to an organization named "Payback," it claims to "work to get your money back."[313] For purchase and sale of cryptocurrency, Payback advises using one of the better-known crypto exchanges and lists Coinbase, Bitstamp, Kraken, Binance and Bittrex. However, everyone is advised to do their own due diligence before choosing an exchange to deal with.[314] The spectacular collapse of Sam Bankman-Fried's FTX is an object lesson.

There are a number of different ways in which cryptocurrency can be stolen. These reportedly can include the following "scams."[315]

There are bit-mining scams. These are scams that invite people to invest in projects to produce or "mine" cryptocurrency, where the promoters simply take the invested funds and disappear without completing the mining promised.

There are "bit wallet" scams that either try to persuade people to place their purchased cryptocurrencies in insecure crypto storage facilities, "wallets," or try to persuade crypto owners using legitimate crypto storage wallets to reveal their passwords or "keys" to their wallets.

There are "pump and dump" scams that try to persuade as many people as possible to invest in cryptocurrencies, which the promoters have previously bought at low prices prior to their promotion. When enough people have been persuaded to invest in the cryptos in question so that their price rises, the scamming promoters will then liquidate their position, making a profit for themselves but causing the value of the cryptocurrency to decline.

There are "pyramid schemes" whereby promoters try to persuade people to purchase a particular crypto product (which may be worthless), promising spectacular returns from rises in the product's value and the promoters urge investors to bring other investors in promising a share of the money these others invest. In these schemes, the promoters may steal most of the money invested without making any of the promised crypto purchases. They will pay early investors a portion of the money put in by later investors, claiming these payments are "dividends" from the investing they have done on your behalf. The scheme collapses when it runs out of new investors. This type of scam is also called a "Ponzi" scheme,[316] recently made more famous by the scheme run by Bernard Madoff until his arrest in 2008, which took in an estimated $64 billion.[317]

There have been a number of allegations that cryptocurrencies can be used to construct Ponzi schemes. The U.S. Securities and Exchange Commission (SEC) has published an "Investor Alert" entitled "Ponzi Schemes Using Virtual Currencies."[318]

---

313. The author has no experience with this organization's recovery efforts. Payback-ltd.com, online, accessed Janary 10, 2022.
314. *Ibid.*
315. The State of California Department of Financial Protection and Innovation provides a database of crypto scams, online at: dfpi.ca.gov.
316. Named for Carlo Ponzi, a Boston, Massachusetts, U.S., conman operating such a scheme in the 1920s.
317. *See* Wikipedia, "Bernie Madoff," online, accessed January 19, 2022.
318. SEC, online, accessed January 19, 2022.

At the beginning of 2022, an online publication called NetAdvisor published a detailed description of cryptocurrency scams and a statement of warnings about investing in cryptocurrency.[319] The article pointed out that about $14 billion had been stolen by crypto-scams in 2021, about double the amount stolen in 2020. Reviewing this article is a useful exercise for anyone considering purchasing or accepting cryptocurrency. Perhaps the most important thing in this review to keep in mind is the following statement:

> Unlike bank accounts for federally regulated currency, there is no such thing as fraud protection or FDIC insurance on the blockchain. When your money gets stolen on blockchain, the only way to get it back is for the recipient to pay you back directly. On a decentralized exchange, that's highly unlikely. And while mainstream crypto exchanges have better fraud and security measures than lesser-known exchanges, there's still no guarantee for investors to recoup stolen crypto.

It should be noted that this lack of guaranteed protection against theft and fraud is not only true for cryptocurrency transactions in the United States, but it is usually the case throughout the world.

Another disconcerting development in the world of cryptocurrency is the number of reported "disappearances" of founders of crypto coin exchanges who vanish, taking billions in cryptocurrency with them.

In November 2019, the BBC reported that Ruja Ignatova, creator of the cryptocurrency OneCoin, and known as "The Crypto Queen," "scammed the world, then vanished."[320] She is a good example of how crypto scammers have gone from being a problem in the cryptocurrency market to becoming some of the world's biggest crime problems.

Ignatova disappeared in 2017 but not before OneCoin had become so popular that it attracted billions of dollars from investors. She was an Oxford-educated businesswoman whose presentation lent significant credibility to a project that she claimed had resulted in the creation of a cryptocurrency that was "a Bitcoin killer." In June 2016, she told a cheering crowd at Wembley Arena that OneCoin would become the world's most popular cryptocurrency "for everyone to make payments everywhere."

At that time, Bitcoin was becoming well known as an investment which could rise in value dramatically making fortunes for its early investors. People who had seen this were looking for another opportunity to get into popular crypto early and make a fortune from an early discovery of a hot investment. OneCoin was purportedly offering that opportunity and many people wanted to be a part of it.

The BBC reported that they had seen evidence that people in Britain invested about €30 million in OneCoin during the first six months of 2016. By March 2017, more than €4 billion had been invested in OneCoin around the world. The Chinese were the

319. For more detail on the types of crypto scams, *see*, M. DeMatteo, "Scammers Stole $14 Billion in Crypto in 2021. Here's How Investors Can Protect Their Coins," *Net Advisor: In Partnership with TIME*, online, January 6, 2022.
320. BBC, "Cryptoqueen: How This Woman Scammed the World, Then Vanished," online, November 24, 2019.

biggest investors in this crypto, with Germans, British and Americans being second, third and fourth.[321]

When Ignatova vanished in 2017, U.S. law enforcement authorities were among the first to charge her with fraud and money laundering offenses. However, she has not been found. The Federal Bureau of Investigation in the U.S. has designated her as one of the FBI's 10 most wanted fugitives. This may or may not help the investors from whom billions have been stolen, but it certainly establishes the Crypto Queen as one of the world's most important financial criminals.

This also moves crypto coin transactions into the arena of being one of the financial markets' most dangerous criminal activities. Since Bitcoin was first introduced, thousands of other cryptocurrencies have appeared that do not appear to have anything involved in their creation except hopes that they might increase in value. This gives effective salespeople such as Ignatova opportunities to attract enormous amounts of money into businesses that may offer no returns whatsoever and that may, indeed, be stolen.

Whether the Crypto Queen will ever be caught remains to be seen. The most recent reports connect her with Dubai, which is one of the countries that she is most associated with.

A legal claim on behalf of those defrauded by OneCoin has been lodged in court at the British Indian Ocean Territory which is apparently a jurisdiction that has been used by OneCoin. It remains to be seen whether that action or legal proceedings in any other jurisdiction connected with OneCoin will lead to any compensation being paid to those that were allegedly defrauded. This is one of the biggest scams in history and demonstrates the power of cryptocurrency to extract money from people all around the world.

Ignatova may still have over 250,000 Bitcoins and is thought to be moving around using high-quality, fake identity documents. She may be the largest holder of Bitcoins.[322]

In April 2021, it was reported that the founder of a crypto currency exchange in Turkey disappeared with $2 billion worth of client cryptocurrency.[323]

In June 2021, it was reported that brothers Ameer and Raees Cajee, founders of a South African-based cryptocurrency investment site, had vanished with over $2 billion worth of Bitcoin belonging to their customers.[324]

Since the first appearance of cryptocurrency, there has been considerable confusion on the part of regulators, courts and governments as to whether these should be considered currency, commodities or investments. Depending on which it is, the legal

321. J. Bartlett, "How This Woman Scammed the World, Then Vanished" *BBC News*, online, November 24, 2019.
322. J. Bartlett & R. Byrne, "Missing Cryptoqueen: Is Dr Rugja Ignatova the Biggest Bitoin Holder?," *BBC News*, online, July 2, 2022.
323. A. Shilov, "Crypto Exchange Founder Disappears with $2 Billion," *tom'sHARDWARE*, online, April 24, 2021.
324. E. Mason, "South African Brother Disappear, Along with $2.2 Billion Worth of Bitcoin," *Forbes*, online, June 23, 2021.

and regulatory status of cryptocurrencies would be different. This points out the need for international cooperation when it comes to regulating cryptocurrencies because it would be very confusing if their status was different from jurisdiction to jurisdiction, although they were being traded internationally.

Again, this points to the dilemma of the Internet. Although those using it may be located in a discreet jurisdiction, their activities have an impact throughout the world. Although there has been a considerable amount of cooperation between countries in formulating international conventions and treaties relating to the Internet,[325] the job is far from over in cyber currencies, presenting difficulties that make it clear that much international work needs to be done in this area.

In fact, it is usually illegal, punishable by severe penalties, to copy an official currency or to issue something which purports to be in competition with official currency. It is generally accepted that efforts to do those things constitute the criminal offense of counterfeiting.

U.S. Federal law says:

> "[w]however, with the intent to defraud, falsely makes, forges, counterfeits, or alters any obligation or other security of the United States, shall be fined ... or imprisoned not more than 20 years, or both." (18 U.S.C.A. Section 471).

The law also forbids possessing any of the tools required to create counterfeit currency and this extends to computers and digital equipment.[326]

The law also prevents the counterfeiting or alteration of any foreign obligations, securities or currencies within the United States.

Within the EU, there are numerous laws and regulations against the counterfeiting of euro notes and coins. A special program called the Pericles 2020 program has been set up to aid the members of the EU in their efforts to protect against the counterfeiting of EU currency.[327]

Under European law, the fraudulent making or altering of currency, or making counterfeits or the distribution of counterfeit currency, or the making and possessing of counterfeiting equipment are all punishable as criminal conduct.[328]

So, where does cryptocurrency fit on this spectrum between being recognized as a "medium of exchange" and the copying of national currencies?

It appears that the law on this issue is not completely settled, with different countries or international groups of countries taking different positions on the legal status of cryptocurrency within their jurisdictions.

325. *See*, E.J. Swan, *Internet Law: A Concise Guide to Regulation Worldwide* (Kluwer Law International, 2022).
326. 18 U.S.C, Chap 25, sections 471-504.
327. Regulation (EU) No 331/2014 of he European Parliament and of the Council of March 11, 2014 establishing an exchange assistance and training programme for the protection of the euro against counterfeiting (the "Pericles 2020" programme) and repealing Council Decisions 2001/923/EC, 2001/924/EC, 2006/75/EC, 2006/76/EC, 2006/849/EC and 2006/850 EC.
328. Directive 2014/62/EU entered into force on May 22, 2014.

The production of cryptocurrency does not really fit the standard definition of counterfeiting, which is "made in imitation of something else with intent to deceive."[329] From this definition, it appears that in order to be "counterfeit," an item must be (1) made in imitation and (2) with intent to deceive.

It appears that in order to cross the line into illegality depends to a significant extent on how the cryptocurrency is marketed to potential recipients.

That may change if cryptocurrencies are adopted by national governments or if national governments decide to issue their own cryptocurrencies.

12.3 ARTIFICIAL INTELLIGENCE

12.3.1 What Is AI?

It is generally accepted that the modern understanding of the term "AI" was first "coined" for the Dartmouth College[330] Summer Research Project held between June 18 and August 17, 1956:

> "For six weeks in the summer of 1956, a group of scientists convened on the Dartmouth campus for the Dartmouth Summer Research Project on Artificial Intelligence. It was at this meeting of the term 'artificial intelligence', was coined. ... The initial conference in 1956 paved the way for the future of artificial intelligence in academia, according to Cade Metz, author of the book '*Genius Makers: The Mavericks Who Brought AI to Google, Facebook and the World.*' ... Conference participants John McCarthy and Marvin Minsky would establish AI labs at Stanford and MIT, respectively, while to other participants, Alan Newell and Herbert Simon, built an AI lab at Carnegie Melon. Taken together, the labs at MIT, Stanford and Carnegie Mellon drove AI research for decades. ... The goal was to build a machine that could do what the human brain could do, Metz said."[331]
>
> "The conference mostly consisted of brainstorming ideas about how AI should work. However, 'There was very little written work record' of the conference, according to computer science professor emeritus Thomas Kurtz,[332] in an interview that is part of the Rauner Special Collections archives."[333]
>
> "Metz said that after the conference, two camps of AI research emerged. One camp believed in what is called neural networks, mathematical systems that learn skills by analyzing data. The idea of neural networks was based on the concept that machines can learn like the human brain, creating new connections and

329. Merriam-Webster's Collegiate Dictonary, 11th ed., (Merriam-Webster, Incorporated, Springfield, MA, 2012).
330. Dartmouth University is one of the eight prestigious "Ivy League Schools" (Harvard, Yale, Princeton, Columbia, Cornell, Pennsylvania, Brown and Dartmouth) in the United States. Dartmouth is located in Hanover, New Hampshire.
331. K. Friel, "A Look Back on the Dartmouth Summer Research Project on Artificial Intelligence," *The Dartmouth*, online at: thedartmouth.com, May 19, 2023.
332. Thomas E. Kurtz, a retired Professor of Mathematics and Computer Science, Dartmouth University.
333. Friel, May 19, 2023, as cited above. The Rauner Special Collections Library holds rare books, manuscripts and archives of Dartmouth College. *See* citation online at: dartmouth.edu.

> growing over time by responding to real world input data. [Other] conference participants would go on to argue that it wasn't possible for machines to learn on their own."[334]
>
> "In about 2010, however, the neural network idea 'was proven to be the way forward,' Metz said. Neural networks allow artificial intelligence programs to learn tasks on their own, which has driven a current boom in AI research, he added."[335]

As can be seen, the modern understanding of "AI" is that AI systems are machines that can do some things the human brain can do, including modifying the performance of the AI system itself in response to data it encounters during the performance of its operations.

Of course, AI machines are not purely "mechanical" machines. They are machines that comprise or include "cyber" or "digital" elements.

12.3.2 What Is the Human Impact of AI?

There is a huge amount of information about AI circulating in the media. It is difficult to know whether the consensus is that AI will benefit, harm, or even bring an end to the human race.

Opinions of this kind make it difficult to know whether AI will be an extension of humanity or an opponent of humanity.

Examination of this quandary requires an injection of realism. From a legal point of view, there will be no division between humanity and AI. AI will not be able to create its own separate world in opposition to humanity.

12.3.2.1 Correcting Fundamental Legal Misconceptions

In discussions of AI, there frequently arise misconceptions about the legal status of AI.

The first is that AI systems can exhibit such independence from their originators and produce such unexpected results in their operation that they constitute an independent being that is separate from humanity.

Indeed, it is sometimes argued that AI systems should be given a separate legal status that entitles them to acquire legal rights that are now only available to human beings.

The second is that one of the difficulties with AI systems is that they are currently "unregulated" and therefore not subject to legal restriction and control.

Neither of these things is true. There will never be a separation between an AI system and human beings. Humans will be the designers, the creators, the operators, the distributors, the owners and/or the users of the AI systems in question.

From a legal point of view, the humans behind an AI system will always be legally responsible for the outcomes the system produces.

334. Friel, May 19, 2023, as cited above.
335. *Ibid.*

Far from being "unregulated," the creation, distribution and operation of AI systems currently is, and will remain subject to, a vast spectrum of existing laws and regulations all over the world.

12.3.2.2 The Human Connection

The real and, indeed, the legal status of AI flows from its connection to its creators, distributors and users.

This connection is shown in the phrase "AI."

The American *Merriam-Webster Dictionary* defines "artificial" as "man-made."

In the *New Oxford Dictionary of English*, "artificial" ... is defined as, "made or produced by human beings, rather than occurring naturally."

In other words, application of the word "artificial" indicates a direct connection between human creation and the thing created.

The term "AI" is defined as "systems able to perform tasks normally requiring human intelligence."[336]

A system that applies AI might be a computer or other contrivance that provides instructions, usually in digital form, directing the tasks in question. Such a device may be called an "AI machine."[337]

Indeed, such devices are usually said to be operating in response to "machine code" or "machine language," which is defined as "a programming language consisting of binary or hexadecimal instructions."[338]

From a legal point of view, the question arises as to what circumstances will permit a break between the creator of an artificial object and the object itself.

The first question is one of legal responsibility. In legal systems, humans are usually assigned a level of responsibility for the results of their actions.

To put it in a popular entertainment context, the "Terminator" was not legally responsible for its actions. Legal responsibility remained with the human creator(s) of the system that brought about the Terminator.

One continuing check on the operation of AI is the fact that the creators of artificially intelligent things will always be legally responsible for the outcomes of their artificially intelligent creations.

The traditional legal concepts of legal responsibility, including DoC, negligence, and compensation for damages, will always be legally applicable to those humans who create and/or use artificially intelligent things or systems. Artificially intelligent creations will never obtain legal independence from those who launch them into the world.

However, because artificially intelligent creations will not automatically possess an understanding of geographic and jurisdictional boundaries, worldwide agreements on the legal responsibilities relating to the use of AI will need to be carefully defined and put into place.

336. The New Oxford Dictionary of English, *Artificial Intelligence* (Oxford: 1998).
337. The New Oxford Dictionary of English, *Machine* (Oxford: 1998).
338. The New Oxford Dictionary of English, *Machine Code* (Oxford: 1998).

That is not to say that there are no existing legal restrictions on the use of AI both within individual jurisdictions and internationally, but these will need to be reviewed to determine how they will apply to any new range of artificially intelligent creations.

12.3.2.3 Application of Machine Law to AI

The complexity and speed with which artificially intelligent things can operate have caused a level of unnecessary confusion with respect to their place in law. The confusion is that they can appear to be so "clever" that they seem to be operating in a sphere that has previously been assumed to belong only to human beings. That sphere is "creativity." The fact that their complexity can allow some AI products to build on and extend their instructions so that they achieve results that were not specifically ordered or even expected by their human creators causes some people to believe that they are, in some ways, a type of superior being.

In some cases, these feelings have extended so far that some people argue that the sophistication of the operations of artificially intelligent things should cause human society to regard them as having legal rights that are now only available to human beings.

For example, in March 2023, a hearing was conducted before the United Kingdom Supreme Court in which an American scientist named Steven Thaler argued that an artificially intelligent "creativity machine" that he had created should be granted patents for two things which the creativity machine produced without any intervention from him. In other words, he was seeking to require the British Patent Office to grant legal rights, in this case patent rights, to a machine.[339] His application was rejected in Britain and also by a court in the United States.

Both courts said that patent rights could only be granted to human creators.

The fundamental flaw in his argument is that without his intervention (in originating the creativity machine), the two subsequent products produced by the creativity machine would not exist.

12.3.3 The Human Element of Law

The purpose of law is to define relations between human beings. Law is intended to be a more desirable substitute for violence and other damaging behavior.

Many different definitions of law have been proposed, but essentially, laws are the rules created by the governors of a society that impose penalties for failure to obey those rules.[340]

Law is itself "artificial" because it is made by humans to govern the behavior of humans within a particular society. The duties and obligations it imposes on humans are not applicable to other objects or life forms. They are not transferable to machines.

339. "Patent Law: Discovery Process," *The Economist*, March 11, 2023, p. 22.
340. P. Shears & G. Stephenson, *James' Introduction to English Law*, pp. 3-5 (London: Butterworths, 1996).

They stay with the humans that are responsible for the creation and operation of machines.

It is true that there are legal "persons" in the form of corporations (limited companies) or partnerships but these are dependent for their creation and governance on the human shareholders and directors behind them. Like the machines discussed above, they are human creations and do not exist without human intervention and participation.

Machines should never have legal rights and responsibilities because no machine exists without a basic starting point of human intervention.

12.3.3.1 A Look at Legal Responsibility for Machines

Essentially, AI machines are a new stage of evolution in the Industrial Revolution. They are a progression of the Age of Machines.

To understand where legal systems currently stand in relation to AI machines and how the laws are likely to evolve, it is useful to see how legal systems dealt with the arrival of the Industrial Revolution and the interaction between humans and the machines that changed their lives then.

12.3.3.2 The Industrial Revolution

The history of the Industrial Revolution began with the invention of steam power. In England, in 1778, James Watt and Matthew Bolton invented a steam engine that could power machines. It was quickly realized that using this source of power to operate machines that could process and weave textiles could greatly increase the volume of textile production and reduce costs, providing Britain with a competitive advantage in the commercialization of textile materials such as wool, flax and cotton. Also, unlike the water power that may have powered some machines, steam power was more easily portable and could be applied most anywhere.

For centuries, Britain had been an enormous producer of textile raw materials such as wool and flax, but these had been largely traded in raw form to markets in the Low Countries, where they were manufactured into textiles that Italian trading companies then marketed all over the known world. At that time, British manufacture of finished cloth had been on a relatively small scale, largely done by hand and often at home using primitive spinning wheels and looms.

The introduction of large, powered textile processing and weaving machines meant that much larger quantities of textiles could be produced at much lower prices. These could be traded throughout the British Empire around the world with significant competitive advantages of speed of production, quantities and prices.

Whereas in 1778, there were no factories in Britain producing large quantities of textiles by powered machines, by 1830, there were over 700 such factories in operation.

12.3.3.3 The Factory Acts

In the 1830s, the British Parliament began to impose laws in response to the changes wrought by the Industrial Revolution that are known as the Factory Acts. These were intended to protect human welfare from the detrimental effects of the expanding use of factories and machines.

There were five Factory Acts between 1833 and 1901.[341]

The first three applied to the textile industry and were aimed at protecting women and children.

The Factory Act of 1833 was aimed at limiting the employment of children in factories. The maximum workweek for children between the ages of 9 and 13 was limited to 48 hours. Their maximum daily workday was limited to 8 hours. For children between 13 and 18, the workday was limited to 12 hours. The employment of children under 9 years of age was prohibited and children under 13 were required to receive two hours of schooling a day. Children under the age of 18 were not allowed to work at night.

Government factory inspectors were appointed.

The Factory Act of 1844 reduced working hours for children between 8 and 13 years to 6 1/2 hours per day. This act also sought to extend protection to women by limiting their workdays to 12 hours and prohibiting women from working at night.

The Factory Act of 1847 limited the workdays of women and children under 18 years of age to 10 hours a day.

The Factory Act of 1867 extended those limitations to all working establishments in which more than five workers were employed.

The Factory Act of 1901 limited the minimum age for work to 12 years. Like the previous act, this rule applied to all working establishments that employed more than five workers.[342]

Although these rules were groundbreaking for their times, as the industrial age and the mechanical marvels it produced spread around the world, rules for the protection of workers, although they undoubtedly differed from country to country, were adopted to protect those employed to work in factories.

12.3.4 The AI Revolution

The introduction of AI into commerce is imposing a similarly dramatic change on the relationship between humans and the means of production.

With the Industrial Revolution, things that were previously being done by humans by hand were now being done by machines. With the present AI Revolution, many intellectual tasks previously performed by humans are now being done by AI machines.

---

341. "The 1833 Factory Act," *The National Archives*, online, factory-artdoc.pdf.
342. "Factory Acts," *The National Archives*, online, factory-artdoc.pdf.

Prior to the Industrial Revolution, there had been no need for laws governing the operation of factories, and certainly no laws restricting the employment of humans in factories.

This is similar to the situation that currently exists with AI. The presence of AI in culture and industry generally is new enough, so significant legal thought as to how its use should be limited is just beginning. New statutes and regulations applying to AI are just beginning to be introduced. As with the early Factory Acts of the Industrial Revolution, a central goal is the protection of children.

12.3.4.1 The Utah Social Media Law

For example. in the United States, the State of Utah has passed a comprehensive law to allow parents to control the exposure of their children to social media available on the Internet. This is the first law in the United States that gives parents the power to restrict their children's exposure to certain social media.[343]

The law gives parents complete access to their children's Internet accounts and permits parents to restrict Internet access from 10:30 P.M. to 6:30 A.M. The governor of Utah wrote:

> We're no longer willing to let social media companies continue to harm the mental health of our youth.

A companion law was passed at the same time, making it easier for parents to bring legal action against social media companies for any financial, physical or emotional harm caused by their posts and imposing fines for any social media companies aiming to advertise that persons under 18.

Although Utah is the first state to impose such laws, it is reported that Ohio, Texas and New Jersey are considering similar regulations and that California has imposed privacy restrictions to protect those under 18.

These things have followed President Biden's recent request for nationwide legislation preventing "Big Tech" companies from collecting the personal data of children and teenagers on the Internet and targeting children and teenagers with advertisements.

In his State of the Union address, President Biden was reported to say:

> We must finally hold social media companies accountable for the experiment they are running on our children for profit.[344]

However, such legislation has not been greeted with universal approval. Some civil liberties groups say that the new Utah law requires the collection of private information about children itself. An official of the political group NetChoice reportedly said that the Utah regulations are counterproductive and unconstitutional because they

343. P. Stubley, "Utah Law Gives Parents Full Control of Children's Social Media," *The Times*, online, March 24, 2023.
344. D. McCabe, "President Biden Will Call for More Limits on Social Media," *The New York Times*, online, March 21, 2022.

will require media companies to collect data about children, verifying their ages and parental relationships. This could put sensitive private data at risk from online hacking attacks.[345]

A significant tool that large ISPs (such as Google and Facebook, etc.) use to collect and process user data involves the use of sophisticated AI programs. Using AI gives them rapid insight into many aspects of the customer data they collect.

As the Marketing AI Institute points out on its website:

> "AI can help you predict outcomes and successful courses of action."
>
> "AI powered systems can analyze data from hundreds of sources and offer predictions about what works and what doesn't."
>
> "AI can also deep dive into data analytics about your customers and offer predictions about consumer preferences, product development and marketing channels."
>
> "AI can be used to unify data across platforms. That includes using the speed and scale of AI to pull together all your customer data into a single, unified view. Artificial intelligence is also capable of unifying data across different sources, even hard to track ones like call data."[346]

It is protection from this kind of comprehensive AI intrusion that the public, particularly children or other vulnerable people, may need or wish protection from.

345. P. Stubley, "Utah Law Gives Parents Full Control of Children's Social Media," *The Times*, online, March 24, 2023.
346. M. Kaput, "AI in Analytics: Top Use Cases and Tools," *Marketing Artificial Intelligence Institute*, online at: marketingaiinstitute.com, April 4, 2022.

CHAPTER 13
Cybercrime

As computing systems become more powerful and sophisticated, they also become increasingly useful tools for cyber criminals (those that use the World Wide Web to commit crimes).

Unfortunately, cybercriminals have found new AI tools to be extremely useful in a number of ways.

13.1 DEEPFAKES

There now has arisen an exceedingly disturbing form of identity theft known as "deepfakes." This is a process of using AI tools to create fakes.

These are representations of people, sometimes well-known celebrities or political figures, or even ordinary individuals, in the form of videos, voice recordings or correspondence.

This involves the theft of more than personal information about someone. It involves theft of their images, their voices, and key aspects of their personalities.

Indeed, as was pointed out in a "Comment" in *The Times*, this constitutes theft of the very things that "make us human."[347]

The author argues that "Now tech can replicate anyone's looks and voice, no person or business is safe from violation."

As an example of how extreme these violations can be, one reads that "deepfakers" have gone so far as to create a porn film using the image of the *Wonder Woman* film star, Gal Gadot. It is often argued that some kinds of pornography can be harmful, but this kind of fraud takes abuse and identity theft to a new level.[348]

Since 2017, deep-faking has been reported appearing on various websites including Reddit. Suddenly, all kinds of deepfakes were appearing on websites. Reddit

347. N. Schick, Comment, "Deepfakes Threaten What Makes Us Human," *The Times*, online, Thursday, August 6, 2020, retrieved August 7, 2020.
348. *Ibid.*

banished them, but this activity has continued to grow and many deepfakes can now be accessed through web searches. They include fake videos using many celebrities, other public figures and private individuals.

Deepfake creation apps and tutorials are also available.[349]

Deep-faking can also be used as a tool of political intimidation. For example, it is reported that an Indian journalist who has been critical of India's ruling party was attacked by a vicious online hatred campaign in 2018 that included a deepfake porn video of her. The video went viral, and she was bombarded with online threats of rape and death. Since this happened, the journalist said, "I have not been the same person."[350]

The writer and commentator Jordan Peterson was reportedly ridiculed using deepfakes from a website entitled NotJordanPeterson.com. Peterson took legal action against the site and wrote:

> Wake up. The sanctity of your voice, and your image, is at serious risk. It's hard to imagine a more serious challenge to the sense of shared, reliable reality that keeps us living together in relative peace.[351]

In another reported incident, a British company lost £250,000 when criminals used a deepfake voice imitation of the company's CEO to telephone an employee and order transfer of that money to an account that disappeared before the fraud was realized.[352]

From these incidents and others, it is clear that more specific controls and legal restrictions need to be put in place to limit the use and abuse of these digital tools.

However, it is important to emphasize that "deepfakes" may already violate many existing laws and regulations on defamation and libel, privacy, and intellectual property.

13.1.1 Response in Estonia

Estonia is one country that has done so in order to counter deepfakes, which were reportedly believed to be from Russian sources, intending to create political disinformation in Estonia. Estonia mobilized digital resources to counter these attacks and increased public awareness of what was going on. These steps have given Estonia a level of protection above that of many other countries.[353]

349. *Ibid.*
350. *Ibid.*
351. *Ibid.*
352. *Ibid.*
353. *Ibid.* Nina Schick if the about of a book on the subject: *Deep Fakes and the Infocalypse: What You Urgently Need to Know.*

13.1.2 Countering Deepfake Crimes and Abuses

The bottom line is that the deepfake problem arose so quickly and has become so serious that specific regulatory and legal attention needs to be focused on it.

13.2 CRIMINAL PUBLIC RELATIONS

Things have reached a point where cybercriminals have become extremely bold, regarding themselves as entrepreneurial heroes to be admired. In August 2020, an article appeared in *The Times* that said:

> Cyberhackers are running sophisticated public relations operations with their own news websites, press releases, twitter accounts and public updates.[354]

It is reported that a number of hacking gangs have set up public relations departments. They have set up new sites where they publicize their attacks. They have adopted brand names and their strategy is reported to be to make those brands as well-known as possible to cause target companies to believe the hackers cannot be stopped and there was no point in trying to defeat them.

13.2.1 Increasing Payments to Hackers

Unfortunately, the hacker gangs' financial successes have been increasing. In the last two years, the average ransom payment hackers have been able to extract from target companies has increased from about $7,000 to about $180,000.[355]

These gangs reportedly love the attention. One calls itself "Evil Corp" and is led by a man who drives a Lamborghini with a license plate that says "thief" in Russian. Another, called "Maze Corp," that is reported to have caused attacks on Xerox, LG and Canon, issued publicity that said its "clients" (targets) should get in touch in three days if they were attacked by Maze Corp; otherwise, they would risk significant "reputational damage."[356]

One criminal group that reportedly calls itself "REvil" is reported to have hosted a competition for hackers offering prizes of $15,000 and an opportunity to work for "REvil."

It is not reported who won.[357]

354. "Hackers Get into the PR Business," *The Times*, online, August 15, 2020, retrieved August 15, 2020.
355. *Ibid.*
356. *Ibid.*
357. *Ibid.*

13.3 REGULATORY LICENSING FOR AI

It can be seen from the above reports that Internet activities by criminal groups are increasing and that AI tools are increasing their power.

In response, it seems necessary to carefully regulate AI tools to limit the types of people that can deploy them and to restrict the kinds of purposes for which they can be used. Perhaps this will entail creation of government regulatory departments to review and license those that create, distribute and use AI systems.

Such regulation exists for financial activities, and it seems that AI will require similar regulatory attention to protect the public and society from criminal abuse of powerful AI tools.

13.4 THE GROWTH OF CYBER CRIME PROBLEMS

In July 2020, *The Times* reported that cybercriminals extorted more than 200 million in ransom from British companies during the previous year.[358]

The pandemic of 2020-2021 made things even worse. It is now not only large companies or institutions or infrastructure that are being attacked by perpetrators of cybercrime but also individuals that have been swindled out of a large amount of money by online scams. One of the most common is the so-called push-payment scams.[359] These are scams where criminals convince people to make payments under false pretenses, such as claiming that the victim has ordered something online or owes money for a non-existent traffic violation.

It is estimated that in 2021, more than half the manufacturers in the U.K. have been victims of cybercrime.[360] It is reported that 63% lost up to 5,000, and around a quarter lost between 5,000 and 25,000. Automotive industries have apparently suffered the most. In 2021, around 62% reported being victimized by cybercrime.[361]

Reportedly, this is done by gangs of hackers, believed to be principally from Russia or Eastern Europe, infecting the commercial computer systems of large companies with malware and then charging those companies large amounts to get back access to their networks. The usual technique of hackers is to encrypt the target's files so that they can be re-opened only with a key sold by the attacker.[362]

It is believed that companies that have been attacked are willing to pay the hackers rather than go to the authorities because they fear damage to their reputations and possible fines from regulators for failing to adequately protect their computer systems and the data stored there.

358. T. Knowles & L. Fisher, "Firms Pay £200m in Ransoms to Hackers," *The Times*, online, July 31, 2020, retrieved on day of publication, https://www.thetimes.co.uk/#.
359. D. Byers, "Internet Giants Are Profiting from Web Scams, Say Banks," *The Times*, online, March 26, 2021, accessed March 30, 2021.
360. MakeUK, "Cyber Resilience The Last Line of Defence," MakeUK Cyber Security Survey 2021, online, May 4, 2021, accessed May 7, 2021.
361. *Ibid.*
362. Byers, above.

Worldwide, it is believed that cyber criminals are extorting around $19 billion per year.

In Britain, it is reported that companies there are suffering around 5,000 ransomware attacks per year.[363] Consequently, about 52% of companies in the U.K. have now acquired insurance cover against cyberattacks.[364]

In fact, the payment total may be much higher, but many companies refuse to admit that they have paid ransoms to hackers.[365]

In addition to the big payments made by companies, there are far too many situations in which cyber criminals tricked individuals into transferring money to them. More than 20% more people were victimized by this type of scam in 2020 than had been in the previous year. There have been approximately 150,000 victims in the United Kingdom alone.[366]

Although much of this fraud involved the bank accounts of the victims, recently, banks have been blaming the large tech companies for much of the problem.

The banks are claiming that the tech companies have not been diligent enough in protecting their platforms from fraudulent scams. Prominent tech websites are often used by criminals to persuade victims to transfer money to fraudsters.

Some in the banking industry claim that the Big Tech companies are not cooperating enough with the banks to put an end to these scams and that they are not making enough of an effort to take down the fraudulent offers that solicit payments. Consequently, some in the banking industry are demanding that tech companies should be made financially liable for frauds that are committed using their platforms.[367]

In the U.K., the Bank of England Governor, Andrew Bailey, has called for amendments to a new government Online Safety Bill to require tech companies to make greater efforts to prevent child abuse, terrorist activities and online financial fraud.

Unfortunately, online criminals continue to expand their activities. It has even been reported that they are offering services to fellow criminals to set up fake websites to service platforms for their illegal activities.[368]

The public relations problem that the major tech companies suffer is that they make money from increased usage of their platforms. In other words, if criminals are increasing their use of tech company online platforms to defraud people, then this increases the revenue to the tech companies. Tech company critics point out that it cannot be right that criminal activity financially benefits the tech companies.

A number of banks have signed on to a voluntary code to make refunds to victims of online financial fraud involving their bank accounts. However, banks are sometimes criticized for not making it easy for victims to recover their losses. In some cases, banks have argued that the losses are due to the negligence of the victims. So, it is not surprising that banks are trying to shift at least part of the blame for financial losses to

363. *Ibid.*
364. MakeUK, above.
365. Byers, above.
366. *Ibid.*
367. *Ibid.*
368. *Ibid.*

the tech platforms where the losses are happening. How this debate is ultimately resolved between the financial and the tech companies remains to be seen.

13.5 TECH COMPANY ANTI-FRAUD EFFORTS

Some major tech companies respond that they are making serious efforts to prevent fraud on their platforms.

Google has said that it has clear policies on the kind of ads it permits to be placed on its platform. They say that they strictly enforce those policies and remove ads that violate them. Google says that it is working around the clock to remove billions of ads that fail to meet its standards.

However, the U.K. government, and undoubtedly other governments, will continue to examine whether tech platforms are doing enough to prevent fraud on their systems that may impose additional regulations if they find that more should be done.[369]

13.6 CYBER CURRENCY INVESTMENT FRAUDS

Many scams involve investment fraud, sometimes aided by AI tools in making false offers to invest in things like digital currencies. Nearly 10,000 people have fallen victim to these kinds of frauds in 2020.

Payments to criminals are usually made in the form of a digital currency, such as Bitcoin, which cannot be traced to the persons paid.

The anonymity of the payments and the reluctance of companies to admit paying combine to give ransomware criminals an almost unfettered opportunity to profit from their crimes free of punishment.

13.7 EXPANDING RANSOMWARE ATTACKS

The possibility of abusive use of AI to create deepfakes of people also raises the possibility that hacking gangs will use deepfakes to blackmail people into paying ransoms to keep embarrassing and humiliating fakes of the Internet or to remove them from circulation.

Apparently, the dangers of suffering public embarrassment, losing data and being fined by regulators are enough to make companies and individuals pay such ransoms without reporting the attacks. The actual total amounts of ransoms being paid may be much higher than is being reported.

This reluctance to report attacks also means that risk to cybercriminals of being caught and punished is greatly reduced.[370]

In the U.K., it is not illegal to pay such ransoms, unless it is known that the payment is going to be used to fund terrorism. However, some Members of the British

369. *Ibid.*
370. *Ibid.*

Parliament have demanded that laws be passed to make the payment of such ransoms illegal.[371]

These reports about British problems are disturbing but become even more so when one recognizes that Britain is number six on the list of countries experiencing ransomware attacks. The first five are the U.S., Italy, Germany, Spain and France. In the United States alone, it is estimated that about $1.3 billion is paid out each year as a result of ransomware attacks.[372]

A frightening aspect of the success that hacker groups have had in extracting money from victims is that these funds make it possible for hackers to purchase ever more sophisticated systems for their hacking and to expand their criminal activities to target even more and bigger victims for their crimes.

In the future, the tools of hacking gangs will probably include sophisticated AI tools.

It is reported that their success has encouraged criminal gangs to advertise for new recruits on the "dark web."[373] Recruits could include AI experts.

The Internet is much more extensive than most users realize. Most of us only use and see the websites that are available to the general public using popular browsers such as Google, Safari and Bing. However, this gives access to only a very small part of the World Wide Web (Web).

There is a part of the Web that comprises an encrypted network that contains websites that can't be reached with the popular browsers. This is the "Dark Web," and the websites on that can only be reached using special "anonymity browsers" such as: The Onion Router, Freenet and f2P. The Dark Web has many uses, but it is a platform favored by cybercriminals to carry out their operations and keep them anonymous.[374]

13.8 INTERNATIONAL COOPERATION NECESSARY

An article published by the World Economic Forum suggests that the best way to deal with cybercrime is greater international cooperation at the highest levels.[375] This article asks national governments to take responsibility for helping to defeat cybercrime. The growing success and sophistication of cyber criminals are going to require greater funding and more resources in order to protect against it. Individuals and companies may not have the funds and resources necessary.

371. *Ibid.*
372. *Ibid.*
373. *Ibid.*
374. "The Dark Web Explained," "The Dark Web and How to Access It in 3 Easy Steps," VPN Mentor, https://www.vpnmentor.com/blog/whats-the-dark-web-how-to-access-it-in-3-easy-steps/?keyword=&geo=9055710&device=&gclid=EAIaIQobChMIhfa6-a_-6gIVjO3tCh3ZZwuREAAYASAAEgJDh_D_BwE, retrieved August 3, 2020.
375. M.S. Muller & A. Zwinggi, "Global Leaders Must Take Responsibility Cybersecurity. Here's Why: And How," *World Economic Forum*, Davos, January 19, 2020. https://www.weforum.org/agenda/2020/01/global-leaders-must-take-responsibility-for-cybersecurity-here-s-why-and-how.

The expanding threat will need to be dealt with at the national and international levels. A number of steps or suggested in order to deal with the problem.[376]

One important requirement is that those who are victims of an attack should be required to report the attacks, cooperate with authorities, and be transparent about the effects of such an attack.

It was reported by the WEF that at least one important international company has followed this path. Norsk Hydro, a large Norwegian metals and energy company, was subject to a ransomware attack. They decided to refuse to pay, report the attack immediately, cooperate with officials, and be transparent about the effects of the attack.[377]

The WEF article recommends that commercial institutions and governments need a well-thought-out anti-cybercrime strategy in order to deal with attacks. This requires that the top management of an organization understand the risks that the organization faces. Training must be provided to working personnel so that they know how to respond immediately in the face of an attack. The funding and resources to provide the knowledge and equipment necessary to improve security against cyberattacks need to be provided. Finally, the reporting of cyberattacks, cooperation with officials and transparency about the effects of the attack is essential to frustrate, defeat, identify and punish cybercriminals.

13.9 CYBERCRIME IN THE PANDEMIC

One thing that seems to be the case is that in times of social stress and or social disruption, Internet crime rises. For example, it has been reported that in Spain, cybercrime has risen by 300% during the COVID-19 pandemic.[378]

In the U.K., it is reported that since the pandemic began, 74% of banks and financial institutions have been affected by some type of financial crime. Their average loss has been approximately £600,000.

Police forces in the U.K. have reported more than 6,000 cases of cybercrime and other COVID-related frauds. In total, more than £34 million has been stolen by fraud and cybercrime since the pandemic began.

Part of the problem is that due to the pandemic, so many people are working from home and using their personal IT systems. IT security is not as strong as it would be if work was being done in offices with professionally constructed and protected systems.

The pandemic has led to a significant increase in online activity from more people working from home and more people shopping on the Internet because of shop closures during lockdown.

This has meant that many more people are putting information about themselves and their financial transactions online. This provides a bigger population of potential

376. *Ibid.*
377. *Ibid.*
378. T. Windterburn, "Cybercrime in Spain Has Risen by 300% During the Pandemic," *EuroWeekly*, online, March 21, 2021, accessed March 23, 2021.

targets for cybercriminals and may provide them with a higher rate of success in their criminal activities.

It has to be understood that with access to AI tools, cybercriminals will have a broader palette of methods with which to conduct ransom attacks and every other kind of fraud and criminal abuse that cybercriminals engage in.

The above circumstances lead to an expansion of computer-user vulnerability that may be the result of people who previously have not had much experience in conducting business and financial transactions online being required to adopt the Internet as a principal method of doing transactions that they used to do in person. This makes them more vulnerable to sophisticated cyber criminals and exposes more computer user information to those that may exploit it for crime and abuse.

Increased work from home also presents a larger population of Internet users that can be vulnerable to the installation of a virus on their computer systems to illegally gather information about the computer owners or to encrypt the users' data and demand that they pay a "ransom" to have the data unlocked.

Although governments and security services are getting better at combating cybercrime, criminals are clever at creating inventive new ways to stay ahead of law enforcement and to locate new locations to practice their illegal activities.

AI is another tool for criminals. It is also the case that the existence of the "Dark Web" and the expansion of the use of cryptocurrencies make it even more difficult to locate and punish cyber criminals.[379]

Although the pandemic has made it difficult or sometimes impossible for many people around the globe to conduct their business and personal activities, it is opened up a myriad of new opportunities for cybercriminals that want to take advantage of us on the Internet.

Ransomware cyberattacks have continued to grow, with some of the worst and most serious coming in 2021 at a time when much of the world was also suffering from the COVID-19 pandemic.

13.10 ATTACKS ON HEALTH, EDUCATION, PUBLIC BODIES AND CHILDREN

It is reported that ransomware gangs are "now routinely targeting schools and hospitals."[380] There have been very upsetting reports of AI deepfakes being used against children.

In 2020/2021, the United Kingdom was reported to have suffered more than 9,000 data security incidents where information was stolen by hackers or mistakenly sent to the wrong recipients. It was reported that 500 private and public bodies were the victims of ransomware attacks, and several hundred more were victims of other types of hacking attacks. Most of these data system breaches were suffered by healthcare and

379. Winterburn, above, reporting on information from Juan Jose Nombela, a computer science expert at the International University of La Rioja (UNIR).
380. J. Tidy, "The Ransomware Surge Ruining Lives," *BBC News*, online, April 29, 2021, accessed, May 11, 2021.

education organizations. The usual tactic of hacking groups is to encrypt the data in the systems of educational or healthcare organizations, depriving those organizations of the use of this data until the ransom is paid.[381]

Other breaches occurred, affecting the systems of police forces in the United Kingdom; these law-enforcement authority systems had an average of approximately eight data incidents a week, which resulted in important data being taken. These statistics are known because whenever a data breach relates to information important to the safety, rights or freedoms of people at risk, the organization holding the data is required to report the breach to the U.K. ICO, which keeps a record of such data incidents.

There is no doubt that AI can create tools (deepfakes) that will allow those that wish to embarrass those working in law enforcement and undermine confidence in law enforcement organizations.

In March 2021, it was reported that attacks on universities, colleges and schools prevented students from being able to return to classrooms in about 80 educational institutions.[382]

This surge in attacks has motivated tech companies and governments to find ways to aggressively and effectively counter these damaging and potentially deadly criminal activities.

In 2021, the U.S. FBI, Amazon, Microsoft and the National Crime Agency of the United Kingdom joined the Ransomware Task Force (RTF) in issuing a report making approximately 50 recommendations for action that governments should take to counter ransomware and other criminal hacking attacks.[383] Those organizations are now looking at ways to counter AI-powered attacks.

However, although hacking gangs found healthcare and educational institutions to be particularly vulnerable to ransomware attacks, they did not forget to attack other sectors. In the retail sector, there were nearly 1,000 attacks, also nearly 1,000 in financial businesses and charities were victimized more than 500 times.[384]

13.11 A VARIETY OF PROBLEMS

Not all data incidents are the result of criminal activity; there are also thousands of computer system incidents whereby data is not sent to the right person. Although many times, such a mistake may not be damaging to the owner of the data and may be easily corrected, there are situations where the mis-sending needs to be reported to the ICO because of risks the misdirection may pose to the data owner.

There is the additional difficulty of the financial problems suffered by companies as a result of declines in business due to the pandemic and the accompanying lockdowns. This has often meant that cost-cutting measures have been necessary,

381. F. Hamilton, "Hackers on Loose as 9,000 Data Leaks a Year Recorded," *The Times*, online, July 5, 2021.
382. *Ibid.*
383. Tidy, April 29, above.
384. Hamilton, July 5, 2021, above.

which have reduced the amount of money available for IT system maintenance and security. This, among other things, has made it easier for criminals to gain access to commercial IT systems. With the dangers that may be posed by AI, cost-cutting in security sectors is even more dangerous.

This represents larger law enforcement issues than simply computer attacks. The money that is paid to criminal gangs resulting from ransomware is used by them to fund other crimes, such as human trafficking and child abuse.

The U.K. National Cyber Security Center reported that there were approximately three times more ransomware attacks in 2020 than in 2019.[385]

There are an increasing number of attacks that affect public services at all levels. For example, in the autumn of 2020, the IT systems of the London borough of Hackney were affected by a cyberattack that interfered with important public services provided online. It was reported:

> The damage done was really significant with things like housing repairs, benefits payments and land registry all impacted. It's going to be months until we are fully recovered, and I can't understand the motivation behind this for criminals.[386]

13.11.1 The Colonial Pipeline Attack

In May 2021, Colonial Pipeline, the largest fuel pipeline system in the United States, suffered a ransomware cyberattack. This system is the Colonial Pipeline, which transports 2½ million barrels a day of fuel, including gasoline, jet fuel and diesel fuel, on the East Coast of the United States.

On May 7, 2021, it was completely shut down by a cyber hacking gang. Fuel availability in 18 states was affected.[387] Fuel prices were affected as a result.

The problem is that modern infrastructure operations are increasingly sophisticated, increasingly digitalized and increasingly connected to computer systems. Consequently, criminals have a variety of portals through which they can seek access to the electronic systems that control important infrastructure operations.

The facts are that the flow of petroleum-based chemicals through the system to the states on the East Coast of America that depend on it is highly evolved technologically. Most of its operations are under the control of electronic systems, switches, gauges and valves that are centrally controlled and monitored by operators on computers.

This kind of control makes much government infrastructure vulnerable to attack by sophisticated computer criminals. As has been said, a devastating attack can begin by opening a single email.[388] There is the danger that use of AI tools will make such attacks even easier for criminals.

385. Tidy, April 29, above.
386. *Ibid.*, quoting Rob Miller, director of information and communications technology for the London Borough of Hackney.
387. J. Tidy, "Colonial Hack: How Did Cyber-Attackers Shut Off Pipeline," *BBC News*, online, May 10, 2021.
388. *Ibid.*

The Colonial Pipeline hack had serious consequences in the United States. There were shortages of fuel in various areas served by the pipeline. In some states, petrol stations ran out of fuel. Rises in the price of fuel were expected to last several months. In some areas, there was "panic buying" of fuels.[389]

The Colonial Pipeline hack is believed to have been caused by a criminal gang known as "Dark Side." They have been reported to have begun attacking computer systems and demanding ransom payments sometime in August 2020. Some sources believe that they are connected to Russia, but there is no certain knowledge that this is true.[390]

It is reported that $4.4 million in ransom was paid to the Colonial Pipeline hackers to get them to release the pipeline.

However, in early June 2021, U.S. government officials were able to trace and recover $2.3 million of this ransom, which was being transferred in the form of Bitcoin by the criminals. Colonial was happy for the "swift work and professionalism of the FBI" in seeking to recover the ransom. A key element of the FBI's recovery was the acquisition of something called the "private key" to the "Bitcoin wallet" of the hackers. No details of how the FBI obtained this information were given, but there has been considerable speculation over whether it was from equipment seized by the FBI, from an informant inside the criminal gang or from a company that the hackers might have used as part of their hacking project.[391]

The increase in ransomware attacks, and particularly the devastating nature of the attack on the Colonial Pipeline has highlighted the issue in the United States and caused people to think that the government needs to do more to protect vulnerable and important IT systems.[392]

As a result of the Colonial Pipeline hack, the U.S. government has called emergency meetings and begun discussions about issuing a presidential Executive Order to increase the cybersecurity requirements for federal agencies and government contractors.[393]

Drafts of such an order have been provided to government agencies and government contractors that provide a cybersecurity program to better protect the United States. The order outlines Government mandated cybersecurity standards that government agencies and contractors would be required to put in place. The proposed standards include "multi factor identification" that requires a second code to be obtained by a different trusted method before a critical system user would be allowed to log in.

Government agencies would also be required to introduce a "zero trust" policy with respect to software vendors. Vendors would be allowed access to government IT

389. *Ibid.*, May 12, 2021.
390. *Ibid.*
391. J. Tidy, "Colonial Pipline, US Recovers Most of the Ransom, Justice Department Says," "A Powerful Message to Hacker Gangs," *BBC News*, online, June 8, 2021.
392. D.E. Sanger, N. Perlroth & J.E. Barnes, "Biden Plans an Order to Strengthen Cyberdefenses. Will It Be Enough," *The New York Times*, online, May 9, 2021, accessed May 11, 2021.
393. *Ibid.*, May 9 2021.

systems only when necessary, and all contractors would be required to comply with certain conditions before any software they supplied would be accepted.

Any violators of the required standards could be banned from government business, which would be seriously commercially damaging.[394]

13.11.2 Other Large Attacks

However, huge and damaging hacking attacks did not end with the Colonial Pipeline. At the beginning of July 2021, there was a massive and devastating ransomware attack that assaulted hundreds of American businesses and many other businesses around the world, affecting companies in about 17 countries.[395]

The suspicion of U.S. law-enforcement authorities was that the attack originated in Russia or in the former Soviet states. The FBI believes that it is being perpetrated by the Russian hacking group known as REvil. Another clue as to the origin of the attack is that the computer code of the attack is structured to exclude the Russian language using computer systems.[396]

The attack involved inserting malicious code into software used by many companies. It has been speculated that the hackers were demanding $70 million to restore service to the companies they attacked.

President Biden directed U.S. security services to do a thorough analysis of the attack to determine who was responsible and how it was done. In a meeting in Geneva shortly before this attack, Biden had warned Putin not to permit attacks on U.S. digital sites to originate from Russia. But it is unclear whether this demand will make any difference to the number or intensity of hacking attacks.

However, the countries that are alleged to sponsor or permit hacking attacks from within their borders should not confidently assume that the hacking abilities within their country are superior to those that can be deployed by the United States or its allies.

It is certainly the case when considering the roles that AI systems and tools can play in both perpetrating and investigating computer attacks that the U.S., with its leadership in AI development, may well be in the strongest position to defend against and/or punish cyberattacks of all kinds, including cyberattacks aided by abusive use of AI.

It seems unlikely that the important infrastructure systems of countries like Russia, China or North Korea are invulnerable to hacking attacks. There seems a little doubt that significant damage can be done to their systems by other countries through the use of the Internet.

It is also the case that countries alleged to be sponsoring hacking attacks have financial and physical resources that can be vulnerable to seizure as retribution for damaging hacking attacks on other countries. Indeed, it has been reported that Mr.

394. *Ibid.*
395. M. Bennetts & A. Dauber, "Joe Biden Takes Aim at Russia Over Crippling Cyberattack," *The Times*, online, January 5, 2021.
396. K. Dilanian, "Code in Huge Ransomware Attack Written to Avoid Computers That Use Russian, Says a New Report," *NBC News*, online, July 7, 2021.

Putin has made efforts to compile a significant fortune with financial institutions outside of Russia.[397]

It is possible that President Biden's warning to Putin did produce a positive response. One of the most notorious hacking groups is the allegedly Russian REvil (also called, "Sodinokibi") suddenly disappeared from the internet after President Biden's warning. REvil's blog and its payment website stopped being available on July 13, 2021.[398] Of course, there are several possible reasons why this occurred. REvil may have decided that given all the scrutiny they were subject to, it might be better for them to lie low for a while. Or, the U.S. or other countries with computer expertise may have successfully hacked their servers and taken them offline. It is also possible that Russian authorities may have been ordered to take action against them. Time will tell whether they will reappear and, if they do, in what form.

13.12 ACTIONS AGAINST CYBERCRIME

One somewhat radical solution to solving the problem of ransomware attacks calls that laws should be passed making the payment of rent somewhere a criminal offense.[399] The former head of the U.K. Cyber Security Center, Ciaran Martin, believes that cybercrime would stop being a way for global Internet criminals to make money if payments to them were banned.

One of the problems with providing effective security against cyberattacks is that a cyberattack on a particular organization creates few, if any, legal obligations on the target. Most are not required to report or publicize the attack, and if payment is made in cyber currency, it may be completely untraceable. This leaves government institutions which are supposed to provide security against cyberattacks with very little information about how to counter them or enforce punishment on the perpetrators.[400]

Martin suggested that regulations similar to those for bidding ransom payments to terrorists should be considered. He says that it makes no more sense to pay Russian cyber criminals than it does to pay Islamic terrorists. Both types of payments are damaging to society in the day and encourage the continuation of attacks that may raise money to fund other kinds of criminality and terrorism.

As of May 2021, the estimated cost of ransomware attacks worldwide was about $120 billion annually. The focus of the attacks has become ever more sensitive, aiming increasingly at educational institutions, healthcare facilities and vital infrastructure. Some experts express the view that a ban on payments may be the quickest way to reduce or even solve the problem or at least to stunt the growth of ransomware attacks.[401]

397. A. Taylor, "Is Vladimir Putin Hiding a $200 Billion Fortune? And If So, Does It Matter?" *The Washington Post*, online, February 20, 2015.
398. "REvil Ransomware Websites Disappear from the Internet," *BBC News*, online, July 14, 2021.
399. F. Hamilton & M. Bridge, "Ban Ransom Payments to Hackers, Urges ex-GCHQ Boss," *The Times*, online, May 14, 2021, accessed, May 17, 2021.
400. *Ibid.*
401. *Ibid.*

There is, of course, a downside in that those that are attacked may lose valuable data because of their failure to pay.

Another problem is that many hackers, rather than threatening to destroy data, threaten to release highly sensitive or deeply embarrassing data about institutions and individuals onto the Internet. The pain, embarrassment and cost of having such data be made available publicly is a serious problem and a key motivation to make payments to hackers.[402] For example, a chain of clinics that provided cosmetic surgery and weight loss therapy to clients, some of whom were well-known public figures, was threatened with public disclosure of a database of client photographs. The disclosure did not happen, but the threat illustrates the delicacy of the problem.[403] Sensitive ways to deal with this type of thing will need to be found.

It seems likely that AI could make stolen personal information of this kind much more useful to criminals who may wish to use it for blackmail of deepfake purposes.

But it is suggested that in the long run, this price is worth paying because it would protect sensitive educational, healthcare and infrastructure providers from a continuous series of attacks of the kind that have recently been experienced in a number of countries.[404]

Martin also urges insurers that provide promises for payment to compensate clients against ransomware attacks to require their clients to put better cyber protection in place. This could be incentivized by tying the level of premiums to the effectiveness of the cybersecurity in place. This would make it more attractive for institutions to improve their cybersecurity.[405]

13.12.1 US International Cybercrime Prevention Act

The growth of cybercrime during the pandemic in general and the devastating Colonial Pipeline cyberattack in 2021 caused the U.S. Congress to reconsider the International Cybercrime Prevention Act (ICPA), which had previously failed to pass in 2018. The bill was aimed at giving law enforcement additional powers to seize computing devices of cyber criminals and created additional criminal violations for which attackers could be prosecuted for disrupting critical infrastructure.

One provision of the ICPA bill would have made any violation of the Computer Fraud and Abuse Act (CFAA) an offense within the Racketeer Influenced and Corrupt Organization (RICO) Act.

The U.S. had previously brought some prosecutions of cyber criminals under RICO. For example, the Justice Department had prosecuted a website for Rico charges relating to the defendants providing hosting services for the distribution of malware.[406]

402. *Ibid.*
403. *Ibid.*
404. *Ibid.*
405. *Ibid.*
406. Department of Justice, “Four Individuals Plead Guilty to RICO Conspiracy Involving ‘Bulletproof Hosting’ for Cypercriminals,” online, May 7, 2021. https://www.justice.gov/opa/pr/four-individuals-plead-guilty-rico-conspiracy-involving-bulletproof-hosting-cybercriminals.

Section 5 of the act would have created a specific violation for serious damage to infrastructure computer systems or for intentionally damaging computers controlling important infrastructure such as election systems, hospitals, power plants and dams.

Section 6 would have made it an offense to use or provide access to a computer infiltrated by criminals within a botnet operated for purposes of cybercrime.

Section 3 of the IPCA would have allowed the law enforcement authorities to confiscate any property used to break data privacy laws.

Section 4 would have allowed provision of injunctive relief against botnets used in cybercriminal activities.[407]

In the end, this bill was not enacted into law.

13.13 ILLEGAL FAILURES TO REPORT DATA BREACHES

A key factor in preventing and punishing cybercrime is that the regulators and law enforcement bodies must have as much information as possible about cybercrime, how it is being conducted and how victims are being targeted.

As shown by press reports, Internet crime victims that failed to report their attacks or to take appropriate steps to prevent damaging data breaches can also be charged with violations of law and/or regulations that can result in large fines and other possible penalties in some jurisdictions.

One dramatic example of this is a report that the French Data Protection Authority fined Uber €400,000, United States authorities fined them $148 million, the Dutch fined them €600,000, and the British fined them 385,000 because Uber failed to timely report a large data breach. The breach occurred in 2016 and exposed data of about 57 million Uber customers around the world. Apparently, the fines were so high because Uber delayed reporting the breach for over a year, hoping to avoid embarrassment, fines and lawsuits. Uber was also accused of failing to have in place basic security measures that could have prevented the breach.[408]

It is important that companies engaged in business on the Internet remember that, as demonstrated by the Uber fines discussed above, most legal jurisdictions will have in place laws and regulations that require the reporting of data breaches exposing personal data and penalties for failing to report or prevent data breaches.

These penalties will differ from jurisdiction to jurisdiction, but one example is the EU GDPR.[409] The GDPR requires that any organization must report certain data breaches that reveal personal information held by that organization. The GDPR requires that the breach must be reported to relevant regulatory authorities without undue delay, usually within 72 hours if that is feasible.[410]

407. S. Igor, "Reintroduced International Cybercrime Prevention Act Would Create New Cybercrime Violations, Increase Forfeiture and Injunctive Relief," *IPWatchdog*, online, June 22, 2021.
408. "France Hands Uber €400,000 Fine over Huge Data Breach," https://www.thelocal.fr/20181220/france-hands-uber-400000-fine-over-huge-data-breach#:~:text=France's%20data%20protection%20agency%20said,million%20clients%20and%20drivers%20worldwide.
409. Regulation (EU) 2016/679.
410. EU GDPR, Article 34.1.

Under the GDPR, the details of the penalties are left to the individual Member States, but they must be "effective, proportionate, and dissuasive."[411]

Uber is by no means the only commercial organization fined for data breaches. For example, the U.K. has imposed a number of large fines because of data breaches:

- In July 2019, British Airways was fined £183,000 because of a data breach that affected 500,000 customers. The regulator found that the security standards of British Airways were not sufficiently robust.
- In the same month, Marriott Homes was fined £99,000 because of a breach that affected millions of customer records. The regulator found that Marriott should have done more to secure its records.
- In October 2018, the U.K. fined Facebook £500,000 (the maximum fine that the U.K. regulator is permitted to impose for breaches) for incorrectly sharing the data of 87 million customers with a political consultant organization. The regulator found that Facebook had failed to adequately protect the data of its customers.
- In September 2018, a company called Equifax was fined £500,000 for failing to make certain that its parent company was adequately protecting the data of Equifax's U.K. customers. It should also be noted that the American FTC fined the parent company $581 million for the breach, which involved the personal data of over 140 million people.
- In April 2019, the U.K. regulator fined a "pregnancy and parenting club" called Bounty £500,000. Bounty provided personal data of over 30 million people to a number of credit rating agencies without permission of the people whose data it was.

These are not the only companies that have been punished for failing to protect against data breaches and/or failing to report them as required by law or regulation.

Others have included Cathay Pacific; Dixon's Carphone; Yahoo; Capital One; Tesco Bank, Target, Anthem, Google, 1&1 Telecom; University of Texas MD Anderson Cancer Center; Fresenius Medical Care North America; Cottage Health, Touchstone Medical Imaging, University of Rochester Medical Center; Jackson Health Systems; DSG Retail Limited; and others. Many of these have been fined and/or penalized by multiple regulators in several jurisdictions. The total of fines and penalties imposed so far is estimated to total more than $1.5 billion.[412]

The above is just a selection of examples.

There have been many other data breach penalties imposed around the world and that is likely to continue for the foreseeable future. It can be seen from the selection above that any company or organization that has and electronic database of sensitive personal information about people can find itself the target of a serious data hack.

Criminal hackers consider any large collection of personal data valuable, not least because those that own it or collect it need the data to run their operations or to live

411. *Ibid.*, Article 84.1.
412. CSO from IDG, "The Biggest Data Breach Fines, Penalties and Settlements So Far," csoonline.com, August 14, 2020, retrieved August 25, 2020.

their lives. Consequently, someone who takes it from them and threatens to make it inaccessible profit from ransom, blackmail, or commercial, political or military advantage.

It is vital that business organizations that hold personal data of people put adequate measures in place to protect that data from improper exposure. Failure to do so can be costly and perhaps devastatingly so. If more than $1.5 billion in penalties seems like a lot, there is a little doubt that the total will keep getting larger.

13.14 POLITICAL PROPAGANDA

Since Britain's Brexit referendum in 2015 and the U.S. presidential election of 2016, serious concern has risen about the ethics and legality of using Internet tools to gather information from the social media posts of individuals and using that information to construct campaigns to change the behavior of the individuals whose data has been mined for the purpose of achieving certain political results.

It seems possible that AI-powered tools could make political interference even more sophisticated and widespread.

Starting in March 2018, Carole Cadwallader and Emma Graham-Harrison began publishing a series of articles that accused Cambridge Analytica of taking data from the profiles of 50 million Facebook users and using that information to manipulate Brexit referendum voters in the U.K. and the U.S. presidential election for the benefit of the Leave campaign end Donald Trump's election team.[413] One article said:

> The data analytics firm that worked with Donald Trump's election team and the winning Brexit campaign harvested millions of Facebook profiles of US voters, in one of the tech giant's biggest ever data breaches and used them to build a powerful software program to predict and influence choices at the ballot box.[414]

In the 2019 Netflix documentary entitled, "The Great Hack," it is strongly agreed with *The Guardian* stories that Cambridge Analytica was hired by both the "Leave" campaign during the Brexit referendum and Donald Trump during the 2016 election to gather data from social media sources, and particularly from Facebook, to create profiles of citizens of the U.K. and the United States to enable the leave and Trump campaign's to change how undecided people would vote.

After these and other revelations about this use of social media data, the situation changed from being embarrassing stories about the activities of Cambridge Analytica to becoming regarded as cyber-criminality.

In January 2019, the parent company of Cambridge Analytica (SCL Elections) pled guilty to violating the DPA because it had failed to provide an American citizen named David Carroll (a Professor at the New School of Social Research in New York

413. C. Cadwalladar & E. Graham-Harrison, "Revealed: 50 Million Facebook Profiles Harvested for Cambridge Analytica in Major Data Breach," *The Guardian*, online, March 17, 2018, retrieved September 27, 2020.
414. *Ibid.*

City) with copies of the data it held on him. They refused to comply with an enforcement notice issued by a U.K. Court and were fined £15,000.

Cambridge Analytica has since gone out of business. It was liquidated amidst allegations that they wanted to avoid having to produce more information about their activities.

13.14.1 Brazil Electoral Interference

In Brazil, there was apparently an attempt by President Jair Bolsonaro to interfere with the electoral process by issuing regulations in September 2021, preventing social networks from removing posts that they consider to be disinformation about the future presidential election.

However, almost immediately following the introduction of those rules, the Senate and Supreme Court of Brazil canceled those rules because Bolsonaro had been using social media to make the claim that he would only lose the election if it were illegally rigged. He appears to have been taking a page from Donald Trump's book on political manipulation.[415]

Mauricio Santoro, a professor of international relations at the State University of Rio de Janeiro, was quoted as saying:

> It's a very positive sign that the Brazilian political class reacted ... The Brazilian leadership is finally understanding how important the Internet is too political life in Brazil.[416]

13.14.2 China

China is reported to be cracking down on political speech in Hong Kong that it judges to be in opposition to government policy. This has been subject to a significant amount of criticism from around the world.

In September 2021, there was an instance where the people that organized the annual Hong Kong commemoration of the 1989 suppression of protest in Tiananmen Square were ordered to take down the content of their commemorative website and also their commemorative comments on social media platforms.

In making these orders, the government was relying on a security law issued last year that allows the government to ban any Internet content that the government, "on reasonable grounds," considers to be a security threat.[417]

415. J. Nicas, "Bolsonaro's Ban on Removing Social Media Posts Is Overturned in Brazil," *The New York Times*, online, September 15, 2021.
416. *Ibid.*
417. K. Kwase, "Hong Kong Police Invoke Security Law to Censor Online Posts," *Nikkei Asia*, online, September 17, 2021.

13.14.3 U.S.: Texas and Florida

In the United States, the Republican administrations of both Texas and Florida have attempted to introduce laws similar to that promoted by President Bolsonaro in Brazil.

Texas

In September 2021, the governor of Texas signed a bill that forbade social media platforms from removing posts because of the political views expressed in the posts.[418]

Under this bill, social media sites:

> cannot remove, play down or otherwise moderate content because of a user's political perspective or ban the user entirely. The companies will also need to publish regular reports showing how often they receive complaints about content and how often they took posts down.[419]

Both the State Attorney General and individual citizens will be allowed to sue social media companies that allegedly breach these rules. The law will apply to any social media providers with more than 50 million users active monthly and to anyone who lives in Texas, conducts business there or receives or distributes social media posts in Texas. Similar bills have been proposed in other U.S. states that have Republican administrations claiming that they wish to prevent "censorship." They justify their attempts to control social media firms in this way by claiming that social media platforms have become a kind of utility or "common carrier" similar to a telephone company.

Florida

As another example, Florida introduced a law, making it unlawful for social media platforms to ban some political candidates from their sites.

However, social media companies brought suit in opposition to this law and the court blocked enforcement of the law until legal challenges to the law could be decided.[420]

U.S. District Judge Robert Hinkle of the United States District Court for the Northern District of Florida said:

> This order preliminarily enjoins enforcement of the parts of the legislation that are preempted or violate the First Amendment.[421]

13.14.4 Foreign Interference in Elections

Using the Internet to interfere with foreign elections has become a significant problem in recent years, and this issue has been raised in many countries, including the recent presidential election of the United States.

418. D. McCabe, "Texas Foribids Political Çensorship' by Social Media Companies," *The New York Times*, online, September 9, 2021.
419. *Ibid.*
420. *Ibid.*
421. K. Singh, "Federal Judge Rules Florida Social Media Law Likely Violates Free Speech," *Reuters*, online, July 1, 2021.

As a result, the number of countries introduced laws to prevent and punish such interference. Because these laws may affect the desire of any Internet user who wishes to use the World Wide Web to express their political views and to persuade others (whether in their own country or in other nations) of the correctness of their political views, it is important to examine the legal status of this issue and the steps that have been taken to correct what is regarded as improper use of the Internet to influence or interfere with elections.

One of the most highly publicized incidents of alleged electoral interference has been highlighted by the conclusion of U.S. intelligence that Russia attempted to influence the U.S. presidential election in favor of Donald Trump during the 2016 presidential election.

After the election, the U.S. Director of the National Counterintelligence and Security Center, William Evanina, issued a report on foreign threats to U.S. elections in which he said:

> Foreign intelligence entities likely view US elections as an opportunity to; undermine confidence in our democratic institutions and processes, sow division in our society, weaken our alliances and promote their political, economic or ideological agendas. These entities operate in the seams of our democratic system to advance their interests, using the tools of traditional espionage, in combination with cyber operations to influence campaigns.[422]

The United States is not the only country that fears this kind of interference and is not the only country which has suffered from electoral interference.

Several countries have taken steps to prevent and punish this kind of interference.

An accepted international legal basis for countermeasures is that such interference can constitute a violation of a country's sovereignty. Several countries have accepted the principle that respecting a nation's sovereignty is a fundamental element of international law set out in The *Tallinn Manual 2.0: on the International Law Applicable to Cyber Operations.*[423]

The countries and international organizations that accept the respect for sovereignty, which is fundamental to international law, include: Austria, Czech Republic, France, Germany, Netherlands, Switzerland and NATO.[424]

An accepted definition of what constitutes a nation's sovereignty was set out in the 1928 Island of Palms arbitration by Max Huber:[425]

> Sovereignty in the relations between States signifies independence. Independence, in regard to a portion of the globe is the right to exercise therein, to the exclusion of any other State, the functions of a State.

422. Office of the Director of National Intelligence, Press Release, "Statement by NCSC Director William Evanina: Election Threat Update for the American Public," online at: dni.gov, August 7, 2020, accessed November 21, 2023.
423. Michael Schmitt, editor, published by the United States Naval War College (Newport, Rhode Island, U.S., 2017).
424. Michael Schmitt, EIJL, October 16, 2020.
425. Michael Schmitt, article, European Journal of International Law, EIJL: Talk!, October 16, 2020.

Singapore

On September 13, 2021, the government of Singapore proposed a parliamentary bill to prevent foreign cyber interference in Singapore politics. The bill is called the Foreign Interference (Countermeasures) Bill. It is targeted at online content that "can cause immediate and significant harm in Singapore."

Social media providers will be required to comply with the law, and ISPs could be required to block harmful political content.

The bill also would permit the blocking of any computer downloads that aid in spreading harmful content. This bill follows the anti-fake news law introduced in Singapore in 2019.[426]

13.14.5 Zero Click Spyware

One of the most sinister developments in online crime, illicit spying and violation of privacy generally has been the development of "Zero Click" spyware that allows hackers to access iPhones and iPads without the owners having to open or click on a file or a link.

This seems to be specific to the iOS operating system.

When this became widely reported in September 2021, Apple took urgent steps to correct this flaw in their system. In mid-September 2021, Apple announced that it had issued security updates to defend against what is described as a malicious PDF file.

This innovative spyware was apparently first recognized at the University of Toronto's Citizen Lab. They said that this spyware affected all Apple devices, including iPhones, Macs and Apple watches.

Toronto also claimed that this flaw was first exploited on an Arab activist's iPhone and that they suspected that an Israeli firm, the NSO group, may have created the spyware.

NSO refused to either confirm or deny its role in creating the spyware. It stated that it would:

> continue to provide intelligence and law-enforcement agencies ... with technologies to fight terror and crime.[427]

Experts pointed out that the use of spyware seems to be limited to specific high-value targets, so it may not be a worry for the general population of Apple users. Apple announced that it had issued defensive software patches in iOS 14.8 and iPad OS 14.8 software.[428]

The Zero Click spyware exploited a gap in Apple's iMessage, which was previously understood to be one of the safest messaging apps.

---

426. C. Lin, "Singapore Submits Bill to Fight 'foreign interference'," *Reuters*, online, September 13, 2021.
427. Joe Tidy, A BBC News Reporter, notes that NSO has been subject to accusations that its hacking has affected innocent people. J. Tidy, "Analysis," *BBC News*, online, September 14, 2021.
428. "Apple Rushes to Block 'Zero Click' Iphone Spyware," *BBC News*, online, September 14, 2021.

This was embarrassing for Apple not only because Apple likes to be known as having one of the most secure operating systems but also because it came to public attention during the time of the year when Apple likes to announce new and/or improved products (September). However, Apple did appear to respond quickly with solutions when it became aware of this problem, and as stated above, risk to average Apple users is pretty low.[429]

13.14.6 Death from Hacking

One of the more frightening aspects of hacking and cybercrime is the fact that many devices and systems critical to healthcare are accessible through the internet. In one sense, that makes it easier to operate and gather information from them about how they are working and how they are contributing to patient care. But on the other hand, this makes them vulnerable to interference from hackers and cybercriminals.

Hospital records, hospital networks, MRI machines and drug infusion pumps are all digitally accessible now. This puts them in danger of being hacked.[430]

One of the most sinister possibilities for hackers is that medically implanted devices could be vulnerable to interference. Among the implantable devices that have been found to be vulnerable are insulin pumps and pacemakers.[431]

There is a fictional story about this in the popular television series *Homeland*, where the actor Damien Lewis's character gives terrorists information about the American Vice-President's pacemaker, which the terrorists use to hack the pacemaker and kill him.[432]

This threat had a real-life parallel in 2013, when the former U.S. Vice-President, Dick Cheney, had the wireless connectivity of his pacemaker disconnected so it could not be hacked and put Cheney's life at risk.[433]

In 2019, the U.S. Food and Drug Administration for that some kinds of defibrillators had vulnerability that might allow unauthorized persons to manipulate them remotely.[434]

Unfortunately, this threat is becoming ever more real.

In September 2020, it was reported that prosecutors in Dusseldorf, Germany, launched a manslaughter investigation after a woman died in a hospital; thereafter, her emergency treatment was delayed for more than an hour. It is thought that her death may have been caused by hackers shutting down the hospital's IT systems. Dusseldorf University Hospital was locked out of its computer systems and a blackmail message was received, giving digital directions for contacting the hackers. The police informed

429. J. Tidy, "Analysis," *BBC News*, online, September 14, 2021.
430. J. McKinley, "5 Medical Devices You Didn't Know Could Be Hacked," https://www.thehealthy.com/healthcare/hacked-medical-devices/.
431. J. Best, "Could Implanted Medical Devices Be Hacked?," *British Medical Journal*, January 14, 2020, https://www.bmj.com/content/368/bmj.m102.full.
432. McKinley, above.
433. Best, cited above.
434. *Ibid.*

the hackers that they had shut down the hospital systems, putting patients in danger. After that, the attack was abandoned, and systems were restored.[435]

13.14.7 Quantum Computing

Another looming challenge to cybersecurity is the dramatic progress that is being made to computer equipment in the form of "quantum computers."

Computers today, or "classical" computers as they are coming to be known, operate digitally in segments of information that are called "bits." A bit can express one of two possible outcomes, 1 or 0. These values represent states that are on or off. All classical computer programs and operations are created from combinations of those two possible positions. Every computing operation we do now is made up of millions of combinations of on or off (1 or 0).

The necessity to operate computers by instructing them with various combinations of those two numbers, some quite long, places limitations on the speed with which computer operations can be completed. Of course, over the past few decades, the computer chips that perform those operations have become increasingly faster, so computer speed is now much greater than it was several decades ago.

However, computer scientists are now working on developing a computer instruction system that operates not in "bits" but in "qubits." This proposed computing system is based on the field of physics known as quantum mechanics. This field of physics was created to try to understand the natural world better. Nature does not operate by choosing between only two possible known outcomes. Nature is more unpredictable. A "qubit," short for "quantum bit," permits examination of many more possible outcomes than just two. Employing this device in computing could make computing operations exponentially faster.[436]

Until late in 2019, it was thought that quantum computing was still a long way away. However, in October 2019, everything changed. In the journal *Nature*, Google announced that a quantum computing system developed by Google had achieved "quantum supremacy," meaning that it could complete calculations much faster than the fastest "supercomputers" existing up until then.

Google's Sycamore quantum system completed a calculation that would take 100,000 classical computers 10,000 years to complete. The truly amazing thing is that Sycamore represents quantum computing at its most primitive. It is expected that soon quantum computers will be much more powerful. Sycamore is a 53 qubit system, but it is believed that future quantum computing systems could operate on billion qubit systems.[437]

What does this mean for cybercrime? Far too much.

435. D. Crossland, "Woman Dies after Hackers Hit A&E," *Times*, online, September 19, 2020, retrieved September 19, 2020.
436. A. Katwala, "Quantum Computing and Quantum Supremacy, Explained," *Wired*, online, March 5, 2020, retrieved September 3, 2020.
437. S. Aaronson, "Why Google's Quantum Supremacy Milestone Matters," *The New York Times*, online, October 30, 2019, retrieved September 3, 2020.

If criminals are able to access quantum tools and the skills that enable them to crack the security systems that individuals and even major companies have in place to protect their information, how much more powerful would criminal hacking groups be? There is no reason not to believe that it would improve their ability to crack protective codes and security systems to an exponential degree. That is a frightening prospect and causes one to wonder whether it will be possible to create any truly safe passwords and security systems in the future when quantum computing becomes more generally available.

Fortunately, scientists are already working to solve this potential problem. Two technological solutions are currently being worked on to provide greater security in the face of potential quantum intrusion.

The first is Quantum Key Distribution (QKD). This is a method of agreeing on encryption keys between distant parties to protect security keys from being observed or tampered with.

The second anti-quantum attack protection method is Quantum Randon Number Generation. This produces numbers random numbers at such high speeds that the numbers can be unpredictable and can form an important part of hacking-resistant security systems.[438]

One can only hope that the development of security technologies can match the pace of the development of quantum computing and the application of this powerful new technology by criminal hacking groups.

This discussion begs the question of whether possession or access to such powerful computing tools should be legally restricted and/or regulated in some way. That is a difficult question. Of course, societies have traditionally used their legal powers to restrict the ownership, possession and use of technological advances that are deemed to be particularly dangerous. Such concerns have resulted in restrictions on firearms, explosives, nuclear technology, automobiles and other technological advances that, although their existence is considered to have benefits, also present different types and degrees of danger to the public.

13.14.8 Online Abuse

It is not news that the Internet, and particularly the social media sites, are full of abusive, insulting and sometimes threatening posts. For Internet service companies and law-enforcement agencies, it is not easy to decide what to do about them.

The first issue has to do with the interstate and international aspects of the Internet. Social media sites operate on the World Wide Web. Who has jurisdiction to control and police them? The second issue has to do with when these posts cross the line from being offensive to becoming criminal activity.

438. UK Government, White Paper, "Quantum Security Technologies," https://www.ncsc.gov.uk/whitepaper/quantum-security-technologies, online, March 24, 2020, retrieved September 7, 2020.

The type of Internet posts that need reaction can be divided into two basic categories. The first is those Internet posts that constitute illegal hate activity. The second constitutes posts which threaten death, destruction or other physical harm.

The first category of activity will depend on what constitutes illegal speech in any particular jurisdiction. This varies from nation to nation. Sometimes, it has to do with insulting or demeaning those of a particular racial or ethnic background. Other times, it has to do with insulting or demeaning particular religious beliefs.

It might constitute insulting, demeaning or challenging government activity.

There is no universal standard for controlling offensive Internet posts. A significant problem in many jurisdictions is that there are often constitutional protections for freedom of speech that excuse a wide range of speech, including Internet posts, which certain individuals or societal might find offensive.

There is the additional consideration in those jurisdictions of when a post has crossed the line going beyond the protections afforded by freedom of speech regulations. This all makes the area of what constitutes online abuse and how to deal with it complicated. The best one can do in this section is to give an outline of when the line of acceptability might be crossed and refer the reader to the jurisdictional sources that may be able to give a more detailed description of how particular posts will be regarded in particular jurisdictions.

Threats of Violence

With threats of violence, it is true that the majority of these do not lead to actual physical harm. However, that is not always the case. Sometimes, people who threaten physical violence act on it.

There have been a number of cases where people who threatened terrorist activity later went on to carry it out by planting bombs or engaging in personal attacks, injuring or killing those they considered to be enemies of their ideology or even innocent persons such as school children.

The standard for judging threatening posts like these seems to be whether a "reasonable person" would consider that a threat was serious enough that it may be expected to lead to criminal acts.[439]

Law-enforcement authorities are in the difficult position of having to judge which threats have crossed the line into criminal behavior. This is often a tricky proposition because a number of countries, such as the United States, have freedom of speech protections written into their constitutions. So, it is generally considered that broad threats such, as let us put Donald Trump back in power, or let us arrest all Democrats, are considered too general to justify prosecution.[440]

439. S. Ovide, "When Is Online Nastiness Illegal?" *The New York Times*, online, April 23, 2021, accessed, April 26, 2021.
440. *Ibid.*

U.S.

In the United States, it is uncommon for someone to be criminally prosecuted based on things they have said, written or otherwise expressed as a type of speech. However, there have been prosecutions that are worth discussing.

For example, a California man who wrote on a blog about cutting off the heads of employees of the FBI did face criminal prosecution based on those expressions. He claimed that his blog was satire and therefore protected speech. He went to trial but was ultimately not convicted. His defense made the arguments that he never made any preparations to follow through with such action and that he had no plans to do so. Neither he nor anyone acting on his behalf had purchased any weapons or taken any actions that could reasonably be thought to be following through to execute those thoughts.[441]

The government of the United States usually sets a high standard before deciding to prosecute someone for things they have said or written that might constitute threats or would otherwise upset people who are the targets of those things.

Generally, only specific threats that would cause reasonable people to believe that the maker intended to follow through with harming persons targeted will lead to prosecution. It is believed that speech that does not rise to this level should be permitted by social media companies that allow people to express themselves on their systems.[442]

The EU

Although it is the case that there are no universal international protection standards against criminal behavior on the Internet, the EU is making efforts to create regulations to protect users. One that has become an international standard is the GDPR of 2018.

There has been no formal universal adoption, but a number of countries outside the EU have used the GDPR as a model for developing their own data protection regulations.[443]

Moving on, the EU is now proposing regulations to govern use of AI. The proposed regulations are outlined in an EU White Paper entitled "On Artificial Intelligence—A European approach to excellence and trust."[444] The Paper says that the EU's goals are to encourage the adoption of AI while dealing with the risks entailed by certain uses of this technology.[445]

441. *Ibid.*
442. *Ibid.*
443. E. Lucas, "EU Is Becoming Policeman of the Internet," *The Times*, online, April 26, 2021, accessed April 27, 2021.
444. European Commission, February 19, 2020, COM (2020) 65 final, online, accessed April 27, 2021.
445. EU Paper, p. 1.

13.15 GROWING INTERNATIONAL COOPERATION

One positive development is that the international growth of cybercrime is beginning to inspire parallel growth in international cooperation against cybercrime.

At their meeting in England in June 2021, the G7 countries agreed to increase international cooperation against cybercrime. Ursula van de Leyen, the President of the European Commission, said:

> We need a robust joint response to cybercrimes especially ransomware. We agreed to step up information sharing and to coordinate more closely on police investigations and diplomatic measures.[446]

13.15.1 The Budapest Convention and Other International Standards

The leading international treaty that provides standards for framing national standards for implementing national anti-cybercrime laws, regulations and guidelines for international cooperation is the Budapest Convention on Cybercrime and the related Protocol on Xenophobia and Racism Online.[447]

The Convention is a binding treaty, and there are currently 66 signatories (including the U.S., the U.K., Switzerland, Canada and most EU countries)[448] and 11 countries that consider themselves observers, such as Ireland, New Zealand, Sweden and Russia).

The Convention's main objective is to bring about a common legal policy aimed at the protection against cybercrime by encouraging the adoption of relevant laws and regulations and promoting international cooperation against cybercrime.

It was the first international treaty to focus on cybercrime, including crimes relating to the Internet and computer networks generally, dealing with such things as infringement of copyright, Internet-related fraud, child pornography and breaches of network security. It provides guidelines for the interception of offending information and the search of computer networks.[449]

---

446. United News of India, "G7 Agrees to Co-operate on Cybercrime Cases: EU," online June 13, 2021.
447. Council of Europe, online portal, https://www.coe.int/en/web/cybercrime/the-budapest-convention.
448. As of this writing, Parties: Albania, Andorra, Armenia, Argentina, Australia, Austria, Azerbaijan, Belgium, Bosnia and Herzegovina, Bulgaria, Cabo Verde, Canada, Chile, Columbia, Costa Rica, Croatia, Cyprus, Czech Republic, Denmark, Dominican Republic, Estonia, Finland, France, Georgia, Germany, Ghana, Greece, Hungary, Iceland, Israel, Italy, Japan, Latvia, Lichtenstein, Luxembourg, Malta, Mauritius, Moldova, Monaco, Montenegro, Morocco, Netherlands, North Macedonia, Norway, Panama, Paraguay, Peru, Philippines, Poland, Portugal, Romania, San Marino, Senegal, Serbia, Slovakia, Slovenia, Sweden, Switzerland, Spain, Sri Lanka, Tonga, Turkey, Ukraine, United Kingdom, and United States of America. The Observer countries are: Benin, Brazil, Burkina Faso, Guatemala, Ireland, Mexico, New Zealand, Nigeria, Niger, Russia (as a Member State of the Council of Europe, South Africa and Tunesia).
449. Council of Europe online portal: https://www.coe.int/en/web/conventions/full-list/-/conventions/treaty/185?module=treaty-detail&treatynum=185.

The Convention is made up of a Preamble and the following Articles:[450]

(1) Definitions.
(2) Illegal access.
(3) Illegal interception.
(4) Data interference.
(5) System interference.
(6) Misuse of devices.
(7) Computer-related forgery.
(8) Computer-related fraud.
(9) Offenses related to child pornography.
(10) Offenses related to infringements of copyright and related rights.
(11) Attempt and aiding and abetting.
(12) Corporate liability.
(13) Sanctions and measures.
(14) Scope of procedural provisions.
(15) Conditions and safeguards.
(16) Expedited preservation of stored computer data.
(17) Expedited preservation and partial disclosure of traffic data.
(18) Production order.
(19) Search and seizure of stored computer data.
(20) Real-time collection of traffic data.
(21) Interception of content data.
(22) Jurisdiction.
(23) General principles relating to international cooperation.
(24) Extradition.
(25) General principles related to mutual assistance.
(26) Spontaneous information.
(27) Procedures pertaining to mutual assistance requests in the absence of applicable international agreements.
(28) Confidentiality and limitation on use.
(29) Expedited preservation of stored data.
(30) Expedited disclosure of preserved traffic data.
(31) Mutual assistance regarding accessing of stored computer data.
(32) Trans-border access to stored computer data with consent or where publicly available.
(33) Mutual assistance regarding the real-time collection of traffic data.
(34) Mutual assistance regarding the interception of content data.
(35) 24/7 Network.
(36) Signature and entry into force.
(37) Accession to the Convention.
(38) Territorial application.

450. Council of Europe online portal: https://rm.coe.int/1680081561.

(39) Effects of the Convention.
(40) Declarations.
(41) Federal clause.
(42) Reservations.
(43) Status and withdrawal of reservations.
(44) Amendments.
(45) Settlement of disputes.
(46) Consultations of the Parties.
(47) Denunciation.
(48) Notification.

There is an Additional Protocol to the Cybercrime Convention that deals with criminalization of racist and xenophobic acts online.[451] It contains 16 Articles dealing with racist and xenophobic threats and insults.[452]

13.15.2 GLACY Project

The original GLACY project (Global Action on Cybercrime) was set up to assist countries around the world in implementing the Budapest Convention. It was hoped that GLACY would result in positive changes in the following areas:

- Involvement of decision-makers.
- Harmonizing legislation.
- Training judges.
- Improving law enforcement capacity.
- Sharing information.
- Reviewing progress.

Its overall aim was to get up to 70 states to cooperate on cybercrime using the Budapest Convention as a common guide. The project ran from November 1, 2013 until October 31, 2016.

13.15.3 GLACY + Project

In October 2016, the EU and the Council of Europe set up a new joint project to combat cybercrime around the world named The Global Action on Cybercrime Extended "(GLACY +)" project.

Its purpose was to continue and use the experience gained under the original GLACY project. The principal participants in the project have been: Bernin, Burkino

451. Additional Protocol 189: Additional Protocol to the Convention on Cybercrime, concerning the criminalization of acts of a racist and xenophobic nature committed through computer systems. This was adopted in 2003 and came into force in 2006. https://rm.coe.int/168008160f.
452. The link to the text of the Additional Protocol is: https://rm.coe.int/168008160f.

Faso, Cabo Verde, Chile, Costa Rica, Dominican Republic, Ghana, Mauritius, Morocco, Nigeria, Paraguay, Philippines, Senegal, Sri Lanka and Tonga.

It was hoped that these countries would be "hubs" to educate other countries in their regions about the value of their experiences. The objectives of the GLACY+ project are formulated to improve the ability of countries around the world to have effective legislation against cybercrime, improve ways to use electronic evidence and improve international cooperation. These objectives were to be achieved by:

(1) Promoting consistent legislation, policy, and strategy.
(2) Strengthening police ability to investigate cybercrime andencourage cooperation between police forces and cybercrime offices around the world.
(3) To smooth and improve processes to prosecute cybercrime and improve international judicial cooperation.

The activities of the GLACY+ project have included:

- Holding workshops around the world, such as one in Burkina Faso in September 2021.
- Holding courses in international cooperation for judges and prosecutors, such as one in Costa Rica in August 2021.
- Holding training sessions improving cybercrime prosecution and the use of electronic evidence, such as one held in Paraguay in September 2021 for 34 magistrates, judges, and judicial training schools.

The above are just a few examples of the kinds of activities arranged through the GLACY+.

Others have included anti-cybercrime activities in Portuguese-speaking African countries, French-speaking African countries, East Timor, Tonga, Belize, etc., plus various international meetings to promote the objectives of GLACY+. Some of these activities are conducted live, others are held online.

In connection with the Project, the Council of Europe also maintains and offers a number of resources to draw upon, such as: reports, webinars, information about connections between cybercrime and COVID-19, and information about cyberviolence.

Cyberviolence is a phenomenon that has been getting more law enforcement attention. It is defined as:

> The use of computer systems to cause, facilitate, or threaten violence against individuals, that results in (or is likely to result in) physical, sexual, psychological or economic harm or suffering and may include the exploitation of the individual's circumstances, characteristics or vulnerabilities.[453]

453. Council of Europe, "What Is Cyberviolence," online at: coe.int, accessed November 21, 2023.

13.15.4 Cyberstalking and Cyberbullying

Using the internet to harass and/or intimidate people has become a widespread problem, and, as a result, a number of legal jurisdictions have adopted laws and regulations criminalizing such behavior.[454]

Cyberbullying is defined in the following ways:

- "Actions that use information and communication technologies to support deliberate, repeated and hostile behavior by an individual or group, that is intended to harm another or others;
- Use of communication technologies for the intention of harming another person;
- Use of internet service and mobile technologies such as web pages and discussion groups as well as instant messaging of SMS text messaging with the intention of harming another person."[455]

Cyberstalking, however, is a repeated pattern of such things as:

- false accusations;
- monitoring;
- making threats;
- identity theft;
- damage to data or equipment;
- solicitation for sex; or
- harassment.

Legislation Against Cyberbullying and Cyberstalking

For example, in the United States, U.S. Federal law does not yet include any specific legislation expressly forbidding cyberbullying or cyberstalking, but legislation criminalizing cyberbullying or electronic harassment has been proposed.

All U.S. states, as well as the District of Columbia, have legislation that criminalizes harassment and/ or stalking. Some specifically refer to such behavior on electronic media, but all are intended to protect the public regardless of the vehicle used.

13.16 THE DUTIES OF INTERNET PROVIDERS AND SOCIAL MEDIA PLATFORMS

As clearly one of the largest and most successful providers of social media platforms, with billions of users, Facebook has reportedly been subject to criticism alleging its failure to properly police the postings of its users.

454. International Human Rights and Privacy Protection Association. Online at ihprpa.org.
455. *Ibid.*

The dilemma is that it is not clear exactly what are the duties of media companies when it comes to editing and controlling how their platforms are used to post information or communicate on and access the World Wide Web.

There is no universal legal regulation governing what level of "honesty" they are required to comply with, what definition of "morality" they must aspire to, how they should decide what their users can do on their platforms, or under what circumstances they must restrict, penalize or ban the activities of their users.

In 2021, a publication in *The Wall Street Journal* alleged what the WSJ believed to be an unacceptable level of hypocrisy on the part of Facebook by publicly posting statements that Facebook knew to be untrue.[456] Among the objections of the WSJ to Facebook's behavior were allegedly allowing celebrities to post things that other users are not permitted to post, being slow to respond to charges that Facebook is used by drug dealers and people traffickers, allowing Facebook to allegedly become a hotbed of anti-vaccination posting when the Facebook founder, Mark Zuckerberg was claiming that Facebook would not be a site for promoting anti-COVID vaccination. Also, Facebook has, allegedly for several years, had information that its Instagram subsidiary causes anxiety and depression in teenagers which, in some cases, can lead to self-harm or even suicide.[457]

These allegations have reportedly led to demands that effective regulation of social media platforms, such as Facebook and others, be brought into force.

One proposal is that the controlling executives of social media companies should be subject to personal liability, possible prosecution, and punishment if a company "breaches fundamental health and safety" rules, leading to "severe harm or death."[458]

456. As reported in *The Sunday Times* (which has the same parent company as WSJ), in the following online article, "Facebook's Hypocrisy Has Been Exposed in Painful Detail," September 19, 2021.
457. *Ibid.*
458. *Ibid.*

CHAPTER 14
Cyberwar

14.1 CYBERWAR IS HERE

In September 2019, PC Magazine published an article entitled "Cyberwar Is Here: Are You Ready?"[459]

The article pointed out that the U.S. and its allies and adversaries have powerful digital weapons at their disposal. But the point of the article was not only that nations are able to deploy these weapons against each other to disrupt military (such as nuclear development projects)[460] and infrastructure systems (such as power grids) that are accessible over the Internet, but that they can be used to affect all of us that use the Internet by disrupting the economic and communication systems that that much of the world's population use and depend on.

Given the fact that any device that can connect to the Internet can be hacked and remotely controlled, cyber war can be used to bring domestic and economic disruption, and perhaps paralysis, to each of us as individuals.

Many people use computer payment systems for shopping, digital security cameras to keep our homes safe, robot vacuum cleaners to clean them, and computer games and media streaming to keep our family members entertained. It is not difficult to imagine how disrupted people's lives could be if these and other Internet-accessible items were suddenly controlled by a hostile party.

And all these domestic disruptions could be in addition to infrastructure attacks on communications, power systems, water and gas grids, transportation systems and military operations systems.

These issues have made countries increasingly aware that important battles in the future will be fought not in the dirt of the earth but in the tech sphere. There is

459. https://www.pcmag.com/news/370753/cyberwar-is-here-are-you-ready.
460. Such as the U.S. and Israel are alleged to have done to Iran by deploying the Stuxnet Worm. http://large.stanford.edu/courses/2015/ph241/holloway1/.

considerable concern among the Western nations and the NATO allies that countries that may prove enemies of theirs in the future, particularly China, North Korea, Iran, and Russia, are developing increasingly more sophisticated ways of attacking the computer-controlled assets of other countries.

It is reported that NATO is subject to cyberattacks almost every day from hackers trying to get access to confidential information. The NATO Secretary General, Jens Stoltenburg, has said that in addition, the individual cellular phones of military personnel in the Baltic states were being hacked apparently to cause disruption of their activities.[461] In response, NATO has conducted military exercises simulating mass cyberattacks on military assets. A policy has also been adopted that in the case of heightened military threats, personnel will be told to turn off their cell phones and remove the SIM cards so that their movements and communications cannot be tracked.

One of the principal purposes of these hostile cyberattacks seems to be to gather information about NATO's military systems so that they can be remotely manipulated in the event of a future conflict.[462]

In March 2021, *The Times* published a report on a Ministry of Defense review of these issues, which said:

> Britain risks losing battles of the future to tech savvy China and Russia "without a shot being fired" unless it adapts, a senior military chief warned.[463]

The report pointed out that in the tech struggle, the power of large armies and conventional weapons will be less important than cyber-sophistication including knowledge of the construction and effective use of algorithms.

It has been reported that General Sir Patrick Sanders, the head of the U.K.'s Strategic Command, believes that:

> Cyber "warriors" will be as vital to protecting Britain as F35 pilots on aircraft carriers, special forces soldiers and some mariners operating the nuclear deterrent . . . .[464]

General Sanders said that included in future defense systems, AI machines would play an important role in defending humans:

> Even the best human operators cannot defend against multiple machines making thousands of maneuvers per second at hypersonic speed and orchestrated by AI.[465]

461. L. Brown, "Enemy Hackers Target Nato with Constant Cyberattacks," *The Times*, online, May 28, 2021.
462. *Ibid.*
463. L. Brown, "Military Chief Warns 'Algorithms Will Be Our Armour in High-Tech Wars of the Future'," *The Times*, online, March 13, 2021, accessed March 15, 2021.
464. L. Brown, "Cyber Warriors as Important to Our Safety as Fighter Jets Says General," *The Times*, online, May 27, 2021, accessed May 31, 2021.
465. *Ibid.*

14.2 CYBER WAR AND LAW

The issue of the importance of Internet-based knowledge in potential future conflicts raises a number of legal questions having to do with access to and the use of such knowledge.

In the present, little thought has been given to the issue of the spread of sophisticated understanding of computer technology and the Internet. This information is generally open to everyone in line with laws widespread in developed Western countries granting and protecting Freedom of Information.

The general approach seems to be that laws and regulations as applied to the cyber sphere are adequate if they can be used to punish misuse of the skills and information necessary to operate at a sophisticated level on the Internet. However, given the ability of the Internet to reach and direct the increasingly growing "Internet of Things," which includes those instruments and data sources that are reachable over the Internet, are these laws adequate? Might there be a need to refashion the legal system applying to the Internet to provide more specialized legal barriers to having certain categories of Internet knowledge at all?

This is not without precedent. Historically, a number of societies restricted certain important tools of communication to a limited number of specially trained and approved persons. For example, in ancient Mesopotamia, the important medium of cuneiform writing was restricted to specially trained and approved scribes who were allowed to use their skills only in the context of certain approved activities—largely related to the formation of commercial contracts but also related to particular governmental and or religious uses. Not everyone was provided with the training or permission to operate within the cuneiform writing system.

In medieval Europe, a similar situation existed with respect to published material. The right to produce published material was limited to printers' guilds such as the Stationers Guild in England. If one wanted to publish any writing at all, it would have to be done through the approved Guild.

It is now virtually impossible to run a nation or individual lives in the developed world without using computer systems connected to the Internet.

In fact, less and less of the data that is important to us as individuals is stored or accessed on our individual computer drives. Increasingly, data is stored in vast server farms that make up the infrastructure of "the Cloud" that keeps so much of the information we need.

It is true that these "cloud networks" are usually operated by digital giants such as Microsoft, Apple or Amazon. Of course, they make an effort to protect their cloud servers with sophisticated security systems. But cyber criminals and hackers, including those employed by government organizations, are constantly working to improve their abilities to get access to protected computer systems. Consequently, the press periodically reports huge data breaches affecting millions, at least one serious power outage, "ransomware" attacks and "denial of service" attacks. These are much more serious than the almost daily irritations that afflict us all, from "fishing" emails, fake "security" alerts, false messages from fake law-enforcement officials, and emails from fraudsters using hacked email accounts of our friends and acquaintances.

The point is that the penetration of the Internet has become so widespread that it can be used not only to irritate and defraud individuals but also to effectively disrupt or destroy the governing abilities of nations.

The impact of these cyber-crimes is huge, but still nowhere near the potential impact cyberattacks could have, given the huge adoption of Internet use currently ongoing and the future potential of the growth of Internet use.

There are currently 3.9 billion users of the Internet worldwide. There are approximately 800 million in China, around 500 million in the EU and about 300 million in the U.S.

It is estimated that within the next 10 years, most of the world's population will be connected to the Internet.

14.3 COLLECTING OUR INFORMATION

The COO of SoftBank believes that there will be over 1 trillion devices connected by the Internet by 2025.[466] The frightening vulnerability of that is that any device that connects to the Internet can be "hacked" and probably controlled by the hacker.[467]

A recent wide-ranging study, done jointly by Imperial College in London and Northeastern University in Boston, Massachusetts, U.S., examined over 80 devices that connect to the Internet, such as speakers, doorbells, smart TVs and other things from major suppliers, including Amazon and Google.

They discovered that most of these devices collected information such as IP addresses, MAC addresses, user habits and location information and sent it to third parties even if the user of the device didn't have any relationship with those parties or any knowledge that this information was being shared with third parties. More than 70 of the devices were found to be making contact with parties other than the device manufacturer. "Smart TV" sellers seem to be particularly guilty of ignoring the privacy of their users. It has been reported that Vizio was sued for secretly recording and marketing usage information about more than 15 million Vizio owners, and Samsung has been criticized for gathering and storing user data. The vulnerability of all these Internet-connected devices to hacking, data gathering and eavesdropping would be of significant interest to national intelligence agencies around the globe.[468]

14.4 ATTACK ON AUSTRALIA

In June 2020, the Australian government reported that it had been the subject of sophisticated state-sponsored cyberattacks on its businesses and institutions. The Australian Prime Minister refused to identify the suspected source of these attacks, but there is suspicion that they emanated from China, a country with which Australia had been having difficult relations. It was pointed out that China, Russia and North Korea

466. venturebeat.com,softbank-believes-1-trillion-connected-devices-will-create-11-trillion-in-value-by-20
467. fastcompany.com/you-can-hack-almost-any-smart-device-with-a-google-search.
468. vice.com,gyzjym/the-internet-of-things-is-still-a-privacy-dumpster-fire-study-finds.

were the only countries with whom Australia was not aligned that had the capabilities to undertake such attacks.[469]

It was reported that such attacks were aimed at "all levels of government," essential services and a number of businesses. The attacks were said to have occurred over many months and were increasing.

Attacks were being observed on "government, industry political organizations, education, health, essential service providers and operators of other critical infrastructure." For example, the Australian National University said it had been attacked by a sophisticated operation that accessed staff and student details.[470]

It was noted that although it has been subject to many attacks, Australia was not unique in this regard, and similar attacks have been identified in other countries.[471]

14.5 INCREASING ATTACKS WORLDWIDE

The overseas threat from hackers that appear to be sponsored by foreign governments is continually increasing.

For example, during the summer of 2017, two major computer viruses attacked sites in the Western world. The first was the WannaCry virus that was believed to be a North Korean-backed hacker attack that encrypted the data of target companies and individuals and demanded ransom money to release the target's data. This affected, among others, parts of the German Railway System and the United Kingdom's National Health System computers. The second was believed to be a Russian attack aimed at businesses in the Ukraine. However, this virus, called "Not Petya," hit what were apparently unintended targets, including the shipping company Maersk and a chocolate manufacturer in Australia.[472]

14.6 BUILDING DEFENSES

A number of countries have taken formal steps to defend against such attacks.

In 2017, the United Kingdom launched its National Cyber Security Centre as part of its national effort to protect the nation against cyberattacks. Ciaran Martin was its first head. From the three years that he had in the organization, he identified three important lessons from his experiences:

(1) Cyberattacks do not operate on their own. They are often part of a coordinated effort by a foreign nation to undermine security by having a target in a nation. Therefore, it is important for security services to counter the hostile

469. "Australia Targeted by 'State-Based' Cyber Attacks," *BBC News*, online, June 19, 2020.
470. *Ibid.*
471. *Ibid.*
472. C. Martin, "GCHQ Chief: The Threat of a Rogue Cyber-Attack Keeps Me Awake at Night," *The Times*, online, August 30, 2020, retrieved August 30, 2020, https://www.thetimes.co.uk/article/gchq-chief-the-threat-of-a-rogue-cyber-attack-keeps-me-awake-at-night-9lf8l6hb0?shareToken=fc12cc7cdfdf136fbe47db90f3361e5.

activities of foreign nationals that are conducted in more traditional ways as well as being sensitive to computer threats from a hostile foreign country.

It is important to be aware of the different kinds of penetration that foreign cyberattacks are aimed to achieve.

For example, Mr. Martin writes that Russian hacker groups tend to focus on national infrastructure targets such as energy systems, medical research and electoral processes.

Chinese hackers, however, have usually tended to seek economic advantages through the theft of intellectual property. However, Chinese hackers now also seem to be attacking important strategic technology as well.

Iranian hackers look for data that can help them track certain people, and they also try to disrupt services in countries that are suffering from unrest.

North Koreans try to use hacking to get money to fund their government.

(2) The second lesson is that a decent level of protection cannot be achieved without careful and skillful security management. Some of this is basic. For example, hacking is far more likely to be effective against organizations with outdated software. So it is important to keep software up to date.

Having good quality and regular backups is an excellent defense against ransom attacks based on encryption of the target's data.

(3) Third, it is important to keep barriers to data entry high. This is particularly important if one becomes the target of a hacker that cannot effectively control the virus being released. This can have a devastating effect on the target's systems and on the systems of others to whom the target is connected.[473]

Although Mr. Martin ceased being the head of the NCSC in 2020, he was recently quoted in *The Times* on the sensitive issue of how Chinese technology should be treated.[474] He predicted that in the future, Western countries, including Britain, would be much more cautious about the use of Chinese technology in computing and communication systems. Mr. Martin said that it had taken the West some time to realize that China was determined to become a strategic competitor and to challenge the West in a way it had not been since the end of the Cold War.

14.6.1 United Kingdom

However, Martin pointed out that the situation was different and more difficult than the opposition presented by the Soviet Union because the West did not have the extensive economic links with the Soviet Union that it had built with China. For example, he pointed to the extensive economic and other links that exist between China and a number of leading Western universities. This has provided China with a pathway to both information and technical penetration in some leading areas of developing Western technology.

473. Martin, above.
474. M. Bridge, "We Have Been Confused About China, Says Former GCHQ Cybersecurity Chief," *The Times*, online, March 15, 2021, accessed March 16, 2021.

This concern appears to be more than speculation. In early 2021, the think tank Civitas express the view that at least a dozen British universities maybe unknowingly helping the People's Liberation Army by exchanging information with universities and companies in China.[475]

This is not a problem that is limited to Britain. Chinese universities and Chinese students have been working hard for many years to establish meaningful relationships and or presence with leading universities throughout the world, including the U.S., Canada and many countries in Europe. What level of surveillance and caution is being exercised in those countries today now that there is a greater understanding of China's desire to increase its political and strategic power around the world?

Mr. Martin, who is now a professor at Oxford University, has urged the British government to clarify its policies on security, defense, development and foreign policy to better define it's response to the expansion of Chinese power enter to provide a better overall understanding of Britain's place in the world.

This increasing awareness of China's aggressive technological role has led to some backlash in Western countries. For example, in 2020, the British government announced that Huawei, the Chinese telecoms company, would be excluded from providing its equipment to British networks by 2027.

However, there is an excellent question as to whether the amount of time that Huawei has had its technology as part of the British system did not provide the Chinese with a long period to learn far too much information about the way that the British communication system is constructed and operated. Will merely replacing Chinese hardware with other substitutes be enough to undo any damage that was done between 2020 and 2027? After all, the reason that the British insisted on the removal of Chinese equipment from its infrastructure was because of the fear that such participation would offer the Chinese a dangerous opportunity to gather intelligence or even conduct sabotage operations in the future.

Does the British government have a detailed record of the extent and location of all Huawei products used in the British communication system? Will it in fact be possible to find and effectively remove all avenues of Chinese penetration into British communications infrastructure? Will the fact that China has had access to this British system for so long mean that British communications infrastructure will be eternally vulnerable to potential malicious Chinese interference?[476]

But although the United Kingdom considers China the "biggest state- based threat" to Britain's economic security, China is still are critically important trading partner to the U.K.[477] U.K. government advisors have reportedly prepared a 100-page report entitled, Global Britain in a Competitive Age, which identifies China's increasing international aggressiveness as an important risk to the interests of the U.K.[478] The report is said to assert that one of the biggest challenges for the U.K. is to maintain and

475. *Ibid.*
476. *Ibid.*
477. L. Brown & S. Swinford, "UK Plans Tighter Security to Allow Trade with 'Biggest Threat' China," *The Times*, online, March 16, 2021, accessed March 17, 2021.
478. *Ibid.*

expand protection of its critical infrastructure in electricity, transportation, and water while simultaneously seeking to establish more extensive trade links with China, including increasing Chinese investment in the U.K.

According to Sir Alex Younger, who was formerly head of Britain's intelligence agency MI6, it is a mistake to think that as China becomes more economically powerful, it will change its policies to become more like Western countries. According to Younger, it is more likely that China will become more attached to its Communist Party ideology.[479]

But the trickiest part for Britain is that having left Europe, Britain is searching for a new role in the world. In that context, they are trying to find the best way to deal with China, which is not only a powerful military and political competitor but also on its way to becoming the largest economy in the world, which presents potential trade opportunities that Britain may not be able to find elsewhere. In Britain's post-Brexit situation, these issues present complex diplomatic puzzles that Britain will have to try to solve very carefully.[480]

To counter this growing Chinese rivalry and threats from other potential international military and economic competitors which may be tempted to engage in cyberattacks and spread this information that affects the U.K., the government of the U.K. intends to create a secure "situation room" similar to what exists in the U.S. White House counter-terrorism officials from the police intelligence agencies and legal advisors gather to evaluate and respond to any such cyberattacks or other forms of terrorism.[481]

The presence of representatives from the legal and judicial sectors in the proposed team of counter-terrorism experts points to the sensitivity to responding to such threats in a way that is compatible with British legal tradition and policy. Although it is certainly important for the U.K. or any nation to respond quickly and forcefully to cyber and physical threats of terrorism or destabilization, it is important that Western democracies do not lose sight of the policies and limitations which support their commitment to democratic processes and the freedom of their citizens.

However, it must be recognized that there will be some conflict between balancing the British desire to maintain a good economic relationship with China in conjunction with protecting itself against cyberattacks on its infrastructure and the desire of some British politicians to punish China for such things as its reported treatment of the Uighur minority in China or its imposition of new laws in Hong Kong that diminish the abilities of the residents of Hong Kong to be able to rely on the protections of democracy.[482]

479. *Ibid.*
480. C. Philip, "'Global Britain' Must Tread a Fine Line Between China and America," *The Times*, online, March 16, 2021, accessed March 19, 2021.
481. Brown and Swinford, above.
482. *Ibid.*

14.6.2 United States

In October 2021, there was a similar reaction in America. It was reported that the U.S. had banned the top Chinese telecoms company, China Telecom, from operating in the United States because of "national security concerns." It was reported that U.S. officials thought that the Chinese government's involvement in that company gave them an opportunity to interfere with U.S. communications in harmful ways including conducting espionage.[483]

14.6.3 Continuing Cyber Threats

One particularly frightening aspect of cyber war that exists because of the markets created on the Dark Web is the fact that countries do not necessarily have to develop their own high-level hacking capabilities.

Expert hacking skills are for sale on the Dark Web. There are experienced hackers selling their abilities to use well-developed and especially well-tested hacking tools that can be put to use for the right price.

There are also hacking specialists that focus on a particular aspect of hacking, such as "system entry specialists" or skilled "data miners" who can be hired by those that wish to put together a team to launch a cyberattack.[484]

Russia apparently has no intention of abandoning its cyber war in the West. In September 2020, *The Times* reported that the software giant Microsoft had warned that Russian military hackers who had interfered with the 2016 U.S. Presidential election remained active, seeking to penetrate the digital data of U.S. political parties, political issue groups and political consultants who were working on the 2020 presidential election. There seems little doubt that future elections will also be targets.

There is also evidence that Russia continues to target news websites with opinion comments from pro-Russian trolls to try to influence international public opinion in favor of supporting Russia.

Their method is basically to insert pro-Russian comments in the opinion sections of articles appearing on Western media sites. The evidence for this is a study done by the Cardiff University Crime and Security Research Institute. This study examined over 30 well-known media websites in 16 countries. For example, the fall of Afghanistan to the Taliban allegedly gave the Russians opportunities to introduce comments that this event was a result of the failure of liberal democracy and the ineffectiveness of NATO. The comments also alluded to the weakness of Western countries supporting those institutions in their support of Ukraine against Russia.[485] The researchers indicated that this is a long-running campaign by Russia that shows no signs of tapering off.

483. "US Revokes License of Top Chinese Telecoms Company," *BBC News*, online, October 27, 2021.
484. Martin, above.
485. G. Corera, "Pro-Kremlin Trolls Target News Website Comments, Researchers Say," *The Times*, online, September 2021.

Microsoft also reported that China and Iran were attempting to access the email accounts of those affiliated with the November 2020 presidential election.[486]

One thing that is clear is that cyber war is becoming ever more intensive. A number of nations have apparently come to the conclusion that it is a low-cost and effective method of disrupting the operations of other countries that they consider to be hostile to them.

In September 2019, Microsoft Corp. reported that hackers in Russia are behind the largest number of cyberattacks on Microsoft customers. During the last two years, Microsoft has issued 13,000 alerts to its customers relating to hacking accounts by nation-states. It says that about 52% of those incidents originated from Russian hackers. The attacks have been a variety of things, including elections. Microsoft also reported that Iran is responsible for about 25% of such attacks and China for about 12%. Other nation-state attacks came from North Korea and a number of other countries.[487]

According to a report in *The Times*, the U.K. military is under daily attack from cyberhackers:[488]

> General Sir Patrick Sanders, Commander Strategic Command, outlined how the Ministry of Defense and its assets were under "constant attack" in cyberspace. Up to ten attacks daily are said to stem from hostile state actors.

The report said that the U.K. has developed cyber weapons to counter, disrupt and "even destroy" computer systems and infrastructure of such attackers.[489]

The U.K. maintains a Joint Cyber Unit in the Ministry of Defense facility in Corsham, Wiltshire, to deal with cyber problems.

There is a constant flow that needs attention. General Sanders said:

> Each year, the systems here manage millions of network and cyber events. Most are dealt with automatically, but around 1,800 per month—or 60 a day—require intervention.[490]

However, the U.K. does not consider its present defense systems to be enough and intends to set up a "National Cyber Force" modeled on one in the U.S., which would:

> fuse expertise in data analytics, machine learning and artificial intelligence, autonomy and robotics, synthetics, quantum, and 5G.[491]

486. H. Zefferman, "Russian Hackers Targeting US Poll, Warns Microsoft," *The Times*, online, September 11, 2020, retrieved September 11, 2020.
487. Bloomberg, online, September 30, 2020, retrieved October 1, 2020, https://www.livemint.com/news/world/microsoft-says-russia-behind-most-nation-state-cyber-attacks-11601444175751.html.
488. L. Fisher, "Military under Daily Blitz of 'Significant' Cyberattacks," *The Times*, online, September 26, 2020, retrieved October 1, 2020, scratchhttps://www.thetimes.co.uk/article/military-under-daily-blitz-of-significant-cyberattacks-5tspjc6nw.
489. *Ibid.*
490. *Ibid.*
491. *Ibid.*

Nations are increasingly understanding the importance of building and maintaining advanced capabilities to both launch and protect against cyberattacks. A phrase that is now commonly used when describing the importance and impact of cyber capabilities is "Information is Power":

> The core element that drives the digital society is digitalized information. Information is the key to how the digital society adds value and redistributes power.[492]

In 2003, the United States published a document entitled *The National Strategy to Secure Cyberspace* that set out the U.S. objectives to profit from the importance of cyberspace and to develop effective defenses against cyberattacks from hostile nations.[493]

A very serious matter is that cyber war may become a nuclear war. Indeed, nuclear powers are already considering that. It has been reported that the United Kingdom is considering the possibility of using nuclear weapons against any stage that inflicted a devastating cyberattack on British systems or infrastructure.[494] The report discussed above, Global Britain in a Competitive Age, said that the U.K. would reserve the right to review its policy on the use of nuclear weapons:

> if future threat of mass destruction, such as chemical and biological capabilities, or emerging technologies that could have a comparable impact, makes it necessary.

14.6.4 The SolarWinds Attack

That necessity is getting increasingly intense.

One of the most clever, sophisticated and devastating nation-state attacks on critical software of another country started in 2019 with penetration of the software of a U.S. company called SolarWinds. This attack is still being investigated and the United States has not yet decided what retaliation to take against the suspected attackers who are believed to be related to Russian intelligence.

SolarWinds is an important U.S. technology firm. They are responsible for creating a software system named "Orion," which is used by thousands of customers across the United States in the world to manage their IT systems. SolarWinds has over 30,000 customers that use Orion. Like any other major software manufacturer, SolarWinds sends periodic updates to its customers.

Many of these customers are large U.S. companies and important federal and state government organizations. The Pentagon, the Department of Homeland Security, the Department of Energy, the Nuclear Security Administration, the State Department and the Treasury are among the many users of Orion. So are Microsoft, Intel and Cisco, among many other high-profile tech companies.

492. S. Park, *Information Is Power* (Springer, 2017), online, retrieved October 1, 2020. https://link.springer.com/chapter/10.1057/978-1-137-59332-0_8#:~:text=Information%20is%20the%20key%20to,once%20shared%20on%20digital%20networks.
493. L. Anderson, "Countering State-Sponsored Cyber Attacks: Who Should Lead?" *information as Power*, online, retrieved October 1, 2020.
494. L. Brown, C. Philip & K. Burgess, "Britain Could Respond to Future Cyberattack with Nuclear Strike," *The Times*, March 17, 2021, online, accessed March 18, 2021.

What the hackers did was extremely clever. They broke into SolarWinds Orion and planted a will hidden malicious software in the updates that SolarWinds sent to its customers. This malicious software allowed the hackers to get access to the IT systems of the customers that received these updates and to gather sensitive and critical information from those IT systems. Although Russia has denied any involvement in this penetration, major software companies like Microsoft firmly believe that the hackers are connected to Russian intelligence.

The extent of the damage of this wide-ranging attack has not yet been fully assessed. But it does come as a major shock to those responsible for securing the safety of critical IT systems in the United States. The U.S. does fund a cybersecurity command that has responsibility for protecting America's online networks. However, they do not seem to have been prepared to fend off this kind of attack.

What the full nature of the U.S. response will be remains to be seen but may involve serious sanctions against Russia and or any other nation-state that is found to have participated in or facilitated this attack.

President of the U.S., Joe Biden, said in July 2021 that he believed that the president of Russia, Vladimir Putin, could shut down the Russian hackers believed to be responsible for a number of important hacking attacks if he wished to do so.

The hacking gang, REvil, is believed to be operating out of Russia. They are thought to have targeted around 250 businesses with ransomware attacks between 2019 and 2021. From this criminal activity, they are believed to have extorted around $100 million. One Russian hacking expert has said, "it only needs one person to come after them: Putin ... If he goes after them they are all done very quickly."

It remains to be seen whether Putin can be persuaded to take decisive action to end the hacking attacks that are believed to originate from Russia. President Biden has said that the U.S. will take action to protect its businesses and infrastructure against hacking attacks and that if Russia took no action to curtail the attacks originating from there, the U.S. would take retaliatory action.[495]

Exactly what that retaliatory action would be is not clear.[496] Biden did say that in his communications with Putin, "I made it very clear to him that the United States expects went around somewhere operation is coming from his soil, even though it's not sponsored by the state, we expect them to act if we give them enough information to act on who that is."[497]

What is clear is that hacking to damage the information systems of third parties either to cripple important infrastructure assets or to extract money will continue for sometime. Major efforts at international cooperation will be needed in order to put an end to the serious infrastructure and economic damage that is now being inflicted on hacking targets.

495. M. Bennetts, "Putin Could Call Off Hackers If He Wanted," *The Times*, online July 11, 2021.
496. D. Charter & T. Parfit, "We Will Retaliate If You Hack Us, Joe Biden Tells Vladimir Putin," *TheTimes*, online, July 10, 2021.
497. *Ibid.*

14.6.5 Russian Hacking Attack on U.S. Food Production

Despite the warnings of President Biden to Russian President Putin, Russian hacking attacks on important U.S. resources do not seem to have let up.

In September 2021, a group of Russian cybercriminals called Black Matter, which is believed to be based in Russia, attacked the computer systems of Neo Cooperative, an organization of soy and grain farmers that has over 8,000 members and forced their systems to close down which interrupted food supply and feeding schedules for millions of chickens, hogs and cattle being raised in the United States.

The hackers threatened to publish Neo Co-op's confidential data unless they were paid nearly $6 million in ransom. In response, Neo Co-op said that they took their systems offline to protect them.[498]

14.6.6 Chinese Attack on Japan

The U.S. and its NATO allies are not the only countries subject to Chinese military cyberattacks. And employee of the Chinese military was accused by Japan of hacking into pop to 200 Japanese organizations including the Japanese space agency. Another Chinese hacking group is thought to be guilty of other cyberattacks against South Korea and Japan. Among the tactics used by these alleged Chinese cyber attackers is the theft of sensitive emails to use them for purposes of distributing malware into the systems of important companies and organizations.[499]

14.6.7 The North Korean Heist

One of the most audacious allegedly state-sponsored hacking attacks by one country on another was an attempt biohacking group, allegedly under orders from the government of North Korea, to try to steal about $1 billion from the country of Bangladesh.

The alleged attempt occurred in 2016. The circumstances are far too complex to describe in detail here but an outline of what happened follows. For a more detailed description of the theft, the BBC published and informative report in June 2021.[500]

Using a complex series of transfers and carefully planned timing, North Korea allegedly tried to steal about $1 billion from the national bank of Bangladesh. They were trying to steal the money from the account of Bangladesh at the U.S. Federal Reserve Bank in New York. Ultimately, the hackers reportedly got away with about $80 million, but they were prevented from getting the whole amount because a small bank in Manila the hackers had chosen to send the money to raised suspicions at the Fed. Nevertheless, losing $80 million was painful for Bangladesh.

498. "Russian Hackers Target US Food and Grain Production," *The Times*, online, September 23, 2021.
499. G. Blair, "Japan Accuses Chinese Military Hacker over Cyberattacks," *The Times*, April 20, 2021, accessed May 7, 2021.
500. "The Lazarus Heist: How North Korea Almost Pulled Off a Billion-Dollar Hack," *BBC News*, online, June 21, 2021.

The worst consequences of the hack were prevented, but this is undoubtedly far from the last North Korean hack attack that the world will experience.

Many reports have been published detailing how North Korea spends a significant part of its national wealth to make itself a powerful force on the Internet.

North Korea allegedly takes children with remarkable mathematical skills at an early age and places them in programs that teach them sophisticated computer skills. Some of the schools that focus on developing the skills are located in China, and others are found in North Korea. But, the alleged intent of these programs is to give North Korea the power to damage and steal from countries that they believe oppose them.

The remarkable thing about the Internet is that it gives a relatively small country with fewer resources the power to do significant damage to those who are believed to be its enemies. Small countries can inflict damage without having the financial, manufacturing, or natural resources to compete with much bigger countries such as the United States.

The secrecy and clandestine manner of these attacks make it possible for North Korea to continuously deny their involvement in such attacks while still reaping the resources and benefits that such international attacks can bring them.

These factors present serious difficulties for countries that are targeted by North Korea, both in terms of proving that the attacks are sponsored by the government of North Korea and deciding how to respond to these hacking attacks.

Because of the international nature of these hacking attacks, it will undoubtedly be necessary to form international organizations and to have in place international treaties to detect, counter and punish such behavior.

14.6.8 Russian Hacking German Parliament

Apparently, U.S. politics is not the only target of Russian hackers.

Reuters has cited a report in *Der Spiegel* that German government officials have found that the email accounts of members of the German parliament have been hacked apparently by a hacking group called "Ghostwriter," which is believed to be a creature of the Russian military intelligence group, the GRU. This is reportedly not the first time that Germany has suffered Russian digital interference. It is also reported that in 2015, emails from Angela Merkel's office were hacked, as was other German parliamentary information.[501]

14.6.9 Former U.S. Intelligence Agents Hack for UAE

One of the more slippery things about the Internet is it it permits users to operate from anywhere in the world. In the peaceful commercial sector, the value of this was shown during the COVID-19 pandemic when billions of employees around the world worked

501. Reuters Staff, "Russian Hackers Target German Parliament Again: Der Spiegel," *Reuters*, March 26, 2021, accessed, September 8, 2021.

from home in order to avoid unnecessary contact that might have contributed to spreading the virus.

However, this flexible ability to work at a distance also enables the intelligence agencies of any country in the world to employ experts from any other country that suits their purposes—whether peaceful or more sinister.

An unfortunate example of the advantages of this flexibility occurred in 2021 when three former U.S. intelligence personnel pled guilty to breaking U.S. laws and engaging in hacking projects for the United Arab Emirates.[502]

The men pled guilty to computer fraud, gaining fraudulent access to relevant devices, and violations of export controls, for which they were fined a total of $1.7 million.

It is reported that they worked for the UAE, allegedly doing things including hacking into server computers and phones around the globe.[503]

14.7 REMOTE OPERATION OF CONVENTIONAL WEAPONS

There is a great deal written above about the power of digital weapons and how they are disrupting the defense, infrastructure and political systems of targeted countries.

However, one of the most sinister developments in digital warfare is the creation of tools that can control conventional weapons over the Internet from a remote location.

One of the most shocking incidents of this type of cyber warfare took place in 2021 when Israel allegedly assassinated Iran's principal nuclear scientist, Mohsen Fakhrizadeh.

It is reported that Israel wanted to kill him for more than a decade, but in 2021, it finally happened using a remotely controlled machine gun mounted on a truck by the side of the road, which unleashed a stream of bullets at Fakhrizadeh's car as he drove it past with his wife as a passenger.

Israeli operatives reportedly smuggled the pieces of this robot machine gun into the country and assembled it to fit in the back of a pickup truck commonly seen in Iran. They also allegedly packed the truck with bombs so that it could be destroyed after the assassination, thereby eliminating much of the evidence relating to the plan.

The robot was controlled via computer systems 1,000 miles away communicating by means of a satellite.

As the car drove by, the remote operator used the machine gun, with the help of computerized cameras also attached to the truck, to target and unleash a stream of bullets that killed Fakhrizadeh almost instantly but left his wife untouched. The truck was then blown up.

Using this type of setup was unexpected and confusing. Iranian news sources first reported that Fakhrizadeh had been killed by a group of assassins in the furious gun

502. "Three ex-US Intelligence Officers Admit Packing for UAE," *BBC News*, online, September 17, 2021.
503. *Ibid.*

battle with the scientist's bodyguards that left several people dead. It took a while for him to understand what actually had happened.[504]

It is reported that over the years, Israel has allegedly arranged for the assassination of a number of Iranian nuclear scientists and military personnel. However, this is the first known instance where the operation was conducted remotely but with extraordinary precision that killed only the target.

This is of course very different than the results that occur when remotely controlled drones are used, which often cause the deaths of innocent bystanders as well as targets for assassination.

There seems a little doubt that hostile nations may continue to order assassinations of those who are considered a threat, and remote-controlled conventional weapons appear to put an important new tool at their disposal.

Beyond that, this type of assassination also alerts other technically savvy countries to the possibilities of conducting remote operations over the Internet using a widening a variety of robot weapons of all sizes, even down to nanorobots.

504. This account is adapted from an article by R. Bergman & F. Fassihi, "The Scientist and the A.I.-Assisted, Remote Control Killing Machine," *The New York Times*, online, September 18, 2021.

CHAPTER 15
EU Law

As a regulatory body, the EU is strongly influential with many of the regulations they have adopted being copied around the world.[505] This is the so-called Brussels effect, where EU policies have become a global standard in many areas, including data protection, financial services and competition law. Many of the areas of law where the EU has been influential are covered in tother publications.

The purpose of this chapter is to concentrate on the influence of EU law on the cyber world, particularly on growing market for AI.

There is no doubt that the EU is keenly interested in the progress of the development of the cyber world.

As early as April 2021, *The Economist* reported that the EU was interested in becoming "the world's super regulator in AI." The EU confirms this by stating:

> The EU aspires to be the global leader in safe AI.[506]

On April 21, 2021, the European Commission first published its proposed regulations on AI. The EU was the first major regulator to propose an overall legal regulation for AI.[507]

The campaign of the EU to establish itself as a world leader in AI is complex involving legislation, regulation and international politics. In each of these areas, the EU has been active and aggressive in moving ahead.

15.1 EU DRAFT AIA

The early proposals evolved into the AIA in 2021.

505. "The EU Wants to Become the World's Super Regulator in AI," *The Economist*, online at: economist.com, April 24, 2021.
506. European Commission, "AI Act Enters into Force," online at: commission.europa.eu, August 1, 2024.
507. *Ibid.*

The EU AIA, which came into force on August 1, 2024, is the first major jurisdiction legislation proposed for comprehensive regulation of AI.

However, the EC states that the AIA "will be fully applicable two years later, with some exceptions, prohibitions will take effect after six months."[508]

The AIA divides AI systems into four categories.[509]

The first includes applications and systems which present an "unacceptable risk." These include government social scoring systems similar to those used in China. These are banned under the AIA.

The second includes "high risk" applications, such as one that scans CVs and ranks job applicants according to specific legal requirements. These must comply with strict requirements such as incorporating risk mitigation systems, high-quality data sets, clear user information, competent human oversight, etc.

The third applies "specific transparency risk" systems, such as chatbots. These are required to clearly inform users that they are interacting with a machine. Also, certain kinds of AI-generated content must be so-labeled.

The fourth category applies to those applications and systems that are neither banned nor listed as high-risk. Examples are: "spam filters" or AI-enabled games. This category will be largely unregulated.[510] Firms producing or using them may wish to comply with voluntary codes of conduct.

The EU's Future Life Institute (FLI) describes AI applications as follows:

> AI applications influence what information you see online by predicting what content is engaging to you, captures and analyzes data from faces to enforce laws or personalized advertisements, and are used to diagnose or treat cancer. In other words, AI affects many parts of your life.

On its website, the FLI expresses the view that the EU AIA could become a "global standard" for AI regulation. They point to a law proposed in Brazil in late September 2021 that is influenced by the EU AIA.[511]

At a meeting of the G7 in Japan in late April 2023, the EU's technology regulation head, European Commission Executive Vice-President Margrethe Vestager, reportedly said that the G7 meeting showed that Europe was not alone in wanting sensible AI regulation.[512]

508. European Commission, "AI Act," online, accessed on October 10, 2024, at: digital-strategy.ec.europa.eu.
509. EC, "AI Act Enters into Force."
510. "The Artificial Intelligence Act," *Future Life Institute*, online at: artificialintelligenceact.eu. This is a website maintained by the Future of Life institute (FLI). The FLI claims that it has two key priorities: first, to promote the beneficial development of AI and, second, to regulate lethal autonomous weapons.
511. FLI, online at: artificialintelligenceact.eu.
512. Kantaro Komiya, "G7 Should Adopt 'Risk-based' AI Regulation, Ministers Say," *Reuters*, online, May 1, 2023.

15.1.1 Second Draft Additions

On April 27, 2023, it was announced that the EU had a preliminary agreement on a second draft of the AIA. Executive Vice-President Vestager announced that the EU hoped to be able to reach an agreement on AI law within 2023. It took a year longer.

Additions in the second draft included specific copyright protection for "generative AI" (AI that creates things such as documents or songs) and such things as transparency obligations for AI-generated music and pictures as well as copyright issues and it noted that perceived educational risks would reportedly be covered by the legislation.[513]

The final EU AIA was projected to deal with such things as fake news and other disturbing products that generative AI is seen to be able to create.

At the G7 meeting in Japan in April 2023, the French Minister for Digital Transition, John Noel Barrow, is reported to have said that France intended to provide relevant exceptions for small AI developers in the final EU AIA.[514]

15.1.2 June 2023 Amendments

In June 2023, EU legislators agreed to add stricter amendments to the AIA.[515]

These included:

- A ban on using AI for biometric surveillance.
- The requirement that any copyrighted data used to train AI systems, such as generative systems like ChatGPT, needed to be disclosed.

Thierry Breton, the EU head of Industry, also agreed to travel to the U.S. in June 2023 to meet with Open AI's CEO Sam Altman and with the Meta CEO Mark Zuckerberg.[516]

Following that meeting, which took place at the end of June 2023, both Altman and Zuckerberg expressed support for the EU's proposed regulation of AI.[517] Breton said:

> [T]hat he and Zuckerberg ... were "aligned" on the EU's regulation of artificial intelligence, ... They agreed on the bloc's risk-based approach and to measures like watermarking.

It is reported that Altman was also in agreement with the EU's approach. He praised the EU for having the foresight to take AI developments seriously and said he looked forward to working with the EU.

---

513. *Ibid.*
514. *Ibid.*
515. F.Y. Chee & S. Mukherjee, "EU Lawmakers Vote for Tougher AI Rules as Draft Moves to Final Stage," *Reuters*, online at: reuters.com, June 14, 2023.
516. *Ibid.*
517. J. Deutsch, "Zuckerberg, Altman Offer Support for EU Regulation of AI," *Bloomberg*, online at: bloomberg.com, June 24, 2023.

Breton was reported to be satisfied with his discussions saying that Meta was willing to submit to "stress tests" on the responses of Meta platforms to AI.

Breton also reported a meeting with Jensen Huang, the CEO of NVIDIA, the chipmaker producing powerful platforms that are important to power AI systems. Huang was also reported as satisfied with the meeting and indicated that NVIDIA may as well invest in Europe.[518]

15.1.3 Further Progress on the AIA

As of the beginning of September 2023, it was the goal of the EU to reach a final agreement on the AIA before the end of 2023. This goal was subject to the EU MPs' position (adopted in June 2023) that they would negotiate with the Member States over the final form of the law.

15.1.4 Statement on Rules

As of June 14, 2023, the European Parliament's statement of the state of the rules under the AIA was as follows:[519]

> "AI Act: different rules for different risk levels"
>
> "The new rules establish obligations for providers and users depending on the level of risk from artificial intelligence. While many AI systems pose minimal risk, they need to be assessed."

The description of the proposed rules under the AIA below is largely copied from the website of the European Parliament (updated as of June 14, 2023). On that website, they also offer an online PDF copy of the AIA available for download.[520]

15.1.5 AIA: Different Rules for Different Risk Levels

The new rules establish obligations for providers and users of AI depending on the level of risk from AI. While many AI systems pose minimal risk, they still need to be assessed.

Unacceptable Risk

Unacceptable risk AI systems are systems considered a threat to people and will be banned. They include:

518. T. Breton, "Excellent Exchange in Santa Clara with Nvidia CEO Jensen Huang," *Posted*, online at: @ThieryBreton, June 24, 2023.
519. European Parliament, "AI Act: First Regulation on Artificial Intelligence," online at: europarl.europa.eu, created June 8, 2023, updated June 14, 2023.
520. European Parliament, News, "EU AI Act: First Regulation on Artificial Intelligence," online at: europarl.europa.eu, created June 8, 2023, updated June 14, 2023.

- Cognitive behavioral manipulation of people or specific vulnerable groups: for example, voice-activated toys that encourage dangerous behavior in children.
- Social scoring: classifying people based on behavior, socio-economic status or personal characteristics.
- Real-time and remote biometric identification systems, such as facial recognition.

Some exceptions may be allowed: For instance, some remote biometric identification systems where identification occurs after a significant delay will be allowed to be used to prosecute serious crimes but only after court approval.

High Risk

AI systems that negatively affect safety or fundamental rights will be considered high-risk and will be divided into two categories:

(1) AI systems that are used in products falling under the EU's product safety legislation. This includes toys, aviation, cars, medical devices and lifts.
(2) AI systems falling into eight specific areas that will have to be registered in an EU database:
   - Biometric identification and categorization of natural persons.
   - Management and operation of critical infrastructure.
   - Education and vocational training.
   - Employment, worker management and access to self-employment.
   - Access to and enjoyment of essential private services and public services and benefits.
   - Law enforcement.
   - Migration, asylum and border control management.
   - Assistance in legal interpretation and application of the law.

All high-risk AI systems will be assessed before being put on the market and also throughout their lifecycle.

Generative AI

Generative AI, like ChatGPT, would have to comply with transparency requirements:

- Disclosing that the content was generated by AI.
- Designing the model to prevent it from generating illegal content.
- Publishing summaries of copyrighted data used for training.

Limited Risk

Limited-risk AI systems should comply with minimal transparency requirements that would allow users to make informed decisions. After interacting with the applications, the user can then decide whether they want to continue using it. Users should be made aware when they are interacting with AI. This includes AI systems that generate or manipulate image, audio or video content, for example, "deepfakes."

15.1.6 Next Steps in 2023

On June 14, 2023, MEPs adopted the Parliament's negotiating position on the AIA. The talks began with EU countries in the Council on the final form of the law.

The aim was to reach an agreement by the end of [2023].[521] But it took a little longer.

That agreement was reached, and the AIA came into force on August 1, 2024.

15.2 THE EU'S EXPANDING DIGITAL ROLE

It is certainly clear that the EU is holding itself out as a model for AI regulation.

In aid of this, the EU has developed several projects to support its regulation of AI. Among the policy measures that it is employing are the AI Innovation Package and the Coordinated Plan on AI:

> Together, these measures guarantee the safety on fundamental rights of people and businesses when it comes to AI. They also strengthen an uptake, investment and innovation in AI across the EU.

In February 2024, the Commission established the European AI Office (EAO) to oversee the Act's enforcement and implementation within the Member States.

The Commission has also introduced an AI Pact. This is a voluntary initiative to support future.

The AI Pact invites AI developers in Europe "and beyond" to comply with the key objectives of the AIA ahead of its full application.

As of the end of September 2024, the EC reports that "over 100 companies have signed EU AI Pact" pledges to drive trustworthy and safe AI development. These were all voluntary pledges.

15.2.1 The EU and the Cyber World

However, the EU's focus on AI is not an isolated interest.

The EU has passed a significant amount of legislation relating to the development and control of the cyber markets. More information about these can be found through the following links:

- Cyber currency dangers in the benefits of EU legislation.[522]
- Fighting cybercrime new EU cybersecurity laws explained.[523]
- Boosting data sharing in the EU what are the benefits?[524]

521. *Ibid.*, accessed September 5, 2023.
522. European Parliament, News, "Cybercurrency Dangers and the Benefits of EU Legislation," online at: europarl.europa.eu, created April 1, 2023; updated May 30, 2023.
523. European Parliament, News, "Fighting cybercrime: New EU Cybercurrency Laws Explained," online at: europarl.europa.eu, created November 10, 2022; updated May 30, 2023.
524. European Parliament, News, "Boosting Data Sharing in the EU: What Are the Benefits?," online at: europarl.europa.eu, created April 6, 2022; updated March 16, 2023.

- EU Digital Markets Act and the Digital Services Act.[525]
- Five ways the European Parliament wants to protect online gamers.[526]

It will remain to be seen how many other jurisdictions follow the models and advice set out in EU legislation, regulation and analysis.

One advantage of the EU legislation is that it does benefit from the input of a process of negotiations between 27 developed European countries. The process of agreeing on EU legislation does demonstrate how technically and commercially advanced countries can achieve consensus on the regulation of the economically important and rapidly developing cyber markets.

525. European Parliament, News, "EU Digital Markets Act and Digital Services Act Explained," online at: europarl.europa.eu, created December 14, 2021; updated August 24, 2023.
526. European Parliament, News, "Five Ways the European Parliament Wants to Protect Online Gamers," online at: europarl.europa.eu, created January 17, 2023; updated January 18, 2023.

CHAPTER 16
U.S. Law

16.1 DOING BUSINESS IN OR TO THE U.S.

The U.S. legal system is very complicated. There are both state and federal laws and legal systems to contend with.

16.1.1 State Law

This is because each of the 50 states has its own legal system that exercises jurisdiction over issues that are principally concerned with life and commerce within that state.

This means that each state has its own laws that deal with many regulatory sectors, including, but not limited to: banking, insurance, investment, transportation, contracts, taxes, crime, etc.

To enforce these laws, each state maintains its own law enforcement and court systems.

It would take an entire library to set out all of the laws and regulations maintained by each state. This book will not attempt to do that. The main message is that anyone doing business in or to any part of the U.S. should be aware of the existence and possible impact of such state laws and regulations.

It is also important to remember that lawyers qualified to practice in one state are not usually, without special permission, allowed to practice or advise on the law of any other state. If any person has questions about the laws and regulations of any particular state, they will need to consult qualified legal advisors authorized to practice law in the state in question.

16.1.2 Federal Law

This is the legal system that deals principally with interstate and foreign commerce. Legislation and regulation to govern these activities come from the U.S. legislative and executive branches of government, including the U.S. Congress, the President, and Federal Agencies such as the U.S. Treasury, the FTC, the U.S. DOJ, the Securities and Exchange Commission, etc.

The federal government also maintains a Federal court system that includes the U.S. District Courts, the U.S. Circuit Courts of Appeal, the United States Supreme Court, and a number of more specialized courts such as tax courts, bankruptcy courts, etc.

Attorneys practicing law in any state where federal courts are located must apply separately to those courts to practice before them. Practice before federal courts usually requires that an attorney be admitted to practice in at least one U.S. state and specific permission to practice before the federal court in question.

16.2 INTERNET LAW

In the United States, the regulation of activities on the Internet is divided between federal and state, as indicated above. This is not unusual under the U.S. legal system. Many areas of commercial activity, such as banking, insurance, and investment business, are subject to separate U.S. Federal and state laws.

The federal regulation of Internet activity began as the regulation of common activities that were migrating from the physical world to the digital world of the Internet. Many of these were commercial activities and, at an early stage of the Internet's development, came under the jurisdiction of the United States FTC.

16.2.1 Federal Trade Commission

The FTC is the U.S. Federal Government agency, the mission of which is defined as:

> protecting consumers and competition by preventing anticompetitive, deceptive, and unfair business practices through law enforcement, advocacy, and education without unduly burdening legitimate business activity.[527]

Their stated goals are:

(1) To protect consumers from unfair and deceptive practices in the marketplace.
(2) To maintain competition and promote a marketplace free from anticompetitive mergers, business practices, or public policy.
(3) To perform these tasks well by managing their resources, people and information technology.[528]

As can be seen, at this point in time, the FTC considers "information technology" an important tool for its own activities and clearly recognizes its importance in U.S. commerce.

527. FTC, "About the FTC, Our Mission," online at: ftc.gov retrieved August 5, 2020.
528. FTC, "About the FTC, Our Strategic Goals," online at: ftc.gov August 5, 2020.

The first interactions of the FTC with the Internet were in the context of enforcing general anticrime and misconduct policies.

As the Internet expanded, a number of activities on the Internet violated established federal laws and policies. This was particularly true of laws and policies against fraud, misrepresentation and theft.

Most of these activities were not confined to the boundaries of a particular state. Electronic communications frequently crossed the state and even international boundaries. Consequently, these activities came within the jurisdiction of the U.S. Federal Government, which is responsible for regulating interstate commerce and foreign commerce. This got the FTC involved.

The FTC's early involvement with the Internet was in the context of investigating and sometimes prosecuting and imposing fines for unfair and deceptive marketing and unfair competition. These are among the duties imposed on the FTC by U.S. Federal law, such as the FTC Act.

Under section 5 of the Act, unfair or deceptive ask-for practices in or affecting commerce are prohibited. These prohibitions apply to all persons engaged in commerce, that is to say, anyone or any entity engaged in an activity for profit. The FTC is given the power to investigate and prevent such acts in order to protect competition and consumers.

The importance of controlling the Internet through the FTC was brought home in June 1991 by President Biden's appointment of Lina Kahn as Chairperson of the FTC. This seemed to be a signal from the administration that the FTC will increasingly focus on the power of the Big Tech companies.

It was noted that Ms. Khan, a 32-year-old professor at Columbia University Law School, has been a vocal critic of the Big Tech companies. In the past, she has advocated the breakup of big companies such as Amazon, Facebook and Google. There seems a little doubt that with her as the head of the FTC, there will be increasing scrutiny of the behavior of Internet companies and robust action against instances where they misuse their power.[529]

Under section 5, consumers can file a complaint with the FTC but consumers may not bring a private legal action in their own right under section 5.

16.2.2 Private Rights of Action under State Laws

This is where state law comes in. Most, if not all, U.S. states have laws prohibiting unfair and deceptive trade practices and unfair competition.

Unlike section 5 of the FTC Act, these state laws usually permit private rights of action. This allows injured parties themselves to bring lawsuits seeking damages or injunctive relief for Internet misconduct that they allege has harmed or is harming them.

529. S. Duke, "Lina Khan, Biden's Choice to Lead Federal Trade Commission Is a Warning to Big Tech," *The Times*, online, June 17, 2021.

For example, New York state law prohibits "unfair competition" and allows parties claiming injury to bring lawsuits seeking remedies for any bad faith misappropriation of material from the Internet. This covers any bad faith misappropriation of the labors or expenditures of another.[530] Note that the case cited is a Federal court case in New York, enforcing New York law rather than Federal law.

16.3 CFAA OF 1986

In 1986, becoming increasingly aware of the importance and uses of computers, the U.S. Congress passed the CFAA of 1986. This makes it a crime to obtain information to which a person is not entitled by accessing a computer without permission.

The intention of this law was to criminalize hacking, fraud and other computer crimes.

However, in a June 2021 decision, the U.S. Supreme Court apparently narrowed the application of this law in a case in which a policeman in the state of Georgia was prosecuted for using his patrol car computer to obtain automobile license plate information in exchange for payment.[531]

In a 6 to 3 decision, the Court said that the officer did not violate the specific provisions of the computer crime law because it did not apply to people who have "improper motives for obtaining information that he is otherwise available to them." The majority's view was that although the law penalizes a person who "exceeds authorized access," this does not apply to someone who improperly uses their authorized access. This case was particularly complicated by the fact that the police officer in question used his access to the license plate database in connection with working with the U.S. FBI on an investigation being conducted by the FBI. The three members of the Supreme Court in the minority argued that the law did apply in this case because the correct interpretation was that a person was not entitled to get information that he is not entitled to, even using a computer system to which he is authorized to access.[532]

16.4 CHILD PROTECTION

When it comes to the privacy of children, there is a federal law that limits information that can be collected by ISPs about children that are using their service. Such activity is governed by the way U.S. COPPA. This prohibits Internet users from collecting data on children under 13 years of age, without their parents' express consent.

In 2019, YouTube was found to be collecting data on children under the age of 13 without obtaining the consent of their parents. The FTC fined YouTube $170 million for this violation of COPPA.[533]

530. Case of *Jeffrey Milstein, Inc. v. Greger, Lawlor, Roth, Inc.*, 58 F.3d 27, 34 (2d Cir. 1995).
531. M. Quinn, "Supreme Court Narrows Scope of Computer Fraud Law with Ruling in Cybercrime Case," *CBS News*, online June 4, 2021.
532. *Ibid.*
533. *The Sunday Times*, online, May 10, 2020.

There are also strict federal and state laws against providing child pornography on the Internet. Just how strictly they can be interpreted was demonstrated in a case before the Maryland Court of Appeals, which upheld a finding that a 16-year-old girl had violated criminal pornography laws by sending a "sext" of herself to friends as a joke.

Even minor child subjects of revenge porn could be treated as child pornographers if they forwarded such postings to others.

Consequently, rather than sending copies of such postings to friends or even adults, child victims of pornography should immediately inform adults and/or the law enforcement authorities of such postings.

If an Internet operator creates videos for children, they are required to label such videos as being created for kids. No personal data about the children viewing these videos can be collected from the views, and no child-targeted ads can accompany the videos. If providers of such videos do not comply, they can be subject to lawsuits and fines.

In 2021, U.S. Congressperson Kathy Castor of Florida proposed new legislation to expand the protections of the COPPA. The additional protections that she proposed are set out in a bill called Protecting the Information of our Vulnerable Children and Youth Act. This would extend the protections of existing law to all persons under 18 years of age and would apply to all sites used by those under 18 years of age. It proposes banning advertising targeted to people under 18 and requires obtaining the consent of teenagers before storing their personal data.

This is a significant extension of COPPA, which now only applies to children under the age of 13 and to sites that are aimed at children under 13. However, there is a wide recognition that children under 13 often gain access to sites aimed at older audiences by lying about their age. It has also been shown that COPPA did not provide adequate protection to children under 13 with respect to collection of their personal data.

Representative Castor's bill is intended to cover gaps in COPPA, which was originally passed in 1998 and is considered to be outdated because of all the changes in the Internet and its use that have taken place since then.[534]

It is reported that the Big Tech companies have for sometime then attempted to deal with child protection laws by developing apps and sites specifically aimed at children under 13 and teenagers under 18. However, these have been subject to a number of criticisms that they do not effectively protect children from inappropriate material. Representative Castor and other lawmakers want to see stricter Child Protection requirements imposed.[535]

534. R. Lerman, "New Bill Would Update Decades-Old Law Governing Children's Privacy," *The Washington Post*, online, July 29, 2021.
535. *Ibid.*

16.5 U.S. ADOPTION OF DMCA

In 1998, the U.S. also passed the DMCA. The purpose of this act was to implement most of the provisions of the WIPO Copyright Treaty (WCT).

16.6 NO ELECTRONIC THEFT ACT

One year prior to that, in 1997, the U.S. enacted the No Electronic Theft Act (NET Act), which established criminal prosecution for those who violate copyright using the Internet or other electronic means.

16.7 DOMAIN NAME OWNERSHIP

Domain names or registries of IP Identifiers (IP addresses) help identify and locate those active on the Internet.

There is also another identifier called a "hostname." These are the labels that are given to domain name systems. This is a component of the Uniform Resource Locators, which are commonly known as "URLs." These are the digital addresses of Internet resources such as websites. Their purpose is to identify Internet resources such as computers, networks, websites, etc.

Domain name registration was originally performed by a man named Jon Postel. Dr. Postel was a UCLA and USC computer scientist who worked on early computer networks such as ARPANET. He is famous for a number of contributions to computing development, such as "Postel's Law" for computer software design, "Be conservative in what you do. Be liberal in what you accept from others." While he was working for ARPANET, he did domain name registration as a "side interest."

In 1983, the Domain Name System DNS was first introduced on ARPANET.

Today, it is managed by the ICANN. ICANN is a U.S. not-for-profit corporation headquartered in Los Angeles, California.

At first, there was not much conflict over who could register a domain name. Originally, there was not a requirement that the registrant be someone who has a natural or commercial interest in a particular domain name; as a result, the number of people who thought they were being clever registered the domain names that appeared to be related to major commercial companies in the hope that these companies would pay them to take over the domain name. It wasn't long before there were complaints about the fact that such a practice was seen to cross the line to fraud, extortion and even blackmail. Consequently, efforts were made to be more restrictive in granting domain name registrations and to resolve disputes between parties that contested rights to particular domain names.

The first formal effort undertaking to create a system for resolving domain name registration disputes was undertaken by ICANN. In 1999, ICANN set up the Uniform Domain Name Dispute Resolution Policy (UDRP). The purpose of the UDRP is to resolve disputes regarding the registration of Internet Domain names. It was set up to solve the problem of the registration of trademarks as domain names by people who didn't have permission from the trademark owner. The UDRP came about as a result of a report, prepared at the request of ICANN and published in 1999. The report recommended a mandatory administrative procedure for solving the problem of abusive registration of the main names. Consequently, ICANN introduced a mandatory agreement in every domain name application, which requires a party to submit to the UDRP procedure if a claim is against it by a third party.

Another important issue that has arisen from Internet use is the issue of who owns and who can use domain names. Domain names are electronic addresses that are posted on the Internet to allow users to connect with the owner of the name. Consequently, it has been important for businesses to acquire Domain names that indicate association with them or their products. However, those that assigned Domain names do not have strict rules about who they will allow to purchase a particular Domain name. There are also multiple Domain name groups, beginning with ".com" and am progressing to groups associated with particular countries (uk, fr, ... etc.), cities or other affiliations. As a result, there are numerous affiliation groups within which one can register a Domain name of one's choice.

Very early in the development of the Internet, this became a problem for major companies that had a valuable brand name they wished to protect. Domain name registrants, known as cyber-squatters, began registering Domain names that indicated affiliation with major companies and then demanding payment from those companies to give up such Domain names.

One can see that for companies like Coca-Cola, Apple and Microsoft, this can be a major headache. The argument of companies wishing to protect their brands is that cybersquatting was a form of fraud on consumers that were being enticed to click on those Domain names.

It did not take much for these major companies to bring this problem to the attention of the U.S. Congress. In response, Congress passed the Anti-cybersquatting Consumer Products Act of 1999[536] (ACPA).

The ACPA permits a lawsuit to be brought for registering, using, or trafficking in a Domain name confusingly similar to a trademark or a personal name. The purpose of this statute was to discourage those who plan to sell Domain names to the legitimate owner of the name or trademark. The owner of the name or trademark can be successful if they show that use of the trade name in question was done in bad faith with intent to profit from its misuse and if the complainant can show that a Domain name is the same or confusingly similar to a well-known trademark or personal name.

Domain names are also protected by the more general, but still applicable, Federal Trademark Dilution Act enacted prior to 1995. This protects trademarks against the registration of Domain names similar or remarkably like trademarks. The ACPA does permit private action against those using trademark-affiliated domain names for deceptive purposes.

536. 15 U.S.C. Section 1125 (d).

16.8 COMPETITION LAW

Another important U.S. law that has a significant impact on Internet use is the Sherman Antitrust Act of 1890. The Sherman Act prohibits two things. Section 1 prohibits agreements in restraint of trade. This includes such things as price-fixing, refusal to deal, bid rigging and other attempts by conspiring partners to control prices and markets for their own benefit. Section 2 prohibits attempts to monopolize markets. Both these issues have arisen with respect to the behavior of certain companies or parties using the Internet and will undoubtedly continue to arise in the future.

16.9 OTHER RELEVANT STATE LAWS

In addition to federal law, there are a number of other state laws that affect Internet transactions.

For example, there is section 5 of the UCC. Because of different state laws, there have been a number of difficulties in doing transactions across state lines in the United States. As a result, an effort was made to create a uniform set of laws for commercial transactions. The result is called the UCC.

The UCC was originally drafted as a joint project of the National Conference of Commissioners of Uniform State Laws and the American Law Institute.

They began drafting their first version in 1942 and the original complete version was published 10 years later in 1952. A number of the top legal scholars in the U.S. participated in the project.

The UCC was developed as a private project. It is not, of itself, law and is not legally binding. Basically, it represents detailed suggestions to the states to adopt uniform commercial laws. When a state adopts all or part of the UCC, those provisions become part of the state commercial law. Over the years, there have been a number of modifications or changes to the original draft of the UCC.

Most states have adopted the UCC, although there may be some variations from state to state. The only significant U.S. jurisdictions that have not adopted most of the UCC are Louisiana and Puerto Rico. This is because, prior to acquisition by the United States, the fundamental laws of these jurisdictions were not based on English common law but rather on the Napoleonic Code. However, it is important to keep in mind that the provisions of the UCC can be interpreted differently by different state courts, which, unlike the Federal court system, do not function within a single jurisdictional framework but operate differently in different states.

The UCC covers many different aspects of commercial relations and, therefore, if dealing with private commercial transactions that involve U.S. states, it should be remembered that sections of the UCC might be relevant, and qualified local legal counsel should be consulted.

The articles of the UCC deal with the following topics:

(1) General Provisions.
(2) Sales and (2A) Leases.

(3) Negotiable Instruments.
(4) Bank Deposits and Collections, (4A) Funds Transfer.
(5) Letters of Credit.
(6) Bulk Transfers and Bulk Sales.
(7) Documents of Title.
(8) Investment Securities.
(9) Secured Transactions.

As can be seen from the titles of these articles, they could have a significant impact on International transactions that involve U.S. states.

For example, Article 5 (letters of credit) regulates a variety of financial instruments that are often used in international banking transactions. And extensive revision of Article 5 was undertaken in 1995 to take account of many changes in international transactions, including that significant parts of the agreement relating to them had become "non-documentary" because of the growth of electronic commercial transactions and the Internet.[537]

A copy of the UCC can be found online at the Legal Information Institute (LII) of Cornell University.[538]

16.10 FEDERAL AND STATE COMPETITION INVESTIGATIONS

Federal Government's concern about the power of major tech companies such as Google, Amazon, Apple and Facebook has been growing.

In response to these concerns, the U.S. Justice Department (DOJ), the FTC and a number of state Attorney Generals have begun investigations aimed at filing competition lawsuits against these companies in an effort to limit their powers and/or punish perceived abuses of the market power of such companies.

A major step in that direction was taken when the FTC and a coalition of 48 U.S. state Attorney Generals filed antitrust cases against Facebook in 2020. However, these cases suffered an embarrassing setback in June 2021 when a federal court dismissed those cases on the grounds that the FTC had failed to define the market in which Facebook operated and that the states waited too long to act against Facebook. U.S. District Judge James Boasberg wrote that the FTC had not provided sufficient detail to support its allegations that Facebook was monopolizing the online social media market. The FTC was given until August 19, 2021, to file a new and better complaint.[539]

These dismissals raise questions as to what will happen in the many cases filed by the Justice Department and state Attorney Generals against Google in the autumn of

537. James G. Barnes, "Internationalization of Revised UCC Article 5: Letters of Credit," *Northwestern Journal of International Law and Business*, Volume 16.2, Winter 1996.
538. Legal Information Institute, Cornell University, https://www.law.cornell.edu/ucc.
539. D. McLaughlin, "Facebook Hit by New U.S. Antitrust Case as FTC Seeks Do-Over," *Bloomberg*, online, August 19, 2021.

2020 and with respect to cases that it is believed may be filed against Amazon in the near future.[540]

However, the FTC has shown itself not to be discouraged by the dismissal it suffered in June 2021. On August 19, 2021, the FTC re-filed their antitrust suit against Facebook with a new complaint alleging that Facebook violated competition laws when it bought Instagram and WhatsApp.[541]

The complaint alleges that these were purchased in order to eliminate them as competitors.

This new filing does have political aspects. There are five commissioners at the FTC—two Republicans and three Democrats. The commissioners voted 3 to 2 to refile a complaint, with Democrats voting in favor and Republicans voting against the filing.

This case is representative of the efforts being made by different governmental branches in the United States to control the powers of the Big Tech companies such as Facebook, Amazon and Google.

The U.S. Justice Department and a number of states have filed several lawsuits against Google. In Congress, legislative bills are being presented to control the expanding business of these companies. One U.S. Senator, Amy Klobuchar of Minnesota, the Chairperson of the AntiTrust Panel of the U.S. Senate, issued a statement supporting the filing, saying:

> Facebook's long history of anti-competitive behavior is no secret ... The company's acquisitions of Instagram and WhatsApp have made the digital landscape less competitive ultimately harming consumers.

16.11 ARTIFICIAL INTELLIGENCE

Because much of the pioneering work on AI originated in the United States, it would be surprising if the U.S. government did not consider what type of regulation makes sense for AI.

The U.S. government has taken a number of steps to impose policies and formal regulations to allow U.S. entities to benefit from the positive elements of AI development while seeking to reduce the risks that AI might pose.

16.11.1 National AI Initiative Act of 2020

On January 1, 2021, the National AI Initiative Act of 2020 became law (AIA 2020). Its purpose was to establish a coordinated AI program throughout the U.S. The AIA of 2020 established the National AI Initiative as a central coordination point for AI research and application in the U.S.:[542]

540. S. Kalhatkar, "What's Next for the Campaign to Break Up Big Tech," *The New Yorker*, online, July 6, 2021.
541. D. McLaughlin, "Facebook Hit by New U.S. Antitrust Case as FTC Seeks Do-Over," *Bloomberg*, online, August 19, 2021.
542. National Artificial Intelligence Initiative, online at: ai.gov, accessed May 15, 2023.

> The mission of the National AI Initiative is to ensure continued US leadership in AI research and development, to lead the world in the development and use of trustworthy AI in the public and private sectors and prepare the present and future US workforce for the integration of AI systems across all sections of the economy and society.[543]

Essentially, the National AI Initiative website acts as a central repository of AI information, including publications, AI development, and sections on:

- Innovation
- Advancing Trustworthy AI
- Education and Training
- Infrastructure
- Applications
- International Cooperation.

It provides information about the more than 20 U.S. government agencies that are dealing with AI.

It also provides news about noteworthy developments in AI, such as a February 13, 2023, report that a U.S. Department of Defense (DoD) team has piloted a fighter jet using AI.[544]

16.11.2 Blueprint for an AI Bill of Rights

In the fall of 2022, the U.S. issued a Blueprint for an AI Bill of Rights (Blueprint) that addressed the issues presented by the development of AI systems. The Blueprint set out how the United States expected to encourage and regulate these new digital products.

The Blueprint was issued by the Office of Science and Technology Policy of the United States (OSTP). The 0STP was established by the National Science and Technology Policy, Organization, and Priorities Act of 1976. The purpose of that Act was to provide the President's office and other government officials with appropriate advice on the scientific, engineering, and technological aspects of U.S. government concerns touching on economy, national security, health, and resources, among other things.[545]

The Blueprint is used to provide guidelines for overcoming the problems identified in connection with the development of AI systems.[546] As the Blueprint says:

> These problems are well documented. In America and around the world, systems supposed to help with patient care have proven unsafe, ineffective, or biased. Algorithms used in hiring and credit decisions have been found to reflect and reproduce existing unwanted inequities or embed harmful new bias and discrimination. Unchecked social media data collection has been used to threaten people's

543. *Ibid.*
544. *Ibid.*
545. OSTP, "About the Office of Science and Technology Policy," online at: whitehouse.gov, accessed May 11, 2023.
546. OSTP, "Blueprint for an AI Bill of Rights," online at: whitehouse.gov, accessed May 11-12, 2023.

> opportunities, undermined their privacy, or pervasively tracked their activity—often without their knowledge or consent.

The Blueprint contains five principles that set out policies intended to guide the rational development of AI while making certain that individual rights and democratic values are protected. A summary of these principles is as follows.[547]

Safe and Effective Systems

The first principle is that people should be protected from unsafe or ineffective AI systems. In order to achieve this goal, the creation of AI systems should be done with consultation from different communities, stakeholders and experts to permit adequate identification of concerns, risks and potential AI system impact.

Algorithmic Discrimination Protections

Discrimination should not be imposed by systems not equitably designed and used:

> Algorithmic discrimination occurs when automated systems contribute to unjustified different treatment or impacts disfavoring people based on their race, color, ethnicity, sex (including pregnancy, childbirth, and related medical conditions, gender identity, intersex status, and sexual orientation), religion, age, national origin disability, veteran status, genetic information, or any other classification protected by law.

Data Privacy

System design choices should, by default, make sure that the collection of data complies with reasonable expectations "and that only data strictly necessary for the specific context is collected. ... Any consent requests should be brief, be understandable in plain language, and give you agency over data collection and the specific context of use. ..."

Notice and Explanation

Designers, developers, and deployers of automated systems should provide generally accessible plain language documentation including clear descriptions of the overall system functioning and the role automation plays, notice that such systems are in use, the individual or organization responsible for the system, and explanations of the outcomes that are clear, timely, and accessible. Search notice should be kept up to date and people impacted by the system should be notified of significant use cases or key functionality changes.

Human Alternatives, Consideration, and Fallback

When appropriate, users should be able to opt out of an AI system and have the opportunity to choose an efficient and effective human alternative:

547. *Ibid.* For the full texts of the Principles, and accompanying material, please refer to the Blueprint itself at the website cited.

> [I]n some cases, a human or other alternative may be required by law.

The instructions on how the Blueprint for an AI Bill of Rights should be applied include the following:[548]

> [T]his framework uses a two-part test to determine when systems are in its scope. This framework applies to (1) automated systems that (2) have the potential to meaningfully impact the American public's rights, opportunities, or access to critical resources or services.

The purpose of the Blueprint is stated to be:[549]

> Considered together, the five principles and associated practices of the Blueprint for an AI bill of rights form an overlapping set of backstops against potential harms. This purposefully overlapping framework, when taken as a whole, forms a Blueprint to help protect the public from harm. The measures taken to realize the vision set forward in this framework should be proportionate with the extent and nature of the harm, or risk of harm, to people's rights, opportunities, and access.

16.11.3 Anti-algorithmic Discrimination Order

In February 2023, President Biden signed an Executive Order requiring federal agencies to eliminate discrimination from new technologies, including AI. The purpose of this Order was to "protect the public from algorithmic discrimination."[550]

In May of that year, the Biden Administration issued a further statement that said:

> The Biden-Harris Administration is developing a National Artificial Intelligence (AI) Strategy that will chart a path for the United States to harness the benefits and mitigate the risks of AI. This strategy will build on the actions that the Federal Government has already taken to responsibly advance the development and use of AI. To inform the strategy, OSTP (Office of Science and Technology Policy) requests public comments to help update U.S. national priorities and future actions on AI.[551]

16.11.4 May 2023 Meeting: Government Officials & Tech CEOs

In early May 2023, the Biden Administration announced that it would introduce policies to address the issues raised by the development of AI.

These policies are intended to determine how federal agencies can acquire and use AI systems. These policies are expected to have an impact on the AI market and regulate how Americans can use AI on government websites and in other government

548. *Ibid.* For the full text and accompanying material, please refer to the website cited.
549. *Ibid.* For the full texts of the Principles, and accompanying material, please refer to the website cited.
550. The White House, "FACT SHEET: Biden-Harris Administration Announces New Actions to Promote Responsible AI Innovation that Protects Americans' Rights and Safety," online at: whitehouse.gov, May 4, 2023.
551. A Notice by the Science and Technology Policy Office on May 26, 2023, "Request for Information; National Priorities for Artificial Intelligence," *Federal Register*, online at: federal-register.gov.

and non-government situations. These policies were announced on a day when government officials met with the CEOs of Microsoft, OpenAI,[552] Google and Anthropic.[553]

A number of government officials participated in this meeting including the Vice-President, the Secretary of Commerce, and other officials with responsibility for science and technology policy, security, domestic policy, and the economy.

The issues that were raised in the meeting included the necessity of reducing the risks that AI potentially posed to individuals, to American society and to international security. The risks that were identified included risks to safety, security, civil rights, human rights, privacy, employment and democratic values.

The CEOs were urged to direct their companies to be models of responsible behavior and to ensure that their companies' actions reflected responsible innovation, necessary safeguards, and protection of the rights and safety of people.

The Big Tech companies were told that they needed to be more transparent both with regulators and with the public about their AI systems and that it was essential to protect any AI systems they employed against penetration and misuse by malicious attackers and actors.

This meeting was one part of the Biden Administration's policy of engaging with a range of participants and stakeholders in the cyber world to promote responsible innovation and reduction of risks with respect to AI.[554]

16.11.5 Progress on AI Regulation

As shown in this chapter, AI activity is already subject to significant regulation under the existing regulatory framework of the U.S. Federal Government. However, there is serious concern that additional regulation by a number of different government agencies and organizations will be necessary in order to focus on the reduction of the risks that may be posed by AI to national security and individual rights, among other things.

There is additional sensitivity to the potential of AI to offer significant improvements to a number of activities, including information, analysis and health protection.

As shown above, several federal government organizations and agencies are giving serious consideration to how AI should be treated. This will undoubtedly result in the development of more specific policies and regulations focused on AI. However, as indicated above, the government is still a considerable distance from determining what these regulations and policies will be and how they should be applied. There will also be additional consideration given to how AI activities should be treated under existing laws and regulations.

552. The creator of ChatGPT.
553. B. Fung, "Biden Administration Unveils an AI Plan Ahead of Meeting with Tech CEOs," *CNN online*, May 5, 2023. Anthropic is an AI safety and research company.
554. White House, "Readout of White House Meeting with CEOs on Advancing Responsible Artificial Intelligence Innovation," online at: whitehouse.gov, May 4, 2023.

Nevertheless, various U.S. officials, including elected officials in the U.S. House of Representatives in the U.S. Senate, have proposed various pieces of legislation to regulate the development, distribution and use of AI systems. Here are some of them.

16.11.6 AI in Nuclear Plants

In 2022, the U.S. government took a serious look at the role of AI in the operation of nuclear plants with the publication in February of that year of a United States Nuclear Regulatory Commission paper, "Exploring Advanced Computational Tools and Techniques with Artificial Intelligence and Machine Learning in Operating Nuclear Plants."[555]

The paper says:

> The report describes the relationships between statistics and AI/ML, and then introduces the most widely used AI/ML algorithms in both supervised and unsupervised learning. The report reviews the recent applications of advanced computational tools and techniques in various fields of nuclear industry, such as reactor system design and analysis, plant operation and maintenance, and nuclear safety and risk analysis. The report presents the insights from the project on the potential applicability of AI/ML techniques in improving advanced computational capabilities, and how advanced tools and techniques could contribute to the understanding of safety and risk, and what information would be needed to provide meaningful insights to decision makers.[556]

16.11.7 AI Training Act of 2022

In October 2022, the Artificial Intelligence Training for the Acquisition Workforce Act (AI Training Act) became law.

The AI Training Act requires the Office of Management and Budget (OMB) to provide an AI training program for the acquisition of the workforces of executive agencies (e.g., those responsible for program management or logistics). The purpose of the Act is to make sure that the relevant workforces understand the capabilities and risks of AI. The program must be updated every two years. Participation should be measured, and feedback from participants should be taken into consideration.[557]

555. United States Nuclear Regulatory Commission, Office of Nuclear Regulatory Research, John Lane, NRC Project Manager, "Exploring Advanced Computational Tools and Techniques with Artificial Intelligence and Machine Learning in Operating Nuclear Plants," published February 2022, online at: inldigitallibrary.inl.gov.
556. *Ibid.*
557. US Public Law No.: 117-207 (October 17, 2022), Artificial Intelligence Training for the Acquisition Workforce or the AI Training Act, online at: congress.gov., accessed July 4, 2023.

16.11.8 Federal Digital Platform Commission Bill

In May 2023, Senator Michael Bennett of Colorado proposed a new version of a bill he had previously introduced to set up a Federal Digital Platform Commission to oversee and regulate AI and other digital technology.[558]

Bennet is quoted as saying:

> Technology is moving quicker than Congress could ever hope to keep up with. We need an expert federal agency that can stand up for the American people and ensure that AI tools and digital platforms operate in the public interest.[559]

Sen. Bennet's bill would give the proposed Commission jurisdiction over data systems that use personal data to either create content or make decisions. It would also require:

> "algorithmic audits" and review of the risks that such systems might cause harm to the public."

The Commission would need to ensure that AI system algorithms are "fair, transparent and safe."[560]

The Commission would also be given oversight of online platforms, including social media platforms and search engines. It was suggested that the Commission should also be given responsibility to review the credentials of and license creators of AI platforms.

This proposal has not been universally met with approval. One critic, Gary Marcus, a professor at New York University, has pointed out that there is a danger that such a commission could fall victim to "regulatory capture." This term describes how industries can gain controlling influence over government agencies set up to regulate them.

Senator Richard Blumenthal of Connecticut has pointed out:

> You can create 10 new agencies, but if you don't
>
> give them the resources—and I'm not just talking about dollars, I'm talking about scientific expertise—[industry] will run circles around them.[561]

16.11.9 AI Disclosure Act of 2023

In June 2023, U.S. Representative Ritchie Torres proposed new legislation requiring all content generated by AI to be accompanied by a disclaimer disclosing its origin. Representative Torres said:

All generative AI should be required to disclose itself as AI. Under the "AI disclosure act of 2023," all material generated by AI technology would have to include

558. B. Fung, "US Senator Introduces Bill to Create a Federal Agency to Regulate AI," *CNN Business*, May 18, 2023, online at: edition.cnn.com.
559. *Ibid.*
560. *Ibid.*
561. *Ibid.*

the following alert—"Disclaimer: this output has been generated by artificial intelligence." It would apply to videos, photos, text, audio, and any other AI-generated material. The FTC would be responsible for enforcement of violations, which could result in civil penalties.[562]

16.11.10 The FTC Investigates ChatGPT

One of the most publicized AI projects is the work done by a U.S. company in San Francisco, OpenAI Incorporated, founded in 2015.

OpenAI's best-known product is an AI machine called ChatGPT. ChatGPT is in the category of "Generative Artificial Intelligence" that interacts in a conversational way that allows it to conduct a dialogue, follow instructions and produce results, including written documents:

> Relative to earlier artificial intelligence models, Generative AI models can digest more complex inputs, and can produce human-like output, making Generative AI more versatile and scalable than prior innovations in AI and machine learning.[563]

It has proved controversial because commentators believe it will allow students to instruct ChatGPT to do their homework, and its capabilities are alleged to threaten a number of professions because it is allegedly capable of searching the Internet for information that allows it to answer questions and do tasks that previously only trained human professionals were able to correctly perform.

This has caused something of a panic fueled by "the frankly insane levels of attention paid to ChatGPT since its launch."[564]

In July 2023, it was reported that the FTC had opened a wide-ranging investigation into ChatGPT.[565]

The FTC investigation reportedly concerns issues of whether ChatGPT has violated consumer protection laws by causing risk to personal reputations and personal data.

In commencing its investigation, the FTC sent a 20-page document demand to ChatGPT's parent company, OpenAI, demanding to know how the company deals with risks associated with its AI products. This investigation by a major U.S. federal agency is seen as a serious threat to OpenAI's U.S. business.[566]

562. U.S. Rep. Ritchie Torres Introduces "Federal Legislation Requiring Mandatory Disclaimer for Material Generated by Artificial Intelligence," online at: ritchietorres.house.gov, 05 June 5, 2023.
563. A.L. Eisfeldt, G. Shubert, and M.B. Zhang, "Generative AI and Firm Values," National Bureau of Economic Research, NBER Working Paper No. 31222, online at: d1e00ek4ebabms.cloud front.net, May 2023.
564. R. Wigglesworth, "The ChatGPT Market Shock," *Financial Times*, online at: ft.com, May 8, 2023.
565. C. Zakrzewski, "FTC Investigates OpenAI over Data Leak and ChatGPT's Inaccuracy," *The Washington Post*, online at: washingtonpost.com, July 13, 2023.
566. *Ibid.*

The FTC's focus on Open AI is the result of the huge amount of publicity that ChatGPT has received citing the potential uses and potential dangers of generative AI systems like ChatGPT.

It is reported that ChatGPT, since its release in November 2022, has become one of the fastest-growing consumer apps in history, creating intense interest and concern around the world. Its success has also caused other tech companies to race to produce similar chatbots.

The parallel interest and concern that this product has created has also resulted in calls for governments around the world to introduce regulations to control the potential uses of such AI systems and to protect against the potential misuse they could bring about.

However, the introduction of appropriate and adequate legislation to encourage the positive uses of AI systems and control the potential harms of such systems can be a slow process. For example, the U.S. Senate Majority Leader, Senator Charles E Schumer, is reported as saying that proper AI legislation will take months to introduce.[567]

This lack of new AI-focused legislation has apparently inspired the FTC to issue statements that many existing consumer protection laws already apply to AI products. This is undoubtedly true not only in the U.S. but also in most jurisdictions around the world.

The FTC's investigation of ChatGPT is a practical demonstration of the application of existing law.

It has long been the position of the FTC that many existing federal laws are applicable to AI and related products.

For example, in April 2020, Andrew Smith, Director of the FTC's Bureau of Consumer Protection, published the following online statement:

> The good news is that, while sophistication of AI and machine learning technology is new, automated decision-making is not, and we at the FTC have long experience in dealing with the challenges presented by the use of data and algorithms to make decisions about consumers. Over the years, the FTC has brought many cases alleging violations of the laws we enforce involving AI and automated decision-making and have investigated numerous companies in this space. For example, the Fair Credit Reporting Act (FCRA), enacted in 1970, and the Equal Credit Opportunity Act (ECOA), enacted in 1974 both address automated decision-making, and financial services companies have been applying these laws to machine-based credit underwriting models for decades. We have also used our FTC Act authority to prohibit unfair and deceptive practices and to address consumer injury arising from the use of AI an automated decision-making.[568]

In June 2023, it was reported that two new pieces of AI-related legislation had been introduced in the U.S. Senate.

567. *Ibid.*
568. A. Smith, "Using Artificial Intelligence and Algorithms," *FTC*, online at: ftc.gov, April 8, 2020, accessed July 17, 2023.

16.11.11 AI Transparency Bill

The first is a bill introduced by the Chairman of the Homeland Security Committee, Senator Gary Peters, along with Senators Mike Braun and James Lankford, that would require U.S. government agencies to tell people when the agencies are using AI to interact with them. People would also be given a way to appeal any decisions being made by AI.[569]

16.11.12 Technology Competition Bill

The other bill is aimed at establishing an office to measure whether the United States is remaining competitive in developing and using the latest technological advances including advances in AI systems. This has been introduced by Senators Michael Bennett and Mark Warner along with Senator Todd Young. The bill is aimed at establishing an office of global competition analysis that would aim to identify ways that the U.S. could stay at the forefront in developing AI systems.[570]

16.11.13 Responses of the U.S. States to AI

As can be seen, many national governments and international organizations are in the process of deciding what their policy should be with respect to AI and attempting to decide what regulations and laws should be put in place to protect against the potential risks of AI while encouraging the development of those AI systems which may offer significant benefits to things such as healthcare and manufacturing.

Many important regulatory areas in the United States are the provinces of the federal government, such as intellectual property and national security. However, each of the 50 states has its own system of laws and regulations covering such things as contracts, investments, crime, tax, healthcare, etc.

Each of the states has officials and politicians that are concerned with developing the economies of their states to expand job creation and tax revenues.

Consequently, states are making specific efforts to develop AI laws and regulations both to protect their citizens against potential risks and to use the potential benefits of AI to benefit their economies. These efforts will no doubt be in process for some time to come and will undoubtedly change over that time.

To give an idea of how states are developing their responses to AI, some of those efforts are described below. However, it should be kept in mind that at the time that this book is being written, intensive concern about AI and related digital topics (such as robotics and automated decision-making) is so new that many of the legislative bills referred to below were still "pending" rather than "enacted" as state law. Consequently, if any reader wishes to know whether particular legislation has become part of

569. Reuters, "U.S. Congress to Consider Two New Bills on Artificial Intelligence," online at: reuters.com, June 9, 2023.
570. *Ibid.*

the law of any state, those readers will need to follow up by consulting qualified legal advisers in the states in question.

Of course, the response to AI is developing rapidly everywhere, so it will be necessary to get updates on a regular basis.

For example, the National Conference of State Legislatures (NCSL) published material online in April 2023 commenting on legislation in U.S. States and territories relating to "AI issues generally." However, their posting said:

> Legislation relating solely to specific AI technologies, such as facial recognition or autonomous cars, is being tracked separately.[571]

The U.S. Chamber of Commerce has also published online information about states that are considering legislation to regulate AI. This is done in the form of an interactive map that allows a user to obtain information about the legislation being considered or introduced in 2021.[572]

Please note that at the time this book was being written (primarily in 2024), publicity and concern about AI were expanding rapidly, and most states were in the process of considering the introduction of new laws and regulations to regulate the development and use of AI. The examples given below are by no means a complete catalog of the measures introduced and implemented by the 50 U.S. states during the writing and following the publication of this book.

Alabama

In 2019, the government of the state of Alabama was tasked with studying AI and reporting on the challenges and opportunities that it presented to the state.

In 2021, Alabama passed a legislative act to create a council on advanced technology and AI, which was directed to examine AI and advanced technologies and report to the governor, the legislature and private parties on the uses in applications of those technologies.[573]

In 2022, Alabama passed a law preventing law enforcement agencies from using facial recognition technology in some criminal investigation activities.[574]

Alaska

The University of Alaska, Center for Alaska Native Health Research has published online material relating to "Artificial Intelligence/Machine Learning Prospects for American Indian/Alaska Native Health."[575]

571. National Conference of State Legislatures, "Artificial Intelligence 2023 Legislation" updated April 18, 2023, online at: ncsl.org, accessed May 25, 2023.
572. U.S. Chamber of Commerce, "State-by-State Artificial Intelligence Legislation Tracker."
573. Alabama Act No. 2021-344, Passed April 27, 2021. Text online at: arc-sos.state.al.us. *See also* C. Kraczon, "The State of State AI Policy (2021-22 Legislative Session)," *Electronic Privacy Information Center*, online at: epic.org, accessed May 24, 2023.
574. Alabama Act No. 2022-420, Passed April 5, 2021. Text online at: arc-sos.state.al.us. *See also*, C. Kraczon, "The State of State AI Policy (2021-22 Legislative Session)," Electronic Privacy Information Center, online at: epic.org, accessed May 24, 2023.
575. University of Alaska, Center for Alaska Native Health Research, online at: canhr.uaf.edu.

In a somewhat remarkable legislative development, it was reported in April 2023 that a member of the Alaska legislature "used Microsoft Bing AI Copilot to write a bill that would legalize gambling on Alaska ferries."[576]

The legislator said that:

> [H]e submitted the idea for the bill to the legislatures lawyers in January [2023], but they failed to get a draft bill back to him.

Arizona

The Legislature of the State of Arizona has introduced a bill setting requirements for AI.[577] The bill demands that AI algorithms must comply with all federal and state laws. It also requires that AI "may not infringe on a human being's constitutional rights."

A state committee on AI was established with a requirement that it review data on AI and submit a report on its findings on or before December 31, 2023.

Arizona has also introduced a bill to regulate the use of AI in ballot processing and adjudication.[578]

Arkansas

A bill has been introduced in the State Legislature, creating requirements for "railroad train defect detectors."

California

California has a number of laws and regulations in the works that affect the use of AI systems.

There is a pending bill that will require the California Department of Technology and other government bodies to inventory all "high risk automated decision systems" that are proposed, used, in development or proposed to be purchased by state agencies.[579]

At the end of January 2023, California introduced more legislation to regulate AI, including Bill 331.[580]

Bill 331 is directed largely at "deployers and developers" of "an automated decision tool." These terms can include a "local government agency."

576. J. Landfield, "Alaska House Representative Uses Artificial Intelligence to write Bill Legalizing Gambling on Alaska Ferries," *The Alaska Landmine*, online at: alaskalandmine.com, April 13, 2023.
577. Legislature of the State of Arizona, House Bill 2685. "Amending Title 18. Arizona Revised Statutes, By Adding Chapter 7: Relating to Information Technology," online at: azleg.gov, accessed May 25, 2023.
578. Arizona Bill 1565, "Relating to the Conduct of Elections," online at: custom.statenet.com, February 28, 2023.
579. California Assembly Bill 302, "Department of Technology: High Risk Automated Decision Systems Inventory,"(Amended), online at: custom.statenet.com, accessed July 3, 2023.
580. California Legislature, Assembly Bill No. 331, "An Act to Add Chapter 25 (Commencing with Section 22756) to Division 8 of the Business and Professions Code, Relating to Artificial Intelligence," January 30, 2023, published, as amended, April 19, 2023, corrected as of April 20, 2023, accessed June 28, 2023.

Bill 331 includes a number of relevant definitions, including the following:[581]

- "Automated decision tool" is defined as "a system or service that uses AI and has been specifically developed and marketed to, or specifically modified to, make, or be a controlling factor in making, consequential decisions."
- "Consequential decision" is defined as "a decision or judgment that has a legal, material, or similarly significant effect on an individual's life relating to the impact of, access to, or the cost, terms, or availability, of any of the following [in summary]: ... 'employment ... education and vocational training ... housing ... essential utilities ... family planning ... health care ... financial services ... criminal justice ... legal services ... voting.'"
- "Deployer" is defined as "a person, partnership, state or local government agency, or corporation that uses an automated decision tool to make a consequential decision."
- "Developer" is defined as "a person, partnership, state or local government agency, or corporation that designs, codes, or produces an automated decision tool, or substantially modifies an artificial intelligence system or service for the intended purpose of making, or being a controlling factor in making, consequential decisions, whether for its own use or for use by a third party."

The Bill is to take effect on or before January 1, 2025. After that, all deployers using automated decision tools would have to do an impact assessment on decision tools that they use. This assessment would have to be documented annually. Those who are subjects of a decision based on an automated decision tool will need to be notified. People would be able to make a request not to be the subject of an automated decision tool. The deployer would need to accommodate that if it is feasible. A governance program would need to be developed by the deployers to incorporate appropriate safeguards.

There are a number of other provisions provided detailing the steps that the deployers would need to take to document their use of automatic decision tools. They would be required to provide certain safeguards, certain opportunities for subjects to object to the use of such tools and they would need to make certain information publicly available about their use of such tools. Generally, certain of these provisions will apply to deployers with 25 or more employees:[582]

- *Pending California Senate Bill 313* requires any state agency that uses AI to communicate with a natural person to provide notice to the person that the communication is being made using AI. Instructions are to be included informing the person how they can communicate with a natural person at the state agency in question.[583]

581. *Ibid.*
582. C. Mitchell, "AB 331: AI Tools," *California Globe*, online at: californiaglobe.com, March 23, 2023, accessed June 29, 2023.
583. California Senate Bill 313, "Department of Justice: Advanced Technology Research (Amended)," online at: custom.statenet.com, accessed July 3, 2023.

- *Pending California Senate Bill 398* provides for a Government Services Advanced Technology Act to develop and implement a comprehensive research plan to study how using advanced technology could improve state and local government services.[584]
- *Pending California Senate Bill 721* creates a California inter-agency AI Working Group to report to the legislature about AI. Members are required to be Californians with expertise in areas such as computer science, AI and data privacy.[585]
- *California Senate Counsel Resolution 17*, introduced on January 30, 2023, affirms the California Legislature's commitment to President Biden's call for safe AI.[586]

Colorado

A legislative bill has been introduced in Colorado restricting the use of facial recognition technology. Certain notices and reports need to be filed to justify the use of this technology.[587]

Colorado has also instituted regulations relating to the use of AI in the insurance business. Essentially, the regulations require life insurance companies to use AI governance measures that are designed to prevent unfair discrimination in the insurance business.[588]

Connecticut

In Connecticut, the Governor and Legislature have undertaken an examination of AI and created an AI bill of rights.

The Connecticut Department of Administrative Services is required to do an inventory of AI systems being used by state agencies. They are to report back on the survey by December 31, 2023.[589]

Delaware

The *Delaware Journal of Corporate Law,* published by Delaware Law School, has published the following statement about the use of AI in corporate governance in that state:

584. California Senate Bill 398, "Department of Technology: High Risk Automated Decision Systems Inventory," (Amended), online at: custom.statenet.com, accessed July 3, 2023.
585. California Assembly Bill 721, "California Interagency AI Working Group," online at: custom.statenet.com, accessed July 3, 2023.
586. California Senate Counsel Resolution 17, "Artificial Intelligence," online at: custom.statenet.com, accessed July 3, 2023.
587. Colorado General Asembliy, SB22-113, online at: leg.colorado.gov. *See also,* C. Kraczon, "The State of State AI Policy (2021-22 Legislative Session)," *Electronic Privacy Information Center,* online at: epic.org.
588. Colo. Rev. Stat. section 10-3-1104.9, online at: leg.colorado.gov.
589. *See* the Act signed in aid of these provisions: SB 1103, "An Act Concerning Artificial Intelligence, Automated Decision-Making and Personal Data Privacy," online at: cga.ct.gov.

> Delaware law requires corporate directors to comply with fiduciary duties of loyalty and care. ... These fiduciary duties include acting in the best interest of the corporation and shareholders and being fully informed prior to making decisions on behalf of the company. ... The use of AI in corporate governance can be beneficial by making the board more effective and efficient in its direction, control, and coaching. ... The board can use AI to track overall trends in how business is allocating funds and extract data to align with the goals of business in various departments. ... (Footnotes omitted). ... In sum, the use of AI can be beneficial to Delaware boards of directors in corporate governance. Due to Delaware laws' emphasis on fiduciary duties of loyalty, care, non-delegation, and oversight, it is unlikely that AI systems will completely replace boards of directors. However, AI systems can potentially be required in corporate governance by Delaware law where the fiduciary duty of loyalty is linked with adopting compliance monitoring systems.[590]

District of Columbia

The Council District of Columbia, the jurisdictional location of Washington DC, has introduced a bill to prohibit users of algorithmic decision-making from utilizing algorithmic eligibility determinations in a discriminatory manner, to require corresponding notices to individuals whose personal information is used, and to provide appropriate means of civil enforcement.[591]

Florida

Florida does not, as of May 2023, have any specific regulation focusing on AI. However, lawyers' groups in Florida are keen for the state to remain at the forefront of the technology business. In aid of this, the Florida Bar has organized a study of AI development. It seems likely that, in the future, Florida will have specific legislation relating to AI.[592]

However, as previously pointed out, Florida does have a range of laws and regulations applicable to AI development, distribution and use, including criminal and consumer protection laws, which are intended to protect Floridians from fraud, misrepresentation, and other abuses.

Georgia

The legislature of the State of Georgia has established a House Subcommittee on AI. Representative Brad Thomas is the Chair of this Subcommittee and the Vice Chairman of the House Technology and Infrastructure Innovation Committee. Mr. Thomas compares the development of AI to the early days of the steam locomotive. He is quoted as saying:

> That was a new thing, an emerging technology and several of them blew up. The American Society of mechanical engineers came out and set standards for the

590. K. Mc Daniels, "The Future of Using Artificial Intelligence in Delaware Corporate Governance," *Delaware Journal of Corporate Law*, May 16, 2023.
591. District of Columbia Council Bill 302, "Stop Discrimination by Algorithms Act of 2023," online at: custom.statenet.com, accessed July 3, 2023.
592. Florida Bar, online at: floridabar.org.

industry which I think is important. We're not experts in AI so we are going to lean heavily on the industry and the appropriate people to make sure that we're doing the things that make sense.[593]

Hawaii

A resolution has been passed in the Hawaii Senate in April 2023, urging the U.S. Congress to begin a discussion considering the benefits and risks of AI technologies.[594]

Idaho

To the extent that Idaho has not enacted specific laws dealing with AI systems, there are numerous laws in effect in that state that can affect the way that AI systems can be developed, distributed and used in ways that may affect residents of the state. These include criminal laws, tort laws, privacy laws, commercial laws, etc.

For example, in March 2019, Idaho passed a criminal procedure statute to the effect that "all pretrial risk-assessment tools shall be transparent":[595]

> "(1) ... (a) All documents, data, records, and information used by the builder to build or validate the pretrial risk assessment tool and ongoing documents, data, records, and written policies outlining the usage and validation of the pretrial risk-assessment tool shall be open to the public inspection, auditing and testing."
>
> "(2) For purposes of this section, 'pretrial risk assessment tool' means a pre-trial process that creates or scores particular factors in order to estimate a person's level of risk to fail to appear in court, risk to commit a new crime, or risk posed to the community, in order to make recommendations as to bail or conditions of release based on such risk, whether made on an individualized basis or based on a grid or schedule."[596]

At least one commentator has called this:

> An example for states committed to using algorithms in pre-trial sentencing while retaining the notions of fairness and due process.[597]

Also, in Idaho, a significant amount of work has been done with respect to examining the use of AI and machine learning in operating nuclear plants. Specifically, the authors of the United States Nuclear Regulatory Commission publication, "Exploring Advanced Computational Tools and Techniques with Artificial Intelligence and Machine Learning in Operating Nuclear Plants" was written by nuclear experts in

593. R. Williams, "Georgia Lawmakers Poised to Study Real and Imagined Threats from Artificial Intelligence," *WABE News* (Live radio broadcasts on BBC World Services), July 5, 2023.
594. Hawaii Legislature. Senate Concurrent Resolution, "Urging Congress to Begin a Discussion Considering the Benefits and Risks of Artificial Intelligence Technologies," online at: custom.statenet.com, April 28, 2023, accessed July 5, 2023.
595. Idaho Legislature, Title 19, Criminal Procedure 19-1910, "Pretrial Risk Assessment Tools," added 2019, online at: legislature.idaho.gov., accessed July 12, 2023.
596. *Ibid.*
597. Electronic Privacy Information Center, "State Artificial Intelligence Policy, State and Local Laws, Idaho Law," online at: epic.org, accessed July 12, 2023.

Idaho, working at either the Idaho National Laboratory or the University of Idaho, both in Idaho Falls.[598]

Illinois

In 2021 and 2022, Illinois introduced legislative acts relating to employment and AI.[599]

One is the *Illinois Future of Work Act,* which created an Illinois Future of Work Task Force responsible for assessing new technologies, such as AI, that could affect employment.[600]

Amendment to the *Illinois Human Rights Act* has also been proposed to provide that an employer that uses "predictive data analytics" in employment decisions may not consider an applicant's race or postal code to reject an applicant in the context of recruiting, hiring, promotion, renewal of employment, selection for training or apprenticeship, discharge, discipline, tenure or terms, privileges, or conditions of employment.[601]

Another is the *AI Interview Act.* This requires employers who are using AI analysis of video interviews in selecting job applicants to report data on the race and ethnicity of applicants who are not selected for in-person interviews and of those who are hired by the Illinois Department of Commerce and Economic Opportunity.[602]

Illinois also introduced the Anti-click Gambling Data Analytics Collection Act. This is intended to prevent any gambling platform from collecting with the intent of predicting how a gambling participant will bet in a particular gambling situation.[603]

Illinois has had a bill introduced to create an *"Innovation and Technology Act."* This is intended to have the Illinois Department of Innovation and Technology establish a Generative AI and Natural Language Processing Task Force to report on generative AI and natural language processing systems.[604]

Indiana

To the extent that Indiana has not enacted specific laws dealing with AI systems, there are numerous laws in effect in that state that can affect the way that AI systems can be

598. United States Nuclear Regulatory Commission, Office of Nuclear Regulatory Research, John Lane, NRC Project Manager, "Exploring Advanced Computational Tools and Techniques with Artificial Intelligence and Machine Learning in Operating Nuclear Plants," published February 2022, online at: inldigitallibrary.inl.gov.
599. C. Kraczon, "The State of State AI Policy (2021-22 Legislative Session)," Electronic Privacy Information Center, online at: epic.org, accessed May 24, 2023.
600. Illinois General Assembly, "Illinois Future of Work Act," Public Act 102-0407, effective date, August 19, 2021, text online at: ilga.gov.
601. General Assembly, State of Illinois, Proposed Amendment to Illinois Human Rights Act, February 17, 2023, regarding use of predictive data analysis in employment decisions, online at: custom.statenet.com, accessed July 5, 2023.
602. General Assembly, State of Illinois, "Artificial Intelligence Video Interview Act" Public Act 101-260, as amended by Public Act 102-47, effective date: January 1, 2022, text online at: ilga.gov.
603. General Assembly, State of Illinois, "Anti-Click Gambling Data Analytics Collection Act," Bill Number H. 2570, Introduced: February 15, 2023, text online at: ilga.gov, accessed July 6, 2023.
604. General Assembly, State of Illinois, "Innovation and Technology Act," Bill Number H. 3563, Introduced: May 18, 2023, text online at: ilga.gov, accessed July 6, 2023.

developed, distributed, and used in ways that may affect residents of the state. These include criminal laws, tort laws, privacy laws, commercial laws, etc.

For example, in May 2023, the Governor of Indiana signed into law a comprehensive privacy act that affects the application of AI systems to the personal data of Indiana residents. The law applies to entities that offer products or services to Indiana residents. Those entities that come within the law or those that control or process the personal data of 100,000 consumers, or if the entities get more than half their revenue from selling personal data involving 25,000 consumers. The legislation is called the Indiana Consumer Data Protection Act (ICDPA) and is modeled on EU privacy laws and those passed by other U.S. states.[605]

Among other things, the ICDPA:[606]

- Prohibits data controllers from processing personal data in ways that violate anti-discrimination laws.
- Gives persons rights to correct, delete, and opt out of personal data processing or sale.
- Requires processors to have security to protect data.
- Requires processors to get consent to process personal data.
- Requires processors to provide persons with clear notices about data processing.
- Provides civil penalties for violations.

Processing entities have until January 1, 2026, to come into compliance with the act which will take effect on that date.

Although, the law does not expressly deal with AI systems, it undoubtedly affects that way that AI systems can be used when processing the data of Indiana residents.

Iowa

To the extent that Iowa has not enacted specific laws dealing with AI systems, there are numerous laws in effect in Iowa that can affect the way that AI systems can be developed, distributed, and used in ways that may affect residents of the state of Iowa. These include criminal laws, tort laws, privacy laws, commercial laws, etc.

Kansas

To the extent that Kansas has not enacted specific laws dealing with AI systems, there are numerous laws in effect in Kansas that can affect the way that AI systems can be developed, distributed, and used in ways that may affect residents of the state of Kansas. These include criminal laws, tort laws, privacy laws, commercial laws, etc.

However, there is involvement of at least one Kansas state supported institution, Kansas State University (KSU), in research and development of AI systems. This is described on the KSU website as follows:

605. A.L. Friel, K.R. Fath, D.J. Oberly, "Follow the Leader: Indiana Becomes Latest State to Enact Consumer Privacy Statute," *The National Law Review*, July 13, 2023.
606. A. Desai, "Indiana Governor Signs a Comprehensive Privacy Act into Law," The Privacy Advisor, International Association of Privacy Professionals (IAPP), online at: iapp.org.

> The center for artificial intelligence and data science of the Department of Computer Science, Carl R. Ice College of Engineering, Kansas State University, is a consortium of several faculty members and the research labs, undertaking research in applied and theoretical topics in the broad areas of artificial intelligence and/or data science. It brings together researchers from Kansas State University, other universities, and industry in pursuit of knowledge and applications related to artificial intelligence and data science.[607]

This activity may lead to significant interaction between state government officials and legislators in defining specific AI regulation for the state of Kansas in the future.

Kentucky

To the extent that Kentucky has not enacted specific laws dealing with AI systems, there are numerous laws in effect in Kentucky that can affect the way that AI systems can be developed, distributed, and used in ways that may affect residents of the state of Kentucky. These include criminal laws, tort laws, privacy laws, commercial laws, etc.

Joining the rapid expansion of academic research on AI and machine learning, the University of Kentucky received a $14 million National Science Foundation (NSF) grant in November 2021 to fund a team of experts from the University of Kentucky's College of Engineering and the College of Arts and Sciences to build a lab that will apply AI solutions in cultural heritage projects.

"Heritage Science" has been practiced at the University of Kentucky for some time in determining the meaning and importance of historical information on how human culture has evolved over the millions of years—"It's the signature on a Bourbon barrel—it's the ancient footprints in Mammoth Cave ..." Heritage science involves the interpretation of these and many other artifacts.

The application of AI will help interpret and classify historical clues in putting together a more cohesive explanation of how world culture has developed.[608]

It is undoubtedly the case that serious research conducted with AI systems by a state institution such as the University of Kentucky will help inform government officials and legislators about the advantages and potential problems of AI.

Louisiana

To the extent that Louisiana has not enacted specific laws dealing with AI systems, there are numerous laws in effect in Louisiana that can affect the way that AI systems can be developed, distributed, and used in ways that may affect residents of the state of Louisiana. These include criminal laws, tort laws, privacy laws, commercial laws, etc.

---

607. Department of Computer Science, Kansas State University, Center for Intelligence and Data Science, website online at: caids.cs.ksu.edu, accessed July 18, 2023.
608. "University of Kentucky Receives $14 Million NSF Grant to Construct World-Class Cultural Heritage Lab," online at: engr.uky.edu, November 5, 2021, accessed July 18, 2023.

According to their websites, both Louisiana State University and the University of New Orleans offer programs in the study of and research on AI and machine learning.[609]

It is undoubtedly the case that serious research conducted with AI systems by educational institutions such as Louisiana State University and the University of New Orleans will help inform government officials and legislators about the advantages and potential problems of AI.

Maine

In June 2023, due to "cyber security risks," the State of Maine banned the use of AI by state agencies for a period of six months.[610]

The ban was imposed by Maine Acting Chief Information Officer Nick Marquis of the Maine Information Technology Agency. An email was reportedly sent to all Maine Executive Branch agencies that said:[611]

> "Generative AI systems have the capacity to automatically process data and information in a way that resembles intelligent human behavior. The risks that Generative AI poses are both known and unknowable and many of these risks transcend security."
>
> "During this time, Maine IT will comprehensively evaluate generative AI technologies within the current regulatory landscape to ensure our approach and adoption cultivates public trust and responsible use of all AI systems while minimizing its potential negative impact."

The State of Maine Office of Information Technology (OIT), also known as Maine IT, was created by state Executive Order in January 2005.[612] Main IT was created:

> To promote statewide information technology solutions and use of information efficiently across the government. ... It also provides networks support for the Judicial Branch, Secretary of State, Attorney General and it supports Maine Citizens through the Maine government web portal, and MSCommNet public safety radio communications networks, among other services.

The Maine IT website contains an extensive list of state of Maine cyber-policies.

Maryland

Four bills on AI were introduced for consideration by the Maryland General Assembly (the state legislature), but all failed to become law.

The first was the Artificial Intelligence Implementation Causing Harm Bill (Bill H 996). This was intended to impose strict liability on persons who intentionally designed

609. For information *see*, Louisiana State University, "Artificial Intelligence," online at: lsu.edu; and The University of New Orleans, "Machine Learning & Artificial Intelligence," online at: uno.edu.
610. E. Tomic, "Maine Bans Artificial Intelligence Use by State Agencies for 6 Months Due to 'Cybersecurity Risks'," *Main Wire*, online at: the mainewire.com, June 21, 2023.
611. *Ibid.*
612. For information, *see*: State of Maine Office of Information Technology (OIT, also known as "MaineIT"), website online at: maine.gov.

and created AI software to cause physical injury or death and imposed damages and civil penalties.

The second was the Artificial Intelligence Impact Advisory Board Bill (Bill H 1034). This was intended to create an Artificial Intelligence Impact Advisory Board to study issues relating to AI and report findings and recommendations to the governor and the Maryland General Assembly.

The third was a bill (Bill H 1068) to create a Commission on Responsible Artificial Intelligence to study issues relating to the use and regulation of AI. They were required to report findings and recommendations to the House Health and Government Operations Committee, the House Economic Matters Committee, the Senate Finance Committee, and the Senate Education, Energy and Environment Committees. This bill was reported as "adjourned," presumably for later consideration.

A fourth bill, (Bill H 1132) reportedly "failed—adjourned" was intended to establish a technology and science advisory commission to study and make recommendations on science and technology in the state of Maryland.

All this makes it appear as though the legislators of Maryland are having difficulty reaching a consensus on how science and technology, particularly AI systems, should be treated under Maryland state law. As some of these bills, as of this writing, have not become law, some were reported to be "adjourned," so it seems possible that versions of these will be incorporated into Maryland law at some point.[613]

Massachusetts

In Massachusetts, a legislator introduced a bill (S.31) that is entitled, "An Act drafted with the help of ChatGPT to regulate generative artificial intelligence models like ChatGPT."[614]

It is not clear if this became law,[615] but Massachusetts has introduced several bills to regulate AI:

- *H.64*: An Act establishing a commission to regulate automated decision-making by the state government. February 16, 2023.
- *H.1974*: An Act regulating the use of AI in providing mental health services. February 16, 2023.
- *S. 31*: An Act drafted with the help of ChatGPT to regulate generative AI models like ChatGPT. February 16, 2023
- *S.33*: An Act establishing a commission on automated decision-making by government in Massachusetts.

It does not appear that any of these have been enacted into law as of September 2023.[616]

613. Summaries of these bill are available on the site of the National Conference of State Legislatures at, online at: ncsl.org.
614. Massachusetts Legislative Information online at: malegislature.gov, accessed June 29, 2023.
615. A legal opinion of a qualified Massachusetts legal advisor will need to be sought.
616. *Ibid.*

Michigan

To the extent that Michigan has not enacted specific laws dealing with AI systems, there are numerous laws in effect in Michigan that can affect the way that AI systems can be developed, distributed, and used in ways that may affect residents of the state of Michigan. These include criminal laws, tort laws, privacy laws, labor laws, commercial laws, etc.

Joining the rapid expansion of academic research on AI and machine learning there are at least 23 colleges and universities in Michigan reported to offer programs in the study of and research on AI and machine learning.[617] Examples are courses offered by the University of Michigan and Michigan State University.

It is undoubtedly the case that serious research conducted with AI systems by educational institutions such as the University of Michigan and Michigan State University will help inform government officials and legislators about the advantages and potential problems of AI.

Minnesota

To the extent that Minnesota has not enacted specific laws dealing with AI systems, there are numerous laws in effect in Minnesota that can affect the way that AI systems can be developed, distributed, and used in ways that may affect residents of the state of Minnesota. These include criminal laws, tort laws, privacy laws, labor laws, commercial laws, etc.

Joining the rapid expansion of academic research on AI and machine learning there are several colleges and universities in Minnesota that are reported to offer programs in study of and research on AI and machine learning.[618] Two of these are University of Minnesota (Twin Cities) and the Mayo Clinic College of Medicine and Science.

It is undoubtedly the case that serious research conducted with AI systems by such educational institutions will help inform government officials and legislators about the advantages and potential problems of AI.

Mississippi

In 2021, Mississippi passed legislation directing the state Department of Education to offer a curriculum in computer science that included lessons in machine learning and AI.[619] This legislation is titled the Mississippi Computer Science and Cyber Education Equality Act. This Act took effect on July 1, 2021.[620]

617. For information *see*, Louisiana State University, "Artificial Intelligence," online at: lsu.edu; and The University of New Orleans, "Machine Learning & Artificial Intelligence," online at: uno.edu.
618. *Ibid.*
619. Caroline Kraczon, "The State of State AI Policy (2021-22 Legislative Session)" Electronic Privacy Information Center, online at: epic.org, accessed May 24, 2023.
620. Mississippi House Bill HB633, 2021, "The Mississippi Computer Science and Cyber Education Equality Act," effective date July 1, 2021, text online at: LegiScan: legiscan.com, accessed May 24, 2023.

Missouri

A bill is being considered by the Missouri Legislature (Bill H 311) to establish the Twenty-First Century Technology Innovation Task Force. It is intended that the Task Force will review the conditions of the state's technology platforms and make recommendations about the use of technology and AI to improve the state's management of records and to allow citizens of Missouri to have more efficient electronic communications and access.[621]

Montana

To the extent that Montana has not enacted specific laws dealing with AI systems, there are numerous laws in effect in Montana that can affect the way that AI systems can be developed, distributed, and used in ways that may affect residents of the state of Montana. These include criminal laws, tort laws, privacy laws, commercial laws, etc.

Joining the rapid expansion of academic research on AI and machine learning, four universities in Montana are reported to offer programs in study of and research on AI and machine learning.[622] They are Montana State University, the University of Montana, Montana Technological University and Montana State University Billings.

It is undoubtedly the case that serious research conducted on AI systems by these educational institutions will help inform government officials and legislators about the advantages and potential problems of AI.[623]

Nebraska

To the extent that Nebraska has not enacted specific laws dealing with AI systems, there are numerous laws in effect in Nebraska that can affect the way that AI systems can be developed, distributed, and used in ways that may affect residents of the state of Nebraska. These include criminal laws, tort laws, privacy laws, commercial laws, etc.

Joining the rapid expansion of academic research on AI and machine learning, colleges and universities in Nebraska are reported to offer programs in study of and research on AI and machine learning.[624] They include the University of Nebraska.

It is undoubtedly the case that serious research conducted on AI systems by this educational institution will help inform government officials and legislators about the advantages and potential problems of AI.[625]

In January 2022, a bill was introduced in the Nebraska legislature that proposed to appropriate $50 million in federal funds to establish an "Artificial Intelligence,

621. The Bill was introduced on April 13, 2023. Text is available online at: custom.statenet.com, under 2023 MO H 311.
622. For information *see*, Louisiana State University, "Artificial Intelligence," online at: lsu.edu; and The University of New Orleans, "Machine Learning & Artificial Intelligence," online at: uno.edu.
623. EduRank, "4 Best colleges for Artificial Intelligence (AI) in Montana."
624. For information *see*, Louisiana State University, "Artificial Intelligence," online at: lsu.edu; and The University of New Orleans, "Machine Learning & Artificial Intelligence," online at: uno.edu.
625. EduRank, "4 Best colleges for Artificial Intelligence (AI) in Montana."

Cybersecurity and High Performance Computing Center" facility at the University of Nebraska, Lincoln, Innovation Campus (NIC). However, the bill appears to have been "indefinitely postponed" in April 2022:[626]

> NIC is designed to facilitate new and in-depth partnerships between the University of Nebraska and private sector businesses.[627]

One project discussed on the NIC website that relates to AI technology is "an AI enabled precision spraying technology for agricultural applications" by Greeneye Technology.[628] In Nebraska, agriculture is a huge business. This seems to be the kind of AI system project that would be natural for NIC to encourage. It will be interesting to see whether future legislative support for this sort of state-supported educational activity relating to AI will develop in Nebraska.

Nevada

A Nevada bill has been introduced creating the Emerging Technologies Task Force within the Department of Business and Industry and it authorizes the Director to create an Opportunity Center for Emerging Technology Businesses as part of the Office of Business Finance and Planning.[629]

New Hampshire

In July 2023, a publication called *New Hampshire Bulletin* published this story online, pointing out that few states have adopted regulations about using AI in hiring and other business activities. Such regulation in New Hampshire is not identified. A Maryland state legislator is quoted as saying:

> Technology always innovates first, and then always seems like a good idea, until it isn't ... That's when legislators step up and try to regulate things as best they can.[630]

To the extent that New Hampshire has not enacted specific laws dealing with AI systems, there are numerous laws in effect in New Hampshire that can affect the way that AI systems can be developed, distributed, and used in ways that may affect residents of the State of New Hampshire. These include criminal laws, tort laws, privacy laws, commercial laws, etc.

Joining the rapid expansion of academic research on AI and machine learning, universities in New Hampshire are reported to offer programs in study of and research

626. LegisScan, "Nebraska Legislature Bill 904, NE LB904, 2021-2022, 107th Legislature," online at: legiscan.com, accessed July 21, 2023.
627. Nebraska Innovation Campus, "About," online at: innovate.unl.edu, accessed July 21, 2023.
628. *Ibid.*
629. Assembly of the State of Nevada, "Emerging Technologies Task Force," Senate Bill Number 165, February 16, 2023, text online at: custom.statenet.com.
630. M. Fitzgerald, "As Employers Expand Artificial Intelligence in Hiring, Few States Have Rules," *New Hampshire Bulletin*, July 18, 2023 (corrected July 19, 2023), online at: newhampshirebulleting.com.

on AI and machine learning.[631] They include the prestigious Ivy League school, Dartmouth College, in Hanover, New Hampshire. Indeed, it is claimed that research on AI originated at Dartmouth:

> In 1956, a small group of scientists gathered for the Dartmouth Summer Research Project on Artificial Intelligence, which was the birth of this field of research.[632]

It is undoubtedly the case that serious research conducted with AI systems by educational institutions such as Dartmouth College and the University of New Hampshire will help inform government officials and legislators about the advantages and potential problems of AI.[633]

New Jersey

A legislative bill has been introduced in New Jersey that requires the Commissioner of Labor and Workforce Development to "conduct a study and issue a report on the impact of artificial intelligence" on the state economy.[634]

A bill has been introduced that requires automobile insurers to provide policyholders with annual documentation demonstrating that there are no discriminatory outcomes created by the insurers' automated underwriting system.[635]

A bill has been introduced that regulates the use of automated tools in hiring decisions to minimize discrimination in employment.[636]

Another bill has previously been introduced also relating to the use of automated tools in hiring decisions that regulates the use of search tools in order to minimize discrimination in employment.[637]

A bill has been introduced relating to the requirements for disclosure and processing of "personally identifiable information." It establishes the Office of Data Protection and Responsible Use within the Division of Consumer Affairs.[638]

A bill has been introduced that requires the Department of Labor and Workforce Development to track and maintain information on job losses due to automation.[639]

631. For information *see,* Louisiana State University, "Artificial Intelligence," online at: lsu.edu; and The University of New Orleans, "Machine Learning & Artificial Intelligence," online at: uno.edu.
632. Darmouth College, "Artificial Intelligence Coined at Dartmouth," website online at: home.dartmouth.edu, accessed July 21, 2023.
633. EduRank, "9 Best colleges for Artificial Intelligence (AI) in New Hampshire."
634. Assembly of the State of New Jersey, "Artificial Intelligence Economic Growth Study," Assembly Number A 168, January 11, 2022, text online at: custom.statenet.com.
635. Assembly of the State of New Jersey, "Automobile Insurers Automated Underwriting System," Assembly Number A 537, January 11, 2022, text online at: custom.statenet.com.
636. Assembly of the State of New Jersey, "Use of Automated Tools in Hiring Decisions," Assembly Number A 4909, April 12, 2022, text online at: custom.statenet.com.
637. Assembly of the State of New Jersey, "Use of Automated Tools in Hiring Decisions," Assembly Number A 1926, March 11, 2022, text online at: custom.statenet.com.
638. Senate of the State of New Jersey, "Personal Identifiable Information Disclosures," Senate Number 3714, March 13, 2023, text online at: custom.statenet.com.
639. Assembly of the State of New Jersey, "Job Loss Due to Automation Information," Assembly Number A 5150, June 2, 2022, text online at: custom.statenet.com.

A bill has been introduced that prohibits certain kinds of discrimination in automated decision-making systems.[640]

Opinions of qualified New Jersey legal advisors will be necessary to determine if any of these bills has been enacted into law.

New Mexico

To the extent that New Mexico has not enacted specific laws dealing with AI systems, there are numerous laws in effect in New Mexico that can affect the way that AI systems can be developed, distributed, and used in ways that may affect residents of the state of New Mexico. These include criminal laws, tort laws, privacy laws, commercial laws, etc.

Joining the rapid expansion of academic research on AI and machine learning, the University of New Mexico is reported to offer a Master of Science in Artificial Intelligence and has created a number of on-campus resources on AI.[641]

It is undoubtedly the case that a serious educational program on AI systems by UNM will help inform government officials and legislators about the advantages and potential problems of AI.

New York

New York City passed Local Law 144, which came into effect on July 5, 2023. Local Law 144:

> prohibits employers and employment agencies from using an automated employment decision tool unless the tool has been subject to a bias audit within one year of the use of the tool, information about the bias audit is publicly available, and certain notices have been provided to employees or job candidates.[642]

New York State has introduced the following bills for consideration.

A bill has been introduced in New York that designates rules for using Automated Employment Decision Tools and creates enforcement criteria for dealing with violations of those rules.[643]

New York has introduced a bill to create a temporary State Commission to Study Artificial Intelligence. The remit of the Commission is to investigate how AI robotics and automation should be regulated.[644]

New York has introduced a bill that requires state government units to use responsible standards when purchasing a product or service that employs algorithmic decision systems. The State Commissioner of Taxation and Finance must adopt

640. Assembly of the State of New Jersey, "Automated Decision System Discrimination," Assembly Number A 1402, October 2, 2022, text online at: custom.statenet.com.
641. S. Velasquez, "UNM Launches AI Resources Website to Highlight Campus-Wide AI Endeavors," *UNM Newroom*, online at: news.unm.edu, August 23, 2023.
642. New York City, "Automated Employment and Decision Tools (AEDT)," *NYC Consumer and Worker Protection*, online at: nyc.gov.
643. Legislature of the State of New York, Assembly Bill A 567, "Use of Automated Employment Decision Tools," January 9, 2023, text online at: custom.statenet.com.
644. Legislature of the State of New York, Assembly Bill A 4969, "State Commission to Study Artificial Intelligence," February 27, 2023, text online at: custom.statenet.com.

appropriate regulations that effectively apply regulations relating to unlawful discriminatory practices to state activities performed through algorithmic decision systems.[645]

North Carolina

A legislative bill has been introduced in North Carolina to establish a committee to study automation in the workforce.[646]

North Dakota

A law was enacted in North Dakota relating to the definition of the term "person." Under this statute, the term does not include "environmental elements, artificial intelligence, an animal or an inanimate object."[647]

Ohio

To the extent that Ohio has not enacted specific laws dealing with AI systems, there are numerous laws in effect in Ohio that can affect the way that AI systems can be developed, distributed and used in ways that may affect residents of the state of Ohio. These include criminal laws, tort laws, privacy laws, commercial laws, etc.

Joining the rapid expansion of academic research on AI and machine learning, a number of colleges and universities in Ohio are offering academic programs in AI, including Ohio State University.[648]

It is undoubtedly the case that a serious educational program on AI systems by such colleges and universities will help inform government officials and legislators about the advantages and potential problems of AI.

Oklahoma

To the extent that Oklahoma has not enacted specific laws dealing with AI systems, there are numerous laws in effect in Oklahoma that can affect the way that AI systems can be developed, distributed, and used in ways that may affect residents of the state of Oklahoma. These include criminal laws, tort laws, privacy laws, commercial laws, etc.

Joining the rapid expansion of academic research on AI and machine learning, the University of Oklahoma is reported to offer studies in such disciplines.[649]

It is undoubtedly the case that a serious educational program on AI systems by the University of Oklahoma and other institutions of higher learning in Oklahoma will

645. Legislature of the State of New York, Assembly Bill A 5309, "An Act To Amend the State Finance Law in Relation to the Purchase of Products That Are or Contain an Algorithmic Decision Systems," March 7, 2023, text online at: custom.statenet.com.
646. General Assembly of North Carolina, Senate Bill 460, April 3, 2023, text online at: custom.statenet.com.
647. Legislative Assembly of North Dakota, House Bill No. 1361, April 11, 2023, text online at: custom.statenet.com.
648. Department of Computer Science and Engineering, "Experiencing AI: Artificial Intelligence Research Is Booming at Ohio State, and It's Opening Doors for Students," College of Engineering, online at: cse.ohio-state.edu, October 6, 2021.
649. "Artificial Intelligence and Machine Learning at OU," online at: ou.edu.s.

help inform government officials and legislators about the advantages and potential problems of AI.

Oregon

In August 2023, the Oregon legislature passed Senate Bill 619, which is a comprehensive consumer privacy law that permits consumers to find out whether a personal data controller is processing the consumer's personal information, the categories of data being processed and a list of the third parties to which the comptroller has disclosed the consumer's personal data.[650]

A consumer can choose to refuse to be subject to being profiled by automatic decision-making systems that will analyze and predict things about their behavior, when these predictions might have legal or professional consequences. The law becomes effective on January 1, 2024. The Bill also provides for reparations for black Oregon residents who can show a heritage of slavery.[651]

Pennsylvania

Pennsylvania has introduced a bill creating an Artificial Intelligence Registry. It would amend the state Administrative Code with respect to the powers and duties of the Pennsylvania Department of Data to provide for said Artificial Intelligence Registry.[652]

That Bill became law in March 2023 by an Act amending P.L. 177, No. 175, of 1929, creating the Artificial Intelligence Registry. The details are set out in a new Section 817, added to the Act of April 9, 1929. That amendment was to take effect in May 2023.[653]

There have been additional amendments to the Public Laws of Pennsylvania relating to the use of AI tools, including HealthCare (HB0155); Education (HB0928); Employment (HB0947); Technology (HB0964) and Securities (HB1402); and others.[654]

Puerto Rico

The U.S. territory of Puerto Rico has reportedly adopted a bill launching an investigation on the use of automated AI systems that may significantly impact the rights and opportunities of persons and institutions in the territory. The bill calls for recommendations to address any potential problems.[655]

650. 2023 Session, "Senate Bill 619," online at: gov.oregonlive.com.
651. *Ibid.*
652. The General Assembly of Pennsylvania, House Bill 49, "Artificial Intelligence Registry," July 3, 2023.
653. Pennsylvania General Assembly, Bill Information—History, "House Bill 49, Regular Session 2023-2024," online at: legis.state.pa.us, March 7, 2023.
654. More information at: Pennsylvania General Assembly, Bill Information—History, "More Bills from This Session under the Same Topics as House Bill 49, Regular Session 2023-2024," online at: legis.state.pa.us, accessed September 20, 2023.
655. Legislative Assembly of Puerto Rico, Senate Resolution, SR 684 "Artificial Intelligence," text online at: custom.statenet.com.

It has also introduced a bill that would create an AI Officer and an AI Council to assist with implementation of AI in Puerto Rico[656] and a bill creating a registry of companies developing or using AI.[657]

Rhode Island

Rhode Island has introduced a bill that prohibits any algorithms or predictive models that use external consumer data in any way that unfairly discriminates based on race, color, national or ethnic origin, religion, sex, sexual orientation, disability, gender identity, or gender expression by insurers.[658]

Rhode Island has also introduced a bill to establish a commission to monitor the use of AI in state government and to make recommendations with suggesting changes in the way that state government uses AI.[659]

Rhode Island has also introduced a bill to prohibit the use of facial recognition technology in betting contexts.[660]

South Carolina

To the extent that South Carolina has not enacted specific laws dealing with AI systems, there are numerous laws in effect in South Carolina that can affect the way that AI systems can be developed, distributed, and used in ways that may affect residents of the state of South Carolina. These include criminal laws, tort laws, privacy laws, commercial laws, etc.

Joining the rapid expansion of academic research on AI and machine learning, there are a number of colleges and universities in South Carolina reported to offer studies in such disciplines, including the University of South Carolina and Clemson University.[661]

It is undoubtedly the case that serious educational work on AI systems by institutions of higher learning in South Carolina will help inform government officials and legislators about the advantages and potential problems of AI.

South Dakota

To the extent that South Dakota has not enacted specific laws dealing with AI systems, there are numerous laws in effect in South Dakota that can affect the way that AI systems can be developed, distributed, and used in ways that may affect residents of the state of South Dakota. These include criminal laws, tort laws, privacy laws, commercial laws, etc.

---

656. Senado de Puerto Rico, "P. del S. 1179," online at: senado.pr.gov, April 18, 2023.
657. National Conference of State Legislatures, "Puerto Rico SjR 412," online at: ncsl.org, accessed September 20, 2023.
658. The General Assembly of the State of Rhode Island, House Bill 5734. "Business Regulation Regarding Insurance Discrimination," text online at: custom.statenet.com, February 21, 2023.
659. The General Assembly of the State of Rhode Island, Senate Bill 117, "Artificial Intelligence in the Decision-Making Process," text online at: custom.statenet.com, February 1, 2023.
660. The General Assembly of the State of Rhode Island, Senate Bill 146, "Use of Facial and Bio Metric Recognition Technology," text online at: custom.statenet.com, February 1, 2023.
661. EduRank, "Computer Science, Artificial Intelligence (AI): North America—United States—South Carolina," online at: edurank.org.

Joining the rapid expansion of academic research on AI and machine learning, there are a number of colleges and universities in South Dakota reported to offer studies in such disciplines including the University of South Dakota.[662]

It is undoubtedly the case that serious educational work on AI systems by institutions of higher learning in South Dakota will help inform government officials and legislators about the advantages and potential problems of AI.

Tennessee

To the extent that Tennessee has not enacted specific laws dealing with AI systems, there are numerous laws in effect in Tennessee that can affect the way that AI systems can be developed, distributed, and used in ways that may affect residents of the state of Tennessee. These include criminal laws, tort laws, privacy laws, commercial laws, etc.

Joining the rapid expansion of academic research on AI and machine learning, there are a number of colleges and universities in Tennessee reported to offer studies in such disciplines including Vanderbilt University.[663]

It is undoubtedly the case that serious educational work on AI systems by institutions of higher learning in Tennessee will help inform government officials and legislators about the advantages and potential problems of AI.

Texas

The State of Texas has introduced a bill to set up an Artificial Intelligence Advisory Council.[664]

Texas has also introduced a bill to establish a program, to be administered by the State Workforce Commission, to train people in skills relating to AI systems.[665]

Texas has also introduced a bill relating to using AI in the provision of mental health services.[666]

Utah

To the extent that Utah has not enacted specific laws dealing with AI systems, there are numerous laws in effect in Utah that can affect the way that AI systems can be developed, distributed, and used in ways that may affect residents of the state of Utah. These include criminal laws, tort laws, privacy laws, commercial laws, etc.

662. EduRank, "Computer Science, Artificial Intelligence (AI): North America—United States—South Dakota," online at: edurank.org.
663. EduRank, "Computer Science, Artificial Intelligence (AI): North America—United States—Tennessee," online at: edurank.org.
664. The Legislature of the State of Texas, House Bill 2060, "Artificial Intelligence Advisory Council," June 13, 2023, text online at: custom.statenet.com.
665. The Legislature of the State of Texas, House Bill 3633, "State Workforce Commission," March 6, 2023, text online at: custom.statenet.com.
666. The Legislature of the State of Texas, House Bill 4695, "Artificial Intelligence Health Services," March 10, 2023, text online at: custom.statenet.com.

Joining the rapid expansion of academic research on AI and machine learning, there are a number of colleges and universities in Utah reported to offer studies in such disciplines including the University of Utah.[667]

It is undoubtedly the case that serious educational work on AI systems by institutions of higher learning in Utah will help inform government officials and legislators about the advantages and potential problems of AI.

Vermont

The State of Vermont has introduced a bill to restrict the monitoring of employment and the use of employment-related automated decision systems.[668]

Virginia

To the extent that Virginia has not enacted specific laws dealing with AI systems, there are numerous laws in effect in Virginia that can affect the way that AI systems can be developed, distributed, and used in ways that may affect residents of the state of Virginia. These include criminal laws, tort laws, privacy laws, commercial laws, etc.

Joining the rapid expansion of academic research on AI and machine learning, there are a number of colleges and universities in Virginia reported to offer studies in such disciplines including the University of Virginia.[669]

It is undoubtedly the case that serious educational work on AI systems by institutions of higher learning in Virginia will help inform government officials and legislators about the advantages and potential problems of AI.

Washington

The State of Washington has introduced a bill relating to the use of "automated decision systems." It is intended to establish guidelines for government procurement and use of automated decision systems. These guidelines are intended to protect consumers, improve transparency and create more market predictability.[670]

West Virginia

To the extent that West Virginia has not enacted specific laws dealing with AI systems, there are numerous laws in effect in West Virginia that can affect the way that AI systems can be developed, distributed, and used in ways that may affect residents of the state of West Virginia. These include criminal laws, tort laws, privacy laws, commercial laws, etc.

667. EduRank, "Computer Science, Artificial Intelligence(AI): North America—United States—Utah," online at: edurank.org.
668. The General Assembly of the State of Vermont, House Bill 114, "Electronic Monitoring," January 25, 2023, text online at: custom.statenet.com.
669. EduRank, "Computer Science, Artificial Intelligence(AI): North America—United States—Virginia," online at: edurank.org.
670. The Legislature of the State of Washington, Senate Bill 5356, "Use of Automated Decision Systems," January 12, 2023, text online at: custom.statenet.com.

Joining the rapid expansion of academic research on AI and machine learning, there are a number of colleges and universities in Virginia reported to offer studies in such disciplines including the University of West Virginia.[671]

It is undoubtedly the case that serious educational work on AI systems by institutions of higher learning in West Virginia will help inform government officials and legislators about the advantages and potential problems of AI.

Wisconsin

To the extent that Wisconsin has not enacted specific laws dealing with AI systems, there are numerous laws in effect in Wisconsin that can affect the way that AI systems can be developed, distributed, and used in ways that may affect residents of the state of Wisconsin. These include criminal laws, tort laws, privacy laws, commercial laws, etc.

Joining the rapid expansion of academic research on AI and machine learning, there are a number of colleges and universities in Wisconsin reported to offer studies in such disciplines including the University of Wisconsin.[672]

It is undoubtedly the case that serious educational work on AI systems by institutions of higher learning in Wisconsin will help inform government officials and legislators about the advantages and potential problems of AI.

Wyoming

To the extent that Wyoming has not enacted specific laws dealing with AI systems, there are numerous laws in effect in Wyoming that can affect the way that AI systems can be developed, distributed, and used in ways that may affect residents of the state of Wyoming. These include criminal laws, tort laws, privacy laws, commercial laws etc.

Joining the rapid expansion of academic research on AI and machine learning, there are colleges and universities in Wyoming reported to offer studies in such disciplines including the University of Wyoming.[673]

It is undoubtedly the case that serious educational work on AI systems by institutions of higher learning in Wyoming will help inform government officials and legislators about the advantages and potential problems of AI.

16.11.14 AI Hardware

NVIDIA Computer Chips

It is the case that AI systems such as the well-known ChatGPT of OpenAI require sophisticated and powerful hardware to perform their functions.

671. EduRank, "Computer Science, Artificial Intelligence(AI): North America—United States—West Virginia," online at: edurank.org.
672. EduRank, "Computer Science, Artificial Intelligence(AI): North America—United States—South Dakota," online at: edurank.org.
673. EduRank, "Computer Science, Artificial Intelligence(AI): North America—United States—Wyoming," online at: edurank.org.

It was reported in May 2023 that a computer chip that has made it possible for AI systems to function at the level they do is made by the California-based computer chip maker, NVIDIA. This association has led to a significant increase in the business of NVIDIA:[674]

> Originally known for making the type of computer chips that process graphics, particularly for computer games, NVIDIA hardware underpins most AI applications today.

Several super computers use NVIDIA chips in their GPUs. For example, it is reported that ChatGPT used 10,000 NVIDIA processing units to train its functionality. NVIDIA is reported to have about 95% of the machine learning GPU market. In 2022, the AI business boomed, increasing revenue by about 40% to around $15 billion.[675]

A positive effect on NVIDIA has been dramatic. NVIDIA has raised its production to meet growing demand and its share price rose almost 30% in May 2023. The AI chips NVIDIA sells to data centers can cost about $10,000 but it is now producing more powerful chips that sell for much more.[676]

NVIDIA was founded in 1993 and initially focused on making better graphics chips for gaming and other sophisticated applications. For important computer tasks such as operating the visual pixels found on a computer screen, GPUs are designed to perform many parallel tasks at the same time.

When it was discovered that such GPUs could increase the speed of mathematics calculations dramatically, the basis of AI was established.[677]

In about 2006, the head of NVIDIA focused their technology on creating a way to make its GPUs programmable which meant that they could be used in many functions other than improving graphics performance. This made it possible for consumer level computers to do much more sophisticated processing than had previously been possible. This was a "breakthrough" which made today's AI possible.

By about 2012, it was possible to use NVIDIA GPUs to "train" AI systems to produce more sophisticated results. This started computer scientists and computer businesses buying such GPUs to massively speed up the processing needed for the operations they were seeking to do.

By 2021, the capabilities of such GPUs produced not only positive outcomes but also made it possible to produce negative and potentially damaging outcomes such as "deep fakes" such as photographic, video and audio simulations that could appear to the real productions by actual people, such as movie stars and others.[678] This reportedly led to a statement by Harrison Ford in 2023 that "I could be dead and I'm still working."[679]

674. Z. Corbyn, "Nvidia: The Chip Maker That Became an AI Superpower," *BBC News*, online, May 26, 2023.
675. *Ibid.*
676. *Ibid.*
677. *Ibid.*
678. *Ibid.*
679. M. MacNamara, "Why Does This Movie Exist? Harrison Ford Explains Reprising 'Indiana Jones' at 80," *Los Angeles Times*, online, May 19, 2023.

It is obvious that there are risks to the expansion of AI systems that will, hopefully, be sensibly dealt with by appropriate laws and regulations.

It is true that the present NVIDIA dominates the GPU market for sophisticated computer applications such as AI systems. However, competitors such as AMD and Intel are trying to catch up. One industry analyst reportedly said:

> NVIDIA is the one with the target on its back that everybody is trying to take down.[680]

So far, NVIDIA has managed to stay ahead of the competition in the race to provide sophisticated GPUs to cutting edge digital creators. In May 2023, it was reported that NVIDIA was on track to become "the first chip company with a $1 trillion market value."[681] When its role in the AI market became more widely known, increases in the price of its stock made NVIDIA the most valuable chip company in the world and the fifth most valuable company in the United States. In 2023, NVIDIA, a company founded in 1993, saw its market value more than double.

16.11.15 U.S. Legal Profession Views

There is no doubt that the growing expansion of AI uses will significantly impact both law and law practice. This has been an expanding topic of discussion by practicing lawyers and professional organizations in the United States.

Many U.S. law firms have published their views on AI developments and have offered to advise on the impact of AI systems. Their views are often stated as publications on their websites.

Professional associations of lawyers have collectively published a number of opinions about the development and impact of AI systems. For example, the American Bar Association (ABA), which is a nationwide voluntary association of lawyers, has issued a number of publications on its website[682] about issues relating to AI, including the following:

- AI and robotics (accessed May 15, 2023).
- AI and the practice of law (April 11, 2023).
- AI: legal, industry, and regulatory highlights (April 4, 2023).

In February 2023, the ABA House of Delegates adopted a resolution setting up three guidelines to improve the use of AI:[683]

- "Developers of AI should ensure that their products, services, systems and capabilities are subject to human authority, oversight and control.

680. Corbyn, May 26, 2023, as cited above, quoting industry analyst, Kevin Krewell.
681. A. Ralph, "Nvidia on Track to Be the First Trillion-Dollar Chip Company," *The Times*, online, May 25, 2023.
682. American Bar Association (ABA), online at: americanbar.org.
683. *Ibid.*

- Organizations should be accountable for consequences related to their use of AI, including any legally cognizable injury or harm caused by their actions, unless they have taken reasonable steps to prevent harm or injury.
- Developers should ensure the transparency and traceability of their AI and protect related intellectual property by documenting key decisions made regarding the design and risk of data sets, procedures and outcomes underlying their AI."[684]

These are clearly good guidelines for developers and users of AI to aspire to. They are also descriptions of goals that legal and regulatory systems should incorporate.

They are not terribly different from guidelines that have been suggested by other commentators, both private and those related to regulatory organizations.

It is hoped that such requirements are included as fundamental regulations in legal systems around the world and in the mission aspirations of both developers and users of AI.

16.11.16 Some U.S. AI Cases

A Chatbot Gets It Wrong

In late May 2023, it was reported that a New York lawyer employed a chatbot (reportedly ChatGPT) to help with legal research used in a legal brief submitted to a federal court in Manhattan in a lawsuit against an airline.[685] Unfortunately, the brief cited a number of supporting court decisions that did not exist and had been reportedly invented by the chatbot.

The lawyer who submitted the citations admitted his mistake and "threw himself on the mercy of the court." He said that he had queried the chatbot whether its citations existed and were correct and accurate. The chatbot replied that the citations were authentic, which was false.

It appears that the chatbot may not only provide false information, but it may also "lie" about its authenticity.

However, the judge, saying that the brief contained "bogus judicial decisions, with bogus quotes and bogus internal citations," ordered a hearing to consider whether to impose sanctions.[686]

Clients hire lawyers and pay them large fees because they believe their attorneys have the legal knowledge and experience to provide them with arguments on their behalf that are the product of careful professional analysis by those lawyers.

Clients are not paying to be represented by chatbots or other AI systems. They are paying for highly educated, well-qualified and appropriately experienced human legal minds.

---

684. *Ibid.*
685. B. Weiser, "Here's What Happens When Your Lawyer Uses ChatGPT," *The New York Times*, online, May 27, 2023.
686. *Ibid.*

It should be clear that no lawyer should rely on chatbots to provide legal research. Chatbots did not study for years to earn a law degree, passed no bar exams, and have no professional obligation to be truthful.

It may be true that in some jobs, AI can be helpful, but in legal representation, actual intelligence is more important.

The recent expansion of the creation and use of AI-related systems means that there is not a long history of litigation and court decisions on issues raised by AI. However, that is changing both in the United States and elsewhere.[687]

In 2023, the U.S. news organization CNBC published a story outlining some of the cases that were being brought because of issues relating to the creation and use of AI systems.[688]

The article said:

> As companies including Microsoft, Google and open AI launch generative AI to the general public, lawsuits are piling up from the creative industries about copyright work co-opted or used by AI.

As examples of the kinds of cases that are being brought to resolve AI-related issues, there are the following examples.

Bev Standing v. TikTok[689]

In September 2021, TikTok reportedly settled a lawsuit brought by the actress Bev Standing.

Ms. Standing reportedly alleged that TikTok was using her voice without permission. An electronic version of what Ms. Standing alleged sounded like her voice was used to speak over videos on the TikTok website.

Lawyers for the parties said the lawsuit had been settled amicably and that TikTok would license Ms. Standing's voice.

Butterick v. GitHub

In November 2022, a class action lawsuit was filed in the U.S. District Court for the Northern District of California against defendants, including GitHub Inc., Microsoft Corporation, and OpenAI Inc.

Among other things, the Complaint says:

> "8. In June 2021, GitHub and OpenAI launched Copilot, an AI based product that promises to assist software coders by providing or filling in blocks of code using AI. GitHub charges Copilot users $10 per month or $100 per year for the service. Copilot ignores, violates and removes the Licenses offered by thousands—possibly

687. *See* for example, the United Kingdom case referred to in an earlier chapter in which a scientist named Stephen Thaler tried to have patents issued in the U.K. to an artificial intelligence system Thaler created. Thaler claimed that certain inventions were independently "created," without human intervention by his AI system.
688. E. Sheng, "In Generative AI Legal Wild West, the Courtroom Battles Are Just Getting Started," *CNBC,* online at: cnbc.com, April 3, 2023.
689. J. Kastrenakes, "TikTok Settles Lawsuit with Actress over Its Orginal Text-To-Speech Voice/She Said TikTok Never Had Permission to Use Her Voice," *The Verge,* online at: theverge.com, September 29, 2021.

millions—of software developers, thereby accomplishing software piracy on an unprecedented scale."

"35. Plaintiffs do not know the exact number of class members, because such information is in the exclusive control of defendants. Plaintiffs are informed and believe that there are thousands of class members geographically dispersed throughout the United States section of joinder of all class members in the prosecution of this action is impractical."[690]

One commentator has said:

> This case is only in its earliest stages but could have a huge effect on the broader world of AI, where companies are making fortunes training software on copyright-protected data.[691]

Matthew Butterick, one of the attorneys who filed the lawsuit, is quoted as saying:

> As far as we know, this is the first class-action case in the US challenging the training and output of AI systems. It will not be the last.[692]

Another online tech commentator has written:

> The current legal cases against generative AI are just the beginning: AI that can generate art, text and more is in for a reckoning.[693]

There is a little doubt that the resolution of this case will have a significant impact on intellectual property protection law in the United States and perhaps far beyond.

Getty Images v. Stability AI

In February 2023, a similar case was filed by Getty Images U.S. Inc. in the United States District Court for the District of Delaware against Stability AI, Inc., also based on an infringement of intellectual property claim.

The Complaint says:

> 1. This case arises from Stability AI's brazen infringement of Getty images' intellectual property on a staggering scale. On information and belief, Stability AI has copied *more than 12 million* photographs from Getty Images collection, along with the associated captions and meta data, without permission from or compensation to Getty Images, as part of its efforts to build a competing business. As part of its unlawful scheme, Stability AI has removed or altered Getty Images' copyright management information, provided false copyright management information, and infringed Getty Images' famous trademarks.

690. Complaint filed on November 3, 2022, available online at: githubcopilotlitigation.com.
691. J. Vincent, "The Lawsuit That Could Rewrite the Rules of AI Copyright," *The Verge*, online at: theverge.com, November 8, 2022.
692. *Ibid.*
693. K. Wiggers, "The Current Legal Cases Against Generative AI Are Just the Beginning: AI That Can Generate Art, Text and More Is in for a Reckoning," *TechCrunch*, online at: techcrunch.com, January 27, 2023.

This case and similar cases are very serious matters for Stability AI and other makers of generative AI systems that produce written, audio or visual output.

If it is necessary for such generative AI systems to be "trained" by reviewing and using protected intellectual property found on the Internet (or elsewhere) and court decisions that hold such "training" is a violation of the legal rights of the owners of such IP, then generative AI creators may be required to pay large damages for their usage of such IP and, if they decide to create such output in the future, may be required to pay large licensing fees in order to be able to do so.

Rulings that are unfavorable to the "training" procedures of generative AI systems may make some uses of search generative AI tools economically difficult or impossible.

Prisma Labs

In March 2023, a Chicago law firm filed a class action lawsuit against Prisma Labs Inc. Prisma marketed an AI-powered photo editing app called Lensa AI. It is claimed that Prisma:

> "Violated the Illinois biometric information and privacy act (BIPA) by collecting users facial geometry without their permission, using it to train/develop artificial intelligence (AI) to see neural networks, and illegally store the data."[694]
>
> It is alleged that: "Prisma Labs Inc. trained ... Lensa Ai by harvesting biometric data from billions of photographs it 'covertly scraped' from the Internet, including facial images of thousands of Illinois residents, ..."[695]

Unlike the previous AI lawsuits mentioned above, this involved as much an invasion of privacy violation as a theft of intellectual property claim.[696]

However, both flow from the "training" procedures involved in providing functionality to an AI system.

It seems that although AI tools might be usable in a variety of crimes and civil law violations, a substantial number of the claims brought in lawsuits against AI systems will flow from the setting-up and "training" of AI tools as much as from violations created by their subsequent operations.

Stephen Thaler Case

On April 24, 2023, it was reported that the U.S. Supreme Court refused to hear a challenge brought by a computer scientist named Steven Thaler to the refusal by the U.S. Patent and Trademark Office to issue patents to his AI system for inventions. Thaler claims were created by his AI system:

694. C. Yasiejko, "Prisma Labs Sued over Lensa AI App's Biometric Data Harvesting."
695. J. Gray, "Lawsuit Alleges Lensa.ai App Illegally Took Users' Biometric Data," *PetaPixel*, online at: petapixel.com.
696. Although intellectual property issues may be involved depending on how the photographs were made and posted and who owned them.

> The justices turned away Thaler's appeal of a lower court's ruling that patents can be issued only to human inventors and that his AI system could not be considered the legal creator of two inventions that he said it had generated.[697]

As shown in another chapter, Thaler also tried to get registrations for his AI system in England as well but was rejected there for the same reasons.

697. B. Brittain, "US Supreme Court Rejects Computer Scientist's Lawsuit over AI-Generated Inventions," *Reuters*, online April 24, 2023.

CHAPTER 17
U.K. Law

17.1 U.K. EFFORTS TO BUILD ITS CYBER ECONOMY

Since leaving the EU (Brexit), there have been many articles and discussions about the economic impact of that decision.

Principal concerns are related to the impacts on international trade, manufacturing, financial services, and agriculture. There has been much disagreement as to whether Brexit will be of long-term benefit or detriment to the U.K. economy.

However, it is clear that the U.K. is seeking to be a leading player in the growing cyber economy, building on its relatively strong educational and scientific sectors.

17.1.1 The U.K. Internet

Sometime after the United States, the U.K. set up its own version of the Internet. By 1983, it had put in place its own network connecting university computers around the country called JANET. It introduced the dot UK (.uk) domain name in 1985, and the U.K. was included in the World Wide Web by 1991.

The first U.K. consumer-priced Internet subscription service, Demon Internet, was introduced in 1992.

The Internet rapidly expanded in the U.K.

It is not possible in a single chapter to review all the ways in which the U.K. economy interacts with the rapidly expanding international cyber economy. Parts of it are considered in other chapters, such as those on competition law, IP law, etc. The goal of this chapter is to show how the U.K. is making efforts to integrate its economy into the expanding cyber markets and how it is seeking to regulate and control those parts of it the government considers most sensitive.

With the rapid growth of the internet economy, the government became concerned that there were dangers of criminal activity and other misuse of the Internet, both within the U.K. and internationally. Parliament introduced laws to protect against that and to regulate activity on the Internet.

17.1.2 The Computer Misuse Act 1990

The first of these laws was the Computer Misuse Act of 1990. It was aimed at preventing and punishing criminal activity on the Internet.

The Act identified three types of Internet activity as criminal:

- The first was obtaining unauthorized access to computer materials.
- The second was unauthorized access with intent to commit or facilitate the commission of offenses.
- The third forbids unauthorized changes to computer material.

This Act was introduced in response to a 1988 criminal case, *R. v. Gold & Schifreen.*[698]

The defendants were two hackers who surreptitiously learned a British Telecom engineer's password to get unauthorized access to the BT Prestel video data system. The Prestel system offered subscribers access to video information on the internet. One of its other early services was a messaging service known as Prestel Mailbox that allowed subscribers to send and receive messages.

Using the stolen access keys, hackers Gold and Schifreen were able to access the private Mailbox information of subscribers, including the private Mailbox of the Queen's husband, Prince Phillip.

However, the defendants were acquitted because their activities did not constitute a specific criminal offense at that time.

Because of the high-profile nature of the defendants' hacking into private and Royal Family information on the Internet and the uproar that caused, Parliament passed the Computer Misuse Act in 1990.

However, the Act came under criticism for not distinguishing between curious hackers like Schifreen and Gold and committed cyber criminals. Consequently, Parliament subsequently passed several acts to prevent and punish cybercrime and amended several other Acts and regulations to include Internet activity.

17.1.3 Dealing with Harmful Content

This scrutiny and control of the Internet has become increasingly important in the U.K., where it is estimated that over 90% of adults are connected to the Internet and where over £190,000 a day is lost to cybercriminals.[699]

In August 2020, a comment in *The Times* argued that one area that U.K. Internet regulation has struggled with is the protection of Internet users against harmful

698. *Regina v. Gold & Schrifreen,* CACD July 17, 1987.
699. BBC.com, January 27, 2019. *See,* Chapter 16.

content.[700] The author said that although ISPs are required to remove terrorist propaganda and childabuse material, users are still subjected to harmful material such as "trolling, disinformation, and self-harm guides" and other content that may be technically legal but "can harm our well-being, our mental health and, in extreme cases, our democracy."[701]

The author, Salma Shah, who is a former advisor to the U.K. Home Secretary,[702] wrote that recent U.K. governments have a poor record of dealing with harmful Internet content. The government had prepared a report (a "white paper") on harmful online content that proposed the creation of a new independent regulator that would exclusively deal with this issue and set a new higher standard for online safety. However, Shah argued that the U.K. government lacked the "courage" to follow through with this groundbreaking plan to regulate the Internet as a special case and that this constituted "a missed opportunity" to effectively regulate harmful content.[703] Shah laments that it was decided to give responsibility for Internet regulation to the "already over-burdened communications regulator," Ofcom.[704]

17.2 DATA PROTECTION AND PRIVACY

17.2.1 BA Data Breach

In 2019, British Airways was found guilty of a data breach that leaked the names, addresses and bank card details of over 400,000 customers and staff. The U.K. ICO required British Airways to pay a fine of £20 million, which is the largest fine it had imposed to date.

The matter also went to mediation instead of a public trial, and a settlement was reached with BA. The terms of the settlement are confidential, although lawyers for the claimants said that the outcome was "extremely positive." British Airways was required to pay compensation to the victims of the data breach.[705]

17.2.2 Protection of Anonymity

Another important question having to do with online privacy is the issue of the protection of anonymity in the Internet age.

In 2014, Lord Neuberger, the President of the U.K. Supreme Court, addressed this issue in his lecture to a group of lawyers and journalists in London, "What's in a name? Privacy and anonymous speech on the internet."[706]

700. S. Shah, "Britain Can't Afford to Miss This Chance to Clean Up the Web," *The Times*, "Thunderer," *Comment*, online, Thursday, August 6, 2020, retrieved August 7, 2020.
701. *Ibid.*
702. Former Home Secretary, Sajid Javid, 2018-2019.
703. Shah, above.
704. *Ibid.*
705. J. Ames, "British Airways Settles over Record Claim for Data Breach," *The Times*, online, July 23, 2021.
706. Online at: supremecourt.uk.

In his speech, one of the functions of free speech that he highlighted as most important is "holding power, particularly governmental power, to account." He identified freedom of the press and privacy as crucial in accomplishing that task.

He noted that there is an unavoidable tension between the right to privacy in Article 8 of the ECHR and the right to freedom of expression contained in Article 10 of the ECHR. Consequently, it is often left to the courts to create a balance between these interests when they come into conflict. The U.K. Supreme Court described both as "vitally important rights" in the case of *Campbell v. MGN*. Lord Neuberger emphasizes that neither has precedence over the other.[707]

The tension between them is particularly acute when a court is asked to grant a privacy injunction.[708] Although this topic has been important for some time, the Internet has raised additional issues to be considered. To begin his analysis of the new privacy issues, Lord Neuberger begins by referring to the Eighteenth-Century problem of "Junius."

Junius was the author of anonymous letters that were printed by a newspaper called *The Public Advertiser*. Junius was a defender of free speech and a harsh critic of the government. It is believed that his attacks on the government may have led to the resignation of the then Prime Minister, the Duke of Grafton, in 1770. He was also a harsh critic of the judiciary, stating in one letter quoted by Lord Neuberger that:

> A judge under the influence of government, may be honest enough in the decision of private causes, yet a traitor to the public.

In 1769, Junius addressed a public letter to King George, which began:

> Sir,—It is the misfortune of your life, and originally the cause of every reproach and distress which has attended your government, that you should never have been acquainted with the language of truth, until you heard it in the complaints of your people.

This publication caused the publisher of the *Public Advertiser* to be tried for seditious libel. Neuberger points out that the debate over this trial, its verdict and its mistrial led to positive changes in libel law.

However, one issue that caused considerable comment at the time, and which, according to Lord Neuberger, has important implications for the regulation of Internet postings, was importance of privacy and anonymity.

Two of the most important political and social commentators of that period, Edmund Burke and Samuel Johnson, defended Junius's anonymity, arguing that it gave Junius the ability to make strong, and often justified and badly needed, public criticisms of the powerful while being protected from prosecution or other harassment by offended powers be they individual or institutional.[709]

---

707. [2004] 2 AC 457 at [12] per Lord Hoffman.
708. This is a topic upon which a committee on super-injunctions (which Lord Neuberger appointed and chaired when he was Master of the Rolls) reported in 2011. The Report can be found at: Online at: judyiciary.gov.
709. Neuberger, pp. 2-5. The identity of Junius has never been discovered, although some of his contemporaries believed that Burke was Junius.

Neuberger compares the bloggers of today to Junius.[710] He points out that the Internet has given many people, at low or no cost, opportunity to publish anonymously and widely. Bloggers often take extra steps to protect their anonymity by using Virtual Private Networks (VPNs) and using "private browsing" modes. However, because of the search and hacking tools available to users of the Internet, it is becoming increasingly more difficult to maintain one's anonymity when using the Internet.

One example is the political blogger, "Guido Fawkes," who was credited with several political "wins," including against a government minister. But he was able to maintain anonymity for only a few months before the *Guardian* newspaper revealed his identity.[711]

To defend their anonymity, some Internet posters have relied on the legal ruling that one does "have a right to be forgotten."[712] This is also known as the "right to erasure." This is a right granted under the EU's GDPR that gives individuals the right to ask organizations to delete their personal data. This is found in recitals 65 and 66 and in Article 17 of the GDPR, which states:

> The data subject shall have the right to obtain from the controller the erasure of personal data concerning him or her without undue delay and the controller shall have the obligation to erase personal data without undue delay.

Under certain conditions, "undue delay" is about a month. The right to erasure is not without limits. It is available under the following conditions as set out in Article 17:

- The data is no longer necessary for the purpose that the organization that originally collected or processed it.
- An organization relies on an individual's consent as the lawful basis for processing the data and that individual withdraws their consent.
- An organization relies on legitimate interests as its justification for processing an individual's data.
- The individual objects to this processing and there is no overriding legitimate interest for the organization to continue with the processing.
- An organization processes personal data for direct marketing purposes and the individual objects to this processing.
- An organization processed an individual's personal data unlawfully.
- An organization must erase the data in order to comply with a legal ruling or obligation.
- An organization has processed a child's personal data to offer their information to social services.

However, there are circumstances in which an organization's right to process someone's data could override that person's right to be forgotten. Such circumstances include:

710. Neuberger, p. 5.
711. *Ibid.*, p. 6.
712. *Google Spain SL. And Google Inc. v. Agencia Espanola de Proteccion de Datos (AEPD and Mario Costeja Gonzalez* (C-131/12)).

- The data is being used to exercise the right of freedom of expression and information.
- The data is being used to comply with a legal ruling or obligation.
- The data is being used to perform a task that is being carried out in the public interest or when exercising and organization's official authority.
- The data being processed is necessary for public health purposes and serves the public interest.
- The data being processed is necessary to perform preventative or occupational medicine:
  - This only applies when the data is being processed by a health professional who is subject to a legal obligation of professional secrecy.
- The data represents important information that serves the public interest, scientific research, historical research, or statistical purposes and where erasure of the data would likely impair or halt progress toward the achievement that was the goal of the processing.
- The data is being used for the establishment of a legal defense or in the exercise of other legal claims.

It should be noted that an organization can request a "reasonable fee" or deny a request if the organization can justify that the request was unfounded or excessive.[713]

However, as Lord Neuberger points out, there is sometimes a public interest to be served by identifying certain people in stories in newspapers on the Internet. Consequently, courts will sometimes override the right to privacy to permit the publishing of the names of persons in the appropriate circumstances, such as:

- It is considered necessary to protect free speech and freedom of the press.
- If, in the interest of privacy, publishers were prevented from naming individuals associated with certain situations relating to public safety or other strong public interest.
- Complete privacy may threaten the viability of newspapers and magazines
  - "because stories about particular individuals are simply much more attractive to readers than stories about unidentified people ... Newspapers and magazines ... can only inform the public if they attract enough readers and make enough money to survive."[714]

Of course, exposing the identity of bloggers may make them reluctant to express themselves candidly on the Internet. This effect cuts both ways.

True, it is sometimes important to reveal information that the government considers "secret" such as the Pentagon Papers or the Watergate Tapes but there are instances when doing that can create situations that endanger lives.

For example, Lord Neuberger points to a situation in which a blogger known as "NightJack" published various allegations and observations about police activity. In a

713. https://gdpr.eu/?s=right+of+erasure.
714. Taken from the opinion of Lord Rodger in *In re Guardian News and Media Ltd. And others*, referred to by Lord Neuberger.

case relating to that, the court ruled that this activity was not a "private activity" where the blogger could have a reasonable expectation of privacy, but was rather an activity of public interest in public information. In that case, the blogger was revealed to be a police detective constable.[715]

17.2.2.1 Common Law Confidentiality

It is important to note here that under English Common Law, a poster's identity may also be protected by well-established principles of confidentiality.

For example, legal professional privilege regarding information received from a client has been held to override a person's legitimate interest in pursuing remedies against the blogger who had revealed confidential information belonging to a person.[716]

17.2.2.2 Comparisons of Anonymous Speech Protection

U.S.

It cannot be ignored that because the Internet currently reaches about 70% of the world's population, it offers unmatchable opportunities to make one's views known around the world. As the U.S. Supreme Court said in the case of *Reno v. ACLU*[717] in 1997, the Internet represents "the most participatory form of mass speech yet developed":

> Through the use of chat rooms, any person with a phone line can become a town crier with a voice that resonates father then it could from any soapbox.[718]

In that case, the U.S. Supreme Court was considering the justification of a law restricting publication of sexual material. However, the court held the law to be overbroad and, therefore, unconstitutional. Justice Stevens wrote:

> The interest in encouraging freedom of expression in a democratic society outweighs any theoretical but unproven benefit of censorship.[719]

EU

Lord Neuberger considers how Internet speech interacts with rights under Article 8 of the ECHR. The EU's attitude toward Article 8 is that it protects not only privacy per se

715. Decision of Mr. Justice Eady, in *Author of a Blog v. Times Newspapers Ltd.* [2009] EWHC 1358 (QB). However, because a *Times* reporter had resorted to email hacking to discover the blogger's identity, the *Times* later made a public apology to the blogger. Neuberger, p. 9.
716. Neuberger, p. 9, citing the case of *SRJ v. Person(s) Unknown being the author and commenters of Internet blogs*, [2014] EWHC 2293.
717. 521 U.S. 844.
718. Stevens, delivering the Opinion of the Court at p. 58.
719. *Ibid.*, at p. 91.

but also covers personal autonomy and self-development as well. Lord Neuberger says, "the Internet offers unprecedented opportunities for such self-development."[720]

Article 10 of the ECHR provides no express protection for the press, but a kind of parallel protection has been found to exist under that Article in European court cases. For example, in the *Goodwin* cased cited by Lord Neuberger,[721] although the press has no express right to publish information freely, the public does have the right under Article 10 to receive accurate information, of which the press can be an important source. Lord Neuberger's view is that this protected right to receive accurate information should naturally also extend protection of anonymous internet bloggers.[722]

As Lord Neuberger points out:

> Throughout history, people's willingness to engage in debate on controversial subjects in the public sphere has always been linked to possibilities for doing so anonymously. The Internet allows individuals to access information and engage in public debate without having to reveal their real identities.[723]

However, the Internet also makes it easier for governments and others to find information about Internet users. Therefore, the Internet has provided opportunities for expression but also made it difficult to be certain that one's posts will remain anonymous.

China and South Korea

Some government regulators have taken steps to eliminate anonymous blogging.

For example, China requires that micro-bloggers on China's "Weibo" platform must register their real names to use the service.

South Korea has introduced a similar regulation.

United States

The United States has taken a very different approach. The U.S. Supreme Court has ruled that the right to freedom of expression includes a right "to read anonymously."[724] Indeed, tools have been developed to help users protect their anonymity such as the free "TOR" app.[725]

The U.S. Supreme Court has gone so far as to approve anonymous political pamphleteering as:

> an honorable tradition of advocacy and dissent [and] a shield from the tyranny of the majority.[726]

720. Neuberger, p. 10.
721. *Goodwin v. UK* (16/1994/463/544) (1996) 1 BHRC 81. Neuberger, p. 14.
722. Neuberger, p. 14.
723. *Ibid.*, p. 11, quoting the Report of UN Special Rapporteur Frank La Rue to the Human Rights Council, A/HRC/17/27.
724. Neuberger, p. 11, citing, *United States v. Rumely*, 345 US, 41, 57.
725. A browser intended to increase privacy and anonymity online. Express VPN, "What Is Tor and How to Use It," online at: expressvpn.com, accessed November 6, 2024.
726. *McIntyre v. Ohio Elections Commission*, 514 US 334 (1995). Neuberger, pp. 11-12.

Generally, freedom of the press and freedom of expression is protected in liberal democracies.

However, there is an important difference between the level of protection in the United States and the protection given in Article 10 of the convention governing EU and U.K. regulation. In the context of a case in which a journalist published and illegally intercepted a telephone conversation, the U.S. Supreme Court ruled that the right to privacy was outweighed by the First Amendment right to publish information of substantial public interest.[727]

Of course, it is difficult or impossible to completely regulate how the Internet is used or what is posted on the Internet. About this, Lord Neuberger argues that the law must always be prepared to adapt to new technology in the case of the Internet, despite the difficulties at present. Because of its international nature and other reasons, both domestic law and international treaties and conventions can put reasonable limits on the use of the Internet and legislators would be remiss in their duty if they did not make significant efforts to impose such reasonable regulations.[728]

Because of the international nature of the Internet, it is necessary for international organizations and groupings of many countries to develop consistent comprehensive regulations to control Internet postings of opinions and political information and to prevent dangerous and illegally offensive postings such as racial attacks and insults.

If it is not possible to put together international treaties or conventions that effectively regulate Internet postings in ways that protect freedom of speech and of the press, but prevent and punish illegally offensive and false information from being broadcast over the Internet, then it is up to the domestic legislatures of individual countries and jurisdictions to provide those regulations.

The Internet has and is growing so rapidly that it is often the case that legislation will be some way behind the latest activities on the Internet, but this must not discourage legislators from making the effort to protect privacy and free speech without permitting the publication of false or dangerous information.[729]

17.3 ONLINE SAFETY ACT 2023

The U.K. proposed to improve its protection from online abuse by introducing an Online Safety Bill. A draft of the bill was proposed in May 2021. However, the main political parties split over who should be members of a "scrutiny committee" to review the bill. Consequently, the Online Safety Act was not passed until October 2023.

The overall purpose of the Act is to protect children and adults online.

727. *Bartinicki v. Vopper*, 532 US 514 (2001). The First Amendment to the U.S. Constitution expressly says, "Congress shall make no law ... abridging the freedom of speech, or of the press."
728. Neuberger, p. 15.
729. *Ibid.*, pp. 15-16.

The Act "puts a range of new duties on social media companies and search services, making them more responsible for their users' safety on their platforms."[730]

Implementation of the Act is the responsibility of the U.K. Office of Communications (Ofcom). The Act requires Ofcom to develop appropriate regulations and codes to effectuate the purposes of the Act. This is an ongoing process. Details as to what codes and regulations are in force, what are being considered and how the Act is being enforced are available online at www.gov.uk and ofcom.org.uk.

The new criminal offenses that the Act brought into effect on January 31, 2024, include the following:

- Encouraging or assisting serious self-harm.
- Cyberflashing.
- Sending false information intended to cause non-trivial harm.
- Threatening communications.
- Intimate image abuse.
- Epilepsy trolling.

The impetus for such legislation was the disgraceful racial abuse posted online after England played in the final of the Euro 2020 football tournament. After England lost in a penalty shootout at the end of the match, several Internet users in the U.K. directed racial abuse and threats at the England players that had missed their penalty shots.

At least five people were arrested in connection with the abusive posts.[731]

The U.K. Prime Minister has condemned the racist internet attacks and says that those responsible will be banned from attending future football matches.[732]

Racism is not the only abuse that is expressed online. In addition to the outrageous racial slurs that appeared on social media after England's loss in the European football championship, another area of Internet hatred and prejudice that has been widely talked about in the press is the presence of antisemitism expressed on social media platforms.

This takes several forms. One of the most prevalent is antisemitic conspiracy theories making outrageous claims of the existence of harmful conspiracies created by members of the Jewish community, including the absurd claim that Jewish people are somehow responsible for COVID-19.[733]

Other absurd abusive posts include bizarre theories about how certain Jewish individuals or groups are seeking to or already running the world or important parts of the world economy such as the financial system.

One area that has been an area of strong focus is the growing AI economy and its relation to media, manufacturing, medicine and defense.

730. Guidance, "What the Online Safety Act does," Department for Science Innovation and Technology, online at: www.gov.uk, May 8, 2024.
731. T. Knowles, "Bukayo Saka Attacks Social Media Giants over Racist Abuse after Euro 3030 final," *The Times*, online, July 16, 2021.
732. O. Wright & E. Courea, "PM Pledges Match Bans to Punish Racist Trolls," *The Times*, online, July 15, 2021.
733. "Social media giants fail to curb 90% of antisemitism," *The Times*, online, August 2, 2021.

17.4 AI REGULATION AND THE U.K.

Since the release of ChatGPT, there have been numerous comments and discussions in all types of media around the world about the need for regulating AI.

Most of these have consisted of general discussions outlining what commentators believe to be the risks that AI systems will present to the human race, usually ending with a call for government regulation of AI. Few of these articles have given specific details of what the authors believe the regulation should be.

One important exception to this is the proposed European AI Law discussed in another chapter.[734]

The response of the U.K. has been the making of strenuous efforts to involve the U.K. in growing the AI business and creating international AI regulations.[735]

17.4.1 U.K./U.S. Summit on AI Regulation

The U.K. outlined its "pro-innovation" position on the development and regulation of AI in a policy paper in 2022.[736]

The U.K. government has stated its intention to "make the UK a science and technology superpower by 2030."[737]

The U.K. has a reputation for leading expertise on AI that was enhanced by its organization of an international "AI Safety Summit" to discuss the development of AI that was held in November 2023.

This was intended to propose international regulations for its safe development and control. The agenda of this summit was agreed upon in a June 2023 meeting between the Prime Minister of the U.K. and the President of the United States. One of the key purposes of the summit was to protect international cyber infrastructure against compromise by anti-western nations such as China and others.[738]

The U.K. government published an online statement about the proposed summit as follows:[739]

- "As the world grapples with the challenges and opportunities presented by the rapid advancement of artificial intelligence, the UK will host the first major global summit on AI safety."
- "This summit will bring together key countries, leading tech companies and researchers to agree safety measures to evaluate and monitor the most significant risks from AI."

734. *See* Chapter 15 above on EU Law.
735. *See* the U.K. Government website on "Artificial Intelligence" at: www.gov.uk.
736. "A Pro-innovation Approach to AI Regulation," copies, and copies of followup documents, can be ordered online at: www.gov.uk, accessed October 30, 2024.
737. Policy Paper, AI regulation: a pro-innovation approach, online at: www.gov.uk, accessed October 28, 2024.
738. Sellman, June 10, 2023, as cited above; C. Smyth, "US will Join Rishi Sunak Summit to Rein in 'Existential' AI Risk," *The Times*, online, June 8, 2023.
739. Prime Minister's Office, 10 Downing Street and The Rt Hon Rishi Sunak MP, "UK to Host First Global Summit on Artificial Intelligence," *Press release*, online, June 7, 2023.

- The PM and President Biden "will take a coordinated approach to the opportunities and the challenges of emerging tech" that were discussed in their meeting in the United States on June 7, 2023.
- "Global companies are expanding their work in the UK as the PM confirms new university scholarships to further UK/US Tech leadership."

The press release states that the summit is being arranged because the U.K. has "a global duty" to make certain that AI is developed and used safely and responsibly.

The U.K. is said to be "a world leader in AI," ranking third behind the U.S. in China. The AI sector is said to employ 50,000 people in the U.K. and to contribute more than £3.5 billion to the U.K. economy. The U.K.'s departure from the EU is said to allow the U.K. to act "more quickly and agilely" with respect to the AI market.[740]

Prior to organizing this AI summit, the U.K. has been engaging in wide-ranging international discussions about international cooperation with respect to AI. It discussed the issues raised by AI development with the members of the G7 at the Hiroshima meeting in May 2023.

Following the November 2023 Summit, the U.K. has continued its drive to establish the U.K. as a leader in the AI development field.

These efforts have included the following:

- The U.K. was ranked third in the world for providing private venture capital funding for AI companies.[741]
- A single regulator for AI has not been proposed. The U.K. has established a Digital Regulation Cooperation Forum (DRCF), which is a new advisory service to support regulators, including Ofcom, the CMA, the FCA and the ICO, in regulating AI. These existing regulators will be responsible for regulating AI that affects the business sectors they already regulate. The U.K. government has announced "over £100 million to help realize AI innovations and support regulators' technical capabilities."[742]
- In October 2023, a joint agreement between the U.S. and the U.K. was published that stated a goal to promote greater Internet platform transparency and consider the impact of new technology, including generative AI. This would involve the sharing of expertise and the launch of a joint children's online safety working group.
- In November 2023, the U.K. government proposed to set aside £17 million in funding to create scholarships for AI and data science courses.
- In February 2024, the Office for AI became part of the AI Policy Directorate in the U.K. Department for Science, Innovation and Technology (DSIT).[743]

740. *Ibid.*
741. Press release, "£17 million to boos skills and diversity in AI jobs," online at: www.gov.uk, accessed October 30, 2024.
742. Consultation outcome, "A Pro-innovation Approach to AI Regulation: Government Response," online at: www.gov.uk, accessed October 30, 2024.
743. Information may be found online at: the DSIT, gov.uk.

- Any businesses that employ AI need to appoint an AI officer to oversee AI safety.

The U.K. government's response and participation in the development and regulation of AI is an ongoing evolutionary process that will continue into the foreseeable future. For details about AI and other cyber regulation, those interested should consult qualified legal advisors in the U.K. and any other relevant legal jurisdictions.

17.5 PREEXISTING REGULATION

Prior to the time that the U.K. considered it necessary to legislate specific AI legislation, the U.K. considered its legislation to be largely "technology neutral."

However, there were in existence a number of laws and regulations which affected both of development and application of AI. A summary review of these is found in a "white paper" published in March 2023 by the U.K. Department for Science, Innovation & Technology.[744]

In the United Kingdom, at the beginning of June, Sajid Javid, a former Chancellor and Home Secretary of the U.K. published a long comment in *The Times* giving his view of how regulation in the U.K. should be approached.[745]

In his comment, Javid talks about both the positive and negative potential of AI. His particular concern is that AI may prove to be dangerously influential on politics:

> "I am especially worried that the UK and US elections next year will become testing grounds for some of the most harmful capabilities."
>
> "But the heart of the debate about AI is its "dual use" potential to enable dangerous and disruptive capabilities. These are particularly troubling when their evolution can be hard to forecast, even by their creators. In the wrong hands, future AI will be able to conduct offensive cyber operations to enable mass fraud, manipulate and generate content to undermine trust and democracy, and initiate deep and personal relationships to facilitate abuse. As former Home Secretary it is also easy to see the capabilities AI brings to serious crime and hostile state activity."[746]

Mr. Javid urged that the policymakers in the U.K. should follow a framework that balances the need for caution with the need to promote innovative technology. He suggested that there should be three parts to this framework. First, he proposes that there be a "system of accountability for AI developers" to allow support, transparent data sharing and increased AI safety resources. Second, there should be an "ethical framework" to protect society. Third, there should be "incentives" that encourage that encourage adherence to "shared global objectives."

744. Department for Science, Innovation & Technology, "A Pro-innovation Approach to AI Regulation," online at: assets.publishing.service.gov.uk, March 2023, accessed May 16, 2023. *See*, Part Two: The current regulatory environment, pp. 14-19.
745. S. Javid, "On Election Day, I Fear We'll See How Harmful AI Can Be," Comment, *The Sunday Times*, online, June 4, 2023.
746. *Ibid.*

There is nothing wrong with these objectives, but they beg the question of whether they will be strong enough to both control the risks of AI and encourage development of its positive aspects. Ethics and incentives are all very good, but given the seriousness of the risks that are being discussed with respect to AI development and its potential abuse, it seems that enforceable laws and regulations will be needed to deter and punish abuse of AI systems and effectively encourage development of helpful AI systems.

One thing that is not emphasized enough in discussions about the need for regulation of AI is the fact that much behavior relating to AI development is already heavily regulated by existing systems of law and regulation. As the originating "home" of the Common Law system, shared to one degree or another in former English colonies, including the U.S., Australia, Canada, and many other now independent nations, it is useful to review how existing U.K. laws and regulations impact AI development.

17.5.1 Equality Act of 2010

This requires data processing systems, such as AI systems, to fairly process data. If AI systems produce data that includes unfair discrimination or bias, that could violate the Act. *See, for example,* Article (5) (1) (a) of the Act, concerning personal data processing. The Act protects against unfair discrimination relating to age, disability, gender reassignment, marriage and civil partnership, race, religion or belief, sex, and sexual orientation.[747]

17.5.2 Product Safety Laws

These require that goods that are manufactured and sold are safe to use.

There are specific laws and regulations requiring safety for electric and electronic goods, such as the Electrical Equipment (Safety) Regulations, HM Government, 2016.[748]

Safety with respect to medical devices is covered by the Medical Devices Regulation, HM Government 2002.[749]

Toys are required to be safe by the toys (safety) regulations, HM Government, 2011.[750]

747. Department for Science, Innovation & Technology, March 2023, cited above, footnotes 54 and 55.
748. *Ibid.*, footnote 56.
749. *Ibid.*, footnote 57.
750. *Ibid.*, footnote 58.

17.5.3 Contract Law and Consumer Rights

In cases where AI-related systems or services are provided under contracts, consumer rights laws and regulations may apply, such as the Consumer Rights Act of 2015 and the Consumer Protection from Unfair Trading Regulations (HM Government, 2008).[751]

Contract terms place a variety of duties on the contracting parties that they are required to meet. For examples, the terms of the contract may require that goods to be of a certain quality, or that they are fit for a described purpose, or that they match other descriptions in the contract.[752]

Failure to comply with those terms may constitute "breach of contract" that may give rise to rights to seek remedies such as money damages, or relief from performance obligations for innocent parties.[753] The requirements of contract law will be likely to apply to providers of AI systems as much as to any other business transactions.

It is important to remember that under many systems of law, including English Common Law, it is possible that contracts can be found to exist from oral agreement, behavior, custom or implication as well as from written documentation.[754]

17.5.4 Law of Torts

A "tort" is a civil wrong (as distinguished from a criminal act). A person injured by a tort may have a right to seek monetary damages or an injunction (to require performance or to restrain from performance of a particular act or acts) as compensation for their injury and/or to demonstrate to the guilty party the impropriety of their injurious behavior.[755]

Under tort law, it is certainly the case that those who believe themselves to be damaged by negligence or other harm caused by AI systems may be able to seek compensation or redress under—depending on the circumstances of their interaction with the AI system in question.

17.5.5 Criminal Law

Criminal law deals with offenses against the State. It is applicable to many types of behavior considered serious and/or dangerous enough to merit intervention by the State to investigate and/or prosecute and punish the authors of such behavior.

Some behaviors can violate both civil and criminal law, such as some cases where damage or harm is caused.

---

751. *Ibid.*, footnote 59.
752. *Ibid.*, cited above.
753. *See*, P. Shears & G. Stephenson, *James's Introduction to English Law*, 13th ed. (London, Butterworths, 1966), pp. 219-285.
754. For examples, *see* G.H. Treitel, *The Law of Contract*, 15th ed. (London: Sweet & Maxwell, 2020).
755. Department for Science, Innovation & Technology, March 2023. *See also*, P. Shears & G. Stephenson, *James's Introduction to English Law*, p. 303.

Creators, sellers and users of AI systems are subject to the restrictions of criminal law as much as any other persons.

17.5.6 Financial Services Law

In many situations where a third party is given authority to decide how another's financial or other assets are to be deployed, that third party may be subject to financial services law and regulation.

That may also be true of any person conducting business relating to AI who may seek others to help fund or promote their business.

In the U.K., the financial services business is generally subject to the Financial Services and Markets Act 2000 (FSMA), as amended, and the regulations thereunder.

17.5.7 Health Law

The medical and health fields are areas where there has been a great deal of discussion about the potential usefulness of AI. However, it has been recognized that there may be potential risks arising from deploying AI in these critical sectors.

Consequently, the U.K. government has paid special attention to the use of cyber-related services in the health sector. There has been established within the U.K. National Health Service (NHS), an AI and Digital Regulations Service for health and social care. This has been funded by the NHS AI lab in the NHS Transformation Directorate.[756] Overseeing these efforts are three government agencies in the U.K.:

- The Medicines & Healthcare Products Regulatory Agency.
- The Care Quality Commission.
- The NHS Health Research Authority.

Their overall goals are to gain benefits to health and social care while ensuring that safety standards are being maintained.

17.5.8 Summary: AI Is Not "Unregulated"

The legal areas discussed above are just a few of the legal and regulatory provisions already in existence that may be applicable to the creation, distribution and use of AI. There are undoubtedly many others including some, such as intellectual property law, which is treated in a separate chapter of this book. Others are cited in other places in this book.

756. *See* information online at: digitalregulaltions.innovation.nhs.uk.

17.6 SPECIFIC AI REGULATION IN THE U.K.

The U.K. government is certainly aware of the potential benefits and risks of AI systems. It is certainly aware that AI businesses, like other businesses that offer both benefits and risks, need regulation. The U.K. remains sensitive to the fact that additional regulation may be needed:

> While AIA is currently regulated through existing legal frameworks like financial services regulation, some AI risks arise across, or in the gaps between, existing regulatory remits. The industry has told us that conflicting or uncoordinated requirements from regulators create unnecessary burdens and that regulatory gaps may leave risks unmitigated, harming public trust and slowing AI adoption. ... Regulatory coordination will support businesses to invest confidently in AI innovation and build public trust by ensuring real risks are effectively addressed.[757]

17.6.1 A Pro-Innovation White Paper

At the end of March 2023, through the Department of Science, Innovation and Technology and the Office for AI, the U.K. government published a "white paper" that indicated that the goal for the U.K. was to become an AI "superpower."[758]

In a "Ministerial Foreword" from Michelle Donelan, the Secretary of State for Science, Innovation and Technology, she said:

> To ensure we become an AI superpower, though, it is crucial that we do all we can to create the right environment to harness the benefits of AI and remain at the forefront of technological developments. This includes getting regulation right so that innovators can thrive, and the risks posed by AI can be addressed.[759]

17.6.2 CMA Review

In early May 2023, the U.K. CMA announced that it was undertaking an initial review of how the development and use of AI would impact competition and consumer protection.[760]

The CMA reports that the purpose of this inquiry is:

> To ensure that innovation in AI continues in a way that benefits consumers, businesses and the UK economy, the government has asked regulators, including the CMA, to think about how the innovative development and deployment of AI can be supported against five over-arching principles: safety, security and robustness; appropriate transparency and explain-ability; fairness; accountability and governance; and contestability and redress.

757. Department for Science, Innovation & Technology, March 2023, cited above, p. 14.
758. *Ibid.*, cited above, p. 2.
759. *Ibid.*
760. Competition and Markets Authority, Press release, "CMA Launches Initial Review of Artificial Intelligence Models," *CMA*, online at: www.gov.uk, May 4, 2023.

The CMA intends to review how "generative AI" could evolve, to look at risks that might affect competition and consumer protection and to publish guidelines that would protect both competition and consumers but which would allow AI to develop productively.

The CMA requested AI-related businesses to provide both their views and other evidence about generative AI development.[761]

17.7 SELECTED U.K. INTERNET CASES

Since it became an important method of communication and commerce, the Internet has been a contentious area of endeavor which has produced numerous disputes and legal cases around the world. That is as true in the U.K. as much as anywhere because the U.K. is one of the world's important financial and trading markets.

It would be impossible to give the details of all the Internet cases that have arisen in the U.K. within this book. Therefore, this volume will discuss only certain U.K. cases of interest. However, it is certainly possible to search databases of U.K. legal material by topic to locate additional cases relating to Internet-related disputes. Among the databases that an interested party might wish to consider are the following:

British and Irish Legal Information Institute (BAILII). An online search of their case database under the word "Internet" should reveal many cases and decisions.[762]

The U.K. Supreme Court. Since 2009, the Supreme Court has replaced The House of Lords as the U.K.'s highest court. Its site includes pdf copies of Decided Cases.[763]

Earlier judgments, in pdf form, from the House of Lords are available online for the years 1996 to 2009.[764]

UKSC Blog. This is a site offered by a barristers' group, Matrix Chambers, providing online access to case reports and commentary on the judgments of Supreme Court cases, developments in case law, and "Case Previews" of upcoming Supreme Court cases.[765] The site does provide a search facility. Searching for "internet case" turns up several comments on relevant and often very recent cases.

"Current Awareness" from the Inner Temple. This is an online source of current information on legal issues, news, case decisions and legislation. It offers helpful resources and tools including daily alerts.[766]

761. *Ibid.*
762. https://www.google.com/search?q=BAILII&rlz=1C5CHFA_enFR936FR936&oq=BAILII&aqs=chrome..69i57.4408j0j15&sourceid=chrome&ie=UTF-8. This database is also connected to WorldLII, an online collection of databases of legal information and case reports of courts and tribunals from 123 jurisdictions (both subscription and non-subscription). This includes collections from countries, regions and other groupings. http://www.worldlii.org/. These are made available by the international group of LII.
763. https://www.supremecourt.uk/. Note that Supreme Court case decisions are also available on the BAILII website.
764. https://publications.parliament.uk/pa/ld/ldjudgmt.htm.
765. http://ukscblog.com/.
766. https://www.innertemple.org.uk/useful-links/current-awareness-blog/.

17.7.1 Online Privacy

Lloyd v. Google LLC [2021] UKSC 50[767]

In 2014, the High Court ruled that U.K. internet users who were suing Google for violating their online privacy could bring suit in the U.K. instead of the U.S.

The court held that the dispute involved complex issues of English law and therefore England was an appropriate place to bring the case where the issues could be resolved by an English court.

The complainant group of internet users asserted that Google was secretly tracking their online habits to identify their personal interests in shopping, hobbies, religion, politics, etc., and was selling this information to advertisers without permission. The claimants alleged that this violated their reasonable expectation of privacy under U.K. and EU privacy law.[768]

In the ultimate decision to the above case, the U.K. Supreme Court, on November 10, 2021, published a judgment in the case of *Lloyd v. Google LLC*,[769] allowing Lloyd to proceed with a collective claim on behalf of about 4 million iPhone users whose internet activity had been recorded by Google in 2011 and 2012 for commercial purposes without the agreement or knowledge of the users.

However, the court also ruled that damages could not be pursued on a collective basis but would have to be determined separately for each individual claimant.

The court said that in the U.K., a "collective action" can be brought under the DPA 2018. The persons affected by a breach of the DPA have the right to appoint a nonprofit organization to bring legal action on their behalf.

In the *Lloyd* case, the collection of data by Google led to many claims against Google in both the U.S. and the U.K.

In their decision, the U.K. Supreme Court said there was both good news and bad news for claimants in mass actions against big tech companies in the U.K.

The "good news" was that the court recognized that representative actions were a legitimate and useful way to protect the similar data rights of many persons who believe their rights to have been violated.

The "bad news" is that court ruled that damages under English Law cannot be assessed on a mass basis but must be determined on an individual basis. This is very good news for big tech companies because it makes it difficult to bring representative actions against them in cases where it is alleged that they have damaged large numbers (millions?) of internet users.

Ruling that damages can be assessed only on an individual basis means that any damage determination of the members of any group of plaintiffs will be tedious and expensive and will probably show that any individual member only suffered very small monetary damage.

---

767. On appeal from [2019] EWCA CIV 1599.
768. J. Croft, "Google Loses UK Ruling on Internet Privacy Case," *Financial Times*, online, January 16, 2014.
769. [2021] UKSC 50.

That will probably make it impossible for future U.K. representative actions to be funded by commercial litigation funding because their potential recovery will be too uncertain.

It is unlikely that any individual member of the claimant group will have the funds or the desire to pursue the action without mass financial support and potential mass financial recovery.

One hopes this case does not hand Big Tech a license to exploit internet users at will in the U.K. without having to worry about the possible financial consequences of collective lawsuit judgment.

The court pointed out, "Parliament has not legislated to establish a class action regime in the field of data protection."

Commentators point out that this recovery gap could be filled by Parliamentary legislation but it remains to be seen whether they will wish to act.[770]

17.7.2 Mass State Data Collection

Judgments in Case C-623/17, Privacy International, and in Joined Cases

In October 2020, the ECJ issued a decision that:

> Confirms that EU law precludes national legislation requiring a provider of electronic communications services to carry out the general and indiscriminate transmission or retention of traffic data and location data for the purpose of combatting crime in general or of safeguarding national security.[771]

Both the U.K. and various European Member States were found to be collecting the communications data of their citizens. However, according to the ECJ, general anticrime or national security concerns do not provide sufficient excuse to permit the mass collection of communications data by the states.

Genuine serious present or foreseeable threats are required to justify "targeted" data collection as a limited exemption to the general rule stated above.

The challenge to data collection in the U.K. was brought by an organization called Privacy International. The Legal Director of Privacy International said that this decision would limit the powers of police and security organizations within the U.K. and EU countries to review the communications data of communications users. The Legal Director said:

> European law applies any time that a national government tries to ask a telecommunications provider to process personal data for the state, including providing access to communications data, or retaining data, even in the context of national security.

770. G. Dunn, "UK Supreme Court Overturns Court of Appeal to Disallow Google Data Privacy Class Action," online, November 11, 2021.
771. Court of Justice of the European Union, Press Release 123/20, online, October 6, 2020.

Commentators have said that this decision challenges some significant pieces of U.K. legislation. For example, the Telecommunications Act 1984 has provisions requiring ISPs to keep and be prepared to provide customers' communications data to U.K. security agencies.

It also calls into question the Investigatory Powers Act 2016, which contains provisions relating to the collection of communications data in the U.K.

Although the U.K. has now left the EU, this decision may require U.K. to modify its surveillance legislation if it wishes to continue to share security data with members of the EU.[772]

17.7.3 Website Blocking Costs

Cartier International AG and others v. British Telecommunications Plc and another

In June 2018, the U.K. Supreme Court ruled that rightsholders such as trademark and patent owners can obtain orders that ISPs should block access to certain websites where counterfeit copies or unauthorized goods of genuine rightsholders are being offered for sale. However, the rightsholders are required to compensate ISPs for the costs and expenses of blocking certain websites.[773]

The litigation relating to this issue was originally brought by Richemont which owns a number of well-known luxury brands including Montblanc and Cartier. They obtained an injunction preventing BT and other U.K. ISPs from hosting websites selling fake copies of luxury goods sold by the rights owners, in this case Richemont. They claimed that they had found thousands or possibly hundreds of thousands of websites where goods and services that infringed the property of rights holders were being offered for sale.

It has been shown that the blocking of such infringing websites is effective protection for rightsholders and that blocking is regularly used by owners of valuable trademarks and intellectual property to protect their rights.

The use of website blocking as rights protection requires a significant amount of ongoing maintenance because infringing websites often reappear under new names. Therefore, the rightsholders will continually need to request ISPs to update their blocking of infringing websites. Performing these tasks, the court ruled will need to be compensated by the rightsholders for the costs and expenses incurred by ISPs in blocking infringing websites

17.7.4 Dark Web Drugs

In October 2021, 24 people were arrested in the U.K. as part of an international investigation targeting a drugs marketplace on the "Dark Web."

772. B. Goodwin, "EU's Top Court Questions Legality of UK Phone and Internet Data Surveillance," online ComputerWeekly.com, October 6, 2020.
773. [2018] UKSC 28. Judgment Date June 13, 2018.

This was one of the largest operations ever against criminal use of the Dark Web.

In the U.K., the operation, which took over six months, was spearheaded by the National Crime Agency cooperating with police forces in the U.K. It resulted in the seizure of a number of drugs, including 50 kilos of cocaine, MDMA, cannabis methamphetamine and ketamine.

The operation began in Germany when authorities there arrested the person who was believed to be the operator of the marketplace, and this gave the German authorities information about how the marketplace was being operated. The German authorities shared their knowledge with enforcement agencies around the world, including those of Australia, Bulgaria, France, Germany, Italy, the Netherlands, Switzerland, the United States, and the United Kingdom and included cooperation from Europol and Eurojus.

CHAPTER 18
French Law

18.1 FRANCE AND CYBER LAW

France is a prominent member of the EU, a major market, and long a leader in legal and technological innovation.

Recently, France is among the principal authors of the proposed EU AIA. There was a little doubt that France will adopt and follow the requirements of the AIA and regulations thereunder.[774]

French legislators have been additionally concerned about all significant developments in the cyber world and to their implications in the legal field.

France, because it is a Member State of the EU, is subject to the EU Internet-related law that was discussed in a previous chapter. It is also subject to the provisions of various international conventions and treaties to which it is a party.

18.2 FREEDOM OF EXPRESSION

French law protecting freedom of expression originates from the Declaration of the Rights of Man and of the Citizen promulgated in 1881.

But not all expression is free in France. There are laws in France against racism, antisemitism, racial hatred and justification of terrorism. These are criminal offenses and punishable by law.

Since 2014, incitement to terrorism and public justification of terrorism or punishable by imprisonment for up to seven years.[775]

774. *See* EU AI regulation in Chapter 5, above.
775. France, Gouvernment, "Everything You Need to Know About Freedom of Expression in France," online, retrieved August 4, 2020.

The Internet has become such an important source of information and entertainment, it is reasonable to ask whether access to the Internet is considered to be a fundamental right in France.

Freedom House, an online organization that reports on internet freedom, rates France 76/100 on "Internet Freedom" and 89/100 on "Global Freedom." Freedom House, has also rated France 4/4 for both "freedom of expression and belief" and "academic freedom and freedom from indoctrination."[776]

The French constitution checks freedom of religion. There are laws that that protect people from religious abuse and from defamation generally. Anti semitic and anti Islamic abuse is also prohibited.

Freedom of the press has long been officially protected in France under the Freedom of the Press Law of July 1881.

However, there are regulations establishing responsibility for content published on the Internet. When illegal content is published on the Internet, several parties may be liable. These could include the author of the material, the host of the internet site and any publishers of the illegal content.[777]

18.3 ARCOM

In 2022, the agency was merged with the High Audiovisual Council to form the Regulatory Authority for Audiovisual and Digital Communication (ARCOM).

18.4 AVIVA LAW ON ILLEGAL POSTING

In May 2020, the Aviva Law was introduced in France. Aviva required the removal of terrorist and child pornography postings within one hour and removal of hate and pornography content within 24 hours.

The Aviva law required online platforms to take down hateful content that had been reported to the platform by users within 24 hours or risk a fine of €1.25 million.

There was criticism as to whether this law was an improper restriction on freedom of speech. Content posters had the option of challenging a decision of removal in court.

In June 2020, a French court, the Constitutional Council of Paris, struck down key revisions of the Aviva law introduced in France in May 2020, stating that they were unreasonable restrictions on freedom of expression.[778]

The Constitutional Council ruled that requiring online service providers to make a legal analysis of content, without a judicial ruling, within such a short time, with the threat of such a large fine, was a danger to freedom of expression because it may cause

776. Freedom House, France, online at: freedomhouse.org/country/france. Accessed November 7, 2024.
777. *See* the official site of the French government administration, online at: service.public.fr. Accessed November 9, 2024.
778. A. Breeden, "French Court Strikes Down Most of Online Hate Speech Law," *The New York Times*, online, June 18, 2020, retrieved August 4, 2020.

service providers to remove any flagged content, regardless of its legal status rather than risk of the statutory punishment.[779]

The court also struck down a section of law requiring platforms to remove content flagged by authorities as a child pornography or terrorist propaganda within one hour because this was too short time and was being required without any independent review.[780]

However, on a more positive note, the court did state that the law's creation of an official online hate speech watchdog would be allowed to remain in place.[781]

A group representing large tech companies in France and other digital advocacy supporters praised the Council's decision, saying that it freed the Internet in France from the law's "abusive censorship."[782]

The reaction of the government in France was disappointment in the ruling and statements that the government was determined to introduce new hate speech laws that complied with this ruling. A spokesperson said that although France did have laws against hate speech that included criminal penalties, existing laws were introduced at a time before the Internet and were inadequate to deal with the complex new problems that the Internet presented.[783]

However, although freedom of speech is an important and often constitutionally guaranteed fundamental right, it has never been an unlimited right.

It has always been the case that France or any society has been held to have the power to limit or illuminate dangerous, defamatory or criminally improper speech as long as an opportunity exists to challenge such restrictions before an impartial forum.

In connection with this restriction on illegal content, the French government has indicated that the posting of antisemitic content would also be excluded under the policy represented by the Aviva law.

18.5 PLEVEN ACT: RACIAL HATRED

In France, promoting racial hatred was made illegal under the Pleven Act in 1972. This referred back to a degree of April 21, 1939, by the then initial Minister of Justice, Paul Machadeau.

This decree permitted a prosecutor to bring an action, even in the absence of a third-party complaint, where it found, "defamation or insult committed against a group of persons belonging, by reason of their original, to a particular race or religion, if it is intended to incite hatred between citizens or inhabitants."

However, France also has its own carefully considered laws and regulations that govern business within France and the use of the Internet. Because the Internet has become such an important source of information and entertainment, it is reasonable to ask whether access to the Internet is considered to be a fundamental right in France.

779. *Ibid.*
780. *Ibid.*
781. *Ibid.*
782. *Ibid.*
783. *Ibid.*

18.6 ARTICLE 33, JUSTICE REFORM ACT, RAVEL AND COMPUTER-AIDED ANALYSIS

In June 2019, France added a section to Article 33 of the Justice Reform Act, which is reported to require that:

> The identity data of magistrates and members of the judiciary cannot be reused with the purpose or effect of evaluating, analyzing, comparing or predicting their actual or alleged professional practices.[784]

This ban was reportedly added because of concern about the work of an organization called "Ravel Law."

Ravel Law states that it has supported the Harvard Law School Library in its work to digitize 40,000 printed volumes of law cases, including over 40 million pages of court decisions dating as far back as the seventeenth century, which have been included in a "Public Case Law Access site":[785]

> Members of the public now have access to one of the largest collections of published case law available online. The site offers robust search and filter functionality, as well as links to PDF images that resulted from the scanning project. ... The public case access contains all US court cases published in official reports from 1658 to 2018. The collection includes over 8 million cases from state courts, federal courts, and territorial courts for American Samoa, Dakota Territory, Guam, native American courts, Navajo Nation, and the Northern Mariana Islands.[786]

The concern of the French legislators, magistrates, and judges apparently had to do with the fact that digitization of legal decisions, such as accomplished with the support of Ravel Law, may give parties the power to "model the decision—making tendencies of judicial decision makers with relative ease ... ."[787]

Article 33 reportedly bans law firms from assembling an overall review of judicial decisions with offenders being subject to a five-year prison term.

Although the French judiciary apparently does not agree, it has been argued that Article 33 interferes with creation of a fairer judicial system:

> Since publication of French court decisions, there have been studies confirming the bias of French judges. AI is now blowing the whistle, alerting us that unbiased judging is not as universal as we once believed.[788]

784. I. Connett, "France Resists Judicial AI Revolution: France Bans Predictive Analysis of Caselaw. Does This Protect or Impede Universal Justice?," *Above the Law*, online at: abovethelaw.com, June 10, 2019.
785. Ravel Law, "Public Case Access," online at: ravel.com, accessed September 27, 2023.
786. *Ibid.*
787. Connett, June 10, 2019, as cited above.
788. *Ibid.*

Ravel was purchased by Lexis/Nexis in June 2017:[789]

> Ravel is a legal search, analytics, and visualization platform. At a time when the amount of legal information is rapidly growing in scale and complexity, Ravel provides insight into what's important, why it's important, and how to use it. We make research radically easier and more insightful.[790]

18.7 AI AND FRANCE

France, like other countries and legal jurisdictions, discussed in other chapters, has in existence many laws and regulations that will bear on the creation, distribution and use of AI systems, without specifically referring to AI.

However, recent reports indicate that France believes that the proper way to regulate AI is through international cooperation and regulation.

France has certainly shown that through its support of the EU AIA legislation.

Going beyond that, it is reported:

> France's top politicians have told CNBC[791] they see the beginnings of global regulation on artificial intelligence coming by the end of this year, with French president Emmanuel Macron saying the country wants to work with the US on rules around fast-growing technology. ... France has looked to position itself as the European hub for AI development ... .[792]

It is quite clear that France's goal is to be one of the leading creators of international AI regulation. They are certainly making efforts within the EU and internationally to achieve that:

> But there is no global consensus on how AI should be managed and controlled with the US, China and the European Union taking different approaches to rules around the tech. Any global regulatory framework would be a huge feat.[793]

France's efforts to shape international AI regulation will require participation in a long process. How successful they will be and how they will affect French domestic law will only be revealed over time.

18.8 CONCLUSION

When discussing French law that affects the Internet or any other part of business, it is important to remember that France is also subject to EU laws and regulations and other international treaties and conventions to which France subscribes.

789. LinkedIn, "Ravel Law (acquired by LexisNexis): LinkedIn," *LinkedIn*, online at: fr.linkedin.com, accessed September 27, 2023.
790. *Ibid.*
791. A U.S. news and entertainment network.
792. A. Kharpal, "France Sees Global A.I. Regulation Ideas by the End of This Year, Wants to Work with U.S. on Tech Laws," *CNBC*, online at: cnbc.com, June 15, 2023.
793. *Ibid.*

Those that wish to know more of the details of laws and regulations applicable in France relating to the cyber world and business generally are advised to consult qualified legal advisers about those laws and regulations that may be relevant.

CHAPTER 19
Chinese Law

19.1 THE INTERNET IN CHINA

About 54% of Chinese people use the Internet. In a population of about 1.5 billion people, this means that about 800,000 people are using the Internet. That is more than Europe and America combined.

However, because almost 80% of the populations of developed Western countries use the Internet, there appears to be a great deal of room for expansion in China. That may mean that in the next decade or so, China will be in an enormous power and influence on the Internet.

Given the enthusiastic and growing use of the Internet in China and the international interaction, personal, commercial, and political that this entails, the laws and regulations that regulate the Internet in China are an important issue, not only for China but also for the world.

19.2 INTERNET FREEDOM IN CHINA

A fundamental question is, "What level of freedom do Internet users have in China?" Freedom House is a private U.S. organization that tracks and ranks countries on issues relating to technology and democracy.[794]

In general, they oppose what they say as a "rising tide" of government control over the Internet. To that end, they produce an annual Freedom on the Net report that ranks countries in terms of Internet freedom. Their 2024 report ranks China among the lowest in the world for Internet freedom with a score of only 9 out of 100.[795] Even Russia ranks higher with a score of 20.[796]

794. Freedom House, "Internet Freedom Scores," online at: freedomhouse.org/, accessed November 12, 2024.
795. https://freedomhouse.org/report/freedom-net.
796. *Ibid.*

This state of affairs begs the question of what exactly China does in terms of restricting Internet freedom.

Freedom House uses three categories to judge Internet freedom. The first is "obstacles to access." These judge the legal and ownership barriers to Internet use in a particular country. There is also the question of how independent regulatory bodies are of political control.[797] The second issue they analyze concerns "limits on content." They look at such things as: legal regulations on content, technical filters and blocking of websites, self-censorship, the diversity of online news media, and the use of the Internet to mobilize opinion on public issues.[798] The third category is an examination of whether there are identifiable violations of user rights. This looks at whether there is surveillance, how privacy is protected, and whether penalties are imposed for online content, which might include imprisonment, harassment or cyberattacks.[799]

China reportedly does very poorly with respect to these tests. There is very little freedom of information. Censorship is strict. The content of all media, whether on or off the Internet, is closely controlled by the government. Information about significant political or public events, such as protests against government control, is not permitted to be shown on the Internet. There is not really any Internet "neutrality." Sources and content are under the total control of the government.

However, despite the lack of Internet freedom, China does have a keen interest in the Internet. This is shown by the fact that it has allowed and encouraged its own gigantic Internet companies to develop, including Alibaba, Huawei, Tencent and China Mobile.

19.3 THE CHINA INTERNET SECURITY LAW

In 2017, the Chinese government implemented the China Internet Security Law (also called "the China Cybersecurity Law").[800]

Under the Cybersecurity Law, the government is entitled to undertake a great deal of control over internet business and to demand a great deal of cooperation from network operators and other internet businesses that the Chinese consider "critical" to national security.

The definitions of those two sectors are very wide. "Network operators" include network owners, managers and providers of any system consisting of computers and related equipment that gathers, stores, transmits, exchanges or processes information. That would seem to include almost all businesses and any individuals that use computers and/or operate on the Internet.

Businesses "critical to national security" include communications businesses, information services, energy, transport, water, financial services, public services and

797. *Ibid.*
798. *Ibid.*
799. *Ibid.*
800. J. Wagner, "China's Cybersecurity Law: What You Need to Know," *The Diplomat*, June 1, 2017.

electronic government services. This puts a large sector of Chinese economic life under scrutiny.[801]

Network operators are required to keep stored within mainland China any data that is gathered or produced within China. This includes any data that is gathered about Chinese citizens within China.[802]

The government is permitted to conduct spot checks and require certifications to ensure that data is being stored within China as required by the law. Network operators can also be asked to provide source code, encryption data or other important information for review by the government. The law requires network operators to accept supervision from the government to bear "social responsibility" and to comply with other standards which permit the network operator very little scope to challenge any government scrutiny and inspection of its computer and data systems.

19.4 CYBERSPACE ADMINISTRATION CHINA

In China, the administration of the Internet is overseen by Cyberspace Administration China (CAC). That organization was founded in 2014 and launched its website in December of that year.[803] Essentially, the function of the CAC is to translate Chinese communist party ideology into technical regulations for the Internet.

19.5 BUSINESS REGULATION IN CHINA

In order to encourage the development of Chinese companies, Chinese regulations make serious efforts to reduce the effectiveness of foreign Internet programs.

Tools that they use include restricting search results or asking international companies to eliminate certain kinds of content. For example, they will sometimes require news aggregating services to remove any content relating to protests against China, such as was done with the Hong Kong protests.

It used to be the case that in former European colonies such as Hong Kong or Macau, many Chinese Internet regulations did not apply. This was a product of what was called the one nation two systems approach that was a key feature of the transfer of political control of those territories from Western nations to China.

An important purpose of that system was to permit these affluent former colonies to continue to produce significant amounts of trade and income for China. However, between 2019 in 2020, this liberality began to disappear. This change was particularly dramatic in Hong Kong when China imposed new laws on the territory, significantly reducing civil liberties there.

801. *Ibid.*
802. *Ibid.*
803. www.cac.gov.cn.

19.6 THE GREAT FIREWALL

One of the CAC's most important functions is to operate the Great Firewall of China, previously operated by the State Internet Information Office (SIIO).

China first connected with the global Internet in 1994. Initially, its priorities were building infrastructure, establishing systems for information security and aiding industrial development.[804]

Initially, the Internet activity was governed by the Ministry of Information Industry (MII). As the penetration of the Internet grew in China, the government became increasingly concerned about the power of that medium.[805]

China turned its concerns into a number of regulatory and technical policies that together constitute a system known as the Great Firewall of China.

19.7 INTERNET CONTROL

These are a number of initiatives to regulate the Internet within China. Their goal is to impose Internet censorship, to block access to a number of foreign websites that do not conform to Chinese ideology, and to regulate international Internet traffic to and from China. Major foreign Internet companies are blocked from operating in China including Wikipedia, Twitter, Google and Facebook.

As time has gone on, China has become even more concerned about controlling the Internet. This has the double effect of both excluding information and communications, which might be contrary to Chinese ideology and permitting Chinese competitors to establish themselves within the expanding Chinese Internet market.

Those non-Chinese Internet companies that are permitted to operate within China are required to adapt their systems to Chinese Internet regulations.

The importance of that is not being underestimated by the government. In 2013, President Xi Jinping said, "the Internet directly relates to the national ideology security and the regime security." In recognition of this position, China has taken the following steps.

19.7.1 Bureau of Internet News Regulation

In 2000, the State Council Information Office (SCIO) created the Bureau of Internet News Regulation. In 2012, China issued a regulation requiring Internet users to give their real names to ISPs.

After the Snowden and Wiki leaks developments, China has become even more determined to regulate Internet activity.[806] This ultimately led to The China Internet Security Law of 2017 discussed above.

---

804. W. Miao (Chinese Academy of Social Sciences, China) & W. Lei (China Radio International, China), "Policy Review, The Cyberspace Administration of China," *Book Review, Sage Journals*, online, December 7, 2016 https://doi.org/10.1177/1742766516680879.
805. *Ibid.*
806. *Ibid.*

19.7.2 Core Infrastructure Initiative

The Internet Security Law includes a number of subsidiary regulations that help define its purposes. There is the Core Infrastructure Initiative (CII).

19.8 AI IN CHINA

Chinese regulators have been concerned about the development of AI products for some time.

In 2018, there was published an Artificial Intelligence Standardization White Paper (AI White Paper) (updated in 2021) that was generally positive about the benefits that could be gained from the applications of AI.[807]

As of March 2022, China introduced new comprehensive regulations for AI-related businesses and products.

Part of those regulations focused on forbidding use of algorithms that use personal information to set different prices for products and services offered to different customers. The rules apply to algorithms that set prices, control search results, recommend videos, and filter content. The regulations also impose restrictions on ride-hailing, e-commerce, streaming, and social media companies.[808]

These regulations are imposed by the Cyberspace Administration of China and are titled "The Internet Information Service Algorithmic Recommendation Management Provisions" (Provisions).

Punishment for violations of the Provisions can include fines, forbidding enrollment of new customers, cancelation of business licenses, or deletion of websites and apps.[809]

There are also regulations on "synthetic content." These apply to fake news, AI-created audio, and "deep fake" pictures and videos.

Creators of AI-generated content must label it as "synthetic," give their real names, and clearly label any "deep fake" content.[810]

Since that time, Chinese regulators have introduced a variety of new laws and regulations affecting the use of AI-related products.

Updated laws on data protection, cybersecurity and personal information have all included provisions that affect AI-related products.

807. CSET, "Artificial Intelligence Standardization White Paper (2021 Edition)," online at: set.georgetown.edu, accessed November 12, 2024.
808. J. Conrad & W. Knight, "China Is About to Regulate AI: And the World Is Watching," *Wired*, online at: wired.com, February 22, 2022.
809. *Ibid.*
810. *Ibid.*

19.8.1 Local AI Regulations

Also, local regulations have been adopted in Shenzhen and Shanghai to both encourage and regulate the development of AI systems in those areas. Both generally follow the ideas set out in the AI White Paper.

19.8.2 Generative AI Regulations

In July 2024, China published new proposed measures focused on regulating Generative AI Services:[811]

- These apply to both online and offline generative AI products.
- The creation of discriminative content is forbidden.
- They also bar "training" that violates IP protections and uses personal data without consent.
- Security assessments need to be provided to the relevant Internet Information Services before generative AI services can be published.

19.9 CONCLUSIONS

Many of the Chinese regulations mirror regulations either introduced or proposed in major competing market centers such as the United States and the EU.

However, others are more locally focused on China. It is not clear yet whether China will cooperate in agreeing to global international treaties regulating AI. China is focused on establishing comprehensive regulations for AI within China.

Anyone doing business there should be aware that many such regulations exist and are being constantly expanded. Consequently, it is sensible for any business doing cyber business to or in China to obtain up-to-date local advice from qualified persons to assist them in offering any Internet and/or AI-related products there.

811. For more information, *see* posting by G. Interesse, "China Releases New Draft Regulations on Generative AI," online at: china-briefing.com, accessed November 12, 2024.

CHAPTER 20
Indian Law

India is the most populous country in the world, with a population of over 1.43 billion. Over 900 million people use the Internet. Internet-related business contributes about 5% of GDP.[812]

India is one of the biggest participants in the world's cybermarkets.

Recognizing the growing importance of the digital world to the economy and people of India, the government has been making strenuous efforts to expand, regulate and protect it.

In 2000, India established an Indian Computer Emergency Response Team (CERT) to protect India's cyber world. There is a Ministry of State Electronics and Information Technology.[813]

20.1 LAWS AGAINST CYBERCRIME

20.1.1 Information Technology Act

The principal Indian law regulating electronic commerce and defending against cybercrime is The Information Technology Act 2000 (ITA) that came into force on October 17, 2000.

20.1.2 Copyright Act

The watching or distributing of child pornography is against the law in India. The penalties can be a fine or imprisonment of up to three years. These offenses are prohibited by the Copyright Act of 1957.[814]

812. Bain & Company, online at: bain.com. Accessed November 13, 2024.
813. "Safeguarding India's Digital Landscape," *Ministry of Electronics and Information Technology*, online at: pib.gov, accessed November 13, 2024.
814. Indian Copyright Act, 1957, sections 63 to 65A.

20.1.3 Other Cybercrime Prohibitions

A definition of "cybercrime" is not found in either the ITA or the National Cyber Security Policy 2013.

There is no specific regulation prohibiting cybercrime as such in India. Cybercrime is brought within the scope of criminal behavior by being recognized as a combination of crimes prohibited by criminal legislation in combination with use of digital technology.

India has digital technology laws dealing with such things as electronic signatures, intellectual property, and privacy and data protection.

"Cybercrime" is recognized as any crime done with the assistance of telecommunication or computer technology or any crime where computers or digital technology is either used in the crime or is the target of the crime. This means that there is really no crime that will not be considered cybercrime if it involves digital or telephonic technology.[815]

20.2 INTERNET CENSORSHIP IN INDIA

Censorship of the Internet in India covers a variety of online activities and is performed by the national government and the state governments. There are significant efforts by both to regulate and remove content. There are also court cases brought by content creators seeking court orders to remove content that appears on the Internet in violation of intellectual property laws and regulations.

Certain websites have been blocked for political reasons by government orders. The first such instance occurred in 1999. Following a military conflict between India and Pakistan over control of Kashmir, the website of *Dawn*, Pakistan's daily newspaper, was blocked by the Indian government-owned telecoms company that provided international internet access to India.[816]

In 2003, all Yahoo groups were banned for about two weeks when the government tried to shut down one Yahoo website that had breached the law by discussing a legal case that was being tried.[817]

There is also a long list of mobile apps banned in India, including TikTok.[818]

815. V. Verma, "Importance of Cyber Law in India," *Legal Service India*, online, retrieved September 9, 2020.
816. "India Blocks Pakistani Newspaper Web Site" *Newswatch.in*, July 5, 1999, online at: bbc.co.uk, retrieved September 9, 2020.
817. S. Thomas, "India Bans One Yahoo Discussion Group," *InfoWar Monitor*, September 29, 2003, online, retrieved September 9, 2020. https://web.archive.org/web/20110917185442/http://www.infowar-monitor.net/2003/09/yahoo-groups-blocked-by-indian-government/.
818. "Government Bans 59 Mobile Apps Which Are Prejudicial to Sovereignty and Integrity of India, Defence of India, Security of State and Public Order," *Press Information Bureau*, June 29, 2020. Online. Retrieved September 9, 2020. https://pib.gov.in/PressReleseDetailm.aspx?PRID=1635206.

India has many internet shutdowns, with as many as 134 in 2018.[819] Many of these shutdowns are for political and/or public order reasons.

20.3 PRIVACY AND DATA PROTECTION

Prior to 2023, India did not have an express internet data protection law, although it did follow international conventions that support rights to privacy.

There are laws that allow persons to seek compensation when there has been improper disclosure of their personal information.

There are rules that restrict businesses in the disclosure of personal data they have collected.

Also, certain regulated businesses in the financial services and telecommunication sectors are subject to regulations about maintaining the confidentiality of the personal information of customers and using it only for certain limited purposes.[820]

On September 1, 2023, the India Digital Personal Data Protection Act 2023 (DPDPA) came into effect.[821] The DPDPA applies to any organization that processes personal data in India, regardless of whether the data was collected in India or otherwise.

It provides data subjects with rights to access, correct and object to uses of their personal data.

Enforcement of the DPDPA is the responsibility of India's Data Protection Authority (DPA). They have powers to order compliance by and investigate and fine data processors.

20.4 INDIAN REGULATION OF AI

India has been rather cautious in adopting regulations specifically targeting AI.

India's Communications and IT minister, Ashwini Vaishnaw, is reported to have said in May 2023 that a number of developed economies were considering what should be the appropriate framework for the regulation of the rapidly expanding field of AI. He is quoted as saying:

> The whole world is looking at what should be the framework, and what should be the regulatory set up. In the G7, all digital ministers (of G7 countries) are seriously concerned about what should be the regulatory framework. So, this is a global

819. "Government Can Switch Off Your Internet in Necessary: The Economic Times," online indiatimes.com, March 8, 2015, retrieved September 9, 2020. https://economictimes.indiatimes.com/.
820. T. Thakore & Associates, "Data Protected: India," online, March 2020, retrieved September 11, 2020. https://www.linklaters.com/en/insights/data-protected/data-protected---india#: ~ :text = Union%20of%20India)%2C%20the%20Supreme,%E2%80%9D%20and%20%E2%80%9Cpersonal%20liberty%E2%80%9D.&text = This%20will%20be%20India's%20first,43A%20of%20the%20IT%20Act.
821. "What Data is Protected by the India Digital Personal Data Protection Act 2023? A Comprehensive Guide to the India Data Privacy Law" online at: secureprivacy.ai, accessed November 13, 2024.

> thing. This is not one country issue. This has to be looked at from the international perspective.[822]

India is not rushing into regulating AI. Its attitude toward the subject has been evolving over the last few years.

At the end of July 2023, it was reported that working groups had been set up by the government to study and report on AI, but reports were not yet available.

However, there has been drafted a Digital Personal Data Protection Bill 2023. Information about that draft has suggested that it may include protections against personal data being used to "train" AI systems like ChatGPT.[823]

20.4.1 AI Crime Reports in India

Offensive uses of AI tools may be considered criminal under Indian law.

There are instances of reports where AI tools have been used to commit crimes in India.

One disgusting example involved an Indian journalist who had been critical of India's ruling party. She was attacked by a vicious online hatred campaign in 2018 that included a deepfake porn video of her. The video went viral, and she was bombarded with online threats of rape and death. Since this happened, the journalist said, "I have not been the same person."[824]

20.5 SELECTED INDIAN INTERNET CASES

1. *Alphabet Inc. (Google India Pvt. Ltd.)* Case (December 2019)

India highest court rules that Google is not liable for certain defamatory posts. This reaffirmed that Internet service and social media companies are not liable for content posted on their services by third parties.

The justices said, Any other result would lead to "strangling the free flow of ideas, which is what the internet is all about."

The case involved a post opposing the manufacture and use of sheets of building material containing asbestos.

Visahaka Industries Ltd., a building materials company, claimed that it was defamed by the post and sued Google for allowing it to be accessed on its search service. They filed a claim against Google India Private Limited in the form of a Petition under section 482 of The Code of Criminal Procedure, 1973.

However, the Supreme Court of India denied their claim, ruling that section 79 of the Information Technology (Amendment Act) of 2008 created an exemption from any

822. "India for International Framework to Regulate AI Platforms like ChatGPT" *The Times of India*, online at: timesofindia.indiatimes.com, May 17, 2023, accessed September 7, 2023.
823. "Why India Can Afford to Wait and Watch Before Regulating AI," *ET Government*, online at: government.economictimes.indiatimes.com, July 31, 2023.
824. *Ibid.*

other law in respect of third-party posts on computer services and social media platforms. "Section 79 is a safe harbour provision."[825]

However, Google did not get off completely. The court ruled that the safe harbor of section 79 did not protect Google from prosecution for hosting such posts in time periods prior to section 79's effective date. The trial against Google for offensive posts pre-section 79 would be allowed to proceed.[826]

2. Section 66A of the ITA, Prohibiting "Offensive Comments" Struck Down. (March 2015)

Section 66A of the Information Technology Act made "offensive" posts a crime punishable by imprisonment.

However, free speech advocates conducted a campaign to have it struck down for being an oppressive restriction on free speech and on the public's right to knowledge. The Supreme Court of India ruled that section 66A's prohibitions against "annoying" or "grossly offensive" posts were so vague, subjective and difficult to enforce that section 66A was unconstitutional.[827]

20.6 CONCLUSION

There is very little doubt that because of the size of its population, its growing Internet penetration and its market power, India will be one of the principal shapers of the cyber world.

825. *Google India Private Appellant(s) v. M/S. Visahaka Industries and Another Respondent(s)*, Supreme Court of India Criminal Appellate Jurisdiction, Criminal Appeal No. 1987 2914. December 19, 2019. Online, retrieved September 10, 2020. Online at main.sci.gov.
826. *Ibid.*, pp. 147-148.
827. "Sec 66A of IT Act Scrapped: 5 Points Observed by the Supreme Court," *Hindustan Times*, March 24, 2015, online, retrieved September 11, 2020.

CHAPTER 21
Japanese Law

Japan hosts the fourth largest e-commerce market in the world after China, the U.S., and the U.K.[828]

Freedom House, in its chart of Internet scores, rates Japan as having the greatest Internet freedom in Asia, with a score of 73 out of 100. That is not far behind the United States, which is given a score of 77.[829]

21.1 JAPAN ON THE INTERNET

Japan has installed high-quality Internet service for most of the population and virtually all substantial businesses. There are over 117 million Internet users in Japan, which represents more than 90% of the population.[830]

Rakuten, Amazon and Yahoo are the major online shopping platforms in Japan.[831]

Japanese law does go a long way in protecting freedom of speech. This protects most forms of communication, including Internet posts and the press. However, there are laws and regulations controlling communication in the e-commerce sector.

Japan's Specified Commercial Transactions Act requires sellers to clearly tell customers prices, delivery costs, ways of payment, and any other costs.[832]

Other laws relating to the sale of any consumer goods include:

- The Electrical Appliance Safety Act.
- The Household Goods Quality Labeling Act.

828. US International Trade Association (UTA), online at: trade.gov.
829. The highest among the 65 countries surveyed. The top-rated is Iceland with a score of 95. Number two is Estonia where the score of 94. https://freedomhouse.org/countries/freedom-net/scores.
830. International Telecommunications Union, Statistics, Percentage of Individuals Using the Internet, Japan, 91.28%, retrieved online July 27, 2020.
831. UTA, above.
832. *Ibid.*

- The Consumer Product Safety Act.
- The Pharmaceutical Affairs Act.[833]

Much of the regulation of the Internet in Japan is self-regulation by ISPs. More formal regulation is provided by the Ministry of Internal Affairs and Communications (MIC). However, the MIC avoids an overly intrusive approach.

21.2 NIPPON TELEGRAPH AND TELEPHONE

Although there is an open market, the principal ISP in Japan is the formerly state-owned Nippon Telegraph and Telephone Corporation (NTT) that was privatized in 1985. In 1999, a new law separated NTT's Internet services from roots Mobile and fixed-line telephone services.

Despite the free market, NTT has remained the dominant service provider in Japan.

The only other big tech companies to establish themselves in the Japanese market have been Apple and Samsung who have had success selling mobile phones. But NTT has no serious competitors in the provision of Internet services.

Use of the Internet both for gathering information and posting it largely operated without government restrictions in Japan. In 2001, ISPs were directed to organize a framework of self-regulation by the 2001 Provider Liability Limitation Act.

21.3 FREE SPEECH

The Japanese constitution protects free speech and forbids most kinds of censorship. However, the government has made efforts to block piracy sites, and there have been arrests and some prosecutions relating to copyright violations using the Internet.

As examples, the government requested ISPs to block piracy sites in 2018. The government also announced that it intends to introduce new laws increase website blocking powers.

In June 2017, a conspiracy law was introduced which permits the police to obtain tap warrants to investigate Internet posts and sites (and other offline locations) which are likely to have links to terrorism.[834]

Japan has passed a statute intended to protect teenagers from Internet content that is too sexual, provides information about how to commit crimes, or contains gruesome descriptions of murder. The statute applies to telecom companies providing Internet services but not to VPNs.[835]

833. *Ibid.*

834. www.refworld.org. The UN Refugee Agency. Retrieved July 29, 2020.

835. Japan, Telecoms, Media and Internet Laws and Regulations, section 6.4, www.iclg.com, retrieved July 29, 2020.Act on the Development of an Environment that Provides Safe and Secure Internet Use for Young People.

21.4 PRIVACY AND DATA PROTECTION

Internet privacy is governed by Japan's general privacy law. This law applies to businesses that have personal information on 5,000 or more people.

There are three principal statutes that protect personal information. They are:

(1) The Act for the Protection of Personal Information (APPI).
(2) The Act on the Protection of Personal Information held by Independent Administrative Agencies.
(3) The Act on the Protection of Personal Information held by Administrative Organs.

These are statutes that apply to call data collection, not only to collection of online information. The statutes require businesses to protect personal information against loss, unauthorized disclosure, or distribution. It is forbidden to transfer personal information to third parties unless the individual whose data it is consents to the transfer.

The government has also instituted a policy that requires all governmental in public administrative bodies to protect the personal data that they collect. The elements of this policy called the Basic Policy on the Protection of Personal Information set out about forty guidelines that were issued in 2010.[836]

The law also requires businesses that have collections of personal data to make the following information available to all those who are subjects of that data:

- The name of the business holding the data.
- The purposes for which the data is being used.
- How to request corrections, disclosure or file complaints.
- Contact information for the entity authorized to accept complaints.

The only cases in which a data collector can't disclose personal information without consent our cases where disclosure is:

- Required by law or regulation.
- Necessary to protect the life, body or property of someone to who it is hard to reach to get consent.
- Necessary for protecting public health.
- Necessary for an authorized governmental entity to conduct its legitimate business.[837]

The Japan Act on the Protection of Personal Information (APPI) requires that those business operations handling personal data must have a system for processing complaints about their treatment of personal data and provide for appropriate and

836. Library of Congress, Law, Online Privacy Law, Japan, www.loc.gov, Retrieved July 29, 2020.*See also*, Japanese Law Translation, online at: japaneselawtranslation.go.jp.
837. *Ibid.*

expeditious handling of such complaints. The data holders are also required to have a similarly well-run system to deal with requests to correct or remove data.

The APPI applies to any holders of personal data on Japanese citizens regardless of where the holders are located, even if outside Japan.

Under the APPI, complaints are to be mediated by local government.[838]

However, the remedies available to data subjects who are unhappy with the way that their complaint is being dealt with are limited. They are not permitted to bring private suits or seek civil damages.[839]

However, in addition to laws specifically designed to protect private online data, Japan also has general criminal statutes that punishes unauthorized computer access. Such violations can be punished by imprisonment of up to a year or a fine of about $6,000. Someone who steals another's password and access ID and uses it to gain access to a computer will be considered to have violated this statute.[840]

The APPI also applies to the collection of data on smartphones in the same way it applies to data collection on computers.[841]

There is no specific government agency for data protection in Japan. Government ministers who have jurisdiction over business are required to oversee online data protection within their sphere of responsibility.[842]

There is no specific statute that recognizes a right to privacy in Japan. That right has been established by court decisions. In 1964, a decision of the Tokyo District court ruled that Article 13 of the Japanese Constitution supported a right to privacy.

Article 13 says:

> All of the people shall be respected as individuals. The right to life, liberty and the pursuit of happiness shall, to the extent it does not interfere with the public welfare, be the supreme consideration in legislation and other governmental affairs.

This right was recognized by the Japanese Supreme Court in a 1969 decision.

In that case, a police officer took photos of people in a protest march. The Court ruled that it was wrong to take photos of people without their consent, unless necessary for public welfare.[843]

A 2008 Supreme Court decision cited this case when ruling that the governmental collection of personal information about persons could violate citizens' rights to liberty in private life, if they disclosed the information to third parties or made the information public without a justifiable reason.[844]

There is an ongoing review of the role of protection of personal data in Japan.

838. *Ibid.*
839. *Ibid.*
840. *Ibid.* The Act for the Prohibition of Unauthorized Computer Access.
841. *Ibid.*
842. *Ibid.* section III.A.
843. *Ibid.*
844. *Ibid.*, footnote 108.

In 2009, the Consumer Commission established a Personal Information Protection Special Research Subcommittee. They recommended that there should be unambiguous rules on a data subject's rights to get, correct and seek to end use of personal information. Other study groups are also examining these issues.[845]

It is fair to say the state of Japanese law and regulation on online activity, generally, and the important sub-issue will continue to evolve as the Internet expands and changes.

21.5 ARTIFICIAL INTELLIGENCE

In April and May 2023, Japan chaired G7 meetings that discussed how AI should be regulated and what agreements the G7 might be able to reach on such regulation.

Japan is reported to be in favor of sensible development of AI and has been supportive of adoption of "reasonable AI uses" by both the public and industry in Japan.[846]

At the G7 meeting in April 2023, Japan's goal reportedly was to seek G7 agreement on providing "flexible" regulation for AI rather than a specific overarching regulation on all types of AI technology, according to reported statements by Japan's Industry Minister Yasutoshi Nishimura.[847]

Japanese Prime Minister Fumio Kishida discussed proposed AI regulation with other world leaders when Japan hosted the G7 summit in May 2023.[848]

It is reported that Japan has been working toward adopting more liberal regulations for AI than are included in EU regulation.

The project team of the Japanese ruling party on the Evolution and Implementation of AI issued a draft act in February 2024, but, as of this writing, no specific law has been enacted.

Japan, like many other countries, wishes to profit from the potential benefits of AI. It is believed that this wish will bring Japanese regulation closer to U.S. regulation than the EU's AIA.

Japan is reportedly hoping to lure AI business away from Europe by being more "AI friendly."[849]

Nevertheless, EU industry official, Thierry Breton, was reported to have visited Tokyo in July 2023 to promote the EU approach to AI regulation. It is not reported that Mr. Breton's efforts are likely to make any difference to Japan's reaction to the EU proposals:[850]

845. *Ibid.* section VI.
846. K. Komiya, "G7 Should Adopt 'Risk-Based' AI Regulation, Ministers Say," *Reuters*, online, May 1, 2023.
847. *Ibid.*
848. *Ibid.*
849. R. Taroh Satoh. "Japan Goes Light on AI Regulation to Court Investment," *Nikkei Asia*, June 19, 2024, online at: asia.nikkea.com.
850. S. Nussey & T. Kelly, "Japan Leaning Toward Softer AI Rules Than EU, Official Close to Deliberations Says," *Reuters*, online at: reuters.com, July 3, 2023, accessed September 29, 2023.

> The chair of the government's AI strategy council, the University of Tokyo's Prof. Yutaka Matsuo, called the EU's rules a "little too strict ... .

Matsuo, who also chairs the Japan Deep Learning Association and is a non-executive director of the Softbank Group, is reported to have said:

> With the EU, the issue is less about how to promote innovation and more about making already large companies take responsibility.

However, officials that are working on the formulation of Japan's AI regulation system have said they were not allowed to talk to the media.

CHAPTER 22

South Korean Law

22.1 EARLY REGULATION

South Korea passed an early Internet regulation law in 1995 with the Telecommunications Business Act (TBA). This law established a regulator for Internet communications entitled, the Information and Communications Ethics Office (ICEO).[851]

The principal functions of the ICEO were to censor posts on the Internet that:

- encroached on public morals;
- might endanger national sovereignty; and
- any other information that could disturb or harm:
  - the character;
  - emotions; or
  - sense of values of the youth of South Korea.[852]

The TBA gave the Minister of Communication the power to order service providers to delete or restrict any offensive material.

This was not a power that the Minister ignored. It is reported that in the first months of 1996, more than 220,000 posts were ordered to be deleted from the Internet.[853]

22.2 POLICIES RELATING TO NORTH KOREA

In addition, South Korean law contains special restrictions on any political speech, contact with or expression of sympathy for North Korea.

851. P. Hwa Ang, "How Countries Are Regulating Internet Content," Nanwang Technological University, Singapore, January 1, 1997. https://web.archive.org/web/20160103124414/https://www.isoc.org/inet97/proceedings/B1/B1_3.HTM.
852. *Ibid.*
853. *Ibid.*

Search communications about North Korea are forbidden. South Korean prosecutors have indicated that they would punish anyone trying to access North Korean pages on the Internet.[854]

It has been reported that a South Korean government official stated that if any South Korean encountered a North Korean on the Internet, he would be required to report this to the police within seven days.[855]

Any posting that reflects criticism of the South Korean government in relation to its policies on North Korea is forbidden. For example, it has been reported that in an incident when a North Korean submarine ran aground, South Koreans who questioned the government's handling of the incident online were investigated for potential violations of law.[856]

However, the strictness of these restraints, including those of the National Security Act of 1948, under which those who praise or express sympathy with an anti-government group can be imprisoned, were challenged in court by the filing of a complaint in August 1999. That complaint charged that provisions of the TBA and an Enforcement Decree under the Act improperly infringed freedom of expression, violated due process and were unnecessarily excessive restrictions.[857]

In that case, a university student went online to question an incident in which North and South Korea warships briefly exchanged gun fire in 1999. The student posted a note on a message board which accused the then President of South Korea, Kim Dae-Jung, of being sloppy.

The court found that the terms in the statutes in question were too abstract and that different officials could make different judgments about whether the laws were being violated. Consequently, those laws could potentially create a "chilling effect" on communications that should not be regulated.[858]

In 2002, a revision of the relevant laws was passed. However, it did not in any way weaken the government's determination to punish what is considered to be improper communication on the Internet.

22.3 FREEDOM OF EXPRESSION

Political expression is still subject to limits under the National Security Act. Inciting or praising anti-government activities is still restricted.[859]

854. *Ibid.*
855. *Ibid.*
856. *Ibid.*
857. Case, 14-1 KCCR 616, 99Hun-Ma480, June 27, 2002, Columbia University, *Global Freedom of Expression*, https://globalfreedomofexpression.columbia.edu/cases/ban-improper-communication-internet-case/.
858. *Ibid.*
859. Diane Kraft, "South Korea's National Security Law: A Tool of Oppression in an Insecure World," *Wisconsin International Law Journal*, Volume 24, p. 627 (2006).

Some concern has been expressed in the Western media that digital communication is becoming too heavily censored in South Korea.[860]

Nevertheless, despite these concerns, Freedom House, which rates 210 countries on their levels of Internet freedom, rated South Korea (at 64 out of 100) as one of the more liberal countries in Asia, ahead of Cambodia (43), China (10), India (55), Indonesia (51), Malaysia (57), Myanmar (36), Sri Lanka (49), Thailand (35) and Vietnam (24).[861]

22.4 AI IN SOUTH KOREA

It is reported that South Korea is seeking to become one of the leading nations in the fields of developing, manufacturing and using AI.

One significant advantage that will benefit South Korea in this area is its dominating position in the manufacture of memory chips—a key component of AI systems.

AI systems require a great deal of digital memory. South Korean firms Samsung Electronics and SK Hynix are reported to produce about 70% of the world's digital memory chips.

South Korea is hoping to become the third largest producer of AI systems after the U.S. and China.

South Korea's Minister for Science, Information and Communications is quoted as saying:

> South Korea seeks to emerge as a prominent player in rapidly growing and promising areas such as AI semiconductors. ... [South Korea] aims to maintain its leading position in memory semiconductor field.[862]

22.4.1 Legal Encouragement of AI Development

To help fulfill South Korea's AI ambitions, the South Korean Parliament has reportedly approved a new set of AI regulations that are reported to be less restrictive than other regulations, such as those of the EU.

For example, in February 2023, a committee of the South Korean Parliament approved a draft law guaranteeing "freedom" to market AI products and services. AI systems will only be restricted if they are found to harm the lives, safety or the rights of people.[863]

860. D. Volodzko, "Is South Korea Sliding Towards Digital Dictatorship?" *Forbes*, online, February 25, 2019.
861. Internet Freedom Scores, Freedom House, online at: freedomhouse.org, retrieved, July 27, 2020.
862. S. Chiang, "South Korea Wants to Be a Top A.I. Hub: Its Memory Chip Dominance Could Be an Advantage," *CNBC*, online at: cnbc.com, July 5, 2023.
863. J. Lee & H. Yang, "Open AI CEO Encourages South Korea to Supply Chips in AI Boom," *Reuters*, online at: reuters.com, June 9, 2023.

To provide industry guidance on AI, the South Korean Personal Information Protection Commission (PIPC) published an English version of its "draft guidance" for AI in July 2021.[864]

The PIPC is the "national data protection authority" of South Korea. It was designated as an "independent regulatory agency in 2020." It has powers to investigate data privacy violations and to adjudicate disputes involving personal data. Under the Personal Information Protection Act of 2011 (PIPA), the PIPC can impose fines for data violations.

The PIPC consists of nine Commissioners, and its chairperson has the status of a government minister.[865]

A "checklist" (Checklist) was created by PIPC for "Developers and Operators." It states:

> This self-checklist was prepared for the purpose of not only complying with the obligations regarding personal information protection, but also providing information on matters necessary for implementing and checking autonomous personal information protection suitable for its technology and service environment in consideration of the fact that AI technology and service are continuously developing and changing ... As it includes guidelines pursuant to the Personal Information Protection Act, personal information controllers in areas other than AI service can also use the checklist.[866]

The PIPC Checklist emphasizes the important connection between data privacy and the operation of AI systems. It states that there are six principles of AI personal information protection that need to be complied with: "legitimacy, safety, transparency, participation, responsibility and fairness."[867]

The Checklist provides detailed additional information about the following eight phases of AI development and operation, where personal information protection requirements need to be considered and implemented by AI developers and operators. These eight phases are:[868]

(1) Planning and design.
(2) Collection of personal information.
(3) Use and provision of personal information.
(4) Storage and destruction of personal information.
(5) AI service management and supervision.
(6) AI service user protection and damage relief.
(7) Autonomous personal information protection activities.
(8) Checking AI ethics.

864. PIPC, "Artificial Intelligence (AI) Personal Information Protection Self-Checklist (May 31, 2021)."
865. The English version of the PIPC website is online at: pipc.go.kr.
866. PIPC, "Artificial Intelligence (AI) Personal Information Protection Self-Checklist" (Checklst), p. 2.
867. PIPC Checklist, p. 5.
868. *Ibid.*, pp. 9-35.

Each of the above includes several things to check when considering any above category.

With respect to number 8 above, checking AI ethics includes in its Appendix a review of "Major domestic and overseas ethical principles."[869] The clear implication of this is that AI developers and operators need to consider both with respect to the development and operation of their AI system.

This Appendix includes a list of ethical standards developed both by international organizations and national governments. It includes ethical standards published by South Korea itself, as well as those published by the OECD and the G20, and standards published by Singapore, the United States, the EU, Canada, Germany, France, the United Kingdom, Australia, China, Japan, and Hong Kong.

In addition to the list of ethical standards publications provided in the first part of the ethical material in the Appendix, there is also a second part that provides "People-centric Artificial Intelligence (AI) Ethical Standards," published in December 2020 by the South Korean Ministry of Science and ICT (Information and Communications Technology).

This section comprises: "Artificial intelligence standards: three basic principles and ten key requirements."[870]

The three basic principles are the following:

(1) The principle of human dignity.
(2) The principle of the public good of society.
(3) The principle of the purposiveness of technology.

All three include more detail about their definition and application.

In addition, there are "10 key requirements—detailed requirements for realizing the basic principles." These ten detailed requirements are headlined as follows:

(1) Human Rights Guarantee.
(2) Privacy protection.
(3) Respect for diversity.
(4) Prohibition of infringement.
(5) Public interests.
(6) Solidarity.
(7) Data management.
(8) Responsibility.
(9) Safety.
(10) Transparency.

Each of the ten contain more detail about their meaning and application.

The Checklist also cites the following additional assistance as being available:

869. *Ibid.*, pp. 38 and 39.
870. *Ibid.*, pp. 39-41.

> For consultation on the sales license checklist and inquiries on personal information protection laws, please contact the 'Personal Information Infringement Report Center' (privacy.kisa.or.kr or call 118).[871]

It is clear from the detail provided in the PIPC Checklist and from public statements by government officials that South Korea is very serious about becoming a major creator and operator of AI systems and is equally serious about playing a prominent role in developing international standards and regulations to promote the advantages of AI systems and to control the risks they may present.

22.4.2 Industry Support for South Korean AI Development

It is not only from the political community that South Korea is receiving support for expanding the AI business. South Korea is receiving strong support from the major international industry players as well. For example:

> ChatGPT-maker OpenAI's CEO Sam Altman, who met with South Korean president Yoon Suk Yeol ..., urged South Korea to play a leading role in creating international AI standards as well as focusing on making the chips needed for the technology.[872]

Among the suggestions reportedly made by Altman were that South Korea should produce semiconductors and the memory needed for AI, that they should encourage AI projects by modifying corporate regulations, and that they should participate actively in setting international AI standards.[873]

Altman also said that he had met with about 100 newly created South Korean digital industry companies.[874]

22.4.3 South Korean AI Companies

South Korea has also been one of the leading countries in developing its own AI-technology-related companies. These include Naver, Kakao and LG.

South Korea is reportedly seeking to expand its AI businesses in areas not already dominated by U.S. and Chinese firms. For example, Kyunghoon Bae, the head of LG AI Research, is quoted as saying:

> In order for Korean companies to have strength in the global AI ecosystem, each company must first secure specialized technology for vertical AI ... . [or AI for specific uses].[875]

871. *Ibid.*, p. 2.
872. J. Lee & H. Yang, "Open AI CEO Encourages South Korea to Supply Chips in AI Boom," *Reuters*, online at: reuters.com, June 9, 2023.
873. *Ibid.*
874. *Ibid.*
875. *Ibid.*

South Korean AI companies are also reportedly trying to develop AI products that cater to cultural sensitivities in areas like the Middle East and meet the needs of non-English speaking countries in the Far East.[876]

Two prominent South Korean AI companies, Naver and Kakao, are also making efforts to shape the regulation of AI by publishing their own statements on what constitutes good ethical behavior in developing and operating AI systems. These two statements are taken seriously by the PIPC and are cited in its Checklist Appendix.[877]

It is the case that in South Korea, most of the AI used in commerce is produced by big South Korean tech companies such as Naver and Kakao.[878]

It is reported that in South Korea, major companies in many industries such as Hyundai Motor, LG, Samsung and Doosan are hard at work implementing AI and robot technologies.[879]

Kakao is a South Korean digital media company founded in 1995 and employing about 4,000 people. It offers products in the fields of communication, media, content, games, lifestyle, fintech, and search.[880] Starting in 2018, Kakao introduced an Algorithm Ethics Charter[881] and educated its employees in ethics for AI and algorithms.[882]

Naver describes itself as a global tech company offering South Korea's leading search portal, "Neighbor." It also has subsidiaries and affiliates that provide a variety of information technology-related products.[883]

Naver produced its "Naver Artificial Intelligence (AI) Ethics Rules" in February 2021.

22.5 CONCLUSION

It seems certain that South Korea is determined to remain one of the major factors in world digital commerce, and that it will make strenuous efforts to expand its role there, including energetic development of the growing AI sector.

876. *Ibid.*
877. PIPC Checklist, p. 38.
878. AI Network, "How Can Korean Big Tech Like Naver and Kakao Keep AI Ethics?," online at: ai-network.medium.com, February 18, 2021.
879. *Ibid.*
880. Profile: "Kakao," *Forbes*, online at: forbes.com, accessed July 28, 2023.
881. This Charter was updated in 2019 and 2020. PIPC Checklist, p. 38.
882. AI Network, "How Can Korean Big Tech Like Naver and Kakao Keep AI Ethics?," online at: ai-network.medium.com, February 18, 2021.
883. For information, *see* Naver website at: navercorp.com.

CHAPTER 23
Singapore Law

23.1 THE INTERNET IN SINGAPORE

In 1996, Singapore directed the Singapore Broadcasting Authority (SBA) to monitor activity and the content of the Internet. The SBA was given the power to regulate ISPs by determining which ISPs should be licensed to operate in Singapore and subjecting them to a Code of Practice for Online Safety (CPOS). The CPOS describes what Internet activity or content is prohibited. Any material that was offensive to public interest, morality, order, security or "national harmony" was prohibited.[884]

23.2 CENSORSHIP IN SINGAPORE

There are also broader general public control laws that can be used against Internet activity or content that is offensive to the government.

For example, Singapore, as a former British colony, kept the British Sedition Act until 2022 because it considered the law necessary against terrorism/and or ethnic conflicts which might endanger the nation's peace and harmony. This law was sometimes used against Internet users that were considered to have crossed the line into abusive or dangerous use of the Internet.

The Sedition Act was repealed in 2022, but some of its key provisions have been transferred to the Penal Code. One example is the provision "ensuring social cohesion between different groups within Singapore."[885]

In 2000, regulation of the Internet was given to a newly created organization, the Infocomm Media Development Authority (IMDA).[886]

884. The Infocomm Media Development Authority (IMDA) online at: imda.gov.sg., accessed November 19, 2024.
885. Ministry of Home Affairs, "Repeal of the Sedition Act 1948," online at: mha.gov.sg., accessed November 19, 2024.
886. The IMDA online at: imda.gov.sg.

The IMDA frequently censors material that it considers to be politically or racially sensitive, creating concern that this can interfere with freedom of speech. For example, satirical websites are carefully monitored and can be subject to censorship.

23.3 PROTECTION OF INTELLECTUAL PROPERTY

In 2014, Singapore amended its copyright law to provide additional protection to intellectual property. All ISPs were required to provide blocks to any websites that "flagrantly infringed" intellectual property rights.[887]

In 2019, Singapore introduced another law that, although it has some virtues, can also be seen as an additional limitation on free speech.

This is a broad fake news law, formally called the Protection from Online Falsehoods and Manipulation Act (POFMA).[888] Under this law, the spreading of false statements of fact that are considered prejudicial to Singapore's security, public safety, public peace or damaging to Singapore's relations with other countries are prohibited, along with some other types of Internet behavior or content.

The IMDA can decide that certain content needs to be removed or have a correction added to it. It can also order tech or social media companies to block posts or websites that spread fake news. The penalties for violating this law can be more than $30,000 for individuals and/or up to five years in jail. If the post is by a fake account or a "bot," the penalties can be more than $70,000 and/or 10 years in prison. Company violators can be fined over $700,000.[889]

The regulators are required to explain why a post is considered fake, and the government has promised that appeals under this law will be fast and inexpensive, but some are concerned that it may be used to suppress free speech.

The Prime Minister of Singapore justified the POFMA by saying:

> If we do not protect ourselves, hostile parties will find it a simple matter to turn different groups against one another and cause disorder in our society.

It is a matter of note that an international journalists' group, Reporters Without Borders, ranked Singapore 74th out of 180 countries on the issue of press freedom in 2023.[890]

The government, legal institutions and legal practitioners in Singapore are certainly aware of the international development and expansion of advanced technology including AI and machine learning. They are aware that significant changes will need to be made to Singapore law and regulations in order to take a proper account of the effects of these things.

887. Intellectual Property Office of Singapore (IPOS), "Singapore's Innovation Performance, 2013-2024," online at: ipos.gov.sg., accessed November 19, 2024.
888. POFMA Office, "Protection from Online Falsehoods and Manipulation Act," online at: pofmao.gov.sg., accessed November 19, 2024.
889. *Ibid.*
890. Reporters Without Borders, online at: rsf.org., accessed November 19, 2024.

However, Singapore's legal community is still in the process of evolving legal and regulatory changes to both control the risks of AI systems and to realize the benefits that they may offer to the small but vibrant nation.

The Singapore Personal Data Protection Commission (PDPC) has issued an online guide to Singapore's approach to AI governance.[891] The PDPC says:

> As Singapore develops its digital economy, a trusted ecosystem is key—one where organizations can benefit from tech innovations while consumers are confident to adopt and use AI. In the global discourse on AI ethics and governance, Singapore believes that its balanced approach can facilitate innovation, safeguard consumer interests, and serve as a common global reference point.

Singapore, like the EU, is apparently hoping that its approach to AI regulation will be copied around the globe.

The rest of the world, when considering the effectiveness of those two sets of regulations, will need to wait until those legal systems have completed their policies on AI regulation before they will be able to judge which, if either, would be worth emulating.

In Singapore, the PDPC has taken the lead in formulating a policy for AI regulation.

Another institution that has been in the forefront of determining how AI should be regulated in Singapore is the IMDA.

The IMDA is a statutory board of the Singapore government. They are tasked with developing and regulating the information communications (Infocom) and media sectors. The goal of IMDA is to encourage dynamic Infocom and media sectors that encourage innovation and business development. The IMDA has established several programs to assist the digital sector, along with other media sectors.[892]

To assist in providing an effective system of AI oversight, the IMDA has published a program called "AI Verify." It consists of a framework to test AI regulation and a software tool kit to assist using the framework:[893]

> The testing framework consists of 11 AI ethics principles which jurisdictions around the world coalesce around and are consistent with internationally recognized AI frameworks such of those from the EU, OECD and Singapore's model AI governance framework. AI verify helps organizations validate the performance of their AI systems against those principles through standardized tests.

The 11 "ethics principles" referred to are:[894]

(1) Transparency.
(2) Explainability.
(3) Repeatability/Reproducibility.

891. The PDPC website is online at: pdpc.gov.sg.
892. The IMDA online website is at: imda.gov.sg.
893. PDPC, "Model AI Governance Framework," "Guiding Principles," online at: pdpc.gov.sg., accessed November 19, 2024.
894. AI Verify Foundation, online at: aiverifyfoundation@sg.

(4) Safety.
(5) Security.
(6) Robustness.
(7) Fairness.
(8) Data Governance.
(9) Accountability.
(10) Human Agency and Oversight.
(11) Inclusive Growth, Societal and Environmental Well-Being.

There is a little question that it is worth considering issues that fall into those categories when reviewing and regulating AI systems.

However, these principles can be subject to very different standards of interpretation. It seems unlikely that any nation would have any significant objections to any of these principles, but recognition of them will not automatically guarantee a consistent international standard of law and regulation.

With respect to the application of AI Verify in Singapore itself, it will take some time to know precisely how these "ethical principles" will be applied as AI systems are developed and used in that nation. For example, will these they be part of legislatively established laws and regulations relating to AI or they will they simply be left as "ethical" standards that may be interpreted differently by AI developers, users and regulators?

Of course, there is not only government interest in the development of AI systems in Singapore. The private legal sector is also keenly interested in understanding how AI should be both controlled and encouraged through law and regulation.

23.3.1 PDPC Guides

In addition to providing a model AI governance framework, the Singapore PDPC also provides several guides to implementation and use of AI.

As a supplement to the Model Framework described above, the PDPC provides an Implementation and Self-assessment Guide for Organizations (ISAGO). This guide was developed in consultation with the World Economic Forum Center for the Fourth Industrial Revolution and with over 60 industry organizations.[895] It provides a list of industry examples and practices to guide organizations in the adaptation and use of AI systems.

To supplement the Model Framework and ISAGO, a Compendium of Use Cases is provided. This Compendium shows how Singapore and international organizations in different sectors can implement and align their AI practices with the Model Framework.

The compendium comprises two volumes. Volume One includes use cases from a selection of major banks and organizations around the Asia Pacific region such as HSBC and Visa Asia Pacific. Volume Two provides cases from the city of Darwin in Australia and from major companies such as Google and Microsoft. It also has a section

895. *See*, the PDPC website online at: pdpc.gov.sg.

on how Singapore implemented its AI Framework in "100 Experiments" projects with organizations such as IBM.

23.3.2 Job Redesign for AI Age

Singapore has also created an Advisory Council of the Ethical Use of AI and Data (AI Advisory Council) to advise the government on how to respond to the effects of development of AI systems on employment.

For several years, there has been concern around the world about how the introduction of AI systems will affect many jobs and professions.

The government of Singapore has been aware of the expansion of AI may affect the job market there. Consequently, the AI advisory Council, the PDPC, the IMDA and the Singapore University of Technology and Design published a Guide in December 2020 that is intended to assist companies on dealing with the impact of AI on employees and how companies can, otherwise, to adapt themselves to the electronic future.[896]

23.3.3 Copyright Protection of AI Products

The Singapore Copyright Act 2021 does appear to have some implications for AI systems. Under section 13(3)(b), the Act is stated to apply to a "computer program," which is said to be protected as a "literary work." However, a literary work is only protected under Singapore copyright law if it has a human author(s).

This would seem to exclude claims that are made by some AI scientists, that AI systems, because they are regarded as possessing a form of "intelligence" that may produce results unexpected by its human creator, should have legal recognition as "Creators" of unexpectedly resulting works. This position has been rejected by courts that have considered that issue in Singapore, as well as in the United Kingdom and the United States.[897] Intellectual property rights have so far only been held to be available to humans.

In the case of *Asia Pacific (Publishers) Pte Ltd v. Pioneers & Leaders (Publishers) Pte Ltd* [2011] SGC 837, the Court of Appeal in Singapore ruled that copyright protection will be granted only to works created by humans.[898]

23.4 SINGAPORE ACADEMY OF LAW

The Singapore Academy of Law (SAL) is a statutorily established organization that characterizes itself as a "promotion and development agency for Singapore's legal industry":[899]

896. *Ibid.*
897. Such as the Thaler cases discussed in other chapters.
898. Similar copyright cases have been brought in the United Kingdom and the United States.
899. The SAL website is online at: sal.org.sg.

> Our vision is to make Singapore the legal hub of Asia. Our mandates are to build the intellectual capital of the legal profession by enhancing legal knowledge, raise the international profile of Singapore law, promote Singapore as a center for dispute resolution, and improve the standards and efficiency of legal practice through continuing professional development and use of technology.

The SAL provides a "knowledge hub for the legal community."

The SAL provides a significant amount of information about Singapore legal cases and legislative developments in private law and practice and also provides online access to international legal developments. As such, the SAL provides a significant amount of information and insight about developments touching on the world of AI.

In its capacity as a legal knowledge center, the SAL, as of this writing in 2024, was providing information about the following AI-related developments in Singapore:[900]

- A SAL innovation program for lawyers and others about how technology is changing the practice of law through machine learning and automation.
- A special issue of the *SAL Journal 2021* on law and technology, including discussion of the "limitations in machine learning."
- A program on data protection law in Singapore reviewing issues relating to AI and machine learning on the local, regional and international levels.

900. SAL online at: sal.org.sg.

CHAPTER 24
Middle East

24.1 UAE

Although its wealth was originally based on petroleum, the UAE, particularly Dubai and Abu Dhabi, has made strenuous efforts to attract a wider range of businesses over the last few decades.[901]

Dubai has become a center for business and commerce of all kinds, particularly commerce related to the financial markets.

In conjunction with that growth, Dubai has put laws and regulations in place to govern financial market participation.

People from all over the world have come to live and work there. Part of the attraction is clearly its warm climate, its proximity to the sea and the effort it has made to build plentiful and sometimes spectacular housing and commercial spaces.

However, Dubai has also developed something of a reputation as an open and light-handed market for financial business. Some may say that this has been a strong attraction to those that wish to avoid legal regulation as much as possible.

Regardless of the truth of those opinions, there was a little question that the financial commerce market will continue to grow and become more important in Dubai and the UAE. Consequently, in order to keep the confidence of market participants, they will undoubtedly have to continually revise their financial market regulations to keep them relevant as the markets change in response to the new cyber world.

24.2 SAUDI ARABIA

Saudi Arabia has been well known in recent decades for the wealth and political power that its abundant oil and gas provides.

901. HSBC, International Business Guides, UAE, online at: business.hsbc.com, accessed November 20, 2024.

However, in more recent years, Saudi Arabia has realized that the cyber world is also a powerful way to earn respect and income.[902]

With its oil and gas wealth as a base, Saudi Arabia has encouraged the development of a financial market and cyber commerce and, in conjunction with that, has issued laws and regulations to control and direct its growth.[903]

24.3 ISRAEL

Since its creation in the late 1940s, Israel has been a vibrant center of commerce and invention. This has become even more true with the introduction of the Internet and ways of doing business and products that the Internet has made possible.

Even a relatively small country like Israel can have a big impact on global commerce over the Internet.

Consequently, Israel has made serious efforts to make certain that its financial commerce cyber business is conducted sensibly and legally.[904]

902. "An Economic Blueprint, Saudi Arabia's Vision 2030," online at: pif.gov.sa., accessed November 20, 2024.
903. "About the Capital Market Authority," online at: cma.org.sa., accessed November 20, 2034.
904. Bank of Israel, "Supervision and Regulation," online at: boi.org.il., accessed November 20, 2034. *See also*, "Israel Securities Authority," online at: gov.il., accessed November 20, 2024.

CHAPTER 25

Future of Global Business Law

There is no doubt that in the last 30 years, the cyberworld has made a tremendous and irreversible impact on international commerce and its regulation.[905]

That impact is only going to grow as new products, new ways of communicating, new instruments for cyber communication, and global reach expand at an increasingly faster pace.

Perhaps the most important thing that this new world of business has shown us is that the necessity for international cooperation between governments and regulators has become increasingly urgent and will continue to be so.

International treaties and conventions that will encourage the growth of international business and control the abuses of the cyberworld are becoming more urgent than ever.

International regulation is the only way to help businesses of all kinds around the world grow with the Internet. Such regulation is also the only way that increasingly creative abuses of the Internet can be prevented and penalized.

905. "E-commerce Wordwide- Statistics and Facts," online at: statistical.com, June 7, 2024.

www.ingramcontent.com/pod-product-compliance
Lightning Source LLC
Chambersburg PA
CBHW070251260926
51849CB00001BA/143
9789403507293